SIMÓN BOLÍVAR

SIMÓN BOLÍVAR
A LIFE

JOHN LYNCH

Yale University Press
New Haven and London

For information about this and other Yale University Press publications, please contact:
U.S. Office: sales.press@yale.edu   www.yalebooks.com
Europe Office: sales@yaleup.co.uk   www.yaleup.co.uk

Set in Minion by J&L Composition, Filey, North Yorkshire
Printed in Great Britain by the MPG Books Group

Library of Congress Cataloging-in-Publication Data

Lynch, John, 1927–
   Simón Bolívar: a life/John Lynch.
      p.cm.
Includes bibliographical references and index.
ISBN 0–300–11062–6 (cl.: alk. paper)
1. Bolívar, Simón, 1783–1830. 2. South America—History—Wars of Independence, 1806–1830. 3. Heads of state—South America—Biography, I. Title.
   F2235.3.L97 2006
   980'.02092—dc22

                                                                                    2005034838

A catalogue record for this book is available from the British Library.

10 9 8 7 6 5 4 3 2

CONTENTS

ILLUSTRATIONS

PREFACE

Simón Bolívar lived a short life but one of extraordinary fullness. He was a revolutionary who freed six countries, an intellectual who argued the principles of national liberation, a general who fought a cruel colonial war. He inspired extremes of devotion and detestation. Many Spanish Americans wanted him to be their dictator, their king; but some denounced him as a traitor and others tried to assassinate him. His memory became an inspiration to later generations and also a battleground. To liberal historians he was a fighter against tyranny. Conservatives redesigned him as a cult. Marxists dismissed him as the leader of a bourgeois revolution. And he still evokes public passions and polemics. He has been appropriated by partisans and co-opted by governments: his current incarnation in Venezuela as the model of authoritarian populism projects yet another interpretation of his leadership and challenges the historian to set the record straight.

Bolívar was an exceptionally complex man, a liberator who scorned liberalism, a soldier who disparaged militarism, a republican who admired monarchy. To study Bolívar is to study a rare and original character, whose mind and will were no less factors in historical change than were the social forces of the time. He knew his own value and protected his reputation, speaking his mind in a flood of words that overwhelm the reader by their eloquence and conviction. Yet he was careless of his archives, gems of originality, which were preserved through the devotion of his followers rather than his own concern. The present book is a history of his life and times based on the Bolivarian documentation and modern research. The commentaries are hardly less prolific than the sources, though it is the sources that enlighten and the commentaries that often obscure.

Why write a new life of Bolívar? There are those who question the importance of biography and reject the cult of the hero. For them the meaning of liberation is to be found in the study of economic structures, social classes and the international conjuncture, not in military actions and the lives of liberators.

In this view Carlyle's claim that the history of the world is the biography of great men is misguided and his assertion that society is founded on hero-worship a curious exaggeration. Yet the independence of Spanish America is incomprehensible without the presence of the liberators and its subsequent history would be empty without the intervention of personal authority. In the action of Bolívar we observe the dynamics of leadership, the power to command and the modes of ruling in the diverse society of Spanish America, not the whole history of the age but a great part of it.

Many words, though not the last word, have been said about Bolívar. In English Salvador de Madariaga's interpretation, extensively researched but basically out of sympathy with its subject, was soon overtaken by Gerhard Masur's more balanced work, which held the field as the leading academic study in English for half a century before it began to show its age. Recently the subject has benefited from further research and new contributions by scholars in the United States, models of accuracy and judgement. In Venezuela Bolivarian writings are part of the national culture and, thanks to the work of generations of historians in the Bolivarian countries, we now have access to an incomparable collection of published documentation, extensive secondary works and numerous specialist studies. For greater understanding of Bolívar, historians everywhere – and none more than the present writer – have long been indebted to Germán Carrera Damas, whose works have illuminated the subject for four decades. The years approaching the bicentenary of Spanish American Independence are likely to see a renewal of interest, a resurgence of congresses, lectures and seminars, and a further upsurge in Bolivarian publications. Yet the life and work of Bolívar remain full of questions and controversies, and his inner motivation and ultimate project continue to challenge the historian. The challenge is one of interpretation rather than facts, although interpretation is impossible without facts, and the facts themselves are often in dispute.

The study of Bolívar, therefore, still provides the historian with space. But there is a deeper sense in which the subject appeals. The study of the Spanish American revolutions of 1808–26 has advanced significantly in recent decades. Historians have adjusted the chronology of Independence to wider dimensions and see the years between 1750 and 1850 as a time of transition when colonial structures were slowly overtaken by nation states. Social change has been more closely investigated and, inevitably, race, class and gender are now required categories for anyone studying Independence. Elites are searched for allegiances and the popular sectors for commitment. Guerrillas are promoted to prominence and the shift from bandits to guerrillas to patriots is seen as a common sequence, adding a new look to military history. Revolution is not the whole story: the Spanish counter-revolution is investigated in greater detail, and Independence is viewed as a war lost by Spain as well as one won by Americans. The political ideas of Independence have been studied by close textual analysis of revolutionary writings, while forms of political sociability have also made their appearance. The idea of American identity has discarded conceptual inhibitions and can now be studied as the development of imagined communities or even the emergence of nationalism in early modern Spanish America. The time has come to integrate Bolívar more closely into the new research, to incorporate the Liberator into the social, economic, intellectual and political life of the society in which he lived, and analyse his policies towards creole elites, mixed races, blacks, Indians and slaves. His history does not end with his death but leaves a legacy hardly less dramatic than his life, and this too is a subject for the historian and one which brings the present work to a close.

I am grateful to Yale University Press for asking me to write this book, to its editorial team for helping to produce it, and to James Dunkerley for encouraging the project. To Germán Carrera Damas I have long been indebted for generous guidance to the thought and action of the Liberator, for practical help in pursuit of sources, and for friendship beyond the world of scholarship. I am grateful too to Carole Leal Curiel, who kindly gave me a vital work of her husband Luis Castro, a historian sadly missed by his colleagues. I am pleased to record my thanks for the help I have received from Peter Blanchard, particularly on the subject of slaves and slavery. Catherine Fuller of the Bentham Project at University College London guided me on the communications between Bolívar and Bentham, and directed me to the sources. I wish to express my debt to the Fundación John Boulton, Caracas, and especially to its Director, Carmen Michelena, for generously making available documents from the Archivo del Libertador Simón Bolívar. I am indebted, too, to Alan Biggins of Canning House, Norman Fiering of the John Carter Brown Library, and Gabriela Carrera of Caracas for help with the illustrations. I am glad to record my appreciation of the services over the years of the Archivo General de la Nación, Caracas, and the National Archives (Public Record Office), London. Particular thanks are due to the British Library, the Institute of Historical Research and the Library of University College London, whose holdings between them make London fruitful ground for Bolivarian research.

I have special words of thanks, inadequate though they are, for my wife, whose support for Bolívar and for me encouraged and sustained the book and helped me to complete it.

South America 1800–30

Caribbean Sea

Atlantic Ocean

Curaçao
Maracaibo • Barquisimeto
Cartagena • Puerto Cabello
Panama — Momipós ✕ Carabobo • **Caracas**
PANAMA Cúcuta • **VENEZUELA** Trinidad
Antioquia • ✕ Boyacá • Angostura
Cartago • **Bogotá** *Orinoco*
NEW GRANADA **GUAYANA**
Popayán • **G R A N   C O L O M B I A**
• Pasto *Japura*
Pichincha ✕ • Quito *Putumayo* *Negro*
Guayaquil • **ECUADOR** *Amazon*
Tumbes • • Cuenca • Tabatingo
Piura • *Marañón* *Amazon*
PERU *Ucayali*
Trujillo •
• Huánuco **B R A Z I L**
Junín ✕
Lima •
• ✕ Ayacucho
Pisco • Cuzco • **BOLIVIA** Pernambuco •
L. Titicaca • La Paz
Arequipa • **(UPPER PERU)** Salvador •
Tacna • Chuquisaca (Bahia)
Arica • • (La Plata)
Iquique • • Potosí *Paraguay*
Paraná
Concepción • **Rio de Janeiro**
Antofagasta • • Jujuy **PARAGUAY**
• Salta São Paulo •
Copiapó • • Asunción
• Tucumán *Uruguay*
UNITED PROVINCES **RIO GRANDE**
CHILE *Paraná* **DO SUL**
Córdoba • **URUGUAY**
Chacabuco Santa Fe • **(BANDA**
Valparaíso ✕ • Mendoza **ORIENTAL)**
Santiago • • San Luis **Montevideo**
Maipú ✕
Rancagua ✕ **OF THE RIO** *River Plate*
Concepción • **Buenos Aires**
Salade
Negro
Valdivia • • Carmen de Patagones **Atlantic Ocean**
DE LA PLATA
Chiloé
Island
P a t a g o n i a

Juan Fernández
Islands

Pacific Ocean

Magellan Strait   Falkland Islands
(Islas Malvinas)

Cape Horn

0	200	400	600 miles
0	400	800	1200 km

Bonaire

Curaçao

Coro

Pto.
Cabello

Caracas

La Guaira

Margarita

Carúpano

Güiria

Barquisimeto

Valencia

San
Mateo

Maracay

La Victoria

Trinidad

Cumaná

nta Ana

Carabobo

Villa de Cura

Barcelona

Maturín

V

jillo

Barinas

E

El Sombrero

Aragua

N

Unare

E

Calabozo

Nutrias

Guanarito

Apure

San Fernando
de Apure

Angostura

Orinoco

Z

Setenta

Mantecal

Achaguas

Payara

Orinoco

U

asdualito

Rincón-Hondo

rauca

G   U   A   Y   A   N   A

E

Caura

L

Caroni

A

0	1250	2500 miles

0	2500	5000 km

Peru and Bolivia

Pacific Ocean

B R A Z I L

P E R U

BOLIVIA
(UPPER PERU)

PARAGUAY

UNITED PROVINCES

Amazon

Paraguay

Paita

Trujillo

Huaraz
Pativilca
Huacho
Chancay
Callao
Cañete
Pisco

Cerro de Pasco
Junín
Jauja
Lima
Huancayo
Ayacucho
Nasca

Cuzco

Arequipa
Quilca
Ilo
Tacna
Arica
Iquique
Cobija
Antofagasta

Lake
Titicaca
Zepita
La Paz
Oruro
Desaguadero River
Condo
Cotagaita
Tupiza

Cochabamba
Santa Cruz
Mizque
Macha
Chuquisaca (Sucre)
Potosí
Tarija
Suipacha
Jujuy

Concepción
Asunción

0   200   400   600 miles
0   400   800   1200 km

Chapter 1

OUT OF A SPANISH COLONY

Venezuelan Homeland

On 26 March 1812 a massive earthquake struck Venezuela. From the Andes to the coast, from Mérida to La Guaira, the earth heaved and cracked, buildings crumbled and people perished in their thousands. The royalist chronicler José Domingo Díaz was there, his journalist instincts aroused:

> It was four o'clock, the sky of Caracas was clear and bright, and an immense calm seemed to intensify the pressure of an unbearable heat; a few drops of rain were falling though there was not a cloud in the sky. I left my house for the Cathedral and, about 100 paces from the plaza of San Jacinto and the Dominican priory, the earth began to shake with a huge roar. As I ran into the square some balconies from the Post Office fell at my feet, and I distanced myself from the falling buildings. I saw the church of San Jacinto collapse on its own foundations, and amidst dust and death I witnessed the destruction of a city which had been the admiration of natives and foreigners alike. The strange roar was followed by the silence of the grave. As I stood in the plaza, alone in the midst of the ruins, I heard the cries of those dying inside the church; I climbed over the ruins and entered, and I immediately saw about forty persons dead or dying under the rubble. I climbed out again and I shall never forget that moment. On the top of the ruins I found Don Simón Bolívar in his shirt sleeves clambering over the debris to see the same sight that I had seen. On his face was written the utmost horror or the utmost despair. He saw me and spoke these impious and extravagant words: 'We will fight nature itself if it opposes us, and force it to obey.' By now the square was full of people screaming.[1]

Thousands died in churches that Holy Thursday, and the churches of La Trinidad and Alta Gracia, which were more than 150 feet high, collapsed into ruins no higher than five or six feet. The great barracks of San Carlos plunged on to a regiment waiting to joint the processions. Nine tenths of Caracas was entirely destroyed.[2] Nothing could resist the heaving of the ground upwards like a boiling liquid and the shocks crossing each other from north to south and from east to west. The death toll reached nine to ten thousand in the city alone. As cries for help were heard from the ruins, mothers were seen bearing children in their arms desperately trying to revive them, and desolate families wandered in a daze through clouds of dust seeking missing fathers, husbands and friends. A group of Franciscan friars carried out corpses on their shoulders to give them a burial.[3] Bodies were burned on funeral piles, and the wounded and sick were laid on the banks of the River Guayra, without beds, linen or medicines, all lost in the rubble. A frightened society suddenly remembered its duties: partners hastened to get married, abandoned children found their parents, debts were paid, fraud was made good, families were reconciled and enemies became friends. Priests had never been busier. But Bolívar had to fight the Church as well as nature, for the catastrophe was exploited by many royalist clergy who preached that this was God's punishment for revolution. Amidst the dust and the rubble he confronted one of the priests and forced him down from his makeshift pulpit. He hated the destruction and disarray with a personal hatred. The earthquake was a double blow, to his birthplace and to his revolution.

'Noble, rich and talented,' an aide recorded of Simón Bolívar, and these were his assets from the beginning.[4] He was born in Caracas on 24 July 1783 to Juan Vicente Bolívar y Ponte and María de la Concepción Palacios y Blanco, the youngest in a family of two brothers and two sisters, and he was christened Simón José Antonio de la Santísima Trinidad. He was seventh-generation American, descendant of the Simón de Bolívar who came to Venezuela from Spain in 1589 in search of a new life. The family lineage has been scoured for signs of race mixture in a society of whites, Indians and blacks, where neighbours were sensitive to the slightest variant, but, in spite of dubious evidence dating from 1673, the Bolívars were always whites. Their economic base was also secure. Basques by origin, in the course of two centuries they had accumulated land, mines, several plantations, cattle, slaves, town houses and a leading place among the white elite. The San Mateo estate, the favourite of the family, dated from the sixteenth century, when it was supported by an *encomienda*, or grant of Indian labour in the valley. In Caracas they lived in a large house in the centre of town. The Bolívars were rooted in the history of Venezuela and had a reputation as *cabildo* officials, militia officers, and supporters of royal policies, accompanied by a claim to aristocratic title. Simón's uncle José Bolívar Aguirre had collaborated eagerly in the suppression of the popular rebellion of 1749.[5] On the maternal side, too, the Palacios were a superior family with aristocratic pretensions and a record as office-holders, their history running parallel to the Bolívars in the public life of Venezuela. There was no doubt that Simón Bolívar was of the elite, but where did his country stand?

Venezuela lay on the southeastern rim of the Caribbean and was the closest to Europe of all Spain's mainland colonies. Bolívar never tired of advising his countrymen to let nature, not theory, be their guide and to cherish the endowments of their native land: 'You will find valuable guidance,' he told the constituent congress of 1830, 'in the very nature of our country, which stretches from the highlands of the Andes to the torrid banks of the Orinoco. Survey the whole extent of this land and you will learn from nature, the infallible teacher of men, what laws the congress must decree.'[6] Travellers approaching Venezuela by sea from Europe first passed Macuro, where in 1498 Columbus encountered mainland America, the Isla de Gracia as he called it, white beaches and lush vegetation with steep jungle slopes behind. Skirting the island of Margarita where prolific pearl fisheries once flourished, they saw further ravishing coastline with clumps of coconut trees, tall palms and shores populated with pelicans and flamingos, and in the dusty ground around Cumaná the *tunales* densely planted with giant cacti and further inland beautiful tamarind trees. Inland in the distant south lay the River Orinoco and Angostura, the pride of Spanish Guayana. Westwards along the Caribbean coast, to the port of La Guaira, the jungle came right down to the beach and mangroves grew on the seashore. At La Guaira sunstroke, yellow fever and sharks were all a hazard before the traveller reached the high plateau inland and the relative safety of Caracas.

Along the west coast, beyond the inland cities of Maracay and Valencia, Coro came into view with its ancient cathedral and vast sand dunes. Regions of great beauty then spread south from the coastal range of mountains into valleys, lakes and rivers, the home of plantations of sugar cane, coffee, cotton and, above all, of cacao. Tropical paradise gave way to the savannahs, or *llanos*, of the east and centre whose vast grasslands were crossed by numerous rivers and subject to relentless droughts and floods, and then in the far west the traveller reached the Segovia highlands with their plateaus, valleys and semi-deserts, and beyond these Lake Maracaibo, where Indian dwellings on stilts gave the Spanish discoverers an illusion of Venice and the country its name. The Venezuelan Andes, running south-west from Trujillo, were topped by Mérida, the roof of Venezuela, recently convulsed by a revolt of the common people against Bourbon exactions.

The German scientist and traveller Alexander von Humboldt, who visited Venezuela in 1799–1800, was overawed by the vastness of the *llanos*: 'The

infinite monotony of the *llanos*; the extreme rarity of inhabitants; the difficulties of travelling in such heat and in an atmosphere darkened by dust; the
perspective of the horizon, which constantly retreats before the traveller; the
few scattered palms that are so similar that one despairs of ever reaching them,
and confuses them with others further afield; all these aspects together make
the stranger looking at the *llanos* think they are far larger than they are.'[7] The
native population of whites and *pardos* were joined in the late eighteenth
century by rebel Indians, fugitive slaves, outlaws and rustlers, rejects of white
society, making the *llanos*, in Humboldt's view, 'the refuge of criminals'. The
llaneros, so remote from the culture of the young Bolívar, were to move nearer
the centre of his life in the wars to come; they were the army's lancers, 'obstinate and ignorant' with low self-esteem, but always treated with consideration
by their general. His first horizons, however, were those of Caracas. Of
Venezuela's 800,000 inhabitants, a mobile population apparently in constant
transit, over half (455,000) lived in the province of Caracas, which was the
prime region of cacao production and of the two new growth exports of
indigo and coffee.[8]

The capital city of Caracas was set in a fertile valley between two mountain
ranges some forty miles and a day's journey by the colonial road, in places little
more than a mule track, which wound its way inland from the coast and the
port of La Guaira. At three thousand feet above sea level the city enjoyed a
warm but more temperate climate than the tropical coast. Central Caracas was
well built around one main square and two smaller ones, with straight, grid-
like streets, many of them paved, and low buildings appropriate to a land of
earthquakes, some of brick, most of adobe. Here the Bolívars owned a number
of properties: in addition to the family house in the Plaza San Jacinto, Simón
inherited from his wealthy uncle Juan Félix Aristeguieta y Bolívar a house on
the main square between the Cathedral and the bishop's palace. Houses of this
kind were decently constructed with spacious patios and gardens watered by
canals fed from the River Catuche, and growing a variety of tropical fruits and
flowers. Gracious living included a distinct, if modest, social and cultural life,
and many homes had libraries they could be proud of. The University of
Caracas began its academic life in 1725 and, while innovation struggled with
tradition, the students were able to study most disciplines of the time and had
access to European thinkers of the seventeenth and eighteenth centuries,
including Spinoza, Locke and Newton.[9]

Humboldt was impressed by the cultural standards of many creoles
(American-born whites), particularly by their exposure to European culture
and knowledge of political matters affecting colonies and metropolis, which
he attributed to 'the numerous communications with commercial Europe and
the West Indies'.[10] He detected among the creole elite of Caracas two tenden-

cies, which he identified with two generations: an older one attached to the past, protective of its privileges and rigid in abhorrence of enlightenment, and a younger one less preoccupied by the present than by the future, attracted to new ways and ideas, firmly attached to reason and enlightenment, and drawn in some cases to a rejection of Spanish culture and a risky connection with foreigners. Bolívar was born into the first group and graduated into the second.

Venezuela was no longer the forgotten colony of Habsburg times, a staging post on the way to the prized viceroyalties of Mexico and Peru. The real history of Venezuela began not with the first conquest but with the second, in the eighteenth century, when Spain reordered the political and economic life of the country and gave it new institutions. The instrument of economic reconquest was the Caracas Company, a Basque-based enterprise that was given a monopoly of trade with Venezuela and soon provided a new impulse to production and export, and a new market for Spain. Bourbon modernization took Venezuela out of the viceroyalty of New Granada and in 1776 gave it an intendant of its own for fiscal and economic administration, and in 1777 a captain-general for political and military control, officials responsible directly to the central government in Madrid and not to an adjacent viceroy. An *audiencia*, or high court of justice, was located in Caracas in 1786 and a *consulado*, or merchant guild, in 1793; Venezuela's legal and commercial business was now its own business and not administered by other Spanish colonies. These institutions did not empower Venezuela: they represented imperial rather than local interests, and Venezuelans were still subject to a distant metropolis. Nevertheless their country now had an identity of its own and was beginning to be conscious of its own interests. It may not have been the heart of the Spanish empire, or the centrepiece of the revolution to come, but as the colonial world receded and Venezuela advanced into a new age, it gave birth to three giants of Spanish American Independence: Francisco de Miranda, the Precursor, Simón Bolívar, the Liberator, and Andrés Bello, the Intellectual.

The Spanish empire was becoming more imperialist. This was not always so. Like all great empires, Spain had the capacity to absorb its colonial peoples. The Habsburg empire had been governed by compromise and consensus, seen first in the growing participation of creoles in the colonial bureaucracy and the law courts, and in the recognition by the crown that colonial societies had identities and interests that it was wise to respect and even to represent. But the years after 1750 saw a de-Americanization of colonial government, the advance of the Bourbon state, the end of compromise politics and creole participation. Bourbon policy was personified in a Spanish intendant, a professional bureaucrat, a generator of resources and collector of revenue.

Creoles were no longer co-opted, they were coerced, and they were acutely conscious of the shift. Juan Pablo Viscardo, the Jesuit émigré and advocate of independence, had been a direct observer of policy trends in Peru and bore witness to the fact that the Bourbons moved from consensus to confrontation, alienated the creole elite, and eventually drove them towards independence. 'From the seventeenth century creoles were appointed to important positions as churchmen, officials, and military, both in Spain and America.' But now Spain had reverted to a policy of preference for peninsular Spaniards 'to the permanent exclusion of those who alone know their own country, whose individual interest is closely bound to it, and who have a sublime and unique right to guard its welfare'.[11] This 'Spanish reaction' was felt throughout America, and not least in Venezuela. Bolívar himself was to complain of the exclusion of Americans from civil, ecclesiastical and financial office, 'perhaps to a greater extent than ever before'.[12] No Venezuelan was appointed to the *audiencia* of Caracas in the period 1786–1810, when ten Spaniards and four colonials held office.[13]

Creoles were aware of their condition, constantly reminded that their country existed for Spain and that their prospects depended upon others. Bolívar himself never forgave or forgot the extreme underdevelopment to which his country was confined, forbidden to compete with the agriculture, industry and commerce of Spain, such as it was, its people forced 'to cultivate fields of indigo, grain, coffee, sugar cane, cacao, and cotton, to raise cattle on the empty plains; to hunt wild beasts in the wilderness; to mine the earth for gold to satisfy the insatiable greed of Spain'.[14] Yet creoles like Bolívar belonged to a colonial elite, well above the *mestizos, mulattos* and slaves toiling at the bottom of society, and as long as their expectations were not too high, with a country estate and a house in Caracas, they could enjoy a life of ease and security under Spanish rule. Few of them were ready to overturn their world.

In Venezuela cacao production and export created a working economy and a regional elite, which in the seventeenth and early eighteenth centuries were largely ignored by the crown and found their economic lifelines in the Americas rather than Spain. From about 1730, however, the crown began to look more closely at Venezuela as a source of revenue for Spain and cacao for Europe. The agent of change was the Caracas Company, a Basque enterprise that was given a monopoly of trade and, indirectly, of administration. Aggressive and novel trading policies, allowing fewer returns for struggling immigrants and even for the traditional planters, outraged local interests and provoked a popular rebellion in 1749. This was quickly crushed and Caracas then had to endure a series of military governors, increased taxation and a greater imperial presence than it had previously experienced. The highest in society were offered capital stock in the reformed Caracas Company, a palliative to secure their collaboration and detach them from popular causes. Thus the new imperialism of the Bourbons, the move from consensus to confrontation, had its trial run in Venezuela. The Caracas experience of regional growth, elite autonomy and royal reaction was early evidence of the great divide in colonial history between the Creole state and the Bourbon state, between compromise and authority. As a leading Bourbon minister observed, colonial peoples will perhaps learn to live without the fruits of freedoms they have never had, but once they have acquired some as of right and enjoyed the taste, they are not going to have them taken away.[15] Bolívar was born into a colony ruled not by consent and devolution but by centralism and absolutism. His parents' generation accepted the innovations in Bourbon government and the loss of traditional creole influence without resistance. The next generation would not be so docile.[16]

Family, Friends and Neighbours

The early life of Bolívar was at once privileged and deprived. He lost his parents while he was young; he had no memory of his father, who died of tuberculosis when he was two and a half; his mother died, also of tuberculosis, when he was nine, and from that point he was left to the tender mercies of uncles of varying qualifications. His father, Juan Vicente Bolívar, had been well known to Caracas society. He followed the family tradition as a colonel in the militia but not apparently in his political views. These revealed divided loyalties, not necessarily between king and independence but between Spaniards and Americans. In 1782 he wrote jointly with two other Caracas grandees a letter to Francisco de Miranda, the Venezuelan officer and dissident who was also wavering in his allegiance, complaining of the 'tyrannical measures' and insults coming from the intendant and his supporters and from every Spaniard, and backed by that 'damned minister Gálvez'. The intendant treated 'all Americans, no matter their class, rank or circumstances, as if they were vile slaves'. They looked to Miranda to help them resist this infamous oppression, for 'you are the first-born son of whom the motherland expects this important service'. But they preferred to await Miranda's advice, for they did not wish to suffer the fate of Santa Fe de Bogotá and Cuzco.[17] Here is an example, if it is true, of political speculation and even of dissidence in the Bolívar family, in thought if not in deed.

Juan Vicente assembled a library of eighteenth-century culture but in other respects he was not a model for his children. A notorious womanizer, 'he was held in fear by women, whites and Indians, maidens and wives'. No girl in his household was safe, as two sisters testified; one, Margarita, had to resist being dragged into a bedroom for sex, and the other, María Jacinta, complained to the bishop of Caracas that 'the wolf, Don Juan Vicente Bolívar, has been importuning me for days to make me sin with him . . . and he sent my husband to the Llanos to [herd] cattle, so as to remain the freer to carry out his evil plans. . . . Do help me for God's sake, for I am on the brink of falling.' But the bishop hushed it all up, more concerned to avoid scandal than to confront the culprit, whom he advised to deny everything.[18] The tactics seem to have succeeded and the serial seducer was able to make a respectable marriage some years later, in December 1773, at the age of forty-six; his bride, Concepción Palacios y Blanco, was an attractive young girl, some thirty years his junior, from a family as distinguished as his own.

Well connected from his parents, Bolívar also had a wealthy cousin, the priest who baptized him, Juan Félix Jerez Aristeguieta y Bolívar, who left him a fortune and various property rights in entail on condition that he remained loyal to God and King. The bequest was additional to his paternal inheritance. The orphan Bolívar, therefore, faced the future more confidently than most Venezuelans, and was less stressed by work, for his income arrived thanks to the labour of others who administered his investments and worked for their yields in various sectors of the Venezuelan economy.

Venezuela was part plantation, part ranch and part commercial market. People and production were concentrated in the valleys of the coast and the *llanos* of the south. Dispersed among the great plains of the interior and the western shores of Lake Maracaibo, hundreds of thousands of cattle, horses, mules and sheep formed one of the country's permanent assets and provided immediate exports in the form of hides and other animal extracts. The commercial plantations produced a variety of export crops: tobacco from Barinas, cotton from the valleys of Aragua, indigo from the Tuy valley and coffee from the Andean provinces. In the 1790s, after a century of economic expansion, these products accounted for over 30 per cent of Venezuela's exports. But the mainstay of the economy was cacao; produced in the valleys and mountain sides of the central coastal zone, cacao expanded until it came to form over 60 per cent of total exports, though vulnerable to competition from Guayaquil.[19] This was the world of the great estates, whose labour was supplied by an ever-expanding slave trade and by tied peons who were often manumitted slaves. Venezuela was a classical colonial economy, low in productivity and in consumption.

Humboldt observed that the Venezuelan aristocracy were averse to independence, because 'they see in revolutions only the loss of their slaves', and he argued that 'they would prefer even a foreign yoke to the exercise of authority by the Americans of an inferior class'.[20] Race prejudice was ingrained in the upper ranks of colonial society. The Miranda family was one of its targets. Sebastián de Miranda Ravelo, father of the Precursor, was a merchant from the Canary Islands. He was appointed, in 1764, captain of the Sixth Company of Fusiliers of the Battalion of White Isleños of Caracas. This provoked a strong reaction from the local oligarchy who branded Miranda a *mulatto* and trader, 'a low occupation unsuitable for white people'; now he could 'wear in the streets the same uniform as men of superior status and pure blood'.[21] The *cabildo* of Caracas, stronghold of the creole oligarchy and guardian of its values, prohibited him 'the use of the uniform and baton of the new battalion, with a warning that if he continued to use them he would be imprisoned in the public gaol for two months'. In the event Miranda was vindicated by the governor and received the support of the colonial authorities, usually more tolerant than the local ruling class. But at a time when *pardos* were striving to improve their legal status, including the right to marry whites and to receive holy orders, the Venezuelan elites continued to identify Canarians as *pardos*, and to impute a racial inferiority to the *isleños*. In 1810 the reservations held by the leaders of Venezuelan Independence towards Francisco de Miranda, the son of a Canarian merchant, were not unaffected by social prejudice against his plebeian origins.

As Bolívar grew up in Caracas his world was a mixture of races and cultures, and he became acquainted with the people who would dominate his public life and determine his political decisions for years to come. The streets of Caracas were becoming more crowded, for this was a growing society: the population of Caracas province probably increased by over a third in size in the years 1785–1810, a growth affecting most racial sectors without altering the balance. The Indians of Venezuela, early victims of disease and dislocation, were mostly out of sight on the margin of society, in remote plains, mountains and forests, or in distant missions administered by friars and unaware of any wider identity. Bolívar's immediate acquaintances were white creoles at the top of a society of castes. Race consciousness was acute and neighbours made it their business to know each other's origins. The whites dominated the bureaucracy, law, the Church, land and the wholesale trade, but they were not a homogeneous group. They consisted of peninsular Spaniards, Venezuelan creoles – comprising a small number of leading families but many more with race mixture in their ancestry and 'passing' for whites – and Canarian immigrants. At the bottom swarmed the *blancos de orilla* (poor whites), artisans, traders and wage-earners, who merged into the *pardos* and were identified with them. Creole Canarians, resident in Venezuela for many generations, also included racially mixed families but were still regarded as Canarians.

Ethnic composition of the Venezuelan Population at the end of the Colonial Period

	Number	Percentage of population
Peninsular Spaniards	1,500	0.18
Creoles of elite status	2,500	0.31
Native Canarians (immigrants)	10,000	1.25
Creole Canarians (*blancos de orilla*)	190,000	23.75
Pardos	400,000	50.00
Blacks (slaves, fugitives and free blacks)	70,000	8.75
Indians	120,000	15.00
Approximate total	800,000	

Source: Lombardi, *People and Places in Colonial Venezuela*, p. 132; Izard, *Series estadísticas para la historia de Venezuela*, p. 9; Báez Gutiérrez, *Historia popular de Venezuela: Período independentista*, p. 3.

People of colour comprised blacks, slaves and free people, and *pardos* or *mulattos*, who were the most numerous group in Venezuela. At the onset of independence, therefore, Venezuelan society was dominated numerically by 400,000 *pardos* and 200,000 Canarians, most of whom would be classified as poor whites. Together, Canarians and *pardos*, many of whom were descended from Canarians, made up 75 per cent of the total population, though they rarely acted together.

The poor whites had little in common with Bolívar's class, the *mantuanos*, owners of land and slaves, producers of the colony's wealth, commanders of the colony's militia. Land was their base and land their ambition, though not necessarily to the exclusion of commerce, and successful merchants were known to invest in land and to marry into creole planter families. The wealthiest *hacendados* were drawn from the oldest families of the province, friends and acquaintances of the Bolívars. They were led by the marqués del Toro, whose annual income was estimated in 1781 at 25,000 to 30,000 pesos and personal wealth at 504,632 pesos, together with numerous properties. Then came a small group of some thirteen individuals with comparable wealth, incuding the first conde de Tovar, followed closely by the conde de la Granja, the conde de San Xavier, Dr José Ignacio Moreno, the marqués de Casa León, Marcos Ribas and Juan Vicente Bolívar. Simón's father owned two cacao plantations, four houses in Caracas and others in La Guaira, sugar cane on the San Mateo estate, three cattle ranches in the *llanos*, an indigo plantation and a copper mine, and he left 350,000 pesos to his family, including the young Simón.[22] At the end of the colonial period the landed aristocracy, the majority of them creoles, comprised 658 families, totalling 4,048 people, or 0.5 per cent of the population. This was the small group who monopolized land and mobilized labour, but whose riches were becoming fragmented as the older generation died and their heirs divided up their estates. The largest share of the Bolívar legacy, 120,000 pesos, went to the eldest son, Juan Vicente junior. A few of the top families were extremely rich, while most of the elites had middling incomes. But they were obsessed with status symbols and titles of aristocracy, most of which were bought, not inherited. They usually lived in town houses and were active in such institutions as Spanish practice opened to them, the *cabildos* the *consulado* and the militia. Almost all the families whose friendship Humboldt enjoyed in Caracas – the Uztáriz, the Tovares, the Toros – had their base in the beautiful valleys of Aragua, where they were proprietors of the richest plantations and where the Bolívars had their historic estate.

The *pardos*, or free coloureds, were branded by their racial origins; descendants of black slaves, they comprised *mulattos, zambos* and *mestizos* in general, as well as *blancos de orilla* whose ancestry was suspect. In the towns they were artisans and an incipient wage-labour group; in the country they were plantation overseers, or engaged in subsistence farming and cattle enterprises, or they were a rural peonage. With the free blacks they formed almost half the total population; their numbers were particularly noticeable in the towns, where the seeds of discontent often grew into open conflict.[23] The *pardos* were not a class but an indeterminate, unstable and intermediary mass, blurring at the edges downwards and upwards. But whatever they were, they alarmed the whites by their numbers and aspirations. From 1760 they were allowed to join the militias, become officers, and enjoy the military *fuero*. By a law of 10 February 1795 they were granted the legal right to purchase certificates of whiteness (*cédulas de gracias al sacar*), which released them from discrimination and authorized them to receive an education, marry whites, hold public office and become priests. The imperial government encouraged this mobility for reasons of its own, which were not entirely clear. It may have been an attempt to release social tensions by allowing *pardos* to compete with whites, at the same time introducing competition into public life and undermining traditional ideals of honour and status.

Few *pardos* invoked this law or ventured into the courts to claim their rights.[24] They might have made their way in the economy but they were still denied social recognition. In a caste society, where law defined status, the advantage was with the whites. The creoles went over to the offensive and opposed the advance of the *gente de color*, protested against the sale of whiteness, resisted popular education and petitioned, though unsuccessfully, against the presence of *pardos* in the militia. Concession to the *pardos*, they declared, was 'a calamity stemming from ignorance on the part of European officials, who come here already prejudiced against the American-born whites and falsely informed concerning the real situation of the country'. The protesters regarded it as unacceptable 'that the whites of this province should admit into their class a *mulatto* descended from their own slaves'. They argued that this could only lead to the subversion of the existing regime: 'The establishment of militias led by officers of their own class has handed the *pardos* a power which will be the ruin of America ... giving them an organization, leaders, and arms, the more easily to prepare a revolution.'[25] A strict distinction was maintained between white and black militias; in Sabana de Ocumare new militia companies were formed, 'four of whites, six of *pardos*, two of blacks, and four of Indians'. [26] In the eyes of the authorities the superiority of white recruitment was taken for granted; even so, the creoles resented imperial policy towards the *pardos*: it was too indulgent; it was 'an insult to the old, distinguished, and honoured families'; it was dangerous 'to enfranchise the *pardos* and to grant them, by dispensation from their low status, the education which they have hitherto lacked and ought to continue to lack in the future'. Race was an issue in Venezuela, usually dormant, but with potential for violence. The creoles were frightened people; they feared a caste war, inflamed by French revolutionary doctrine and the contagious violence of Saint Domingue, the future Haiti.

These forebodings were intensified by horror of slave agitation and revolt. Again the creole aristocracy lost confidence in the metropolis. Slaves were everywhere in colonial society, carrying for their masters in the streets, working as domestics in houses, labouring in workshops. But most of them worked in plantations and without them Venezuela's production would have stopped, and families such as the Bolívars would have seen their profits plunge. For some reason slave imports into Venezuela began to diminish in the 1780s, a time when an expanding economy had removed trade laws restricting imports and planters were ready to pay more for slaves.[27] The young Bolívar's widowed mother complained about the price of slaves and their failure to reproduce. On 31 May 1789 the Spanish government issued a new slave law, codifying legislation, clarifying the rights of slaves and duties of masters, and in general seeking improvement of conditions in the slave compounds. The creoles rejected state intervention between master and slave, and fought this decree on the grounds that slaves were prone to vice and independence and were essential to the economy. In Venezuela – indeed all over the Spanish Caribbean – planters resisted the law and procured its suspension in 1794.[28]

The following year both reformers and reactionaries could claim to have proved their point when a black and *pardo* revolt convulsed Coro, the centre of the sugar cane industry, the home of fifteen thousand slaves and *pardos* and the base of a white aristocracy so class conscious that 'the families of notorious nobility and purity of blood live in terror of the day that one of their members should surprisingly marry a *coyote* or *zambo*.'[29] The revolt was led by José Leonardo Chirino and José Caridad González, free blacks who were influenced by the ideas of the French revolution and the race war in Saint Domingue. They stirred up the slaves and black labourers, three hundred of whom rose in rebellion in May 1795 with the proclamation: 'The law of the French, the republic, the freedom of the slaves, and the suppression of the *alcabala* and other taxes.'[30] They occupied *haciendas*, sacked property, killed any landowners they could lay hands on and invaded the city of Coro. This was an isolated and ill-equipped rebellion and was easily crushed, many of its followers being shot without trial. Yet it was only the tip of a constant underlying struggle of the blacks against the whites in the last years of the colony, when slave fugitives frequently established their own communes, remote from white authority.

The creole elite was conditioned by disorder. The conspiracy of Manuel Gual and José María España frankly sought to establish an independent republic of Venezuela, attacking 'the bad colonial government' and invoking the example of the English colonies in North America. The two Venezuelan leaders, white creoles and minor functionaries by career, were prompted by a Spanish exile, Juan Bautista Picornell, reader of Rousseau and the *encyclopédistes*, and a confirmed republican. Recruiting *pardos* and poor whites, labourers and small proprietors, and a few professional people, the conspiracy surfaced in La Guaira in July 1797 with an appeal for 'liberty and equality' and the rights of man, and it had a plan of action for taking power and installing a republican government. The programme included freedom of trade, suppression of the *alcabala* and other taxes, abolition of slavery and of Indian tribute and distribution of land to the Indians, and it pleaded for harmony between whites, Indians and coloureds, 'brothers in Christ and equal before God'.[31] This was too radical for creole property-owners, many of whom collaborated with the authorities in suppressing the 'infamous and detestable' movement and offered to serve the captain-general 'not only with our persons and *haciendas* but also by forming armed companies at our own cost'.[32] España was taken and executed in the main square of Caracas, accompanied by tolling bells, solicitous priests and a military detachment, and his limbs were displayed on pikes on the highroads, while his wife was imprisoned for protecting him. The conspiracy may have been small and fleeting but it gave voice to ideas of liberty and equality and left traces of discontent.

Two years later Humboldt observed some of the repercussions of the rebellion. On the road from La Guaira to Caracas he encountered a group of Venezuelan travellers discussing the issues of the day, the hatred of the *mulattos* for the free blacks and whites, 'the wealth of the monks', the difficulty of holding slaves in obedience, and bitterly disputing with each other on all these matters. They had to take shelter from a storm: 'When we entered the inn, an old man, who had spoken with the most calmness, reminded the others how imprudent it was, in a time of denunciation, on the mountain as well as in the city, to engage in political discussion. These words, uttered in a spot of so wild an aspect, made a lively impression on my mind.'[33] He also had an impression of anticlericalism, though this was not an obvious trend in Venezuela.

Religion, reputed to be severe in the Hispanic world, was worn lightly by Venezuelans, and while Bolívar received a large legacy from a clerical cousin he seems to have received little else from the Church. The clergy of this poorly endowed colony had few opportunities of preferment. According to Bishop Mariano Martí few of them deserved it. In the course of his pastoral visitations he became totally disillusioned with his clergy, many of them local creoles, hardly distinguishable from their parishioners in moral behaviour. Negligence, ignorance and incompetence were the norm among parish priests, who seem to have been by-passed by both Counter-Reformation and Enlightenment.[34] Martí himself was a model of a Bourbon bishop, an agent of both Church and state, his work an amalgam of functions, inspired by the conviction that priests should be warned against subversion as well as sin and that his visitation should yield a total view of Venezuela, both secular and religious. A Spaniard by birth, he was a reformer, determined to improve the Christian and moral level of America. After heading a diocese in Puerto Rico he became bishop of Venezuela in 1770 at the age of forty-one.

Martí saw his episcopal role as an almost constant *visita*, lasting from 1771 to 1784, and covering the Venezuelan coast, Andes and *llanos*: Indians, Africans, slaves, Spaniards and mixed races, rural and urban society, priests and people, no one escaped his interrogations. As he travelled the mountains, valleys and plains of his diocese he invited the people of each town to confide the details of their 'sinful' behaviour – and that of their neighbours – which he then proceeded to record and judge, leaving for posterity a vivid picture of how Venezuelans were living. Life was evidently not all work. His records (seven volumes in their modern edition) list over fifteen hundred individuals singled out for accusation, primarily of sexual misdeeds. Adultery, fornication, concubinage, incest, rape, bigamy, prostitution, lust, homosexuality, bestiality, abortion and infanticide, these were the various practices across the land, while drunkenness, gambling, witchcraft, murder, theft and idolatry competed for the people's pleasure and the bishop's attention. He took a wide view of sin and his reprobates included *hacendados* who were cruel towards their slaves, village priests who were harsh towards mission Indians, and merchants and shopkeepers who levied usurious charges on their customers.

Nearly 10 per cent of clerics in the province came under criticism, and even the governor of Maracaibo was denounced. Not surprisingly, the bishop's probing earned him the enmity of many regional elites, as well as some local clerics.

For his part Martí was not impressed by the reluctance of the upper classes to marry their children to racial inferiors, and he insisted that unions be solemnized according to Christian morality, not left informal. But in practice he could not defeat social prejudice and prevent informal partnerships, a practice that avoided interracial marriages. In any case Martí did not challenge prevailing standards and he usually imposed punishments on female slaves rather than the slave owners who seduced them. There was an ingrained bias in religious culture, which regarded women as occasions of sin and blamed their allure, behaviour and dress for all sexual temptations, rather than men and conditions, a mentality characteristic of the Church throughout the Americas.

It was easier to describe the ways of Venezuelans than to change them. Bishop Martí tried to impose a moral code and to encourage Christian behaviour in social and sexual relations. He issued proclamations prohibiting dancing and he proscribed improper dress for women. On his visitation he exhorted priests to preach and apply the commandments. But it was a losing battle to apply the rules of the Church at every level of colonial society, or to narrow the gap between morals and behaviour. In one village drunkenness would be 'the main sin', in another robbery. For the majority of Venezuelans, especially the popular classes, marriage was an optional institution, virginity an ideal rather than a practice, illegitimacy acceptable and casual unions not uncommon. For those with little or nothing to lose, marriage and legitimacy were not a particular advantage. They were, it is true, assets to the upper classes, as Bolívar's marriage documents make clear, but for reasons of inheritance and public office rather than moral repute, and in Hispanic society infidelity was not regarded as a serious threat to marriage.

Martí's visitation points to an enduring truth about colonial Venezuela, and equally the whole of Spanish America. Faith was not in doubt. The Church preached its doctrine and performed its liturgy in a society that easily accepted both. During his visitation the bishop saw many signs of religious fervour. Of the white, *mestizo*, *mulatto* and black population of Tinaquillo he wrote that they are 'a devout people, many of them daily mass goers; they frequent the sacraments and come to say the rosary at 3 o'clock'. Of Ocumare he reported: 'The parish priest tells me the nature of these people is such that if they are invited to a dance they all go; equally, if they are invited to a church service they all go. There is no particular vice among them.' In the small village of Parapara the people were 'docile, of good disposition, and frequent the sacraments'.[35] There was evidently much popular piety in Venezuela. Christian morals, however, were a different matter, accepted by most in theory but ignored by many in practice.

A Youth of Independent Means

Bolívar's formative years lacked the structure of school and university, and he was denied even the props of family life. His mother, loving in nature but frail in health, was only thirty-three when she died, leaving him an orphan at the age of nine. His memories were mellowed by time and distance and his Caracas childhood came back to him as a period of joy. When the one uncle he trusted, Esteban Palacios, returned from Spain to Venezuela in 1825, Bolívar, who was in Peru at the time, was much moved by the news: 'I learned yesterday that you were alive and living in our dear homeland. How many memories crowded my mind at that moment. My mother, my dear mother, so like you, rose from the dead and appeared before me. My earliest childhood, my confirmation and my godfather at that event were focused into one as I realized that you were my second father. . . . All my memories rushed back to reawaken my earliest emotions.'[36] The reality was not so idyllic. When his mother died he went to live with his grandfather, who assigned his uncles to him as guardians. Esteban was permanently absent in Spain, ineffectually trying to secure the family's claim to nobility. So his real guardian was the nearby Carlos, something of a misanthrope, anxious to get his hands on his nephew's inheritance, and a racist who referred to *mulattos* as a 'rabble'. Taking precedence in the child's esteem was his black nurse Hipólita, a slave from the San Mateo estate, who became a mother and father to him. Years later he asked his sister to look after her: 'Her milk has nourished my life and she is the only father I have known.'[37] An indulgent father, it seems, and he emerged from her care unaccustomed to discipline.

His solicitude for Hipólita was accompanied by concern about his own reputation as a youth. Stung perhaps by malicious rumours spread by his enemies and by the French traveller Gaspar Mollien that he was uneducated, he later wrote to his colleague Santander, 'It is not true that my education was badly neglected, for my mother and tutors did all they could to ensure that I applied myself to study: they secured for me the leading teachers in my country. Robinson [Simón Rodríguez], whom you know, taught me reading and writing and grammar; geography and literature were taught by the famous Bello; Father Andújar, so much esteemed by Humboldt, set up an academy of mathematics especially for me. . . . Still in my youth I took lessons in fencing, dancing, and horsemanship.'[38] For 'academy' perhaps we should read 'classes', given for a small number of pupils in Bolívar's own home, but otherwise his claim that he was educated as well as any American child of good family could possibly have been under Spanish rule was more or less correct. It is later historians who have exaggerated the influence of Rodríguez, Venezuela's star of the Enlightenment.

In 1793 the ten-year-old Simón was enrolled in the Escuela Pública de Caracas, along with 113 other pupils, who were taught reading, writing and arithmetic, and religious doctrine. The young Rodríguez was a conscientious if dissatisfied teacher in this ramshackle institution, where education was rudimentary; pupils arrived at any hour, some paid, some did not.[39] The boy came to hate both the school and the man appointed to be his guardian, his uncle Carlos Palacios, and in 1795, at the age of twelve, he fled from both to the house of his sister, María Antonia, and her husband. She received him with open arms, convinced that he needed protection not only against his uncle but also against his own inclination 'to wander by himself through the streets of Caracas, on foot and on horseback, mixing with boys who are not of his class'. He showed an early determination to take command of his life, not only in mixing easily with other classes but in standing up to the *audiencia*, telling them they could do what they liked with his property but not with his person, and that if slaves had the freedom to choose their masters, so did he have the right to choose where he lived.[40] But Carlos Palacios did not intend to allow this family asset to slip so easily from his grasp. After an ill-tempered lawsuit and spirited resistance by the boy he was propelled back to school and to the house of his teacher, Rodríguez; this was a motley ménage not apparently to his liking, which he soon abandoned for his guardian's house. His education was subsequently advanced through the tuition of Father Andújar, a Capuchin missionary priest, who held his classes in Bolívar's home, and the young Andrés Bello, who taught a few private pupils before entering the colonial bureaucracy and who later described Bolívar as a talented but restless young man, deficient in application.[41]

It is often assumed that the most influential of Bolívar's teachers was Simón Rodríguez, but whatever their subsequent relationship they had only brief contact in Caracas, and the boy's resistance to authority in 1795 seems to have been directed against his teacher Rodríguez as well as his uncle. Already a dissident, the teacher left Caracas in 1797 and, taking the name of Samuel Robinson, spent the next years in the United States and Europe before he met Bolívar again. His contribution to the intellectual life of the time was that of a pedagogue rather than a philosopher, and his principal concern was securing education for citizens of the new republics, believing that without popular education there could be no true society and without society no republic. His conversion to Rousseau's *Emile* could have had little influence in Caracas where he was teaching not one-to-one but in a school of over a hundred pupils.

In the tradition of his family Bolívar enrolled at the age of fourteen as a cadet in the elite militia corps, the White Volunteers of the Valley of Aragua, which had been founded by his grandfather and commanded by his father. Here natural powers of leadership emerged, and he was promoted to second lieutenant after a year; he completed his military training, which was probably not extensive, with a good report. This was a typical step among the creole elite. So, too, was the decision of his guardian to send him to Spain, the American equivalent of the grand tour, there to continue his studies in a style appropriate for an upper-class creole. Carlos Palacios sent him to his uncle Esteban with a mean recommendation, warning that the boy had already spent extravagantly on the journey, so 'it is necessary to control him, as I have said before, first because otherwise he will become accustomed to spending money without restraint or economy, and second because he is not as wealthy as he imagines. . . . You must talk to him firmly and put him in a college if he does not behave with the judgement and application he should.'[42] The unstated conclusion of this letter was probably 'otherwise he might waste the family fortune and we shall all suffer'.

Old Spain, Young Love

Bolívar left Caracas for Spain at the age of fifteen. Behind him lay an affluent if troubled childhood, a family life with its ups and downs, and only brief contact with his teachers, two of whom, Rodríguez and Bello, would return to his life in later years. Here was a youth deprived of strong family supports but not of his wealth and confidence. Self-pity he had none and the modern tendency to attribute a person's later behaviour to a disturbed childhood was totally absent from his thinking. He was no rebel and knew when to back off, but he already showed signs of a strong will and power of decision, qualities enhanced by some military training and inclination, while freedom from close family control enabled him to socialize easily with lower-class people and to show an early trace of that *noblesse oblige* that became a hallmark of his character.

He sailed from La Guaira on 19 January 1799 on the *San Ildefonso*, a Spanish warship that had to navigate warily; Spain was at war with England, and Havana, the port of rendezvous for convoys returning to Spain, was blockaded by the enemy, as he explained in a letter to his uncle Pedro Palacios Blanco, an early lesson for the boy in relative sea power.[43] The delay in Veracruz, where the ship loaded Mexican silver, gave Bolívar time to make a quick visit to Mexico City before the Atlantic crossing; this was made without incident and the vessel docked at Santoña, Vizcaya, on 13 May 1799. From there he made his way to Madrid.

Bourbon Madrid, a city of palaces, grand houses, historic squares and streets, with an active cultural and social life, presented a sensational contrast to the urban existence Bolívar had known in Caracas. Behind the façade, however, Spain was in deep recession, and had little to teach an American except the illusion of power. Since 1789 the entry of French revolutionary ideas and invasion by French armies would have tested any regime. But this was a special regime, headed by a king, Charles IV, whose vacant benevolence, depicted by Goya, was also characteristic of his political attitudes, and Godoy recalled how each night the king would ask him, 'What have my subjects been doing today?'[44] Queen María Luisa of Parma was a source of scandal in Spain and speculation abroad. Spaniards believed that she took lovers even before she met Manuel Godoy and was not averse to them thereafter. But she knew what she was doing in selecting Godoy and grooming him to be first minister, creature of the monarchs, their support and adviser. Godoy was expected to deal firmly with France, but he took Spain into a ruinous war with its neighbour and then, in 1796, to an expensive peace. The Spain that Bolívar entered in 1799, therefore, was not a metropolis to inspire confidence: what he observed was a satellite of France and an enemy of Britain, a costly dilemma from which the old regime would only escape after a decade of destruction.

Bolívar lodged first with his two uncles, Esteban and Pedro Palacios, in a house belonging to Manuel Mallo, a minor South American courtier with Godoy-like pretensions and a lifestyle of doubtful propriety. As they were a family unit the three soon moved out to a house of their own, where being permanently short of money and observing the high-spending lifestyle of their nephew, the uncles were anxious for Bolívar to pay some of the bills. Esteban had a modest government sinecure that kept him alive while he lobbied unsuccessfully for a noble title for the family; lacking top contacts, hovering on the fringes of court life, and always impecunious, he was no advertisement for the Bolívars. Fortunately for Simón he found a more serious patron in the marquis of Uztáriz, another Venezuelan who, after a good education in Caracas, had secured an official career in Spain; when Bolívar went to lodge with him in 1800 at 6 calle de Atocha, he was Minister of the War Council.

Uztáriz was the first stable influence in Bolívar's life, effectively his guardian and tutor in Madrid, a father figure always remembered with respect.[45] Under his direction and in his extensive library, the young man studied philosophy, history, mathematics and languages, and in his circle he was able to develop his social skills, to listen and to learn. And there he met María Teresa Rodríguez del Toro y Alayza, daughter of a Venezuelan father and Spanish mother, a nineteen-year-old, whose dark eyes, pale complexion and, above all, shy and gentle nature captivated Bolívar. Seventeen as he was, he quickly declared his love. Romance was accompanied by calculation. The entail bequeathed to him by Aristeguieta depended on his making a good marriage, so he began his campaign without delay, 'to avoid', he said, 'the damage I would cause by failing to have an heir'.[46] He was betrothed in August 1800 and became her *novio*. He was impatient when the widowed father took her off to their house in Bilbao, 'lovable enchantress of my soul', and at the same time seems to have suspected that his love was greater than hers. With Uztáriz's departure from Madrid to a posting in Teruel, the capital suddenly became empty for Bolívar, and he experienced some obscure hostility from the authorities. So he moved to Bilbao in March 1801 and then made a quick visit to Paris in January–March 1802, where he came to the conclusion that 'Spain was a country of savages compared to France'.[47] In April 1802 Bolívar was given leave to return to Spain and he rushed to Madrid to renew his pursuit of María Teresa and, on 5 May, to make a formal declaration of intent to marry, unimpeded by 'any vow of chastity or other canonical impediment'. By now her father had relented, persuaded no doubt by the marriage agreement and a glance at the figure of 200,000 duros as the young man's assets. Bolívar described María Teresa as 'a jewel without a flaw, valuable beyond esteem', but his lawyers helped him to place a value on her and he settled a handsome sum of money (100,000 reales, one tenth of his liquid assets) on the bride, 'in consideration of her distinguished birth, her virginity, her spinsterhood, her personal qualities, and her readiness to leave Spain with her husband'.[48] Immediate return to Venezuela, in fact, was Bolívar's next priority. They were married in the church of San Sebastián on 26 May 1802; he was eighteen, she twenty-one. They left promptly for La Coruña and took ship for Caracas on 15 June. Since the Peace of Amiens in March the Atlantic was a peaceful sea and they made a good crossing to La Guaira, arriving on 12 July. Their home in Venezuela, however, was not to be a haven.

Bolívar owned various properties, a town house on the corner of Las Gradillas, south-east of the main square of Caracas, an estate in the valley of Seuse on the southern edge of the city, the *hacienda* of Yare, where he established extensive indigo plantations, and the San Mateo estate in the Aragua valley, the historic seat of the family. It was here that Bolívar took his young wife, who began to set up home while he supervised the work of the estate and took exercise on foot and horseback.[49] His joy was brief. María Teresa contracted a malignant fever, weakened rapidly, and on 22 January 1803 died, just eight months after her wedding. Bolívar was distraught, overcome by immense grief and the loss of young love.

The next months were ones of unrelieved sadness. Everywhere he looked in Caracas there were problems, and the emptiness he felt at home was filled by a series of trying frustrations in his affairs. He had to rebuke his uncle Carlos

Palacios for sharp practice in the accounting of his inheritance; he was forced to complain to the authorities against his neighbours at Seuse who were encroaching on his estate; investments had to be made in his coffee and indigo plantations and arrangements for the export of their products; and negotiations for transfer of funds to Europe were proving difficult. All these troubles strengthened his decision that it was time to get out. Years later he unburdened himself.

> I loved my wife dearly, and her death caused me to vow that I would never marry again; I have kept my word. See how things have turned out: had I not been widowed perhaps my life would have been different; I would not be General Bolívar, nor the Liberator, though I agree I was not made to be the mayor of San Mateo. . . . But when I arrived in Caracas from Europe with my bride in 1801 [1802], let me say at once that my mind was filled only with the emotions of passionate love and not with political ideas, for these had not yet taken hold of my imagination. When my wife died and I was left desolate from that premature and unexpected loss, I returned to Spain, and from Madrid I went to France and then to Italy. It was then that I began to take an interest in public affairs, politics began to concern me, and I followed the different changes then emerging. . . . Without the death of my wife I would not have made my second journey to Europe, and it is probable that the ideas I acquired on my travels would not have taken root in Caracas or San Mateo, nor would I have gained in America the experience and knowledge of the world, of men, and of things that have been so valuable to me in the course of my political career. The death of my wife propelled me early on the road to politics.[50]

Personal tragedy not only sent him back to Europe to study and learn; he there acquired the knowledge and experience to equip him for a political role. When he returned there was no one to equal him.

Chapter 2

LESSONS FROM THE AGE OF REASON

Life in Paris

Once he had ordered his affairs and secured his finances in Caracas, Bolívar set sail for Spain in October 1803 and reached Cadiz by the end of the year. But, as he planned his life anew, Spain did not satisfy his interests. He paused in Madrid, long enough to see his father-in-law and share his grief, and by mid August 1804 he was in Paris.

At the age of twenty-one Bolívar's looks, though restrained, were those of a young man somewhat arrogant and pleased with himself, fresh-faced, if the surviving miniature is correct, with regular features and frank eyes already questioning. Other sightings of those years remain elusive, though we know that he was of medium height, about five foot six, slim and narrow-chested. Fifteen years later his appearance had changed and he had become the Simón Bolívar known in the classic portraits. Daniel Florencio O'Leary, his loyal aide who saw him most days, recorded in his private notes a recognizable description:

> Gl B's forehead was very high, but not unusually broad. It had many wrinkles. His eyebrows were thick, but well shaped; his eyes were dark and keen; his nose rather long and handsome. . . . His cheek bones were salient, his cheeks sunken ever since I first knew him (May 1818). His mouth was ugly, his lips being thick, the upper one long. His teeth were regular, white and beautiful. He took particular care of them. His jaw bones and chin were long. His ears were large. His hair, which he wore long (until it began to turn gray, 1822), was extremely black and curly. . . . His skin was dark and rough, his hands and feet remarkably small and pretty.[1]

In 1804 the days of youth were his glory, wrinkles and grey hairs unimagined.

In Paris he rented a house in the rue Vivienne and took up with other exiles from South America. If the gossip can be believed, he passed with unseemly haste from grieving widower to profligate playboy, plunging into a crazed life of gambling and sex, feeding legends that he did nothing to dispel. Did he have countless women? Perhaps. There was certainly a favourite. Among the parties he attended were those of Fanny Dervieu du Villars, who presided over one of the more liberal salons of the time much frequented by the chattering classes and fringe elements of the *demi-mondaine.*

In 1804 Fanny du Villars was a young woman, not yet thirty, married to a man, Count Dervieu du Villars, almost twice her age. Fair of face, with large blue eyes, smooth voice and languid movements, she immediately attracted Bolívar, who became a frequent visitor to her house. Was she the lover who assuaged his grief, unlocked his heart, released his spirit and satisfied his desires?[2] In letters written years later she insists that he had loved her 'sincerely' and reminds him that he gave her a ring which she still wore; he had confided in her and shared 'great plans', while she had wept tears to prevent him leaving. Her looks may have gone with the years, but she was the same woman. Could he come to her assistance and enable her to buy the house in Paris where he had known her? She calls him 'cousin', asks him to look after their godson, Simón Briffard, and slyly hopes that he is 'the only godson you have in Europe'.[3] Were these fanciful recollections or calculating appeals? The letters were written between 1820 and 1826 and she seems to have been hoping to revive their relationship in times of hardship when she had three sons and a seventy-six-year-old husband to look after, and Bolívar had gone on to glory. Bolívar left Paris in 1806 and they never met again. He ignored her appeals and maintained a discreet silence.

It was probably in Fanny du Villars's salon, in September 1804, that Bolívar met Alexander von Humboldt, recently returned with Aimé Bonpland from their American travels. The conversation passed into history and became another Bolivarian fable. Bolívar referred to the glittering destiny of a South America freed from the yoke of oppression, and Humboldt replied that although the country was ready for liberation there was no one capable of leading it. An apt exchange, except that there is no evidence that it ever took place.[4] The time was not yet right for a meeting of minds between an unknown liberator and the distinguished liberal. In public Humboldt was politically discreet about the Hispanic world. Over-impressed, perhaps, by the opinions of affluent creoles, he thought that the Spanish colonies were recon- ciled to their condition and did not wish to exchange peace and security for revolutionary upheaval. As for Bolívar, his political ideas were still unformed and he was not so presumptuous in 1804 to imagine himself a leader of a liberation movement. In the event Humboldt, unlike Bonpland, was not impressed by Bolívar. Half a century later he admitted to O'Leary his early doubts. In 1804, he wrote, he had met the young man in Paris and noticed his love of liberty and lively conversation, but saw him as a dreamer: 'I never believed he was destined to be leader of the American crusade.' During his sojourn in America, he added, he had not encountered serious opposition to Spain, though once the struggle began he then saw the deep hatred that existed: 'But what most surprised me was the brilliant career of Bolívar, so soon after our separation in 1805 when I left Paris for Italy.'[5] Subsequent relations between the distinguished scientist and the young creole were distant and intermittent. Bolívar was deferential to Humboldt and in a letter of 1821 called him 'a great man' who had served America well and become for its people a model of high moral purpose.[6] Humboldt had no contact with Bolívar in the years 1806–21, but then wrote three letters of recommendation on behalf of European visitors, expressing his admiration for 'the founder of the liberty and independence of your beautiful homeland'. A trace of scepticism remained; as one who had seen the divisions in American society he believed that peace would prevail only if correct social institutions and wise legislation preserved the republic from civil dissension.

Political Awakening

Bolívar's years in Europe from 1804 to 1806 were not consumed by his social life: they were above all the time of his intellectual awakening, when he began to read, observe and experience politics. His innate curiosity was stirred as the international situation developed before his eyes. Now the weakness of Spain was impossible to ignore, threatened as it was by imperial France and confronted by the sea power of Britain, the victor of Trafalgar. In a changing world, what did the future hold for Spanish America? And what did Spanish America promise for Bolívar? The slavery of his country and the glory of freeing it were a personal challenge. The prospect of power attracted him, but what were his chances? It was in Paris that the Napoleonic myth first entered his mind. It is not certain that Bolívar was actually in Paris when the empire was instituted on 18 May 1804 and Napoleon, previously first consul, was proclaimed emperor at St Cloud. But he was in Paris on 2 December, that bitterly cold day when Napoleon warmed the hearts of Frenchmen, crowning himself emperor in Notre Dame in the presence of Pope Pius VII. Bolívar was attracted and repelled. The sources are divided, as were his own responses.

According to O'Leary, Bolívar was invited to attend the ceremony in the suite of the Spanish ambassador, and he not only refused but shut himself in his house the whole day. The reason? For Bolívar, Napoleon was no longer the hero of the republic, 'the symbol of liberty and glory, the object of his political admiration' that he had been two years previously when he ratified the peace of Amiens, but a tyrant and a hypocrite, an enemy of freedom.[7] There is another version of his thoughts, as reported in the diary of Peru de Lacroix, a Frenchman who had served in the army of the emperor before gravitating towards Bolívar's campaigns. There he expressed himself inspired by the event, less for the pageant than for the spontaneous outpouring of love that more than a million people lavished on the French hero, an experience that he saw as the supreme ambition of man.

> The crown which Napoleon placed on his head I regarded as a miserable thing and a gothic fancy: what seemed great to me was the universal acclaim and interest that his person inspired. This, I confess, made me think of my country's slavery and the glory in store for the man who would free her. But how far was I from imagining that such a fortune awaited me! Later, it is true, I began to flatter myself that one day I would be able to participate in her liberation but not that I would play the leading role in so great an event.[8]

Notre Dame was not Bolívar's last opportunity to see Napoleon. Between social distractions and serious reading, Bolívar's life in the French capital reached a time of decision. Influenced perhaps by Simón Rodríguez, whom he met again in Paris, and his political instincts aroused by the events around him, he embarked on a tour of Italy early in 1805. The influence of Rodríguez on Bolívar's intellectual formation is difficult to define, intermittent as it was, though attested by Bolívar himself: 'You formed my heart for liberty, for justice, for the great, for the beautiful. . . . You cannot imagine how deeply engraved upon my heart are the lessons you gave me.'[9] Rodríguez was an inspiring teacher, perhaps, but not a contributor to the thought of the Enlightenment or the philosophy of the eighteenth century. For Bolívar, however, he seems to have been a channel of independent thinking.

In April 1805 Bolívar took his leave of Fanny du Villars and sealed the parting with a ring. With a Venezuelan friend, Fernando del Toro, son of the marqués del Toro, and accompanied by Simón Rodríguez, he set off on a walking tour to the south, though how much actual walking the trio did is a matter of conjecture, as is the notion that this was a health cure after months of dissipation. Via Lyons and Chambéry, in deference to Rousseau, they crossed the Alps to Milan, where the triumphant entry of Napoleon and the throng of people to welcome him were unforgettable sights. Near Castiglione they witnessed a great march past with Napoleon seated on a throne on a small incline, and Bolívar was struck by the emperor's plain clothing in contrast to that of his officers.

Bolívar continued his tour, travelling via Verona, Vicenza and Padua to Venice, whose beauties he could not ignore, but the glory of Venice, from which his country took its name, had been exaggerated in his mind and he was disappointed. In Florence he paused to admire the monuments and art but not, apparently, the writings of Machiavelli, whose ideas provoked in him an instinctive dislike for their amorality. Long afterwards, a few months before his death, Bolívar visited O'Leary in Cartagena and, seeing on his table a new edition of the works of Machiavelli, observed that he should have better things to do with his time. In the course of a conversation on the merits of Machiavelli, Bolívar appeared to be quite familiar with the contents of the edition and O'Leary asked him if he had read it recently. Bolívar replied that he had never read a word of Machiavelli since he'd left Europe twenty-five years before.[10]

On the approach to Rome, Bolívar's excitement grew as he recalled the history of ancient Rome and gazed upon the sites of former glories; a mind already filled with the classical past and modern philosophy was now fired by hopes for the future of his country and himself. The ruins of the Capitol stirred his imagination and in the August heat he hurried to the Aventine, the Monte Sacro where Sicinius led the people of Rome in protest against their patrician rulers. Mind and heart responded to the scene. 'On Monte Sacro,' writes O'Leary, 'the sufferings of his own country overwhelmed his mind, and he knelt down and made that vow whose faithful fulfilment the emancipation of South America is the glorious witness.'[11]

The vow was made on 15 August 1805 in the presence of his mentor Rodríguez and his friend Toro. The lengthy preliminary, where the pen of Rodríguez may well have prevailed, reviews the history and civilization of ancient Rome, its heroes and traitors: 'This nation has examples for everything, except for the cause of humanity. . . . For the emancipation of the spirit, the elimination of cares, the exaltation of man, and the final perfectibility of reason, little or nothing. . . . The resolution of the great problem of human freedom seems to have been something inconceivable, a mystery that would only be made clear in the New World.' In this review of European civilization there is a curious silence on the great ages of Christian Rome, explained perhaps by awareness that to have included such a reference would be to say that it too had given nothing to 'the great problem of human freedom', which had to await its resolution in the New World, and Bolívar at any rate would not wish to say that.[12] The final statement, the oath itself, contained no ambiguity: 'I swear before you, I swear by the God of my fathers, I swear by my fathers, I swear by my honour, I swear by my country that I will not rest body or soul until I have broken the chains with which Spanish power oppresses us.'[13] Bolívar never forgot the vow of Rome. For him it became a great truth.

'Do you remember,' he asked Rodríguez years later, 'how we went together to the Monte Sacro in Rome, to vow upon that holy ground to the freedom of our country? You cannot have forgotten that day of eternal glory for us, a day when we swore a prophetic oath to a hope beyond our expectations?'[14]

O'Leary received the details of his narrative from Bolívar himself and from many of the people who were in Rome at the time, where it aroused much comment. In the same way he heard of an episode that occurred a few days later in the Vatican and created a greater sensation than the action on Monte Sacro. Bolívar accompanied the Spanish ambassador to an audience with Pius VII and refused to kneel and kiss the cross on the shoe of the pontiff, shaking his head when the ambassador insisted. The pope noticed the embarrassment and said in a sympathetic way, 'Let the young man from the Indies do as he pleases,' and extended his hand to Bolívar to kiss his ring, which he did respectfully. The pope, aware that he was a South American, asked some questions of him and seemed pleased with his replies. On the way out the ambassador reproached the young man, who replied, 'The pope must have little respect for the sign of the Christian religion if he wears it on his sandals, whereas the proudest sovereigns of Christendom place it upon their crowns.'[15]

After his time in Rome, Bolívar visited Naples where, contrary to legend, he did not climb Vesuvius with Humboldt, or with anyone else. He made his way back to Paris in April 1806, though not to Fanny, who was herself travelling in Italy. He was resolved to return to Venezuela and a serious life. Bolívar's political attitude in 1805–6 was a mixture of determination and diffidence, a young man anxious to do something for his country yet unsure of his role. In later reflections he rejects the idea that he was chosen by God: 'Circumstances, my nature, character and passions were what set me on the road, and my ambition, constancy, spirit and insight kept me there.' On his own estimate he did not see himself as the sole author of the Spanish American revolution and suggested that in default of himself another leader would have emerged during the struggle.[16] But there were few others available at the time with the qualifications already acquired by Bolívar in 1804–6 when his sojourn in Paris, his journey to Italy and his act of commitment on the Aventine were all steps towards political maturity. During this time too his knowledge of the international politics of Europe was growing. He was aware of the threat from Napoleon, who might swallow Spanish America as well as Spain. If subjection by France was avoided there was still the possibility of control by Britain, whose sea power before and after Trafalgar gave the country a decisive role in South America. How many Venezuelans were aware of these things in 1804–6? How many, even among the enlightened, knew that liberty in itself was not enough and would never be an answer unless it was accompanied by independence?

A Spanish American in the Age of Revolution

It was in these years that Bolívar began his serious reading of classical and modern authors. In Caracas he had received a basic, if not very systematic, primary and secondary education. Family tradition and social convention then placed him in the militia, not the university. In Madrid, he tells us, he had studied mathematics and foreign languages. Now in Paris he began a lifetime's reading of the works of Locke, Candillac, Buffon, D'Alembert, Helvetius, Montesquieu, Mably, Filangieri, Lalande, Rousseau, Voltaire, Rollin and Vertot, and of the classical literature of antiquity, Spain, France, Italy and, he adds, 'a great many English authors'.[17] It was a purely secular course of reading, devoid of religious sources. Religion had a place in Bolívar's idea of education, as he later explained to his nephew, though simply as a useful moral code 'in the form of religious maxims and practices conducive to the preservation of health and life'. When he returned to Venezuela and threw himself into the struggle for independence he continued to read and study, and for the next twenty years he could be regarded as self-taught. On campaign and in politics his books were an essential part of his baggage, hardly less important than his equipment, his weapons and his horses. His library did not compare with that of Miranda but was still impressive for the conditions in which he assembled it. His first library, which he had with him until 1816 when it fell into the hands of the Spaniards as booty, was replaced in the following years through friends and contacts in all parts of South America; as he travelled from north to south and back again he always had cartons of books with him for immediate use, leaving the bulk in store in the major towns.[18] According to O'Leary, he rarely had a book out of his hands, reclining in his hammock in his spare time, reading his favourite authors, which in these years were Montesquieu and Rousseau. Other observers cited Voltaire as his particular choice. His preferred discipline was history – ancient, American and world history. Bolívar himself advised his nephew to study history, inverting normal chronology and proceeding 'from the present day backwards by stages to ancient times'.[19]

Bolívar reflected the age in which he lived and so we see in him evidence of Enlightenment and democracy, of absolutism and even counter-revolution. In addition to Montesquieu and Rousseau, O'Leary lists other authors who especially impressed him: Hobbes and Spinoza, Helvetius, Holbach and Hume. But it does not follow that these thinkers exercised a precise or exclusive influence. Bolívar read widely as an exercise of the mind in order to educate himself, to acquire general knowledge rather than a specific programme of knowledge. He studied ancient history for the quality of its narrative, the interest of its wars and politics, the character of its leaders, not for practical lessons or exemplary institutions; the messages from Athens, Sparta and Rome, he would explain at Angostura, were mixed, yielding icons rather than laws, and not suitable for imitation in modern state building. In his reading of the philosophers of the seventeenth and eighteenth centuries he found sources that appealed to his mind and developed his ideas, but his reading seems more likely to have confirmed his scepticism than created it, to have enlarged his liberalism than implanted it. Precision in tracing ideological influences and intellectual causation is notoriously elusive, not least in a leader like Bolívar, whose ideas were a means to action and whose actions were based on many imperatives: political, military and financial, as well as intellectual. To insist too much on the intellectual origins of Bolívar's revolution and to overemphasize the influence of the past is to obscure his real originality. Bolívar was not a slave to French or North American examples. His own revolution was unique, and in developing his ideas and policies he followed not the models of the Western world but the needs of his own America.

Bolívar read not to imitate but to equip his mind for independent analysis in preparation for new policy. Beyond philosophy he was interested in applied enlightenment, practical liberalism. He was the model of the revolution to come. Asked what was the cause of American protest, he would reply *American interests*, and as for *ideas*, they were there to test and explain. Spain's deconstruction of the creole state, its replacement by a new imperial state, the alienation of the American elites – these were the roots of independence as he saw it. Creole resentment was accompanied by popular unrest – Venezuelans had observed this in neighbouring colonies and experienced it in their own – with potential for social revolution rather than political change. In this sequence, ideology does not occupy prime position and is not seen as a 'cause' of independence. Nevertheless, this was the age of democratic revolution when ideas appeared to cross frontiers in North America and Europe and to leave no society untouched. In Spanish America too Bolívar heard the language of liberty in the last decades of empire. Then, after 1810, as Spanish Americans began to win rights, freedom and independence, Bolívar would invoke ideas to defend, to legitimize and to clarify the revolution, drawing on his wide reading to provide arguments and examples.

In the maturity of his political thought Bolívar addressed the Congress of Angostura in 1819 and he described the Spanish American revolution as he saw it: 'A republican government, that is what Venezuela had, has, and should have. Its principles should be the sovereignty of the people, division of powers, civil liberty, prohibition of slavery, and the abolition of monarchy and privileges. We need equality to recast, so to speak, into a single whole, the classes of men, political opinions, and public custom.'[20] These few words not only embody his hopes for the new Venezuela; they also describe to perfection the model of revolution developed in the Western world since 1776. Looking at the world from the vantage point of France, Bolívar saw an age of revolutionary change in Europe and America, a time of struggle between the aristocratic and the democratic concept of society, between monarchical and republican systems of government. Reformers everywhere put their faith in the philosophy of natural rights, proclaimed ideas of popular sovereignty and demanded written constitutions based on the principle of 'separation' of powers. To what extent was Bolívar influenced by the ideas of the age and a protagonist of democratic revolution?

The political and intellectual movements of the time were marked by diversity rather than unity. The concept of a single Atlantic revolution inspired by democracy and nurtured on the Enlightenment does not do justice to the complexity of the period, neither does it discriminate sufficiently between minor currents of revolution and the great wave of change unleashed by the most powerful and radical movements of all. The age of revolution was primarily that of the Industrial Revolution and the French Revolution, a 'dual revolution' in which Britain provided the economic model to change the world, while France provided the ideas.[21] Yet this conceptual framework does not accommodate all the liberation movements of the time, and it cannot provide an obvious home for the movement led by Bolívar.[22]

As Bolívar's ideas of revolution developed, they did not conform exactly to political trends in Europe. Even the most liberal of Spanish Americans were guarded towards the French Revolution and its potential for political violence. As Francisco de Miranda observed in 1799, affected no doubt by his own tribulations in France, 'We have before our eyes two great examples, the American and the French Revolutions. Let us prudently imitate the first and carefully shun the second.'[23] Bolívar was too young to feel the first shock of the events of 1789, but the French Revolution in its imperial phase cast its spell over him and he was impressed by the achievements, if not the titles, of Napoleon. Moreover, he saw that indirectly, in terms of military and strategic consequences, events in France carried a warning for Spanish America, first in 1796 when they drew the hostility of Britain on France's ally Spain, thus endangering the Atlantic crossing and isolating the metropolis from its colonies, then in 1808 when France invaded the Iberian peninsula and deposed the Bourbons, thereby precipitating in Spanish America a crisis of legitimacy and a struggle for power.

Bolívar was conscious of the influence of Britain, not so much from reading as from experience. The Industrial Revolution found a valuable outlet for British textiles and other products in Spanish America, whose underdevelopment made it a captive market. Moreover, it had a vital medium of trade, silver, so Britain valued its trade with Spanish America and sought to expand it, either via Spain and the Caribbean or by more direct routes. During times of war with Spain, while the British navy blockaded Cadiz, British exports supplied the consequent shortages in the Spanish colonies. These were precisely the years when Bolívar began to be conscious of the wider Atlantic world. He saw a new economic metropolis displacing Spain in America. As a young Venezuelan planter and exporter, Bolívar experienced the frustrations of seeking freer commerce against the rules of Spanish monopoly and the constraints of British blockades. It would be an exaggeration to say that British trade undermined the Spanish empire, or made revolutionaries out of opponents of monopoly, but the stark contrast between Britain and Spain, between growth and depression, left a powerful impression on Spanish Americans. And there was a further twist to the argument: if imperial Britain could be evicted from America, by what right did Spain remain?

Bolívar and the Enlightenment

As Bolívar surveyed the European and Atlantic worlds in the years around 1800 and tried to make sense of politics and policies in an age of revolution, what intellectual resources could he draw upon? What ideas were appropriate to the age? What were the ideological roots of his responses? Spanish Americans, unlike the North American colonists, had no experience of a free press, a liberal tradition going back to the seventeenth century, or local assemblies where freedom could be practised. But they were not isolated from the world of ideas or from the political thought of the Enlightenment. Bolívar was not the first or the only Spanish American to glory in the age of reason. His own Venezuela was a pioneer in political speculation. The publications inspired by the conspiracy of Gual and España included a translation of the French *Declaration of the Rights of Man* in its more radical 1793 version; it was Miranda who propagated Viscardo's revolutionary *Letter to Spanish Americans* across northern South America; already before 1810 a translation of Rousseau's *Social Contract*, probably undertaken by José María Vargas, was known in Venezuela, as was William Robertson's *History of America*.[24] Liberal and republican ideas were there for the reading, and readers were growing bolder. But reading was not the same as action, and active revolutions of the kind recently seen in North America and France, while they were known as potential models for Spanish America, did not have direct impact there.

Bolívar and other leading creoles were familiar with theories of natural rights and social contract and their application to government. From these they could follow the arguments in favour of liberty and equality, and some would go further along the road of Enlightenment to insist that these rights

could be discerned by reason, and reason, as opposed to revelation and tradition, was the source of all human knowledge and action. Ideas of hierarchy,
custom and submission were giving way to belief in personal freedom and
private virtue. A few would venture into further reaches of eighteenth-century
thought to declare that intellectual progress should not be hindered by religious dogma and to identify the Catholic Church as one of the principal
obstacles to progress. Bolívar shared the anti-clericalism of the Age of Reason
and regarded the Church as another agent of the old regime. In 1812 he would
blame religious fanatics and their allies, soon, he believed, to be reinforced
from Spain, as yet further enemies of the young republic: 'The religious influence, the empire of civil and military power, and all the prestige they can use
to seduce the human spirit will be so many more instruments available to
them to subdue these regions.'[25] As secularism challenged religion, many saw
the object of government as the greatest happiness of the greatest number,
happiness being judged to a large extent in terms of material progress
achieved through human agency.

Hobbes and Locke, Montesquieu and Rousseau, Payne and Raynal, all left
their imprint on the discourse of independence. But did these thinkers exert
an exclusive influence? An alternative interpretation insists that the *doctrinas
populistas* of Francisco Suárez and the Spanish neo-scholastics provided the
ideological basis of the Spanish American revolutions, with the corollary that
Spain not only conquered America but also supplied the arguments for its
liberation. In arguing for independence in 1811, a number of Bolívar's
contemporaries, graduates of the University of Caracas, employed the argument of 'popular sovereignty', which insists that power reverts to the people
when the sovereign tyrannizes or abandons them.[26] This idea, while similar to
the doctrine of Suárez, was not peculiar to any one school of political thought
and did not exclude a pact of a Rousseauan kind. A variant of the argument
suggests that neo-Thomism was a vital component of Hispanic political
culture, the basis of the patrimonial state and an ideological accompaniment
of independence. There is no sign of these influences in the thought of
Bolívar, which was characterized by derivations from classical republicanism
and the Enlightenment, and showed no evidence of reading in Catholic
sources. In the early nineteenth century Catholic emphasis on tradition and
authority did not sit easily with the kind of liberty that preoccupied Bolívar.

Classical republicanism tripped easily off the tongue of Bolívar, fed by rapid
reading of the classical texts in French translation, especially Caesar and
Tacitus, rather than a profound analysis of the ancient world and its institutions, which for him were sources of useful quotations rather than basic principles. It was the French authors of the Age of Reason who unlocked the minds
of Americans and infused the thinking of Bolívar. This did not mean that

Bolívar was an uncritical disciple of Enlightenment thinkers. The chronology and the depth of their intellectual influence are difficult to determine.[27] His approach to knowledge was empirical, not metaphysical, and he was not interested in creating a new philosophy. He could quote from Voltaire, Rousseau and the *philosophes*, but he did not follow them into purely intellectual speculation and he could be scornful of theories. Place, conditions, circumstances, these set the limits of theories and the limits of Bolívar's enlightenment. His realism always held back the full flow of ideas. Analysis of his own writings show that he was just as familiar with ancient and modern treatises of the art of war as he was with the stars of modern writing.[28] The basic objectives were always liberation and independence, but liberty did not mean simply freedom from the absolutist state of the eighteenth century, as it did for the Enlightenment, but freedom from a colonial power, to be followed by true independence under a liberal constitution.

The texts of liberty were at the heart of Bolívar's reading programme in the years 1804–06, and John Locke led the way as a guide to natural rights and social contract. Citing Acosta, Locke argued that the original inhabitants of the Americas were free and equal and placed themselves under government by their own consent. He also argued that people lose the freedom and independence gained by contract 'whenever they are given up into the power of another'.[29] This was an argument for freedom but not specifically for freedom from colonial power. Montesquieu was a favourite source for Spanish American intellectuals, and most of them were familiar with his statement that 'The Indies and Spain are two powers under the same master, but the Indies are the principal one, and Spain is only secondary. In vain policy wants to reduce the principal one to a secondary one; the Indies continue to attract Spain to themselves.'[30] Montesquieu seemed not unsympathetic to the idea of a nation establishing colonies abroad, as long as it was a free nation and exported its own commercial and government systems. But this did not deter Bolívar, who drew on Montesquieu throughout his political life, and for whom *L'esprit des lois* was a constant work of reference. The debt can be seen in his analysis of the forms of government and the characteristics of a republic, in the insistence on the separation of powers and admiration for English government. In the Jamaica Letter he used Montesquieu's concept of oriental despotism to define the Spanish empire, and his entire political thought was imbued with the conviction that theory should follow reality, that institutions are really agencies of survival and not expressions of abstract principles, that legislation should reflect climate, character and customs, and that different peoples required different laws.[31] But even Montesquieu did not go all the way that Bolívar wanted.

Rousseau provided some of the leading texts of the Enlightenment and had many readers among educated creoles, as they struggled with concepts of liberty. Could reason not only justify freedom but even compel men to be free? Could a state created by the will of its citizens enforce obedience on them?[32] Bolívar was familiar with the principal ideas of Rousseau – the social contract, the general will and the sovereign people – though it is difficult to believe that he accepted, or even followed, the theoretical arguments by which the French philosopher reached his conclusions. Although he did not name Rousseau among the unrealistic philosophers whom he so scorned, the Frenchman fits the bill, and Bolívar made it clear that an idealized Sparta or Rome provided no model for Spanish American society. Even if Bolívar accepted that man is born free, he recoiled from the idea of absolute liberty or that authority is contrary to nature. As for equality, while he knew the difference between social and legal equality, he did not believe that an absolute social equality should exactly balance natural inequalities. And we can only conjecture what he made of Rousseau's search for 'a form of association which will defend and protect with the whole common force the person and goods of each associate, and in which each, while uniting himself with all, may still obey himself alone, and remain as free as before', a search so unreal that it amounted to establishing an organic whole without its parts being subordinate to one another.[33] In some respects Bolívar identified with Rousseau's secular view of life, and he was probably captivated, as many were, simply by the philosopher's personality and prose.[34] Particular details had less appeal: whether he accepted the argument that man originally lived in a purely natural paradise of happiness and goodness, exempt from servile work, and without trace of original sin or inclination to evil, is doubtful. And he had no time for Rousseau's idea of a state-created religion as a prop to public order.

The liberty of the *philosophes* was not enough for Bolívar. Liberty could be an end in itself and stop short of liberation. This was the belief of the Spanish liberals in the Cortes of Cadiz, who subscribed to the freedoms of the Enlightenment and offered them to Spanish Americans, but with equal determination refused them independence. The Enlightenment, in other words, could be invoked to grant greater freedom within a Hispanic framework, to justify reformed imperialism. Was the Enlightenment, then, a source for independence as well as for liberty? European intellectuals of the eighteenth century were blind to the existence of nationality as a historical force. The cosmopolitanism of the *philosophes* was inimical to national aspirations; the majority of these thinkers disliked national differences and ignored national sentiment. They seem to have been totally unaware of the possibility of new and embryonic nationalities, of the need to apply ideas of freedom and equality to relations between peoples, or of any right of colonial independence. Rousseau, it is true, made a gesture to the theory of nationality, arguing that if a nation did not have a national character it must be given one by appropriate institutions and education. Rousseau, moreover, was the leading intellectual defender of political freedom against the despotic monarchies of the eighteenth century. But even he did not apply his ideas to colonial peoples. And the fact remains that few of the eighteenth-century progressives admired by Bolívar were revolutionaries. Neither Montesquieu, nor Voltaire, nor Diderot went to the logical conclusion of advocating revolution; even Rousseau stopped short of sanctioning violent political change.

None of them, of course, had seen a colony at first hand or witnessed the social inequality and racial discrimination endemic in Spanish America. Humboldt had the advantage over other leading liberals of having travelled extensively in these societies and spoken to their people. Yet even Humboldt did not direct his thoughts towards the issue of independence. It is true that in private he was extremely critical of colonialism. In Guayaquil in 1803, for example, he noted: 'The colony is a land in which one claims to be able to live in freedom because one can mistreat one's slaves without fear of punishment and can insult the whites as long as they are poor.' He observed that 'the idea of a colony is itself an immoral idea, this idea of a land which is obliged to pay dues to another country, a land which should only attain a certain degree of prosperity and in which industry and enlightenment are only allowed to spread to a certain degree'. But during his time in America Humboldt did not express his criticisms in public; he confided them to his diary or to close friends, presumably in order not to jeopardize his relations with Spain, on which his researches depended.[35]

Instead, Humboldt posed a different question. How could a minority of European Spaniards hold on to so vast an empire for so many centuries? He argued that they did it by pre-empting the creole majority: 'The European party in all the colonies is necessarily augmented by absorbing a great mass of Hispano-Americans.' These reject the cause of independence because they prefer security and peace to violence. Some see in revolutions nothing but the loss of their slaves, the spoliation of the clergy and the introduction of religious toleration. Others are too committed to their property and privilege to want to share them or confer rights on others; they prefer Spanish rule to an authority handed over to Americans of a lower caste: 'They abhor every constitution founded on equality of rights.' Yet others, living on their country estates and untouched by the authorities, would no doubt prefer a national government and full freedom of commerce to colonial status, but this desire is not strong enough to exceed their love of peace and an easy life or to induce them to undergo long and painful sacrifices.[36]

These questions also exercised Bolívar and he would address them in his Jamaica Letter, where his answers focused on Spanish oppression and American identity rather than pre-emption and indifference, and his language bore a harder edge than that of Humboldt. 'During my time in America,' Humboldt later wrote, 'I never encountered discontent; I noticed that while there was no great love of Spain, at least there was conformity with the established regime. It was only later, once the struggle had begun, that I realized that they had hidden the truth from me and that far from love there existed deep-seated hatred.'[37]

The Enlightenment, therefore, did not reach the point of applying the idea of freedom and equality to relations between peoples, and did not produce a concept of colonial liberation or war of independence. It needed the makers of North American and Spanish American independence to do this. In most parts of the Atlantic world post-Enlightenment liberalism was not in itself an effective agent of emancipation. Jeremy Bentham was one of the few reformist thinkers of the time to apply his ideas to colonies, to advocate independence as a general principle, and to expose the contradictions inherent in regimes which practised liberalism at home and imperialism abroad.[38] But Bentham was exceptional, and most liberals, reflecting the interests of the new bourgeoisie and their desire for captive markets, remained no less imperialist than conservatives. Bolívar, therefore, would find little direct inspiration for ideas of emancipation, either from European or from Hispanic sources. Like the authors of the North American revolution, he had to design his own theory of national self-determination, which he did in the course of the struggle for independence, and this was a contribution to, not a derivation from, the age of revolution. Bolívar was a prime example of one lesson of the Enlightenment, *think for yourself*, and of Rousseau's encouragement to *be yourself*.

Enlightenment thinkers could give only a limited education to a young creole seeking ideas on revolutionary change. Two exceptions were Thomas Paine and the Abbé Raynal. Paine's *Common Sense* (1776) was an outright justification for colonial rebellion, defending American independence as a 'true interest', on account of miseries endured, redress denied and the right to resist oppression: 'There is something absurd in supposing a continent to be perpetually governed by an island.' This impressed Spanish Americans as an exact statement of their own case, as did his later conclusions: 'What were formerly called revolutions were little more than a change of persons or an alteration of local circumstances. . . . But what we see now in the world, from the revolutions of America and France, are a renovation of the natural order of things.'[39] Paine was cited and paraphrased by Viscardo, and read by many more. In 1811 a Venezuelan enthusiast published in the United States an anthology of Paine's works translated into Spanish, which circulated from hand to hand in Venezuela and was an influence on the constitutional thinking of the republic.[40]

Paine was also cited by the Abbé Raynal, a minor *philosophe*, whose *Histoire des deux Indes*, a clutter of colonial history, irritated many in the Hispanic world for its prejudice and inaccuracy, yet drew approval from the few Spanish Americans who read it for its support of the North American revolution against the British Crown, and its conclusion that 'the new hemisphere must one day be detached from the old'. Some were also impressed by Raynal's imitation of Paine: 'By the laws of bodies, and of distance, America can only belong to itself.'[41] Raynal was more significant for his influence on Dominique de Pradt, a French archbishop and supporter of Napoleon, who, though scathing of the flaws in Raynal's work, recognized its originality in theme and structure. De Pradt, whose views were recommended by Bolívar in the Jamaica Letter, was the first Enlightenment thinker to advocate the absolute independence of the Spanish colonies as a matter of principle and policy; this was made inevitable, he argued, by the example of the United States, Spain's decline as a colonial power and revolutionary change in Europe – influences that Spain was impotent to stop and which hastened the tendency inherent in colonies to grow to maturity and break away.[42]

The Church as well as the state came under the scrutiny of the Enlightenment. Deistic and freethinking writings, first introduced from England, acquired a new lease of life in France in the eighteenth century. When deism emerged into the open with the writings of Voltaire and the *encyclopédistes*, it was not a precise theology but a vague form of religion used as a sanction for politics and morals and a cover against the charge of atheism. The growth of scepticism in religion and the specifically anti-Christian offensive of the *philosophes* not only represented intellectual positions, but also supported proposals to increase the power of the state over the Church and even to create a state religion which, however spurious, was regarded as necessary for public order and morals. Bolívar seems to have been marked by some of these influences, though whether they totally destroyed his belief it is impossible to say. He usually handled the subject of religion with caution, but beneath his outward observance there was an element of scepticism, and in private he ridiculed some aspects of religion. Did he then reject the religion as well as the government of the *ancien régime*? According to O'Leary, an Irish Catholic, Bolívar was 'a complete atheist' who believed only that religion was necessary for government, and whose attendance at mass was purely formal. 'Sceptic' rather than 'atheist' would be a closer approximation to Bolívar's mentality, and still leaves a question: When did his scepticism begin? Was it in France in 1804–06 when he read himself into the modern mind? Or did those shoots grow in the years ahead? Again, we do not know. O'Leary hints that Bolívar's mentor, Simón Rodríguez, had deliberately instilled in the young man a philanthropic and liberal view of life rather than a Christian one, and had introduced Bolívar to the works of eighteenth-century sceptics and materialists. 'Yet in spite of his scepticism and consequent irreligion, he always believed it necessary to conform to the religion of his fellow citizens.'[43] And he continued to attend mass.

In the absence of strong religious motivation, Bolívar seems to have embraced a philosophy of life based on utilitarianism, not necessarily the most convincing of moral absolutes but one in vogue among contemporary liberals. The evidence for this comes not simply from his contacts with James Mill and Jeremy Bentham – he described himself as a 'disciple' of Bentham and a follower of his doctrines – but from his own writings, where the greatest happiness principle emerges as the driving force of politics. Spanish Americans, he argued, held unrealistic expectations of proceeding directly from servitude to freedom, from colony to independence. He attributed this to their eager search for happiness: 'In spite of the lessons of history, South Americans have sought to obtain liberal, even perfect institutions, doubtless out of that universal human instinct to aspire to the greatest possible happiness, which is bound to follow in civil societies founded on the principles of justice, liberty and equality.' A few years later, in his Angostura Address, he stated that 'the most perfect system of government is that which results in the greatest possible measure of happiness and the maximum of social security and political stability'. In 1822, writing to the vice-president of Colombia, Francisco de Paula Santander, at a time when there were fears that congress might revise the constitution of 1821, Bolívar observed: 'The sovereignty of the people is not unlimited, because it is based on justice and constrained by the concept of perfect utility.'[44] Some years later political circumstances would force him to revise his support for the public application of Benthamite principles, but not necessarily to abandon the philosophy of utility.

Bolívar's response to the Age of Reason was inspired by what he saw in contemporary Europe as well as by what he read; he saw the limitations as well as the achievements of the Enlightenment, and asked himself what could be useful, what irrelevant, to Americans. Yet his intellectual journey was not purely pragmatic: while directing the military course of the revolution he would also engage with basic conceptual problems such as the limits of liberty and the nature of equality. Liberty had to conform to the history and traditions of a people, and purely abstract concepts of liberty drew his scorn. In the same way he would define the meaning of equality in the context of American society. And he was always conscious that imperfect human nature precluded perfect political solutions, a criticism of theoretical arguments if not a restatement of original sin. While the experiences of 1804–06 do not give us the whole picture of Bolívar, they already reveal that his world would be based on rational and secular values and would have an intellectual as well as a political framework.

Return to Venezuela

From his travels in Italy Bolívar returned to Paris in the spring of 1806, but not to the pleasures of his previous life. Events in his homeland disturbed him. In 1806, despairing of help from Britain, Miranda led a tiny and ill-prepared expedition to Venezuela, where he was coldly received by creole landowners and denounced as a 'heretic' and 'traitor'. Bolívar seems to have regarded the action as premature and more likely to harm Venezuelans than their rulers. Meanwhile his own resources were tied up in the colony by the British blockade. In the autumn of 1806, determined to return to Venezuela and resume an American life, he took his leave of Fanny du Villars, without great drama on his part. On borrowed money, he took ship at the end of November, not from France or Spain, which were at war with Britain, but from Hamburg under a neutral flag, and he sailed not directly to Venezuela but to the United States. He landed at Charleston, the worse for wear after ocean conditions and the onset of fever. He remained in the United States long enough to visit Washington, New York and Boston, and then sailed from Philadelphia for La Guaira, where he arrived in June 1807. Little is known of these travels, though he later recalled that 'during my short visit to the United States, for the first time in my life, I saw rational liberty at first hand'.[45] A rare vision in the Americas, as he was to discover.

The personal events of Bolívar's life in the years 1804–07 were not chronicled in any detail, either by himself or his friends, and early biographers felt free to fill the gaps with fables. The public history of the time, however, was well known. When Bolívar left Europe in 1806 a number of pieces were coming into place, preparing the ground for revolution in South America and for his own leadership. Spain was finished as an imperial power, its role now a satellite of France, its colonial resources a prop for its ally. Spain no longer controlled America. From the beginning of empire conquest had outstripped control, and claims exceeded the capacity to enforce them.[46] Now, having lost power in the Atlantic and with it the route to its own possessions, Spain was not able to secure the trade and loyalty of its colonial subjects. Here was a prize for the taking. For whom? France or Britain? Would Spanish Americans willingly exchange one metropolis for another? This was the situation as read by Bolívar. He had seen that Europe was a threat as well as an inspiration to America. He had begun, if not completed, his political education and learned the realities of the European and Atlantic worlds from observation as well as from study. This was not a unique insight. But how many Venezuelans were as qualified as Bolívar to understand what was happening? How many, even among the enlightened, concluded that liberty in itself was not enough and was not the same as independence? Not all Americans had advanced so far. As long as Spain remained politically intact, defence of creole interests and criticism of Spanish government were made within the confines of the existing regime, as Humboldt suggested. Even when, from 1800, Spain's economic and political power was in headlong decline, and leading creoles had ever greater reason for criticizing Spain's commercial and fiscal policies, the threat of rebellion was slight. Bolívar's thinking was ahead of its time.

The young Bolívar was not an uncritical reader of the texts of freedom and his scepticism would grow in successive stages of the revolution. While the Enlightenment remained the prime source from which he drew to justify and defend his actions, before, during and after the revolution, ideology in itself was not enough. When he returned from Europe to Venezuela he had to appeal to interests as well as ideas. American interests and American arguments would now be decisive in his thinking and actions. Some of his contemporaries also saw these things at first hand, without, however, possessing his motivation or genius. Power and glory were not everyone's ambition, but they were central to Bolívar's world. Alongside the slavery of his country he was conscious of 'the glory that would come to him who liberated it'.[47] Bolívar was not made to live unseen and unknown, to remain 'a mayor of San Mateo'. He returned to Venezuela an independent spirit with leadership potential and opportunities ahead.

Chapter 3

CREOLE REVOLUTION

Grievances of a Colony

Bolívar returned to Venezuela in 1807 convinced that the independence of his country was imperative and inevitable. His conviction came not simply from life in Caracas or work on his estates but from his experience in Europe, where the international situation alerted him to impending change and the ideas of the age made a deep impression on his mind. He found that few people in Venezuela shared his views and that political consciousness in the colony was not raised enough to question loyalty to the king and support for the existing order. His arguments convinced his brother Juan Vicente but no one else among his family and friends, who had little awareness of crisis in the Hispanic world or changes in the balance of power. Bolívar's convictions and his distance from creole opinion explain his political position in the events of the next four years. In this phase of his life he confronted a host of discordant voices without the power to impose his own.

At heart a revolutionary, he outwardly conformed. These were years when Bolívar followed the same occupation as the rest of the creole aristocracy: he managed his revenues and cultivated his estates. At San Mateo to the west of Caracas on the road to Maracay, at La Concepción near Ocumare and Yare in the Tuy valley, his plantations produced the tropical products that Caribbean and European markets demanded; his labourers were blacks, many of them slaves, and he himself worked among them, hands on. His property in Yare had an ongoing boundary dispute with the adjacent estate of the family of Antonio Nicolás Briceño, and in September 1807 there was a violent stand-off between Briceño and Bolívar, when the former led a group of his slaves armed with pistols, machetes and knives to prevent Bolívar and his labourers working on land they regarded as their own. Bolívar's lawyers stepped in to defend his position and Briceño was subsequently arrested, though the case died out amidst the political turmoil of the time. Meanwhile, as he produced and sold from his estates, Bolívar observed the reality of making a living in colonial conditions, where the metropolis promoted its own interests without protecting those of its American subjects. And he came to different conclusions from most of his neighbours. A product of the colony, he was to become the colony's fiercest enemy.

Venezuelan whites were always aware of the superior numbers of *pardos* and blacks, and of the hostile eyes around them. Until the last years of the colonial regime the creoles saw no alternative to the existing power structure and they accepted Spanish rule as the most effective guarantee of law, order and hierarchy. But gradually, between 1789 and 1810, force of circumstances eroded their loyalism. In an age of revolutionary change, when Spain could no longer control events either at home or abroad, creoles came to appreciate that their place in the world depended on gaining an immediate political objective – to take exclusive power instead of sharing it with officials of a debilitated metropolis.

Their economic world was also changing. The Venezuelan economy underwent some diversification in the late eighteenth century, as planters moved away from total dependence on cacao and added coffee, indigo, tobacco and cotton to what they produced. Bolívar took a close interest in his indigo plantations and was concerned about their prospects in the export market. The Venezuelan economy responded positively to the greater opportunities for export once the monopoly of the Caracas Company was removed in 1784 and imperial free trade was extended to Venezuela in 1789. Exports and imports doubled in value in the period 1783–90, and in 1790–6 agricultural exports to Spain doubled over those of 1782–9, while its share of American colonial trade noticeably improved.[1] But the great proprietors were still frustrated by Spanish control of the import–export trade, and campaigned against what they called in 1797 'the spirit of monopoly under which this province groans'.[2] The departure of the Caracas Company left the way open for a new breed of Spanish merchants operating in open market but still protected by the colonial monopoly of Spain and clashing now with local *hacendados*. The Venezuelan economy, moreover, was a victim of the European wars which overwhelmed Spain and exposed even more glaringly the flaws of colonial monopoly – the great shortage and high cost of imported manufactures and the difficulty of getting the colony's products to foreign markets.

From 1796 Spain was dragged through France's wars against Britain in a satellite role, forced to subsidize its imperial neighbour and sacrifice its own interests. Colonial trade was the first victim and the profits of empire the immediate loss. The British navy blockaded Cadiz and cut the transatlantic route. To supply colonial markets and preserve some returns for itself, Spain allowed neutrals to trade with America, by decree of 18 November 1797. This was revoked eighteenth months later, but the revocation was ignored and neutral vessels continued to trade into the colonies when Spanish vessels simply could not make the crossing. The dominant interest groups in Venezuela responded in different ways to the crisis. Colonial officials were alarmed by the loss of revenue, merchants by the erosion of their monopoly, *hacendados* by the damage to their exports.[3] Their discordant voices added to Spain's political problems. After a brief respite during the peace of Amiens (1802–3), the renewal of war with Britain speeded the decline of imperial trade. A series of naval reverses, culminating in Trafalgar, deprived Spain of an Atlantic fleet and further isolated her from the Americas. Spanish policy was driven by various pressures, from the central government dependent on colonial revenue, from peninsula exporters demanding a monopoly market, and from the colonies anxious to maintain trade and supplies. To satisfy as many interests as possible, the government again authorized a neutral trade and from 1805 neutral shipping dominated the Spanish Atlantic. The future of Spain as an imperial power was now in the balance. The economic monopoly was lost beyond recovery. All that remained was political control, and this too was under increasing strain.

As the French Revolution became more widely known it appealed to some, frightened others and threatened defenders of the traditional order. A slave revolt in Coro in 1795 proclaimed 'the law of the French'. From 1796 the British navy cut the trade routes between Venezuela and Spain, and Britain captured Trinidad in February 1797. In the same year Gual and España made their social protest, claiming equality as well as liberty. A sense of crisis was developing, and people felt it in their pockets as defence expenditure rose and with it taxation. Spain's new war with Britain from 1805 revived the economic depression of the 1790s. Venezuela was shaken by two attempted invasions, in April and August of 1806, when Miranda, with the connivance of British naval authorities in the Caribbean, attempted to revolutionize the colony. Defences remained firm, but there were renewed fiscal demands from Spain at a time of economic depression and in the midst of a series of damaging droughts. Spain's response to the British blockade was to reopen trade to neutrals and to sell licences to foreigners to trade with its colonies, yet this still failed to revive exports and secure vital imports. As colonial merchants were taxed so they were subject to bewildering policy changes. Yet in spite of war-induced hardships and inconsistent royal policies, veering between liberalizing and restricting trade, the local planter and merchant leaders did not respond to Miranda's invasion, and they welcomed his defeat, donating men and money against that 'abominable monster'. Caught in a crisis of authority, they made no move to challenge authority. From 1808, when the reversal of alliances in Europe ended the maritime war with Britain and export quantities improved, the economic prospects of Venezuela looked more favourable. But did this really matter, as long as the colony had to conform to imperial trade rules, deter foreign traders and send large remissions to Spain? The Venezuelan aristocracy were living in a dream world, but the dream was about to end.

Realism prevailed when the aristocracy came to appreciate that they themselves were better guardians of the existing social structure than was the metropolis. The colonial elites were more worried by the hostile presence of *pardos*, blacks and slaves, the 'volcano at our feet', as Bolívar later described it, than about cacao prices and consumer shortages.[4] There would be no cacao without slave labour, no leisure without a servile work force. Violence in Coro, conspiracy in La Guaira, banditry in the *llanos*, these movements had racial connotations, threatened security of life and property, and raised the spectre of black power. Social protest from below frightened the Venezuelan elites into the shelter of the colonial state. But if the colonial state itself was unstable, could they find security outside?

1808, the Critical Year

The balance between obedience and dissent was disturbed not by economic depression or colonial grievance but by the shock of events in the metropolis. When they saw the state collapse and interests struggle for power at the centre of the Spanish empire, the peoples of colonial Venezuela also went into action, as Spaniards and creoles interpreted events and decided their moves.

In 1807–8 Napoleon decided to destroy the last shreds of Spanish independence and invaded the Iberian peninsula. Bourbon government was already divided against itself and the country was defenceless against attack. In March 1808 a palace revolution at Aranjuez, masking an aristocratic reaction against the Bourbon state, forced Charles IV to dismiss Godoy and to abdicate in favour of his son, Ferdinand. But the French were the winners. They occupied Madrid, and Napoleon induced Charles and Ferdinand to proceed to Bayonne for discussion. There, on 10 May 1808, he forced both of them to abdicate and in the following month proclaimed his brother, Joseph, king of Spain and the Indies. The predictions of Bolívar were coming true.

In Spain the people began to fight for their independence and the liberals to plan for a constitution. Provincial *juntas* organized resistance to France. Deputies were sent to England to secure peace and alliance. In September 1808 a central *junta* was formed, invoking the name of the king and, from Seville in January 1809, issuing a decree that Spanish dominions in America were not colonies but an integral part of the Spanish monarchy with rights of representation. But as French forces penetrated Andalusia, the *junta* was driven into a corner and in January 1810 it dissolved, leaving in its place a regency of five instructed to summon a cortes that would represent both Spain and America. Spanish liberals were no less imperialist than Spanish conservatives. The cortes of Cadiz produced the constitution of 1812 which declared Spain and America a single nation. But while Americans were granted representation they were denied equal representation, and while they were promised reform they were refused freedom of trade.

What did these events mean to Spanish America? The two years after 1808 were decisive. The French conquest of Spain, the collapse of the Spanish Bourbons, the implacable imperialism of Spanish liberals, all delivered a profound and irreparable shock to relations between Spain and America. The spectacle was unbelievable: a king deposed, local autonomies rising, foreign forces occupying the land. A crisis of political legitimacy confronted Americans. Could they too achieve the unimaginable? They could not have the Bourbons, they did not want Napoleon, they did not trust the liberals. Whom then should they obey? And how should power be distributed between imperial officials and local elites? Once autonomous decisions were taken on these issues, independence could hardly be avoided.

News of the French conquest of Spain was first known to the authorities in Venezuela, a country without newspapers, at the beginning of July 1808 when two issues of *The Times* of London dated 31 May and 1 June reached Caracas, courtesy of the governor of Trinidad. The *Times* reports, specifying the abdication of the Bourbons and the takeover by Napoleon, were translated by Andrés Bello, then an official in the colonial service, for the benefit of Captain-General Juan de Casas, who promptly rejected them as 'lies invented by the perfidious English'.[5] He was soon disabused. On 15 July two ships arrived at La Guaira almost simultaneously. The first, a French brigantine, carried agents of Napoleon to demand submission to the French, as the monarch himself had submitted. The other was the British frigate *Acasta*, commanded by Captain Philip Beaver, who announced that the Spanish people had risen in resistance to the French and had the alliance of Britain. Captain Beaver was not impressed by his official reception, and he preferred to visit the streets of Caracas, fielding questions and testing public opinion. He was struck by the people's sense of judgement and reported, 'I venture to say that these people are extremely loyal and passionately devoted to the Spanish branch of the House of Bourbon; and that so long as there is some probability of the return of Ferdinand VII to Madrid, they will remain loyal to the present government. But if this does not happen soon, I believe I can affirm with equal certainty that they will declare independence for themselves and then they will look to England as the only means of assuring their freedom and expanding their trade.'[6]

Beaver hit the mark. Casas was in a panic and dithered. Spanish officials feared for their jobs. The *cabildo*, the establishment and many people wanted recognition of Ferdinand VII as legitimate king and the establishment of a *junta*, comparable to the responses in Spain. And Bolívar? Events were proving the force of his position on absolute independence. The first reaction in Caracas envisaged a union of the local ruling class, officials and leading citizens, in support of Ferdinand VII and the Spanish resistance movement, almost in patriotic parallel to the *junta* movement in Spain itself. While the Spanish bureaucracy hesitated and drew back from the idea of a *junta*, leading creoles began to meet and talk. The authorities were alarmed by intelligence of a republican conspiracy, premature though it was, and arrested a number of people, including Captain Manuel Matos, a friend of Bolívar, who were alleged to have plotted in the country house of Bolívar near the River Guaire.[7] The captain-general sent his son to give Bolívar an informal warning against associating with subversives. Bolívar, not yet ready to raise his profile, protested that he was 'anxious to escape from unwelcome hangers on who came uninvited', and that he was leaving for his *hacienda* the following day, innocent of any wrongdoing.[8]

Nevertheless, leading creoles continued to meet in Bolívar's house, some to socialize and talk politics, some to take the initiative and press for an independent *junta*, and some to listen and report to the authorities.[9] Bolívar and his brother joined actively in these discussions, though their ideas were well in advance of the rest of the company, and Simón reserved his position. He had acquired his political convictions in Europe and was unwilling to compromise them amidst conflicting opinions in Caracas or moves towards appeasement with the monarchy. But the creole establishment, or as they said, 'la mayor parte de los Caballeros de esta ciudad', in effect forty-five signatories headed by the conde de Tovar, José Félix Ribas and Mariano Montilla, and mobilized by the Spaniard Antonio Fernández de León, a powerful landowner in Maracay and future marquis, presented a petition to the captain-general on 24 November 1808, rejecting the jurisdiction of the Seville junta in Venezuela, and requesting the establishment of an independent *junta* to exercise authority on behalf of Ferdinand VII.[10] This was not a revolutionary move: rather it was a traditional form of response in defence of the legitimate monarch by 'representantes del pueblo', which meant leading planters, merchants, military, clerics and others from the colonial elite, and it included Spaniards as well as creoles. It did not, however, include Simón Bolívar. Along with others who would take a revolutionary position in 1810, he refused to sign the petition to the captain-general as it did not go as far as he wished, and he left Caracas for San Mateo.[11] Bolívar thus distanced himself from the *juntista* movement; his goal was independence and anything less was a blind alley.

The Caracas government proved his point; it arrested the marqués del Toro, the conde de San Javier, and Fernández de León, the future marqués de Casa

León, the Tovar brothers, Mariano Montilla, Pedro Palacios, José Félix Ribas, and others. The authorities clamped down hard on the movement with shock tactics and arrests in the night, actions which appalled the elderly conde de Tovar, a confirmed monarchist who was the first to sign the petition. In the event, sentences of imprisonment and exile proved to be fairly lenient, though other tactics were more insidious and played upon latent social tensions. Government propaganda sought to persuade European Spaniards that their lives were at risk, while warning the *pardos* and lower classes, already alerted to the implications of *juntista* power, that the creoles would enslave them. The idea that the revolution was exclusive to the white elite and held nothing for the lower orders was an argument favoured by the Spanish authorities to stir up black resistance and slave rebellions on creole estates.[12]

The regime survived attempts on 14 December 1809 and 2 April 1810 to depose the new captain-general of Venezuela and governor of Caracas, Vicente Emparan. Emparan was a mass of contradictions. A Spaniard of the Enlightenment, formerly an efficient governor of Cumaná, a partisan of France and Napoleon, yet on friendly terms with many of the creole *juntistas*, he was well enough liked by local interests for his liberal interpretation of the colonial trading laws. He arrived from Spain in May 1809 in the company of Fernando Toro, Bolívar's close friend, and was soon at odds with opponents of the *juntistas* led by Miguel Joseph Sanz and his son-in-law Captain Francisco Antonio Rodríguez, who denounced him to the government of Spain for disloyalty. Toro was aware of the opposition towards his brother Francisco and friends, and recruited Bolívar to back him up. Armed with sabres, they marched across Caracas to Sanz's house to confront Rodríguez and berate him.[13] Emparan intervened to arrest Rodríguez and expel Sanz, and the matter subsided. But no one showed up well. Emparan appeared weak and partisan. Toro overreacted. And Bolívar behaved with an extravagant sense of solidarity, his judgement not yet fully mature. He disagreed with the politics of the Toros, but felt obliged to stand at the side of Fernando out of friendship, displaying in the process a certain public swagger. A curious incident that underlines the crossing of political and social lines in Caracas in a time of confusion.

Events in Spain sharpened the crisis. The transfer of the central *junta* to Seville, its announced intention to enfranchise some deputies from America, and the treaty of alliance with Britain were all reported in April–May 1809 in the recently established *Gaceta de Caracas*, Venezuela's first newspaper and government mouthpiece.[14] But creoles soon found that no government in Spain was willing to grant equality of representation to Americans. And that was not the end of the Spanish nightmare. The central *junta* dissolved itself at Cadiz in February 1810 in favour of a regency. Why should Americans accept these manoeuvres and obey a so-called regency? The question was asked in all the Spanish colonies, and the answer led to revolutionary movements throughout the subcontinent. But Venezuela heard the news first and took action on 19 April 1810. The captain-general still refused to collaborate in the creation of an autonomous *junta*, so the radicals took matters into their own hands, orchestrated by a maverick canon of the cathedral, José Joaquín Cortés Madariaga, one of the many minor characters with walk-on parts in the story of Bolívar. While young activists mobilized a crowd in the main plaza of Caracas, the *cabildo* met independently of the Spanish authorities and was joined by creole revolutionaries representing various interests. On the balcony of the *cabildo*, Emparan was shouted down by the crowd and decided to concede the day. The *cabildo* became the nucleus of a new government of Venezuela, the *Junta Conservadora de los Derechos de Fernando VII*, which refused to recognize the regency in Spain.[15] They deposed and deported the captain-general, the intendant, half the judges of the *audiencia*, and senior army officers, while their place in the tasks of government was assumed by the local ruling class, not by officers of the crown to which they were supposedly loyal. While the pace of revolutionary change quickened in Caracas, other provinces were joining the movement, and throughout Spanish America independent *juntas* made their appearance. Bolívar, however, remained aloof in his *hacienda* of Yare, absent from the events of 19 April, their preliminaries and their conclusion. Not for him adhesion to an absent king and spurious institutions in Spain, or to those in Venezuela who took these things seriously. Full independence was the only serious choice.

The *junta* represented the creole ruling class, but this class did not speak with one voice. It was divided between conservatives who saw themselves as holding the fort for a captive king and the traditional order, autonomists who wanted home rule within the Spanish monarchy, and supporters of independence who demanded an absolute break with Spain.[16] At first the conservatives were in the ascendancy, and it was they who forbade the entry of the veteran revolutionary Miranda, whom they saw as an invader, deist and anticlerical. Where did Bolívar stand now? The patriot government was at last in place and giving orders. It was not what he wanted, but he could not remain aloof indefinitely, without a voice and without influence. So he offered his services to the new government in a diplomatic capacity, which would enable him to express his patriotism without identifying closely with the new regime in Venezuela. The *junta* promoted him from captain to lieutenant colonel in the infantry militia, and in June 1810 appointed him on a mission to London to make contact with the British government and seek its support, a proposal previously canvassed by Miranda. Some disapproved of the appointment, for they resented Bolívar's obvious aloofness from their movement and suspected his judgement, but as he undertook to pay the expenses of the mission and the treasury was empty, they could hardly refuse his offer. So they added Luis López Méndez, a graduate with administrative experience, as second commissioner and a restraining influence, and Andrés Bello as secretary to the mission; it was a group that mirrored the revolution, an aristocrat supported by middle-class professionals. Admiral Sir Alexander Cochrane, commander of the British Windward Fleet, sent the naval vessel *Wellington* to transport the trio, who left La Guaira on 9 June and arrived in Portsmouth on 10 July. Waiting for them in London was Francisco de Miranda, a man with a prolific past, soldier, politician, intellectual, revolutionary, anglophile, an exile anxious to return to his embattled country.

The London Mission

The three great causes for which Miranda stood throughout his public life were independence, liberty and unity. In 1810 in a circular letter to Spanish Americans he wrote: 'My house in this city is the fixed point for the independence and liberties of the Colombian continent, and it always will be.'[17] From 1802 that house was 27 Grafton Street (now 58 Grafton Way) and it served not only as a home for Miranda, his companion Sarah Andrews, his two sons, Leander and Francisco, and his secretary Tomás Molini and his wife, but also as a resource centre for Latin American affairs. As such it housed his library, meeting rooms and the editorial offices of *El Colombiano*. And now, in the summer of 1810, it became the effective headquarters of the delegates from Venezuela. They had been warned by the Caracas *junta* to beware of Miranda who was suspect to some creoles as a French revolutionary extremist, but in the event they would have been nothing without Miranda. According to López Méndez, the delegation arrived in London lost and disorientated, and it was Miranda who rescued them from oblivion:

> The only person we could consult with confidence and who could give us the preliminary briefings we needed was our compatriot; he more than anyone else, with his extensive experience and travels, his long contacts with this government, and his well-known exertions for America, was in a position to give us wide and reliable advice. Even his enemies have never dared to deny his extraordinary knowledge, experience, and talents. He was extremely helpful to us and placed his knowledge, his books, his influence and his contacts completely at our disposal.[18]

Andrés Bello was equally impressed: 'That great exile personified in himself the Spanish American revolution. He was already sixty years old. But in spite of his age he seemed to be at the height of his youth and ideals, and he persisted in all the plans for promoting the independence of Spanish America, never losing hope of seeing this desire fulfilled.'[19] Bolívar, according to O'Leary, eager no doubt to put the best gloss on his hero's relations with Miranda, 'had long recognized in Miranda not only great military genius but also the veteran who had been the first to try and rescue Venezuela from oppression. He believed that . . . he had discovered in Miranda the man whose happy destiny reserved for him the glory of realizing the splendid project of emancipating South America.' Bolívar urged Miranda to return to Venezuela to serve the cause 'for which he had suffered so much'.[20]

More immediately Miranda spent hours arranging meetings and interviews for the delegates and briefing them in appropriate arguments, introducing them to his friends and contacts, including Nicholas Vansittart, the duke of Cumberland, the duke of Gloucester and the recently arrived Blanco White, and taking them to the houses of Samuel Enderby, John Turnbull and William Wilberforce, where on one occasion they arrived when the family was at prayer and were kept waiting for some time.[21] Miranda put Bolívar in touch with significant institutions such as Joseph Lancaster's school in Borough Road, as well as taking the group to the tourist sights of London: Greenwich, Richmond, Kew Gardens and Hampton Court. On other occasions, from his rooms in Duke Street, Bolívar made his own way around London. He was thrown out of a brothel when one of the girls mistook him for a homosexual demanding services that were not on offer. When he tried to calm her with banknotes she threw them into the fire and raised the rest of the house: 'Imagine the scene, I spoke no English and the prostitute no Spanish. She seemed to think that I was some Greek pederast and created a scandal that made me leave faster than I had entered.'[22]

Bolívar found his argument on the need for absolute independence confirmed in the ideas of Miranda, and independence was the agenda that Miranda urged them to follow in their negotiations, rather than loyalty to Ferdinand which they had been instructed to maintain. But British support was a lost cause and the Venezuelans were unlikely to make any impression on the foreign minister, the Marquis of Wellesley. Miranda knew the situation from memory.

The instructions of the mission, which did not assert Venezuelan independence, were to explain that it had been necessary to disavow the authorities in Spain as they had no constitutional legitimacy and that, as in Spain, each province of the monarchy had a right to form a *junta*. Only in the event of the Spanish cause collapsing in the peninsula would Venezuela seek British protection for its independence. The country was prepared to defend the rights of Ferdinand VII but not to accept the measures of the regency. Finally, the delegates were instructed to seek facilities to buy arms, to ask for protection for their commerce and to seek recognition on the part of the British authorities in the Caribbean.

Britain was in a difficult position: the war in the peninsula was at a critical stage and Wellesley would not risk offending Spain by recognizing the new Venezuelan government. Neither did he wish to offend the Venezuelans by refusing to receive the mission, for they might soon be independent of Spain and British authorities in the Caribbean were already dealing with the independent *junta*. In any case there were commercial advantages at stake: the Foreign Office thought that 'by use of the bond of allegiance to Ferdinand England may preserve her colonies to Spain yet compel Spain to alter her commercial system'.[23] He therefore decided to receive the Venezuelans privately at his home; hence the meetings at Apsley House. They were conducted in French, a language in which Bolívar was fluent.[24]

At the first meeting, on 16 July, Wellesley, whose manner was strictly formal, pointed out that the action of the Caracas government was inopportune, for it was based on the false premise that Spain was lost, whereas in fact its cause was more favourable than ever. So they had to begin by asking whether the action of the Caracas government was the result of abuses in colonial administration, which could be corrected, or whether the province had decided to break with Spain and establish an independent state. Bolívar, who led the Venezuelan side and undertook the burden of its case, spoke with force and passion, in contrast to the English minister. He reviewed events in Venezuela since July 1808, described the pro-French position of the authorities and their refusal to allow leading citizens to form a *junta*, and highlighted the French occupation of Andalusia, which precipitated the decision to remove the Spanish administration and place authority in the hands of the citizens. He made the Venezuelan position clear: while loyal to Ferdinand VII, the Venezuelans regarded the regency as illegal and unacceptable. Wellesley, however, insisted that to reject the regency was to declare independence; any province could do the same, which would mean the disintegration of the Spanish empire and the triumph of France in the peninsula. Britain regarded this as incompatible with the Anglo-Spanish alliance.

Bolívar was not finished. He denied that the disavowal of the regency was critical to the case, as Venezuela was ready to continue helping the cause of the Spanish patriots in the best possible way, as could easily be proved. Wellesley then showed his ignorance of Spanish colonial practice: he argued that, although the delegates' instructions enjoined them to act in accordance with the fundamental laws of the monarchy, the Venezuelan revolution itself had broken one of the fundamental laws by expelling the Spanish officials, for the laws stipulated that all authority in the colonies rested with *peninsulares*.

López Méndez corrected him: there was no such law. Wellesley came back with a totally legalistic argument. The basis of all government was a central authority uniting all parts in a common obedience, and whoever sought to damage the central power was threatening the constitution; this could only be justified on principles of the rights of man, which had provoked the French revolution and were now completely discredited. Dependence on Spain, he argued, was purely nominal as long as they refused to recognize its government; Caracas should recognize a reformed colonial government.

The delegates tried another line. They argued that the independence won by Venezuela was the result of special circumstances and was designed to protect the province from the danger of France and its allies in Caracas. Caracas wished to remain united to Spain as long as it continued to resist the French, but their instructions did not allow them to consider any agreement with the regency. The Venezuelans would rather die than submit to an illegal power. All they could do was to thank the minister and submit his suggestions to their government. They also reminded Wellesley of the benefits that would accrue to Britain from support for Caracas, namely new markets and greater popularity in Spanish America. True, he replied, but this was less important than the independence of Spain, which was vital for the liberty of Europe and the permanent interests of Britain. To this Bolívar replied that it was expecting much of the colonies not to take account of their own interests, which demanded new agreements; no one better than Wellesley knew the vices of the Spanish administration. Wellesley recognized that the central *junta* had been corrupt and inefficient but he had great hopes of the council of regency. Bolívar concluded by observing that Venezuela was too small a part of the Spanish empire for its action to have a significant effect on the war in Spain.

Wellesley smilingly complimented Bolívar on the zeal with which he defended his country's cause, and Bolívar replied that Wellesley defended the interests of Spain with even greater zeal, drawing the response that publicly and privately Wellesley had always worked for the well-being of the Spanish colonies, to the point of offending the previous Spanish government. The conversation continued spiritedly without producing new arguments. The proceedings ended with Wellesley expressing pleasure that Caracas had decided to approach the British government and asked the deputation to give his best regards to the Venezuelan government. He saw them off cordially and invited them to another meeting two days later, on Thursday 19 July.

The deadlock was never resolved in spite of further meetings and exchanges of compliments, and the Venezuelans were left with informal expressions of friendship and assurance of protection against France, but without the sign of recognition they requested or even specific permission to purchase arms. The

Venezuelans sought to reassure the foreign office that theirs was not an extremist movement: 'The deputies say there was little expression of popular feeling in the revolution, the people of all castes being in total ignorance were easily led.'[25] The argument was wasted on Wellesley. The negotiations leave the distinct impression that he was putting off the Venezuelans and that Britain was more concerned to placate Spain than to influence Venezuela. Bolívar could perhaps feel some satisfaction that while the British government did not approve of the action of Venezuela, neither did it express disapproval or act against the government in Caracas. Moreover, the British favourably received the Venezuelan request that Britain should instruct the commanders of its fleets and colonies in the West Indies to promote friendship and commercial relations between British subjects and Venezuelans, and to preserve the neutrality of the British navy.[26] Andrés Bello thought the result was as satisfactory as could be hoped for in the circumstances. And Britain allowed two of the Venezuelan agents, López Méndez and Andrés Bello, to stay in London; and there they remained to work for Venezuela – López Méndez to raise troops for Bolívar's army, and Andrés Bello to speak and write for Spanish America.

The Apsley House discussions, inconclusive for Venezuela, were an education for Simón Bolívar. In previous stages of his life he had sought, found and defined his political objectives. But it was not enough to identify Independence. He had to acquire the public skill and stature to achieve it. This was his first political outing: after a period of plantation work among his slaves and of frustrating arguments with his peers, he was now exchanging verbal blows with the British foreign secretary; from a small corner of the Hispanic world he was on stage at the centre of the British empire. Political stature, that was the first gain from London. The second was to put his eloquence on display. Bolívar's style came through strongly in these exchanges. Not for him quiet, cool debate but a presentation vigorous and passionate, pursuing his object inexorably, like a hunter his prey, always making a point. Wellesley was impressed enough to congratulate him on his ardour. And his ardour did not overstep diplomacy: the Venezuelans did not once allude to Britain's experience of North America independence. Bolívar did not hesitate to take responsibility for the team's argument and to assume the lead for the Venezuelan side. Here was a milestone in his political life, when it gained confidence and impetus. He returned to Venezuela a leader in waiting.

Bolívar left England on 22 September 1810 in the *Sapphire*, a vessel of the royal navy, and reached La Guaira on 5 December. Miranda too wanted to take this ship and he even loaded his luggage and sixty-three volumes of documents on board. He had already asked Wellesley for authorization to leave, but the British government was reluctant to provoke the Spaniards further by exporting a revolutionary into their midst and the vessel sailed without him. Finally, on 3 October, he informed Wellesley that he was going anyway, and on 10 October, accompanied by Molini but without his family, he sailed on a packet boat and reached La Guaira on 11 December. Bolívar had paved the way for the Precursor. He brushed aside the social, political and personal prejudices of the creole elites against Miranda and helped to prepare public opinion to accept him, not only as a recruit to the cause but as a leader. He went down to La Guaira to meet Miranda, with other creoles, and orchestrated his welcome back to Caracas. The reception was mixed. The Precursor expected to be treated as the leader. But many Venezuelans regarded him as a foreigner and most of the revolutionaries saw him as an old man. In fact he was sixty. The royalist chronicler José Domingo Díaz could barely contain his outrage: 'I saw Miranda enter in triumph, welcomed as a gift from heaven, with the hopes of the worst demagogues resting on him. He was about sixty-five years of age, serious looking, tirelessly loquacious, friendly towards the scum of the people, who were always ready to support his pretensions. He was a political sage to the young and wild, to moderates a danger to the state.'[27]

Independence, Declared and Destroyed

The early legislation of the *junta* was a model of liberal self-interest: it abolished export duties and the *alcabala* on essential consumer goods; it decreed freedom of trade; it ended the Indian tribute and proscribed the slave trade (though not slavery). The colonial *audiencia* was replaced by a high court of appeal, headed by the marqués de Casa León. It then held elections in all the towns under its rule, on a franchise restricted to adults (minimum age twenty-five) owning not less than two thousand pesos in movable property. The national congress met on 2 March 1811; thirty-one deputies from seven provinces, all from great landed families and the majority favouring the 'autonomist' position and the rights of Ferdinand VII. Congress replaced the *junta* by a new executive consisting of three rotating members, an advisory council and a high court. As colonial institutions collapsed, questions were asked of the colonial caste structure. The caste system generated tensions between its groups which threatened to destroy the traditional order in a holocaust of socio-racial violence. The *pardos* saw new opportunities for themselves: they participated in 'popular assemblies' associated with the early stages of the revolution, gatherings abhorred by the creoles. *Pardos* used the revolution to advance themselves and to penetrate various bastions of privilege, especially the army. The elite began to take notice and become alarmed.

In London Bolívar had relied on Miranda. In Caracas Miranda had the support of Bolívar, and soon he had a constituency when his election to congress was arranged as representative for the minor province of Pao. These two were the leaders of a small radical group who stood for absolute independence. They operated from within the *Sociedad Patriótica*, an organization founded in August 1810 for 'the development of agriculture and livestock', but which soon transformed under the impetus of Bolívar into a political club and a pro-independence pressure group advocating a harder political and military policy, and controlling the *Gaceta de Caracas* as a mouthpiece in the press. Compared to these activists, the moderates looked like amateurs. The liberal lawyer Juan Germán Roscio, however, was convinced that the radicals of the *Sociedad Patriótica* were lightweight critics with rash ideas and that Miranda pursued extremist goals while more serious people were getting on with the task of governing.[28] The membership of the society was almost as exclusive as that of congress itself, though the creoles made a gesture towards democracy by allowing a number of *pardos* to attend meetings. The fact is that the radicals no less than the conservatives stood primarily for the advancement of creole interests, but they believed that these could best be served by national independence.

Bolívar himself, who caught the eye in any group through his strong personality, nervous energy and imperious gestures, took the lead in proclaiming this view in congress in the session of 4 July 1811, his penetrating voice matching the vigour of the words: 'The Patriotic Society rightly respects the national congress; but equally congress ought to listen to the Patriotic Society, centre of enlightenment and of all revolutionary interests. Let us banish fear and lay the foundation stone of American liberty. To hesitate is to perish.'[29] It was a seductive call. Independence was declared on 5 July and, amidst some resistance and repression, the first Venezuelan republic was born.[30] Miranda unveiled its flag – yellow, blue and red. José Domingo Díaz recorded his disgust. And for Bolívar euphoria was tempered by the tragic loss of his brother, Juan Vicente, who did not live to see the new republic; sent to the United States on a mission similar to Bolívar's in England, he died on the way home when his ship sank in a storm off Bermuda in August 1811. The republic had its enemies as well as its martyrs. There was a series of royalist outbreaks in 1811 and on 11 July a group of sixty Canarians rose in revolt in Los Teques. Poorly armed and organized, they were easily repressed, but the republic executed some sixteen of the rebels and displayed their heads in Caracas. The saintly Roscio approved of the executions, here and in Valencia: 'Without spilling blood our rule would be weak and our independence unstable.'[31]

The creole concept of the new society was revealed in the Constitution of December 1811, a constitution strongly influenced by that of the United States, with occasional deference to the French Declaration of the Rights of

Man. Its authors, Juan Germán Roscio and Francisco Iznardi, also deferred to regional forces: just as Caracas asserted its independence from Spain, so did the provinces claim rights from Caracas, and the document allowed various gradations of autonomy, to the horror of Bolívar. The constitution was weak in executive power, and hierarchical in its social values.[32] These had been first announced by congress in its declaration of the *Derechos del Pueblo* (1 July 1811): 'Citizens shall be divided into two classes, those with right of suffrage and those without. . . . The latter are those who do not have the property qualifications specified by the constitution; these shall enjoy the benefit of the law without participating in its institution.'[33] The elite were already setting the limits of freedom and equality.

The supreme *junta* had already decreed (25 June 1811) that militia battalions of whites and blacks were to remain segregated, and the two senior officers of the black militia were to be white; and as in the colony, the black militia officers were still paid less. Now the republican government called the citizens to arms in a decree (13 July 1811) which still maintained racial segregation: they were to assemble for enlistment 'in the Plaza Trinidad, the whites in front of the church, the blacks on the east side, the *mulattos* in the south', while the slaves were ordered not to leave their masters' homes except on government authority.[34] The constitution, it is true, established 'liberty, equality, property and security'. And it was egalitarian in the sense that it abolished all *fueros* (corporate rights) and all legal expressions of socio-racial discrimination: 'The old laws which imposed civil degradation on one part of the free population of Venezuela known hitherto as *pardos* are revoked and annulled in all their parts.'[35] But legal inequality was replaced by a real inequality based on the franchise, which confined voting rights, and therefore full citizenship, to property-owners. To the *pardos*, therefore, there was an illusion of equality. And the slaves remained slaves. The constitution confirmed the suppression of the slave trade, yet preserved slavery. The new rulers, indeed, ordered the establishment of a 'national guard for the apprehension of fugitive slaves; they shall patrol and search fields, *haciendas*, highlands and valleys; they shall enforce law and order among that sector of the population assigned to agricultural labour, preventing them from evading such labour through caprice, idleness, vices or other reasons prejudicial to the tranquillity and prosperity of the country.'[36] The creole message was unmistakable, and it soon reached the blacks and *pardos*. Electoral disqualification and social barriers alerted them to the policy of the republicans and they looked for other ways forward.

As independence simultaneously raised and frustrated expectations, so the blacks fought their own revolution, that '*insurrección de otra especie*', another kind of insurrection, as a Spanish official described it. The royalists were quick to exploit the situation. The archbishop of Caracas instructed his clergy in the plantation areas to preach to the slaves the advantages of Spanish government compared to rule by landowners.[37] Royalist agents moved through the coastal zone provoking and sustaining black insurrection. Creole leaders such as Bolívar were appalled by this 'revolution of the blacks, free and slave, provoked and sustained by agents of Monteverde. This inhuman and atrocious people, feeding on the blood and property of the patriots, committed in those valleys, especially in the village of Guatire, the most horrible assassinations, robberies, violence and destruction.'[38] The slaves, of course, were creatures of the society which bred or bought them, and they seem to have fought less for liberty than to enslave their masters; alternatively they massacred the whites and destroyed their property. This upsurge of racial violence alienated most creoles from the cause of abolition and many creoles from the cause of independence. The royalist ranks began to swell. The army of Miranda, which forced Valencia to surrender, was virtually all white; so it was obvious for the royalists to arm the *pardos*, and it set a significant precedent. The *pardos* also found a place in the royalist camp under the 'popular' caudillos. In June 1812 a violent *pardo* and slave rising in the Tuy valleys east of Caracas lost the republic many of its supporters, as they preferred to surrender to Monteverde than stay with Miranda.

War with Spain and with Nature

The first republic was established and controlled by the creole elite of Caracas. It was not accepted by all the provinces, or by the popular sectors, both of whom saw themselves excluded from decision-making. Guayana, Maracaibo and Coro, all with strong regional oligarchies, remained aloof. So did the *pardos*, the blacks and the Canarians. But these disparate elements needed a strong leadership if they were to act together. From bases in Puerto Rico and Santo Domingo, Spain could launch combined naval and military operations to reinforce its supporters. One such operation was commanded by Domingo de Monteverde y Ribas, a native Canarian of rich and noble family but one with numerous relations among creole Canarians and poor whites, whose resentment of the Venezuelan elites he shared. A naval captain and a natural caudillo, Monteverde made Coro a base for the counter-revolution, and there he recruited people and priests to his cause.

Bolívar always cited the failure of the first republic to declare Coro insurgent territory and attack it by land and sea as a basic strategic flaw and another example of that fatal restraint towards the Spanish enemy which undermined the republican cause. Coro was where the rot set in; insignificant in itself, it became the source of counter-revolutionaries from the west who eventually marched into Caracas unopposed.[39] The Canarians in particular, resentful of the predominance and exclusiveness of the republican oligarchy, and heirs of their colonial masters, became the backbone of the royalist reaction, and they were immediately rewarded by Monteverde, while his naval companions were given senior appointments in the administration and the army. Monteverde in effect behaved like a caudillo prototype rather than a representative of the king. He rewarded his clients, the Canarians, and they became his principal power base. Eventually they became a particular target of Bolívar.

The republicans, therefore, found that they faced a determined enemy, if anything more united than they were themselves. Resistance in Valencia presented a serious challenge and one which the republic's military leader, the marqués del Toro, was incapable of crushing. Miranda was called on to provide a more professional approach. Miranda seemed determined to downgrade Bolívar and prevent him marching with the Aragua militia, describing him as 'a dangerous young man'.[40] Since their return to Caracas relations between the two had foundered, partly through Bolívar's friendship with the Toros, notorious enemies of the Miranda family, partly through policy differences, Miranda favouring a more indulgent policy towards Spaniards than did Bolívar. Perhaps too he wished to curb the status and ambition of the young revolutionary and remind Venezuelans of his own reputation as an experienced professional soldier who had fought in Europe as well as America. Or perhaps he was pressured by Bolívar's opponents in congress. Whatever the reason, it was a pointless gesture. Bolívar succeeded in joining the vanguard under Toro as they moved westwards on Valencia and he fought bravely when they encountered heavy resistance, earning the commendation of Miranda for his distinguished service along with other officers.[41] In Valencia two groups whom Bolívar would subsequently identify as problems for the republic made their presence felt. The *pardos*, frustrated by denial of full rights of citizenship, rose against the whites and vigorously repelled the republican forces. Many Canarians, resentful of their second-class status, also took the royalist side. Miranda himself assumed command of the campaign, imposed a blockade on the city and, with the advantage of superior numbers and artillery, forced the town to capitulate on 13 August 1811. He was criticized for his tactics and the heavy casualties he took, and was summoned to Caracas to give an account of his actions to congress, which he did convincingly. But there were lapses in the high command. While the royalists fought without pity and without scruple, the congressional leaders were victims of their own social bias; inflexible towards the coloureds, they were too lenient to the royalists and allowed many to escape and regroup. And Miranda soon made it clear that he preferred defence to attack.

José Domingo Díaz, who despised republican government, regarded late 1811–early 1812 as the last months of the old Venezuela, 'a country now without a government but surviving a period of tranquil anarchy through the rule of Spanish laws, the habit of obedience, and public satisfaction in the midst of plenty, unperturbed by the threats of the enemy'. But Spanish and republican peace alike were soon to be shattered.

On 26 March 1812, an oppressively hot day, the air calm and the sky cloudless, calamity struck the people of Caracas, crowded into churches for Maundy Thursday.[42] A massive earthquake tore across Venezuela from the Andes to the coast, reaching Caracas at seven minutes past four in the afternoon. The first shock was powerful enough to make the bells of the churches toll, followed by a tremendous subterranean roar, louder than the rolling of thunder, and now the ground was in a continuous undulating movement, bringing everything above crashing down. Thousands died in churches on this Holy Thursday, soldiers perished on campaign, towns collapsed around the patriots, and in Caracas destruction and casualties were traumatic. 'The processions,' wrote Humboldt, 'had not yet set out, but the crowd was so great in the churches that nearly three or four thousand persons were crushed by the fall of their vaulted roofs. . . . Estimating at nine or ten thousand the number of the dead in the city of Caracas, we do not include those unhappy persons, who, dangerously wounded, perished several months after, for want of food and proper care.'[43] Bolívar was never closer to the revolution than on that hot afternoon; in his shirtsleeves amidst the dust and debris of the stricken capital, beside himself with rage and helplessness, he hurled defiance at nature and vowed to fight back. The evidence for the scene gains credibility from its source, for it comes precisely from José Domingo Díaz, royalist chronicler and enemy of the republican cause. Bolívar had to fight the Church as well as nature, for royalist clergy blamed the revolution for bringing down God's anger on Venezuela. He personally remonstrated with one of the priests preaching repentance in the square. But he could not hold back the royalist reaction, as people returned to the fold through fear. A second earthquake struck on 4 April, raising the death toll to more than twenty thousand.

Seismic disturbance also struck the patriot war effort and the republican cause swiftly collapsed. Monteverde advanced unchallenged out of Coro at the head of royalist troops reinforced from Puerto Rico and supported by Juan de los Reyes Vargas, an influential Indian who had changed sides. Soon, without even a serious battle, he recovered the whole of western Venezuela. The republic reacted to these disasters by appointing Miranda *generalísimo*, commander-in-chief with dictatorial powers, on 23 April 1812. But the aged revolutionary could not recover the nerve of his youth or stem the tide of royalism that swept over the republic. He evacuated Valencia and on 3 May Monteverde entered the city with the connivance of the inhabitants and began to reinforce his troops. In the *llanos* the guerrilla leader Boves joined the royalist cause.

These national disasters enclosed a personal crisis for Bolívar. On his way to Caracas to collect troops and supplies, Miranda stopped at San Mateo and appointed Bolívar political and military commandant of Puerto Cabello. Bolívar saw the appointment as another attempt to marginalize him, as he wanted to fight at the front against Monteverde, but he accepted, 'not without reservations'.[44] Puerto Cabello was strategically important, commanding communications with the interior and defence against attack from the sea. The fort of San Felipe protected the town and was a prison for leading royalist prisoners, as well as holding a store of arms and supplies; the combination was risky and unprofessional, and discipline was lax. Bolívar took command on 4 May.[45] Did he have time to unravel the situation and improve security? Or was the task beyond his training and experience? Whatever the answers, it was vital that he hold on to this important seaport, a difficult task made more hazardous by Monteverde's dominance in Valencia just to the south, the presence of traitors within, and the non-cooperation of the local authorities.

Bolívar, therefore, inherited a danger and he was isolated. Neither was he helped by the commander of the Fort, Colonel Ramón Aymerich, who decided to visit the town and gave command of the fort to a treacherous subordinate, one Vinoni. The traitor promptly released and armed the prisoners, seized the garrison for the royalist cause, and directed the batteries on the city while also controlling the harbour. It is fair to say that since taking command of Puerto Cabello Bolívar had pointed out the danger of keeping top political prisoners, who had wealth and influence, in close proximity to an arms store. Now he had to deal with the consequences. He offered to pardon the 'prisoners, officers, corporals, and soldiers who have taken possession of San Felipe' if they surrendered within an hour. The offer was repudiated. For six days he held off the rebels and the enemies outside while the guns bombarded the town, and his own meagre forces, with inferior firepower, suffered heavy casualties, desertions, and defeats. Fearing an attack by Monteverde, he urgently requested reinforcements from Miranda and urged him to attack the enemy in the rear, or he would be lost. 'That is the way of the world,' commented Miranda. Bolívar had to extricate his headquarters and retreat along the coast; he reached La Guaira on 7 July along with a few officers, whose good name he defended. For him it was a bitter occasion causing deep humiliation. Ideas, ambitions, hopes for Venezuela, his whole life so far, were now suddenly destroyed by military defeat. After years of mental preparation he became the runner who fell at the first hurdle. His pride hurt, he wrote to Miranda a detailed report on the loss of Puerto Cabello, and an account of his own ignominy and demoralization, ashamed to see him face to face:

General, my spirits are so depressed that I do not have the heart to command a single soldier. I was presumptuous enough to believe that my desire to succeed and my ardent zeal for my country would supply the talents that I lacked as a commander. I therefore beg you either place me under the orders of your lowest ranking officer or grant me several days leave to compose myself and to recover the confidence that I lost in losing Puerto Cabello. On top of this there is the state of my physical health, for after thirteen sleepless nights and extremes of responsibility and anxiety, I find myself in a condition of virtual collapse. . . . I did my duty, General, and had but a single soldier stayed with me, I would have fought on, but they abandoned me through no fault of mine.[46]

'Venezuela is wounded in the heart,' observed Miranda and he himself began to weaken. His army for an attack on Valencia was more impressive in numbers – five thousand – than in quality and he soon saw his appeals to Valencians ignored and his forces reduced by desertions. He seemed to have had no plan of campaign. He retreated to Maracay where he wrote wordy proclamations and pleaded for international help, but allowed Monteverde to advance further. He retreated to La Victoria, where he stood down his army for weapons cleaning. Again Monteverde attacked and this time the patriot army gave a good account of itself and twice could have turned strong resistance into advance on the enemy had it been allowed to do so, but against the pleas of his officers Miranda halted the troops and withdrew them to defensive lines.[47] As he lost the military initiative so he was beginning to lose his own credibility among the military and the politicians, and there were mutterings against him and criticisms of his use of power, harsh personality and defensive tactics. The republic had wasted its assets in Valencia and the west and retreated to a narrow strip of territory from La Victoria to Caracas and La Guaira, and in June the towns and cities of the east began to desert to the royalist camp. The core of the republic was under virtual blockade. Miranda decided to call it a day and negotiate surrender terms with Monteverde.[48]

The pact was signed at San Mateo on 25 July 1812. The terms protected the lives and property of the patriots, granted a political amnesty and offered passports to those wishing to leave the country. Miranda took leave of the army and returned to Caracas, but seeing no place for himself in Monteverde's Venezuela he decided to leave the country before the latter occupied the capital. He therefore went discreetly to La Guaira with the intention of embarking immediately for Curaçao. Many Venezuelans, especially among the military, deplored the San Mateo pact. Bolívar was openly horrified when he read the order announcing the disbandment of the army, an army superior to the enemy's in the number of its troops and the quality of its officers. He tried, though in vain, to organize a resistance movement among his fellow officers. He was convinced that Miranda's decision to leave the country without awaiting Monteverde's arrival in Caracas, and knowing that the capitulation would not be observed, was a step that would expose his fellow citizens to certain retribution. He himself had already begun to plan his own departure and to arrange for transfer of funds in the next months to his destination abroad. Two trunks of his luggage, including fifteen hundred silver pesos in cash and sixteen hundred ounces of silver, were taken to La Guaira and loaded on to HMS *Sapphire* for shipping to Curaçao. This was the same vessel that had brought him from England and it was also waiting to take off Miranda with his books and papers and money from the treasury.[49]

Determined to prevent Miranda's departure, and to escape Monteverde, Bolívar himself moved to La Guaira where, together with Colonels José Mires and Miguel Carabaño and Commander Tomás Montilla, he approached Dr Miguel Peña, the governor, and Colonel Manuel María de las Casas, the military commander of the port, to collaborate in a plan to detain Miranda. According to O'Leary, Bolívar's intention 'was limited to seizing Miranda and obliging him to remain in the country, in order to demand from Monteverde full compliance with the articles of capitulation'. The plan may have been limited but it was hardly realistic, and it involved an act of deceit, luring the general into a false sense of security, when he decided to stay a further night ashore rather than board the *Sapphire* immediately. The men awoke Miranda in the night, to be greeted with reproaches of '*bochinche, bochinche*' (calumny, calumny). Bolívar and Montilla arrested him and, in the early morning of 31 July, Mires took him up the hill to the fort of San Carlos and left him in chains. Would Bolívar have gone further? Colonel Belford Hinton Wilson, trusted aide of Bolívar in his later years, informed O'Leary that the Liberator had always insisted that 'he wished to shoot Miranda as a traitor, but was with-held by others'. Colonel Casas, in collusion with Monteverde and anxious to make peace with the victor 'even at the cost of his honour', handed Miranda and effectively all the other refugees who had failed to make ship, over to the enemy.[50] A predictable end to an extraordinary action. As the first republic died amidst angry recriminations, Monteverde entered Caracas in triumph and established what he called 'the law of conquest'. The conquering 'army' numbered less than three hundred.

Bolívar left La Guaira for Caracas, where the ubiquitous Spaniard, the marqués de Casa León, gave him asylum in his house and another Spanish royalist, Francisco de Iturbe, a friend of the Bolívar family, requested from Monteverde a pass for him to leave. Very few such passes were being granted, but O'Leary records that Monteverde told Bolívar, 'You have done a worthy service in arresting Miranda, and that makes you merit the King's favour.'

'Since that was not my intention when I seized General Miranda,' Bolívar retorted, 'I deny all right to the merit you wish to attribute to me. The reason for my conduct was quite different. I considered him to be a traitor to my country.' Monteverde then had second thoughts until Iturbe intervened and he grudgingly agreed to grant the passport, which Bolívar described as an example of his 'stupidity'.[51] On the other hand it could have meant that the young colonel was not recognized as a great leader in the making. Stupid or not, it was a fatal decision for Spain.

The Defeat of the First Republic

The *patria boba*, as the first republic came to be called, was shackled by the social structure of the colony. The Spanish royalists, with the support of some creoles and most of the Canarians, fought for the old order. The supporters of independence fought for creole supremacy. The *pardos*, blacks and slaves fought for their own liberation. So there were a number of movements and each confronted or exploited the other, while many simply stayed at home as they saw the ancient peace of Venezuela shattered by alien causes. These divisions were ideal conditions for the restoration of royal power. Miranda himself subsequently cited four factors to explain his capitulation: a shortage of provisions in Caracas; the uprising of blacks to the east of Caracas; the effects of the earthquake; and the conflict between Spaniards and Americans. His decision was honourable, if misjudged. He had superior forces which could have done more, and he failed to take the measure of Monteverde. Did he decide to cut and run? Not according to one witness. He seems to have been relocating rather than deserting, with the idea of starting again from Cartagena, rather like Bolívar himself.[52] Instead, he spent the next four years a captive of Spain and died in a prison in Cadiz, a tragic and abandoned figure.

The chronicle of Bolívar's life in the years from 1810 to 1812 is not good reading for those who seek perfection in a hero. These were years of ordeal by battle when relentless events tested his will and judgement and gave him lessons in leadership. He emerged a deeper and a wiser man, but a scan of his record reveals a number of shadows that cannot easily be banished. The loss of Puerto Cabello, his fault or not, was a strategic disaster and a blow to his morale; the arrest of Miranda was an ignoble action, 'perfidy' in Andrés Bello's view, a punishment undeserved by one who had worked so long for the American cause; and the passport to safety was gained through influence with royalists which Miranda himself had never enjoyed.[53] These are episodes that reveal flaws of temperament and behaviour which his own excuses and those of his partisans only magnify. There was an emotional streak in Bolívar, times when reason retreated and passion took command; his endless denunciation of Miranda as a '*cobarde*' was unforgiving, hardly excused by belated recognition of him as '*ilustre*'.[54] Nevertheless from the ruins of the first republic emerged the unmistakable signs of a leader: a commander's ruthlessness, an inner fortitude, a resolution in the face of adversity, and an ability to pick himself up from calamity and come back fighting. Superficially cast down, he still retained deep within him the will to win. The Spanish American revolution re-enacted the scene many times in the next twenty years: his individual survival amidst collective failure.

Bolívar sailed from La Guaira in a Spanish vessel, the *Jesús, María y José*, and arrived in Curaçao five days later. There his baggage was confiscated by an unfriendly British governor and he lived, no longer the aristocrat, politician and officer in a new republic, as a refugee with conditions to negotiate and a role to establish. He relied on friends, especially Iturbe, to administer his properties, protect his revenues and look after his interests in Venezuela, where his personal wealth was his only power base for the future. Meanwhile, 'indifferent to bad luck', he had some books to read, an inevitable friend in need, and time to calm his mind and recover his spirit.[55] At the end of October he managed to procure a thousand-peso loan and sailed for Cartagena, while in Caracas the counter-revolution exacted its revenge.

Chapter 4

WAR TO THE DEATH

The Cartagena Manifesto

Cartagena was an obvious choice for Bolívar. Caribbean port and fortified outpost of South America, once a depot for the Atlantic slave trade and now the home of a diverse population of blacks, *mulattos* and Indians, it opened an alternative route to independence. Its hinterland of great rivers, plains, jungles and mountains, of tropical vegetation and bleak plateaus, contained a similar mixture of resources as Venezuela – with the addition of gold deposits, now less profitable than formerly. Like Venezuela, New Granada was in the second league of Spanish colonies, though elevated to a viceroyalty in the eighteenth century. A population of 1.1 million inhabitants in 1825 contained the familiar divisions of whites, blacks, Indians and mixed races, and was characterized by extensive *mestization*.[1] It was a normally docile society, though fiercely protective towards its perceived rights. Creole grievances were expressed within traditional structures and did not threaten the colonial state until that state itself collapsed when Spain began to falter in the years after 1808. Then New Granada reproduced the prevailing pattern of colonial dissent, from loyal *juntas* to independent government. Following the example of Quito, other towns of New Granada formed separate *juntas* of creole elites in competition with those in Spain, overtly supportive of Ferdinand VII and of Spanish resistance to Napoleon but by 1812 independent of the Spanish connection.

Independence, however, led to disunity, and disunity to destruction. Bolívar knew the sequence well. The republic was immediately divided into centralist and federalist factions. Cundinamarca, the most important of the provinces, was a centralist base, its president, Antonio Nariño, a dissident voice since the 1790s; but the other provinces refused to subordinate themselves to the rule of Santa Fe de Bogotá and grouped themselves into the Federation of New Granadan Provinces, with its capital Tunja. And, in the worst scenario, provinces began fighting each other. The revolution thus became self-defeating and the country was engulfed in civil war before it was even fully independent. The Spaniards simply had to wait for New Granadans to destroy each other.

Cartagena, a port long anxious for free trade, sought to extricate itself from Spain and from the surrounding chaos. There the revolution had a broader social base, as the merchant elite mobilized the *pardos* in support of the *junta* and then in the push for complete independence.[2] This was accompanied by the adoption of a republican constitution and the emergence in effect of an independent Cartagena state from November 1811, hostile to Spain, isolated from surrounding regions, and like Caracas vulnerable to counter-revolution. This was the refuge sought by Bolívar in October 1812.

Bolívar entered Cartagena with a prepared agenda for the next stage of his life. First, he wrote the conceptual framework of his project, then he acted it out in the field. He planned to restore his military reputation in New Granada, but before that he displayed his political credentials. He began by writing to the congress of New Granada, briefly explaining the reasons for the collapse of the Venezuelan republic. The earthquake of 26 March and the loss of twenty thousand people he described as of only secondary importance. The primary causes were the political errors committed by the government, especially the failure to crush the resistance of Coro before it infected the rest of the country. There were other failures: lack of military recruitment and budget control; indulgence towards perfidious Spaniards; religious fanaticism 'hypocritically directed by the clergy' to keep its control over a superstitious people; and the weakness of federal government. The republic's army had been capable of winning, in spite of which its general 'with unmatched cowardice' failed to pursue the enemy and instead concluded a capitulation. Now the few who escaped 'the clutches of those raging beasts' implored the protection of New Granada; to earn this they wished to join the struggle between the new state and the province of Santa Marta. Their service to South American freedom encouraged them to look to the liberal spirit of the people of New Granada. 'Caracas, the cradle of Colombian independence, surely deserves deliverance, like another Jerusalem.' And fellow republicans here, learning from us, can become the liberators of their captive brothers, thus recovering the freedom of South America and restoring 'its natural rights'.[3]

The natural rights of South America received closer attention in Bolívar's first major statement of his political ideas, the so-called 'Cartagena Manifesto', in which he gave vent to his intellect and expounded his vision. Here he further analysed the failings of the first Venezuelan republic and probed its political assumptions, offering these 'terrible lessons' as an example and a warning.[4] The reasons for failure, he argued, lay in the adoption of a constitution ill-adapted to the character of the people; excessive and misguided tolerance towards the enemy; reluctance to recruit professional military forces, relying instead on undisciplined militia forces; financial incompetence leading to the issue of paper money; the earthquake, physically and morally destructive, compounded by a weak central government incapable of repairing the damage, and the religious fanaticism unleashed by the event; and, finally, the factionalism which subverted the republic from within, the 'fatal poison that laid the country in its tomb'. Popular elections, he maintained, allowed the ignorant and the ambitious to have their say and placed government in the hands of inept and immoral men who introduced the spirit of faction. Thus, 'our own disunity, not Spanish arms, returned us to slavery'. Peoples so young, so innocent of representative government and of education, could not be immediately transformed into democracies; their system of government should not advance beyond social realities. He insisted on unity and central-ization; a 'terrible power' was needed to defeat the royalists, and constitutional susceptibilities were irrelevant until peace and happiness were restored. This was the beginning of his permanent opposition to federalism: it was contrary to the interests of an emerging state, for a federal government was weak and complex, whereas America needed strength and unity.

Bolívar appealed for continental collaboration and more immediately for New Granadan support for the liberation of Venezuela. The recovery of Venezuela, he urged, was essential to the security of New Granada and to the liberty and independence of South America. He returned to a favourite analogy. If royalism in Coro led to the fall of Caracas, could not counter-revolution in Venezuela endanger the whole of America? 'Coro is to Caracas what Caracas is to America.' The appeal to self-interest was also an appeal to seize the opportunity. Spain was on its heels, deserted by creole troops and slow with reinforcements; for the moment the route to Caracas was open and patriots were waiting in welcome. The good name of New Granada depended upon it taking over the task of marching into Venezuela 'to free that cradle of Colombian independence' and bring liberty to all.

The Cartagena Manifesto presents Venezuela as a lesson in politics. But there is a subtext running through the document, taking its significance beyond the immediate political and military context into conceptual problems of political ideas. Bolívar steps back from the Age of Reason and distances himself from many of its liberal assumptions. For the first time we can judge him against the thought of the Enlightenment and observe him exercising his own critical perceptions.[5] He sees that a society's ability to survive militarily and politically depends on the efficiency of its institutions. So he warns New Granada not to fall into the same errors as Venezuela, errors which could be traced to the lack of realism in the Constitution of 1811. The flaws of that constitution derived from its individualist and federalist character and were rooted in the ideas of the Enlightenment. Institutions were created according to abstract and ratio-nalist principles far removed from concrete reality and the needs of time and place. Bolívar coined the phrase '*repúblicas aéreas*', ethereal or abstract republics, to show how distant from reality was the thought of the Enlightenment as expressed in the Caracas constitution.

> The codes consulted by our magistrates were not those which could teach them the practical science of government but those designed by certain worthy visionaries who, conceiving in their minds some ethereal republic, have sought to attain political perfection, assuming the perfectibility of the human race. So we were given philosophers for leaders, philanthropy for legislation, dialectic for tactics, and sophists for soldiers. This subversion of principles and affairs shook the social order to its foundations, and inevitably the State made giant strides toward its general dissolution, which soon came about.

The next stage of the argument was to show that institutions that are adopted for their philosophical content (possibly valid for other countries and times) were fatal and condemned to military and political failure. The vacuum left by the fall of the Spanish empire had to be filled by institutions appropriate for that purpose, based on American reality and not on imported ideas. This meant shunning absolute democracy, which legitimizes the government by the electoral process without incorporating moderating elements into the organization of the state; these are needed to provide defence against dema-gogues and political schemers looking for their own exclusive interests. 'What most weakened the government of Venezuela was the federal form it adopted in keeping with the exaggerated principles of the rights of man. By author-izing self-government, this principle undermines social contracts and reduces nations to anarchy.' So each province, then each city, claimed independence 'on the theory that all men and all peoples have the right to establish whatever form of government they choose'. There were of course alternative explana-tions to those of Bolívar. Does federalism provoke or placate localism? Was it possible that Venezuelans had not yet achieved a sense of nation, and people still looked primarily to towns and cities as the focus of their political interests, as they had in colonial times?[6] Valid questions, though Bolívar would blame ignorance and inexperience among the people, not lack of identity.

The Western Front

First the word, then the action. Bolívar was determined to prove that Venezuela could earn the support of its neighbour. He was in fact an asset to

Cartagena, a boost to its revolution and a focus for further resistance. He was the most distinguished of a group of Venezuelan officers who sought refuge in the port and were accepted into the army: José Félix Ribas, friend and relative, Antonio Nicolás Briceño, neighbouring *hacendado*, Francisco and Miguel Carabaño, Mariano and Tomás Montilla, and others. The Cartagena government gave Bolívar command of a corps in the division headed by Colonel Pierre Labatut, a French mercenary of mediocre talents and provocative ways, who posted him to the town of Barranca near the mouth of the Magdalena River with instructions not to move, effectively not to detract, from the Frenchman's command. Fifty years previously a missionary friar who had travelled the same route described the Magdalena as a pleasure and a paradise, a delight to the senses of all who sailed it. Bolívar saw it as a gateway to great things. Beyond the river lay the royalist territory of Santa Marta, a colonial outpost and frontier against unconquered Indians. He decided to attack the Spaniards at the fortified town of Tenerife and open up the river. Pausing only to recruit volunteers and, it is said, to conduct a brief affair with Anita Lenoit, a young Frenchwoman, he proceeded upriver and seized the initiative through tactics of secrecy and surprise rather than superior force; he had only two hundred poorly armed men, but the startled Spaniards abandoned their supplies and boats as well as Tenerife itself.

Never one to miss an opportunity to speak of liberation, he stood at the head of his small army and assembled the inhabitants on the riverbank. There he reproached them for their previous royalism and loyalty towards tyrants 'who have enslaved your men, plundered your homes and raped your women, for where the Spanish empire rules, there rules desolation and death'. He went on to describe the new regime that was taking shape as though he were giving a class in constitutional law, concluding: 'Now we have come to open up for you a great future of glory and fortune, declaring you members of a society which has as its foundations absolute equality of rights and the rule of law, which never favours birth or wealth, but always virtue and merit. In short, you are now free men.'[7] Thus, on the banks of the Magdalena, in a clearing in the tropical forest and among an uncultured community, Bolívar summarized his republican hopes and the liberation that military victories could bring. He asked these people if they would swear loyalty and obedience to the sovereign government of Cartagena, and they answered with a unanimous, 'Yes, we do swear'.

Continuing upriver, Bolívar reached Mompós on 27 December and was acclaimed military commander of the district by grateful patriots. Recruiting along the route, he then occupied El Banco on 1 January 1813 and advanced to defeat the Spaniards at Chiriguaná. Then he seized Tamalameque by surprise and occupied Puerto Real and Ocaña without any opposition. This ended the campaign to free the upper Magdalena and clear the way to the interior of New Granada, previously cut off by the Spanish ships on the river.[8] On 8 January he reported to congress in Tunja that he had opened the Magdalena to navigation in just fifteen days. The government of Cartagena was impressed and ignored Labatut's complaints about the victor's insubordination.

For his next campaign Bolívar was authorized by the president of Cartagena to march on the Spanish forces under Ramón Correa occupying the valleys of Cúcuta, and thus close the gap in the eastern defences of New Granada. It was also the route to Venezuela. This involved leading troops accustomed to the tropics through harsh mountain conditions where the terrain and the climate were a severe test of endurance even before battle was joined; at San José de Cúcuta the Spanish forces were defeated by a mixture of smart tactics on the part of Bolívar and brave charges led by his friend Ribas. The royalists fled, abandoning valuable ordinance and merchandise. San José was a major victory, Bolívar's first, an early example too of his response to the challenge of landscape; above all, it established his credentials for leadership.

He crossed the Táchira River in early March and in the Venezuelan town of San Antonio addressed his troops in the first of many such proclamations: 'Your liberating arms have reached Venezuela, bringing life and protection to the first of its towns. In less than two months you have concluded two campaigns and begun a third, which will end in the country that gave me birth.'[9] He thus pre-empted the liberation of Venezuela and likened it to the crusades 'which liberated Jerusalem'. He was subsequently given military promotion to the rank of brigadier general in command of the federation armies. He established his headquarters at Cúcuta and followed his military victories with political initiatives. He knew that he still had to sell his project to president and congress in New Granada and persuade them to support an invasion of Venezuela. Now he showed his talents not only as a soldier who could win battles but also as a politician who could win a difficult argument. His case was muddied by military rivalries. Colonel Manuel Castillo, his second-in-command, a native of Cartagena and early fighter for independence, resented the intrusion of a Venezuelan into his revolution, and reported to congress that Bolívar had misused the booty taken at Cúcuta and was rushing into an unauthorized invasion of Venezuela. Bolívar defended himself vigorously and his eloquence, plus the support of Camilo Torres, patriot pioneer and president of the United Provinces, induced congress to grant him permission to invade Venezuela, but only as far as Mérida and Trujillo; in May 1813 he was required to swear adhesion to this commission and throughout the campaign he dutifully reported his progress to congress.

Castillo remained a thorn in his flesh for the next two years, opposing most of his initiatives and splitting the army between Venezuelans and New

Granadans. Preparations for the move into Venezuela were hampered by these personal rivalries. Castillo resigned from the division which was then commanded by one of his supporters, Major Francisco de Paula Santander, a rising officer in the New Granadan army, who appeared to be reluctant to order the unit forward. Bolívar ordered Santander to march, but the latter indicated that he was not prepared to obey. 'There is no choice,' retorted the general. 'March! For either you will shoot me or I will certainly shoot you.' The division left but without Santander, who remained on frontier duties in La Grita.[10] This was another rivalry that endured. Bolívar had shed two awkward subordinates but they were influential officers and for the moment their absence cost him the confidence of other officers and the enthusiasm of the troops. The support of Colonel Rafael Urdaneta, a young officer from Maracaibo who was to prove one his most loyal followers, was more than welcome: 'General, if two men are enough to free the country, I am ready to go with you.'

Bolívar's military service in New Granada earned him, if not the respect of his rivals, at least credit with congress, and this enabled him to secure a base on the border and to recruit an army of invasion. It was a small army – estimates vary between three hundred and seven hundred men – and its prospects depended upon striking at the heart of royalist power before Monteverde could concentrate his scattered forces. Its strength lay in the confidence of its general, the quality of officers such as Ribas, Urdaneta and Girardot, and the commitment of its troops. And for once Bolívar had been able to assemble adequate arms and supplies. Anyone taking stock of Bolívar's war at this point would conclude that since entering Cartagena he had written his own script. First, he had mounted an intellectual assault pinpointing the flaws of the revolution and the prospects of overcoming them. Then he had applied a military strategy, partly of his own making, partly the fortune of time and place, beginning with a river campaign to clear the Magdalena of Spanish occupation, followed by a major battle to finish the war in New Granada and lead him back to Venezuela. Now he simply needed a short, sharp campaign to lead him to Caracas.

In Caracas Monteverde had taken the title of 'commander general of the army of pacification', and was subsequently appointed captain-general and *jefe político* under the Spanish Constitution of 1812. He established his own regime, oppressive certainly but not at first violent. He did not consider himself bound by the capitulation and he promptly began to jail patriots and confiscate their property. Soon the fortresses of Puerto Cabello and La Guaira were full of *independentistas* and of many who were mere suspects. The caudillo based his rule on upper-class creoles, royalist clergy, and his compatriots, the *canarios*; many personal scores were settled and much property changed hands. But this military dictatorship was not an unmitigated blessing to Spain. It alienated the legitimate Spanish bureaucracy and outraged moderate royalists by its greed and cruelty. Monteverde had usurped authority from his Spanish superiors in 1812 and therefore needed a power base against the official Spanish party as well as against the creole republicans. He found this among the lower social groups, not *pardos* or blacks but poor whites, most of whom were Canarians, 'usually regarded in Venezuela', commented the *audiencia* judge José Francisco Heredia, 'as synonymous with ignorance, barbarism and coarseness'.[11] Royalism had less success in attracting *pardos* and slaves. Were Spanish masters any improvement on the aristocratic republic? The slaves once more burst out of their plantations; at Curiepe they armed themselves with machetes and knives and marched on La Guaira. The *pardos* of the coast were still restless and in November 1812 conspired to overthrow the dictatorship. Bands of insurgent peons and *llaneros* continued guerrilla actions against white property-owners. These part-bandits, part-rebels were no asset to either side; they preyed upon the economy and terrorized the countryside. Yet their mere existence served the cause of independence. They provided a source of recruits for the republican forces when the struggle was renewed. Meanwhile they demonstrated to the creoles that restoration of royal power was no guarantee of social order.

War by Terror

Bolívar left Cúcuta and moved quickly out of New Granada in May 1813. Mérida fell without a fight on 23 May and added reinforcements to his army and the name of Liberator to its commander. Trujillo quickly followed, and soon he was on the road to Barquisimeto, Valencia and Caracas.[12] Venezuela now endured a new and bloodier conflict; cruel and destructive, it was total war. This was a measure of the insecurity felt by each side, neither of which held preponderance of power or could afford to allow the other to grow. Monteverde tried to tip the balance in his favour by terrorizing the population and allowing his subordinates to kill civilians as well as belligerents. Bolívar reported news of the killing of one hundred victims in Caracas. The cruelty of the Spaniards was nowhere worse than at Maturín and Aragua and no one more monstrous than the officer Antonio Zuazola, who burned, mutilated and murdered indiscriminately, encouraging his soldiers to shoot wounded insurgents; he exhorted his troops to 'spare no one over seven years' – 'a detestable man', as Bolívar called him, who destroyed even the foetus in the mother's womb.[13]

Atrocities were committed on both sides in different parts of Venezuela. Antonio Nicolás Briceño, a *hacendado* neighbour of Bolívar, hard-line revolutionary and fellow exile, who became known as *El Diablo* among his colleagues, had his own terrorist agenda outside the control of the authorities in New Granada. He presented to Bolívar a plan of action (16 January 1813), in which he proposed to kill all European Spaniards. Bolívar gave approval only for those found arms in hand; Briceño offered promotion to his officers and men in return for the heads of Spaniards, and this tactic too was repudiated.[14] But he killed and decapitated two elderly Spanish civilians and sent a head each to Bolívar and Castillo, an action for which he was denounced and disavowed by Bolívar. In an independent expedition to Barinas he continued his bloody ways, but was captured and with twenty-five of his men and twelve other prisoners was executed by Spanish forces – rough justice perhaps but an outrage to Bolívar. According to O'Leary, 'this event was one of the immediate causes of the declaration of war to the death.'[15]

In Bolívar's view the enemy was waging an undeclared war of extermination, killing prisoners whose only crime was that they fought for freedom. He believed that his people were fighting at a disadvantage, conceding impunity to the Spaniards, who denied such a right to the patriots. He could not ignore the injustice without compromising his leadership. He therefore resolved upon a new policy – war to the death, pardoning only Americans, in order to give the patriots parity of menace. 'Our tolerance is now exhausted, and as our oppressors force us into a mortal war they will disappear from America and our land will be purged of the monsters who infest it. Our hatred will be implacable, the war will be to the death.'[16] In the upland village of Mucuchíes, near Mérida, the army executed the first victims of American vengeance, and in Mucuchíes too, according to legend, Bolívar was presented with a dog of the celebrated local breed that followed him with its young Indian companion until they both died in the battle of Boyacá.

On 15 June, in the celebrated decree issued at Trujillo, Bolívar made the position even clearer in words that were carefully calculated:

Any Spaniard who does not collaborate against tyranny in favour of the just cause, actively and effectively, shall be considered an enemy and punished as a traitor to the country, and in consequence shall be inescapably executed. . . . Spaniards and Canarians, know that you will die, even if you are simply neutral, unless you actively espouse the liberation of America. Americans, you will be spared, even when you are guilty.[17]

The exception was significant. This was a civil war, in which Americans predominated on both sides. And Bolívar could not bring himself to wage war to the death on Venezuelans, even though they might be royalists: 'It is not right to destroy men who do not wish to be free.'[18] Nor was it feasible to do so.

Knowing that he could not win this war without American support, both that of landowners and of the other creoles, he promised the creoles that they could count on absolute immunity. The Trujillo decree ruthlessly distinguished between Spaniards and Americans; it sought to cut through categories such as royalism and republicanism and to make this a war between nations, between Spain and America. More simply it aimed to terrorize Spaniards into submission and to encourage creoles to support independence. In fact it did not accomplish either, neither was it rigidly enforced. But it added to the violence.

Armed with the Trujillo decree, Bolívar's army increased its numbers from volunteers and enemy deserters and advanced eastwards. To fulfil his mission and to sustain his army he had to advance, even if it meant ignoring the instructions he had received from congress. His strategy, 'the initial effort of an inexperienced warrior', was to attack along the route to Caracas, and rapidly, in order to give the enemy no respite and to prevent his own forces from starving. Speed was the key weapon: 'If we move rapidly our armies can feed off the country until we reach Caracas.'[19] On his left flank he had to beware of royalist Maracaibo and beyond that Coro, of sinister memory. In Barinas, to his right, Monteverde had positioned a sizeable force under the command of Antonio Tizcar; if this managed to invade Trujillo and Mérida it could take New Granada and cut off Bolívar's own army. Somewhere in front was Monteverde himself with his forces from the east. Bolívar made a characteristic pre-emptive strike. Crossing the mountain range into the Barinas plains he made a rapid advance on Tizcar, forcing Monteverde to evacuate Barinas so hurriedly that he left valuable arms and ammunition to the patriots. Meanwhile by frontal attack Ribas won a decisive victory on the Niquitao heights, adding four hundred American prisoners to the patriot ranks and putting all the Spaniards to the sword. He went on to face a bitter and bloody struggle to take Barquisimeto and eventually join up with Bolívar, who had already occupied San Carlos. Bolívar immediately marched against the royalists and overwhelmed them on the savannah of Taguanes (31 July), where he employed the tactic of two men to a horse to give his infantry greater mobility, and caused great casualties among the enemy. Monteverde, already defeated in the east, had to make a rapid escape from Valencia to Puerto Cabello, piling up atrocities on the way and incurring equal reprisals.

In addition to speed, Bolívar valued the word, and on this campaign his words soared. As he liberated so he praised, and still more often preached: you have done well but we want more – money and volunteers. Governors were warned that unless their people yielded supplies, horses, mules and money, their provinces would be treated as enemy country.[20] He also appealed to women, new fighters for the cause, and praised their support, denouncing the

Spaniards for their cruelties. In Carache 'they have directed their deadly arms against the fair and tender breasts of our lovely women, spilling their blood and killing not a few . . . and our women are fighting against the oppressors and competing with us to overcome them'.[21] And as he advanced he reminded all of the terms of war to the death.

Bolívar occupied Valencia on 2 August and assigned Atanasio Girardot, a young veteran of New Granada's wars, to cover the enemy at Puerto Cabello. He himself went on towards Caracas where virtual anarchy prevailed and the authorities, lacking political leadership and military defences, saw no alternative but to capitulate. Frightened *peninsulares* and Canarians, who were the principal government and military officials, began to abandon the country. As royalist forces disappeared and republicans stood back, the *pardos* began sacking houses and public buildings, and menacing the lives of whites. While the capitulation was being negotiated the captain-general, together with military and civil authorities and many Spaniards, fled from the city and embarked at La Guaira, leaving their compatriots to face an angry populace. The city authorities sent another deputation to Bolívar begging him to come quickly to protect the lives and property of the inhabitants. He agreed but insisted that Monteverde too should ratify the agreement. 'Caracas remained almost deserted, because its joyful inhabitants went out to welcome the conqueror, who entered his native city on 6 August 1813, amidst the cheers of a grateful people.'[22]

Caracas, showing the scars of earthquake and occupation, was not too gloomy to celebrate. A great crowd of people turned out to greet him, with cries of 'Viva el Libertador de Venezuela'. A troop of young girls in white broke through the crowd and took the bridle of his horse, and as he dismounted crowded round to crown him with laurels and press flowers in his arms. Church bells rang and bands played as he moved in triumph through the streets of the capital, responding to the embraces of the crowd and the greetings of supporters.[23] That night he danced at a ball given in his honour and there he began his relationship with Josefina Machado, 'Pepita', one of the girls in white, an amiable twenty-year-old, not a great beauty but assiduous in her attentions and her opinions, who also brought her mother and sister along. She was his acknowledged mistress for the next four or five years, and if court gossip was to be believed a source of patronage for office-seekers.[24] Glory on campaign, power in government, a woman in his bed – Bolívar took it all as his due.

The Liberator

The eloquence of victory was left to Bolívar. Two days later he presented to the people of Caracas the results of the Admirable Campaign in the war to restore laws, liberty and independence to Venezuela:

Your liberators have arrived, from the banks of the swollen Magdalena to the flowering valleys of Aragua and the precincts of this great capital, victorious they have crossed the rivers of Zulia, of Táchira, of Boconó, of Masparro, Portuguesa, Morador and Acarigua; they have traversed the bleak and icy plateaus of Mucuchíes, Boconó and Niquitao; they have made their way over the deserts and mountains of Ocaña, Mérida and Trujillo; they have triumphed seven times in the battles of Cúcuta, La Grita, Betijoque Carache, Niquitao, Barquisimeto and Tinaquillo, and have left beaten five armies, which to the number of 10,000 men were devastating the fair provinces of Santa Marta, Pamplona, Mérida, Trujillo, Barinas, and Caracas.[25]

The itinerary had given Bolívar himself a vivid lesson in the geography of his country, and five pitched battles opened him to new knowledge in the art of war.

Events of equal importance were taking place in the eastern part of the country. There too Monteverde had imposed the rule of conquest and crushed the patriot movement. But a group of its leaders, Santiago Mariño, José Francisco Bermúdez, Manuel Valdés, Manuel Piar and Antonio José de Sucre, decided to fight back and liberate Venezuela. On 11 January 1813 Mariño, like Bolívar a product of the colonial elite, headed a small expedition, the famous 'forty-five', from Trinidad to Güiria, leading his band from his *hacienda* to operate in territory where he had property, relations and dependants.[26] The enterprise flourished and the royalists began to retreat and scatter before the eastern caudillos. Mariño captured Maturín and, later in the year, Cumaná and Barcelona. He established his leadership through his style, his victories and his violence. He repaid cruelty with cruelty. In Cumaná he had forty-seven Spaniards and creoles shot in reprisal; in Barcelona he executed sixty-nine conspirators, because 'the life of such men was incompatible with the existence of the State'.[27]

But Mariño was a challenge as well as an ally. Naming himself 'chief of the independent army', he established not only an independent military command in the east but a political entity separate from Caracas and from the government of Bolívar. The Liberator, on the other hand, insisted on establishing a central authority for all Venezuela. While it made sense to have two military departments, it was essential to have one central government uniting east and west: Venezuela and New Granada. 'Only a Venezuela united with New Granada could form a nation that would inspire in others the proper consideration due to her. How can we think of dividing her into two?'[28] Thus, Bolívar's first projection of a greater Colombia, united for national strength and economic viability, was presented as an alternative to the anarchy of local caudillo rule.

With the exception of Maracaibo and Guayana, Venezuela was now in republican hands with an army of trained veterans, hardened by combat in Bolívar's Admirable Campaign. Royalist officers told Heredia that in the battle of Araure 'the insurgents had fought with prodigious courage and manoeuvred with as much speed and dash as the most battle-hardened European troops'.[29] Bolívar's victory was so complete – or thus it appeared – that he was able to establish a virtual dictatorship, and with military success behind him he was in a position to dictate policy and appoint his own nominees. He was determined to avoid the mistakes of the first republic. He spoke of 're-establishing the free forms of republican government', but he really wanted new and strong executive power; this he procured on 2 January 1814 when a representative assembly granted him supreme power. And in spite of the reservations of the Venezuelan aristocracy, who regarded him as a tyrant and sought to restrain him by reinforcing the *cabildos* and the judiciary, he established a hard-line revolutionary government; his policy was to offer no mercy towards Spaniards, and to Americans an amnesty for those who surrendered, but the death penalty for those who disturbed public order and peace. Hard in government, soft in leisure, this was the stereotype of Bolívar now circulated by his enemies and given credence by the malicious Ducoudray-Holstein, a foreign adventurer who did not get the promotion he thought was his due: 'Bolívar, like most of his countrymen, loved ease and his pleasures better than exertion. His favourite occupations were being in the company of his numerous mistresses, and lying in his hammock surrounded by his flatterers.'[30]

Now politics as well as war occupied his mind. As he himself said, he was forced to be a soldier and a statesman, 'simultaneously on the battlefield and at the head of government . . . both a chief of state and a general of the army'.[31] Bolívar was a dictator when he wrote these words, served by known supporters and backed by the army. Bolivarian dictatorship, however, was not caudillism. It was less personal and more institutional; it dealt in policies as well as patronage. His intention was to concentrate authority in order to defend and extend the revolution. There was some resentment, however, and he convoked an assembly on 2 January 1814, to which he explained his dictatorship: 'My desire to save you from anarchy and to destroy the enemies who were endeavouring to sustain the oppressors forced me to accept and retain sovereign power. . . . I have come to bring you the rule of law. Military despotism cannot ensure the happiness of a people. A victorious soldier acquires no right to rule his country. . . . I am a simple citizen, and the general will of the people shall always be for me the supreme law'[32] Did he persuade himself that this was true, or was he reciting a familiar liberal text? Subsequent Bolivarian dictatorships, in Peru and Colombia, embodied the same principles; they were a response to emergency, they represented policies not interests, and they restored law as well as order. Meanwhile, in 1813, Bolívar was dictator of only half of Venezuela – the west. The east was won by Mariño, who also saw himself as a liberator.[33]

Bolívar expected the Church to conform and support the republican cause. His religious policy was coloured by deference to the Enlightenment and hatred of Spain. So he deplored the post-earthquake superstition and attacked the alliance between the hierarchy and its Spanish patron. He made it clear to bishops and priests that their only option was independence, no matter what their conscience told them, and that support for the Spanish enemy had to stop. Soon after his arrival in Caracas he wrote to the archbishop of Caracas:

> The time is past for obstructing government decrees, and the full weight of the law will fall upon offenders. Consequently, as Your Grace's orders are inspired by the same spirit, you should require all the parish priests, preachers and confessors of the archdiocese, under penalty of the powers reserved to you, to explain each week the just principles of American emancipation and persuade them of the obligation to accept and defend them, if necessary at the cost of personal interests and life itself. . . . As for the confessional, abuse of this sacred ministry by any who seek to undermine political opinion favouring the present government could be prevented by suspending them from their duties for this fact alone.[34]

His dispute was with clericalism, rather than religion. And he always distinguished between royalist and patriot priests, some of whom he recognized had also suffered at the hands of the enemy. But the spirit of Bourbon regalism was obviously still alive.

Bolívar's writ might run in Caracas, but elsewhere the war raged on. In Puerto Cabello Monteverde refused to surrender and refused to receive the Spanish peace commissioners. This left to their fate more than four thousand European Spaniards, the victims of Monteverde's intransigence as much as the republicans' vengeance. Reinforcements from Spain gave Monteverde a brief respite, but he wasted his resources in a premature break out from Puerto Cabello; the Spaniards were driven back with heavy losses in the battle at Bárbula on the Valencia road, and he himself was badly wounded in the fighting at Las Trincheras. The republicans too paid a high price – the loss of Girardot, whose death deeply affected Bolívar and the whole army. The war was by no means over and the royalists were recruiting further support; Bolívar had to send General Urdaneta with a division to protect the western front, where the enemy was still raiding from Coro and Maracaibo.

When Bolívar returned to Caracas, the municipality called a meeting of prominent citizens on 14 October 1813 in order to reward the achievements of the commander-in-chief. The assembly conferred upon Bolívar the rank of 'Captain-general of the armies' and the title of 'Liberator of Venezuela'. The title was unique and became his greatest distinction, the essence of his identity for all time. In an elegant reply he accepted the title as 'more glorious and satisfying for me than the crown of all the empires of the world', and deferred to his commanders Ribas, Girardot, Urdaneta, D'Eluyar, Elías and the other officers and troops as the true liberators.[35]

Was the hero of liberation also the author of terror? Bolívar and his colleagues insisted that it was Monteverde who first imposed 'the law of conquest' and gave his subordinates a loose rein to terrorize, and Heredia, regent of the *audiencia* of Caracas, admitted that Monteverde broke the capitulation on the question of amnesty.[36] They specifically cited the atrocities commited in eastern Venezuela by Spanish officers: first Cervériz, 'young, impetuous, and cruel', according to Heredia, whose coarse and brutal ways became a byword for unrestrained terror, promising a peso for every ear of an insurgent, and then Antonio Zuazola, whose mutilations and killings of prisoners were recorded by appalled Spanish officials.[37] In justifying his action to the British governor of Curaçao, who sought to mediate on behalf of Spanish prisoners, Bolívar insisted on his right 'to deprive the tyrants of the incomparable advantage of their organized methods of destruction' and he cited the action of Zuazola in the village of Aragua: 'Men and women, old and young, had their ears cut off, were skinned alive, and then thrown into contaminated lakes or put to death by slow and painful methods . . . unborn babes were destroyed in the wombs of expectant mothers by bayonets or blows.'[38] The English volunteer Richard Vowell, who was with Bolívar in the fighting in the *llanos* in 1818, saw the war to the death at close quarters. At Calabozo, observing Bolívar's response to the spectacle of royalist atrocities, he concluded that 'his own troops would now have torn him to pieces, had he not consented to retaliate to the utmost extent of his power.'[39] Retaliation gave him credibility with his own men. So Bolívar intended to terrorize, to establish a balance of fear, to reassure his followers that he was as ruthless as the enemy, and to convince his own side including the caudillos of the east that he was a leader to be reckoned with. From Caracas he reported to the congress of New Granada: 'After the battle of Tinaquillo I advanced without delay through the cities and villages of Tocuyito, Valencia, Guayos, Guacara, San Joaquín, Maracay, Turmero, San Mateo, and La Victoria, where all the most criminal Europeans and Canarians, were shot.'[40] He insisted that 'a government of a country in revolution must follow routes very different from the ordinary'.

Some five years later, defending his extremism, Bolívar conceptualized his policy:

Extreme measures, though terrible, are indispensable in sustaining an enterprise lacking in resources. Simply recall the violent expedients I have had to adopt to gain the few successes that have kept us alive. In order to hold on to four guerrilla bands who had contributed to our liberation, we were compelled to declare war to the death; to gain a few faithful followers, we had to free the slaves; to recruit the two armies of last year and this we had to resort to the oppressive martial law. . . . A mere glance at all this will show you that it amounts to nothing. To achieve this nothing, we have been obliged to employ all our resources; for it is a general rule that, in an ill-constructed machine, the engine must be enormously powerful to produce the slightest result. Experience has taught me that much must be demanded of men in order that they may accomplish little.[41]

Bolívar captured the infamous Zuazola, 'executioner of countless men, women, and children whose throats he cut with his own hands', four Spaniards and a number of Americans, near Puerto Cabello in September 1813. Zuazola was promptly hanged, the four Spaniards executed and the Americans pardoned.[42] He demanded the surrender of Monteverde in Puerto Cabello, together with his armaments, funds and ships: 'This is the only way left to him to save the numberless Spanish and *isleño* prisoners in my power, and I have made him understand that on the slightest delay they shall be exterminated.' Bolívar hesitated before the enormity of this execution; he was ready to compromise and do a deal with Monteverde to save the four thousand Spanish captives he held, through an exchange of prisoners, but Monteverde refused to listen and imprisoned the messenger. He rejected another proposal to exchange them for an equal number of Americans of similar rank; again he imprisoned the messenger.[43] When all attempts failed, and in the face of the atrocities of Boves and other Spaniards, and reports of conspiracy to escape, he signed the order condemning to death the Spanish and Canarian prisoners in La Guaira. Juan Bautista Arismendi, military governor of Caracas, was more than ready to carry out the order and eight hundred victims were sacrificed on 14–16 February 1814, in spite of the pleas for mercy from Archbishop Coll y Prat. Bolívar defended the action in uncompromising terms to the archbishop: 'The welfare of the country demands it . . . indulgence would only increase the number of victims . . . yesterday in Tinaquillo they murdered twenty-five of its garrison. . . . Boves has not yet given quarter to a single one of our men taken prisoner. . . . The enemy, seeing our ruthlessness, will at least know he will pay dearly for his atrocities, and he will no longer be encouraged by impunity.'[44]

Counter-Revolution

By the beginning of 1814 Bolívar had reason to believe that his policies were working and that the second republic was safe. Monteverde had been forced to abandon Puerto Cabello, and further victories in the east and west secured the revolution. But bloody battles lay ahead and the year ended in abject defeat. The reasons soon became clear. The social base of the second republic was no wider than that of the first. The cause of liberation had not yet won the minds and hearts of all Venezuelans. It was a matter of great bitterness to Bolívar that 'the greater part of the Spanish forces were composed of Venezuelans. . . . American blood continued to be shed by American hands. Sons of America were among the most obdurate enemies of independence.'[45]

Divided against itself the creole upper class was also challenged by the mass of the people and of two particular groups: the slaves and the *llaneros*. The slave rebellions of the first republic were fresh in minds of the Venezuelan aristocracy, and reinforced its rejection of manumission and any other concession. When Bolívar's army occupied Caracas in August 1813 it identified the slaves as a major focus of resistance and dispatched a punitive expedition against them. And *hacendados* pressed Bolívar to revive the national guards and patrols 'in order to pursue robbers, apprehend fugitive slaves, and preserve estates and properties free from all incursions'.[46] 'We are going to fall into the hands of the blacks.' This was the persistent fear of white creoles in the years around 1814. Slaves converged into *cumbes*, armed bands, and continued their own autonomous struggle, independent of Spaniards and creoles alike. When race-conscious black forces fought on either side, it was from opportunism, not conviction. And they consistently singled out the whites of the opposing force for extermination. After an engagement with a royalist unit on 6 September 1813 a patriot officer reported: 'The deaths [twenty-six] comprise whites, Indians and *zambos*, with only one black, and face to face we have noticed that black casualties are invariably the least, a fact on which the government can reflect in the interests of our tranquillity.' The slaves could take lives but not power. Like the blacks and *mulattos* they were formless and leaderless. Not so the *llaneros*.

In the interior a new royalist leader rose to resist the revolution – José Tomás Boves, an Asturian who had entered colonial Venezuela as a pilot in the Spanish merchant marine with contraband as a sideline. After a brush with the law he retreated to the *llanos* and became a cattle-dealer at Calabozo. When the revolution began, the strong, cunning and sadistic Spaniard was already at one with his new environment, the wide plains of the interior. This endless expanse of flat grassland, scorched by the sun in the dry season and in the wet turned by torrential rain into great swamps and lakes, was the home of a wild and warlike breed, a racial mixture from Indian, white and black stock, hardened by their savage surroundings and capable of great endurance on horseback. The *llanos* became a refuge for vagrants, fugitive slaves, bandits and the simply impoverished, and for most of the *bandidos* survival was more important than ideology:

> It is not uncommon to observe in these vast territories groups of bandits who, without any political motivation and with desire of pillage their only incentive, come together and follow the first caudillo who offers them booty taken from anyone with property. This is how Boves and other bandits of the same kind have been able to recruit hordes of these people who live by vagrancy, robbery and assassination.[47]

'Of all the monsters produced by the revolution in America or elsewhere,' wrote O'Leary, 'José Tomás Boves was the most bloodthirsty and ferocious.'[48] Insulted by the patriots in 1812 and jailed in Calabozo for insubordination, Boves was freed by the royalists in May 1812 and soon became a caudillo of the *llaneros* and the scourge of Bolívar. Tall and well built, with a large head, blond hair, staring blue eyes and fair complexion, his appearance contrasted with that of the followers he cultivated, but he more than matched them in physique and endurance. After initial defeat, in October 1813, at the hands of the republican forces led by Vicente Campo Elías, Boves retreated southwards to recoup and fashion the *llaneros* into a powerful lancer cavalry. On 1 November he issued a notorious circular from Guayabal calling on all *llaneros* to join him and promising them booty at the expense of their wealthy enemies. The brutalities inflicted by the republican Campo Elías on the rural population also helped his cause.

What was the Boves magic? Why did men flock to his band? Was he a genuine populist, a leader of an agrarian revolution? In the proclamation of Guayabal, Boves decreed war to the death against his creole enemies and the confiscation of their property.[49] But the killing of prisoners was common on both sides. So was pillage. The decree simply meant that Boves, like Bolívar and other military leaders, royalist and republican, took property from the enemy to finance the war effort and pay his followers. His followers, it is true, were blacks and *mulattos*, and it was the property of whites which he promised them. A potent mixture of race and reward, therefore, animated the *llaneros* and gave Boves and other royalist caudillos their troops. He also attracted the Canarians, who were drawn to Boves partly because he was anti-creole and anti-elite, and partly because he rewarded his followers with land and booty. It is doubtful whether he was a true populist offering agrarian reform to the *llaneros* or absolute freedom for slaves. But the fact remains that

he was able to recruit a following among blacks and *pardos* because he promised them white property and because the creole oligarchy of the first republic
had been responsible for further land concentration and cattle privatization in
the *llanos* to the detriment of the popular classes. This was the reason why the
llaneros joined Boves against the republic – to fight for their freedom and their
cattle.

Boves recruited blacks and *pardos* by preference; in his forces they became
officers and were promised wealth at the expense of whites, and he often
referred to the *llanos* as belonging especially to *pardos*, as their property and
their fortress. According to José Ambrosio Llamozas, chaplain in the army of
Boves, it was the caudillo's principal policy and system to kill whites and
reward *pardos*. Llamozas enumerated specific occasions when whites were
killed, amounting to some four thousand victims: 'He constantly and publicly
reminded his troops of the declaration of war to the death on whites which
he had made at Guayabal: he always told them that the property of these
people belonged to the *pardos*.'[50] In the army of Boves, which in December
1814 consisted of seven thousand men, there were only sixty to eighty white
soldiers and forty to fifty white officers. The result of this system was a
dramatic fall in the white population of the provinces under his control and
rising expectations among the blacks and mixed races, 'the slaves fired by their
longing to be free, and the *mulattos* and other castes by their expectation of
civil representation and appointments'.[51]

Bolívar was acutely aware of the deep racial divisions in Venezuela and of
the reckless exploitation of race prejudice by both sides in the conflict. To
some extent this limited his own options. The class hatred infusing the *llanero*
followers of Boves horrified the creole aristocracy and confirmed their determination to gain political power on their own terms. Heredia, the creole
regent of the *audiencia* of Caracas, spoke of the 'mortal hatred' between whites
and *pardos* in Venezuela during the first republic and commented, 'The guerrilla band that later joined the king's side encouraged this rivalry, and it was
commonly said by the European extremists that the *pardos* were loyalists and
the white creoles were revolutionaries whom it was necessary to destroy.' This
was the policy, he added, of José Tomás Boves and other bandit chiefs, nominally royalists but in fact 'insurgents of another kind', who waged war on all
white creoles: 'And so he became the idol of the *pardos*, who followed him in
the hope of seeing the dominant class destroyed'.[52] When Boves occupied and
plundered Valencia in June 1814, the Spanish authorities looked on helplessly;
when he took Caracas, he refused to recognize the captain-general or to have
his *llanero* forces incorporated into the royal army.[53] His was a personal
authority, expressing violence rather than legitimacy, and loyal to only a very
distant king. Bolívar grimly observed these developments. He noticed that

royalist caudillos incited slaves and *pardos* to plunder in order to increase their commitment, morale and group cohesion. And he could not fail to see that some of his own insurgents 'were reluctant to fire on *hombres de color*'.[54]

Bolívar was struggling. Monteverde, wounded in the battle of Las Trincheras on 3 October, was removed from command at Puerto Cabello and replaced as captain-general by Manuel Cagigal, a more conventional Spaniard. The royalists were resilient. In November 1813, at Barquisimeto, inferior royalist forces, apparently defeated, were allowed to recover when a mixture of panic and mistakes caused the patriot infantry to flee, to the fury of Bolívar, who renamed this battalion the *Sin Nombre* (Nameless), and suffered the loss of a thousand men. He had to swallow his pride, and from Valencia he sent an urgent request to Mariño to come to his assistance. He managed to recruit an army and marched to San Carlos to join with Campo Elías and his troops. At Araure, on the plains between San Carlos and Guanare, Bolívar forced the royalists to fight a set battle on 5 December, addressing his 3,000 troops (against the enemy's 3,700) with rousing words. His infantry, the *Sin Nombre* battalion under Urdaneta, kept ranks and discipline under heavy artillery fire and advanced on the royalist infantry while the cavalry came up in support. But the royalists fought back strongly and when the situation became dangerous Bolívar placed himself at the head of his select dragoons; he launched a sudden attack on the enemy cavalry, and managed to turn near-defeat into victory. He now named the *Sin Nombre* the 'Victors of Araure', for they finally charged with fixed bayonets and routed the solid Spanish line. By this important victory he had managed to regain the west, but it was his last big victory for the second republic.

He knew he was stretching things. To win this victory he had to assemble all his available troops, leaving the rest of the liberated territory unprotected and many fronts from Coro to Caracas dangerously exposed. The prisoners taken from the royalist army were mostly Venezuelans, and promptly after the victory he addressed a proclamation from his headquarters at San Carlos offering a full pardon to all provided they presented themselves at a patriot camp within a month's time. The invitation was ignored, and the royalists continued to recruit troops from Venezuelans, and 'American blood continued to be shed by American hands'. Also by Spanish hands. They too waged war to the death and took no prisoners: when Ribas entered Ocumare he found three hundred corpses in the church – men, women and children who had taken no part in the fighting.

Bolívar would have to confront Boves who, having devastated the *llanos* from the banks of the Orinoco to the Valles de Aragua, destroying all the towns along his route and terrorizing their inhabitants, was threatening Valencia and Caracas. Bolívar's position, already weakened by a rival dictatorship in the east, was now wrecked by the intervention of this guerrilla chief turned general who fought to destroy the republic in collaboration with hard-core defenders of the colonial order. Mariño eventually brought his forces to join those of Bolívar and fought alongside him in February and March 1814. The joint army regrouped at Valencia and Bolívar yielded the command to Mariño, 'as a sure sign of his high opinion of his person and services, and also in this way to ensure the adhesion of the eastern officers to the common cause of Venezuela'.[55] But neither the eastern caudillos nor their forces distinguished themselves in these engagements.

After Boves defeated Campo Elías at La Puerta, Bolívar assembled all available troops and took up a position on his own estate at San Mateo. But he was soon surrounded, without hope of reinforcements, and this did not become a victorious last stand on his patrimonial soil. Campo Elías was killed, and the young Captain Antonio Ricaurte in blowing up the defenders' military stores in the manor house killed himself as well as the attackers.[56] Bolívar was forced to retreat to Valencia, and it was left to Ribas to hold Boves at bay, defeating him temporarily at La Victoria on 12 February 1814. It was now that Bolívar signed the order condemning to death the Spanish prisoners in Caracas and La Guaira. But this made little difference to the strength or the morale of the royalists, who again assembled an army and threatened to destroy the republic. Again Bolívar had to respond, this time with the united forces of Cumaná and Caracas, Mariño and Bolívar. The two armies fought on the savannahs of Carabobo on 28 May 1814 in heavy rain, eastern and western patriots side by side; they won a 'signal victory', but to little avail. With his endless supply of *llaneros* Boves always emerged hydra-like from any slaughter.

Boves advanced again from Calabozo and mounted another attack on La Puerta, where Mariño had stationed his weakened forces in sound defensive positions in a gorge with his artillery on a hill. The arrival of Bolívar from Caracas with his secretary, a chaplain and a few aides, changed defence into attack, not a wise decision; on the plains Boves's cavalry were able to destroy the patriot forces within a few hours and started killing prisoners, reducing the patriot ranks by about a thousand. Diego Jalón, who had recently benefited from a prisoner exchange, was invited to lunch by Boves who had him beheaded immediately afterwards. This defeat, on 15 June 1814, was the beginning of the end of the second republic. Bolívar, Mariño, Rivas and a few other officers escaped to Caracas, while Boves occupied the fertile valley of Aragua and cut communications between the capital and Valencia. There the garrison held out stubbornly until forced into a negotiated surrender, according to which the lives and property of the citizens and garrison would be guaranteed. Boves swore to this before the eucharist during mass. The next evening, while their wives danced, he had the husbands killed and the massacre continued until all the patriots were eliminated.[57]

In Caracas Bolívar desperately sought a way out of the calamity. There were not enough supplies to sustain a siege or enough money to pay an army. From churches he took silver and jewels, filling twenty-four boxes, and sent them eastwards. His token resistance to Boves approaching from the west was brushed aside and panic overcame the people of Caracas. He began to evacuate the capital, taking a few troops he had managed to save and those who had come by sea from the siege of Puerto Cabello. Pepita Machado was sent to St Thomas. A mass of civilians swarmed eastwards, fleeing in terror from Boves and his hordes, an exodus of hopeless refugees, ravaged by hunger, disease and trials of the terrain; the survivors reached Barcelona twenty days later and some of these made it to Cumaná. There was a brief pause to organize some resistance at the patriot headquarters at Aragua de Barcelona, but Bolívar could not avoid another humiliating defeat, this time at the hands of another royalist chief, Francisco Morales, or prevent his undisciplined troops deserting at the mere sight of the enemy. Indeed, he was not even in command in this engagement, which took place in Mariño's territory under the command of his lieutenant, Francisco Bermúdez. Morales killed all civilians in Aragua; altogether 3,700 patriots lost their lives in the battle of Aragua de Barcelona, and 1,011 royalists.[58] Most of the casualties were Venezuelans, a further commentary on the war to the death. Hunting and killing refugees on the way, Morales made for Barcelona, which he entered on 20 August.

Boves reached Cumaná in October and quickly occupied it, beginning another reign of terror and the final destruction of the second republic. A thousand victims were slain in this city alone, including many of the unfortunate families who had fled from Caracas. The eastern caudillos now began to dispute with western officers and among themselves. Mariño had wanted to evacuate Cumaná and concentrate resistance in Margarita or Güiria. Ribas insisted that the patriots should hold Cumaná at all costs. He won the argument but Cumaná was not exactly a prize, for the royalists already had it in their sights and the patriot leaders fled further east, together with most of the inhabitants. Maturín was the next target. There Bermúdez wanted to keep the patriot forces in defensive posture, while Ribas insisted on marching out to attack Boves. His opinion prevailed and the patriot army of some three thousand met Boves at Urica with a force twice as large. The patriots were slaughtered and few managed to escape to Maturín. The life of Boves ended in that fatal battle, killed by a patriot lancer, but so did the life of the second republic. It only remained for Morales to mop up in Maturín, which he did with as much cruelty as his former chieftain, and his followers boasted of having raped every woman in the place. It was here that Ribas was taken in flight, shot and dismembered; his head was cooked in oil and taken to Caracas, where it was displayed topped by his red cap.[59] By the end of January 1815 the entire province was in the possession of the royalists and independence seemed as far away as ever.

Bolívar was not an actor in these tragic scenes. When he reached Cumaná on the night of 25 August 1814 he found utter confusion, civilian refugees, disorganized troops, no supplies and no possibility of establishing order or organizing resistance. Once more, as yet another of his constructs collapsed under the dread hand of chaos, he had to decide to leave the republic to its fate. But even escape was difficult.[60] The next day he sailed with Mariño for the island of Margarita, carrying the church silver and jewels, which he was obliged to share with the corsair Giovanni Bianchi, the commander of the vessels conducting the evacuation of patriots. There they found another caudillo in control, Manuel Piar, an ambitious *mulatto* staking out space for himself in eastern Venezuela, who declared the two liberators outlaws. Bolívar was seething and never forgot the affront. They returned to the mainland and, landing at Carúpano on 3 September, found that Ribas too had turned rival and declared them deserters of the republic, making himself supreme chief of the west and Piar supreme chief of the east. He arrested Mariño and forced Bolívar to turn over the remaining boxes of church wealth and the supplies on their ships. He then allowed them to board their vessel and sail to Cartagena, one of his last acts before his own undoing. It was painful for the Liberator to fail and flee yet again.

Before sailing he issued his 'Manifesto of Carúpano', in which he defended himself and explained the failure of the second republic, a moving document expressing his sense of helplessness and determination, his failure and his defiance.[61] He deplored the divisions in American society that caused so many to reject their liberators. 'It appears that heaven, to our humiliation and glory, has determined that our conquerors shall be our brothers and that only our brothers shall triumph over us.' The army of liberation might destroy the enemy, but, as Bolívar insisted, it could not force men to be free. How could political philosophy, he asked, prevail over vice and greed? 'The choice of liberty over ambition and avarice, and with it our fate, lay in the hands of our compatriots who were deluded and pronounced against us.' Look for the original source of all misfortune – human frailty. 'To expect politics and war to march in step with our plans is like seeking to achieve, through human resources, results attainable only by a divine power.' He accepted that he was not blameless and was the ill-fated instrument of the country's miseries, but while his conscience may have advised him wrongly or ineffectively it had never been party to wilful error or act of malice. Let the supreme congress of New Granada be his judge. 'I swear to you that as Liberator, alive or dead, I will always be worthy of the honour you have accorded me; nor is there any human power on earth which can hold back the course which I have set for myself – to return a second time, by that western road already drenched with so much blood and adorned with so many laurels, to make you free.'

But for now the western road was closed.

Exit and Exile

On his journey across the Caribbean, Bolívar's morale was undiminished. Beaten and banished in the east, he was still held in respect in New Granada, and in Cartagena, where he arrived on 19 September 1814, he promptly took up residence in the palace of the absent bishop. He himself was still a general and Liberator and as such held senior military rank; he was expected to play a leading part, as yet undefined, in a country divided into rival factions and a weak confederation. Within a month he was moving up the Magdalena River towards the seat of congress in Tunja, when he met the troops of General Urdaneta, who had fought his way out of western Venezuela and was also on his way to Tunja apparently on a rival mission. Urdaneta's troops broke ranks and presented themselves to Bolívar with cries of 'Viva el Libertador!' Urdaneta had to accept the inevitable, and Bolívar to hail and also to rebuke the troops, which he did in memorable words:

> Soldiers! You have filled my heart with joy. But at what cost? At the cost of discipline, of subordination, which is the first virtue of every soldier. Your chief is the distinguished General Urdaneta; and he deplores as I do the excess to which your love has led you. Soldiers! Do not repeat these acts of disobedience. If you love me, prove it by your loyalty and discipline and submission to your chief. I am only a soldier who comes to offer his services to this sister nation. For all of us our native land is America; our enemies are the Spaniards; our ensign is independence and liberty.[62]

They escorted him into Tunja on 22 November, where he gave an account to congress of the rise and fall of the second Venezuelan republic and received the warm support of its president, Camilo Torres. 'The congress of New Granada will give you its protection because it is satisfied with your record. You may have been an unlucky soldier but you are a great man.'[63] He was appointed captain-general of the Colombia State Federation and given command of all troops with a mission to bring Cundinamarca into the union and Cartagena to heel. But Bolívar needed New Granada for another mission – to recover Venezuela. Could he reconcile the two?

After the capture and exile of Nariño, who opposed the confederation and preferred a strong central government, Cundinamarca was governed by Manuel Bernardo Alvarez, a political incompetent and religious fanatic who refused to accept the union. Bolívar marched his troops up to Santa Fe de Bogotá and offered conciliation, but Alvarez rejected this and launched criminal accusations against Bolívar and the Venezuelan troops, declaring for good measure that they were excommunicated from the Church. Alvarez and his clerical allies allowed their political prejudices and poor information to make them look fools when one week they excommunicated Bolívar for coming to sack churches and rape virgins, and exonerated him the next as a good and faithful Catholic. What a farce, thought Bolívar. In repudiating the accusations, he denied that he ever intended to declare war to the death in his approach to Santa Fe, 'nor will I ever do so in this peaceful country, where the Spaniards have behaved very differently than in Venezuela'.[64] But his troops were forced to fight their way into Santa Fe street by street until, on 12 December 1814, they were able to occupy the city. Bolívar could rightly claim that he had come as a liberator and a unifier.

The congress moved from Tunja to Santa Fe in January 1815 and became the union congress; it then named Bolívar captain-general of the union armies and approved his plans for the defence of the frontiers and invasion of Venezuela. His own message to congress was a plea for unity and solidarity against external threats and the enemy within: if so far we have experienced horror and disaster 'it is through our own fault and not the power of the enemy'. 'Let us persuade the people that this half of the globe belongs to those whom God has ordained to be born here and not to transatlantic defectors who wish to establish here the tyranny they are leaving at home.'[65] The most urgent task for Bolívar was the security of the Atlantic front, where the Spaniards possessed a vital bridgehead, and the stability of Cartagena, where Castillo was stirring up trouble. He liberated Ocaña and Mompós, but before he could reach the last Spanish base at Santa Marta he was fatally diverted.

The stubborn refusal of Cartagena to accept the authority of Bolívar or of any central institution, and the personal animosity of its commander, Colonel Manuel del Castillo, trapped the Liberator in a civil war. For six weeks from Mompós he tried negotiation and conciliation, but it became obvious that Castillo would never cooperate with a man whom he personally disliked, considered an invader of his space and scorned as an inferior strategist who wasted the military resources of New Granada on wild adventures in Venezuela. Against his better judgement Bolívar agreed with his military colleagues to lay siege to Cartagena and on 27 March he established his headquarters in the monastery of La Popa on the hill overlooking the city. He took measures to secure his supply routes and Castillo countered by having

La Popa's water reservoir poisoned; while Castillo's military sorties failed, Bolívar's army was disappearing through desertions. This was a battle neither side could win: the only victor would be the royalists. As Bolívar fought to bring Cartagena within the mainstream of the revolution, the royalists were able to recover lost ground in the Magdalena valley and open a gap through which the republic could be invaded. Bolívar agonized. He signed a peace pact with Castillo, resigned his commission – something he had been trying to do since March – and, despairing of resolving New Granada's problems, left for Jamaica. A Spanish expedition under General Pablo Morillo landed at Santa Marta in July 1815. Cartagena maintained a suicidal resistance to a siege that lasted a hundred days, and was finally occupied on 6 December. The town was dead, its streets and houses were littered with corpses, and the few patriots still alive were butchered by the royalists. Castillo was taken and executed.

Bolívar departed in a vessel belonging to the English merchant Maxwell Hyslop and reached Jamaica on 14 May 1815. Before embarking he took a rueful leave of his soldiers, lamenting the campaign they had been forced to wage, not against the tyrants but against their own countrymen; yet while he had to leave the decisive action, they were to continue the struggle for freedom and on them depended the republic.[66] The lesson he took with him was clear: they were defeated not by Spaniards but by Americans. 'In New Granada,' he wrote, 'the excessive powers of the provincial governments and the lack of centralization in the federal government have reduced that fair country to its present state. For this reason its enemies, though weak, have been able to hold out against all expectations.'[67] America needed strong, not liberal, government.

The years 1813–15, the time of the Admirable Campaign in Venezuela, victories in New Granada, and the triumph of the counter-revolution, were another chapter in the history of Bolívar's personal progress and public frustration. His own analysis pointed to an inescapable conclusion: when he personally imposed his policies and projects they worked. His success stopped when other interests intervened, and creole hostility and caudillo rivalry crowded in to obstruct him. The caudillos presented the next challenge. So far, glory was his, but power remained beyond his reach.

Chapter 5

TOUCHSTONE OF THE REVOLUTION

The Jamaica Letter

In 1814 Ferdinand VII, returned to Spain, restored absolute government and began to punish liberals. In America his policy was equally bereft of ideas and deaf to pacification. Here restoration meant reconquest and the revival of the colonial state. On 16 February 1815 an expeditionary force sailed from Cadiz under the command of General Pablo Morillo, a rough professional soldier, veteran of the peninsular war, who ruled by order and discipline. The original destination, the Río de la Plata, was changed in favour of Venezuela, the focal point of revolution and counter-revolution, from which New Granada could be reconquered, Peru reinforced and the way opened to the Río de la Plata and Chile. In three centuries this was the largest expedition Spain had sent to America – forty-two transports, five escorting warships and over ten thousand troops, followed by annual reinforcements.[1] But size exceeded morale, and once in America numbers were soon reduced by death and desertion. The Spanish troops were conscripts, not volunteers. Colonial war was not a popular cause in Spain, and neither troops nor officers wished to risk their lives in America, least of all in Venezuela, where the environment and the fighting were notoriously cruel.[2]

They were soon in action and in the beginning numbers and professionalism prevailed. In April Morillo occupied Margarita before proceeding to the mainland. In May he entered Caracas, 'to forgive, to reward and to punish'. And in July he moved on to New Granada where, in a brisk and uncompromising campaign, he completed the reconquest by October 1816. Santa Fe de Bogotá was subjected to an unprecedented reign of terror and the patriot elite wiped out in an orgy of hanging, decapitation and shooting, cynically described as 'pacification', while peasants were herded into labour gangs to turn the colony into a supply base for Morillo's army. The year 1816 was the blackest year of the American revolution, the year of the gallows in New Granada and of reaction and retribution throughout the subcontinent.

The Spanish king spoke piously of mercy and reconciliation. But there had been too much carnage; creoles had lost lives and property; the *pardos* had advanced. The clock could not be put back, and the counter-revolution imposed itself as a violent reconquest. Morillo needed money and supplies. In 1815 he proceeded rapidly and without due process of law with the confiscation and sale of rebel property, rebels being defined widely enough to include leaders, supporters, passive followers and emigrants. In Venezuela the *Junta de Secuestros* sold almost 1 million pesos worth of property in 1815–16 for the royal treasury. Over two hundred *haciendas* were confiscated, most of them in the coast and mountain valleys of the north, the property of a small elite comprising 145 individuals, among them the Tovars, Blancos, Toros, Machados and Palacios. Bolívar himself lost five estates and other properties valued at 80,000 pesos, the largest single confiscation made by the royalists, indicative of his total wealth of some 200,000 pesos and his position as one of the richest men in Venezuela.[3] This was not the way to reconcile the Venezuelan elite. Here as elsewhere counter-revolution proved counterproductive.

As news of these events unfolded with dreaded familiarity, Bolívar revised his first plan, which had been to proceed from Jamaica to England 'in search of help'.[4] Spanish action on the mainland demanded proximity to events. His reaction was unfailing: first intellectual analysis, then preparations to strike back. His celebrated 'Answer of a South American to a Gentleman of this Island', usually known in Spanish as *Carta de Jamaica*, was dated from Kingston on 6 September 1815, and addressed to Mr Henry Cullen, a friend and admirer, of Falmouth on the north coast of Jamaica, and implicitly to the wider English-speaking world.[5] A requiem to past failure and a celebration of future prospects, Bolívar's eloquence raises the Spanish American revolution to the heights of world history and his own role to its intellectual as well as its political leadership.

Bolívar was not the first statesman to construct a theory of colonial emancipation. In North America Richard Bland, John Adams, Thomas Jefferson, the declarations of the Continental Congress, and the Declaration of Independence itself had all made crucial contributions to the colonial debate. But Bolívar was convinced that the North American experience was different to that of his own people and could never be their model. He had to design his own theory of national liberation, and this was a contribution to the ideas of the Enlightenment, not an imitation. Here the Liberator is seen striving to achieve a total vision of America, beyond Venezuela and New Granada.

Yet the Jamaica Letter was an exercise in applied liberalism rather than a theoretical discourse, though it contains certain political and moral assumptions: that people have natural rights; that they have a right to resist oppression; that nationalism has its own imperatives; that deprivation of office and economic opportunity justifies rebellion. He began by arguing that the unjust policy and oppressive practice of Spain had severed its ties with America and authorized the sixteen million Americans to defend their rights, the more so when counter-revolution increased the oppression. These rights were natural rights, granted by God and nature. True, 'a principle of loyalty' had bound Americans to Spain, seen in the enduring habit of obedience, community of interest, understanding, religion, goodwill and, on the part of Americans, a regard for the birthplace of their forbears. But all these bonds were broken, as affinity changed to alienation and the elements of community turned into their opposites and became – though Bolívar did not use the word – signs of incipient nationalism. And there were problems of identity. Americans by birth, they were neither Indian nor European, but in an ambiguous position between usurped and usurpers. Under Spanish rule their political role was purely passive: 'America was denied not only its freedom but even an active and dominant tyranny.' Most despotic rulers, he argued, had at least an organized system of oppression in which subordinate agents participated at various levels of administration. But under Spanish absolutism Americans were not allowed to exercise any functions of government or even of internal administration. Thus, he concluded, they were not only deprived of their rights but kept in a state of political infancy.

Bolívar gave significant examples of inequality and discrimination, arguing that Spain deprived Americans of economic opportunity and public office, reducing them to a source of labour and a consumer market. They were not allowed to compete with Spain and supply themselves, either in agricultural products or manufactured goods. They were allowed to be no more than producers of raw materials and precious metals, and the export even of these was controlled by the Spanish trading monopoly. Moreover, he added, this applied today, 'and perhaps to a greater extent than ever before', an observation confirmed by modern research, which shows that *comercio libre* (freedom of trade) was intended to expand Spanish colonial trade and channel it more effectively through the peninsular monopolists. The new imperialism of the Bourbons also sought to restore Spanish domination over appointments. Bolívar states that Americans were barred from senior offices and prevented from acquiring any experience in government and administration. 'We were never viceroys or governors, save in exceptional circumstances; seldom archbishops and bishops; diplomats never; as soldiers only subordinates; nobles, without real privileges. In brief, we were neither magistrates nor financiers and seldom merchants.' Modern research concludes that Americans had ample access to public office (mainly through purchase) in an earlier period of colonial history (1650–1750) but were then restricted in a 'Spanish reaction' which Bolívar himself lived through.[6] Bolívar went further. He maintained that Americans possessed 'constitutional rights' to public offices, deriving from a pact between Charles V and the conquerors and settlers, whereby in return for their own enterprise and risks they received lordship over land and administration. As history the idea is questionable, but there is a contractual concept embedded in the argument which Bolívar sought to transplant in American soil.

In the Jamaica Letter Bolívar consciously saw himself on the side of change against tradition, in favour of revolution against conservatism. It is character-istic of civil wars, he argues, to form two parties, 'conservatives and reformers'. The former are commonly the more numerous, because the weight of habit induces obedience to established powers; the latter are always fewer in number although more vocal and learned, so numbers are counterbalanced by moral force. Polarization causes prolonged conflict, but he upholds the struggle in hope, because in the war of independence the masses are following the reformers. The international situation, too, he saw in terms of division between conservatism and liberalism, between the Holy Alliance and, in effect, Great Britain. Speaking of Spanish America's isolation (in 1815) and the need for a sympathetic ally, he wrote: 'As soon as we are strong, under the patronage of a liberal nation that will lend us its protection, we will reach agreement in cultivating the virtues and talents that lead to glory.'

Bolívar's view of the old regime and of revolutionary change was not that of a European or a North American, and there were basic limitations on the extent to which outside models could serve him. He lived in a world with a different history, capacity and social organization, and worked among a people with different expectations. As he searched for appropriate forms of government we can see him once more recoiling from the political ideas of the Enlightenment. Political solutions and modes of government, he appre-ciated, must conform to American conditions and satisfy American needs. One of the greatest needs was for strong, central authority. Americans had risen rapidly in the revolution without previous experience of public affairs. This made it difficult for them to organize their independence or to benefit from liberal institutions. Creatures of the Age of Reason, no sooner did they have the opportunity than they set up popular *juntas* which in turn summoned congresses; these established democratic and federal govern-ment, declaring the rights of man, providing for a balance of powers and passing general laws in favour of liberty of the subject, of the press, and of other freedoms. His conclusion was uncompromising: 'Events in *Tierra Firme* have proved that wholly representative institutions are not suited to our character, customs, and present knowledge. In Caracas the spirit of party arose in the societies, assemblies, and popular elections; and parties led us back into slavery.'

The Jamaica Letter is more important as a reflection of Bolívar's thinking and a source of the springs of action than as a call to the American people, for in 1815 the American people did not hear it. It was first published in English, in 1818, and it was only in 1833 that the first known Spanish version was issued. But the Liberator drew on the Letter, sometimes word for word, in other more public utterances in the years to come, and thus it became part of the political currency of the Spanish American revolution. Well might Camilo Torres, on being informed of Bolívar's exile in Jamaica, declare that he did not despair of the fate of the revolution, for 'where Bolívar is, there is the republic'.[7] This was Bolívar's own assessment: he made himself the measure of the revolution.

While he was in Jamaica, Bolívar sought to influence British opinion in the island in the cause of independence and indirectly to seek the support of the British government, through letters to the press and to his own contacts. These did not have the intellectual content of the Jamaica Letter and were mainly exercises in propaganda, not all of it convincing. In a letter to the *Royal Gazette* he claimed that the government of New Granada would be able to raise troops capable of defeating the Spanish army and besieging Cartagena, while the people of Venezuela had seized all the inland provinces and were poised to drive the enemy into the sea.[8] In another he described in lurid detail the atrocities committed by the Spaniards in Venezuela against the old and infirm, the women and children, in their attempt to 'annihilate the New World and remove its people'.[9] In an article in the same periodical, presumably seeking to reassure British interests in the Caribbean, he painted an idyllic picture of race relations in Spanish America between whites, Indians, blacks and mixed races, totally at odds with his own experience and subsequent opinions.[10] The whites, though a minority, can claim equality through their intellectual qualities. The Indian is peace loving, 'the friend of all', content with his security, his land and his family, and protected by the equality conceded by the government. The slaves on the *hacienda*, 'taught by the Church that it is their duty to serve, are born into domestic dependence, their natural state as members of the families of their masters, whom they love and respect'. The Spanish caudillos, ignorant of the true causes of the revolution, have sought to raise the coloured people, including the slaves, against the white creoles, encouraging plunder and bloodshed, but in the end these abandoned the Spanish cause and came to support independence, so that we can now affirm that 'all the sons of Spanish America, whatever their colour or condition, are joined in fraternal and inalterable affection'. He also renewed contact with Sir Richard Wellesley, pressing the arguments he had already used in London and hoping that a word to the British government might remind it of South America's need.

Jamaica was a grim exile for Bolívar, a paradise turned purgatory, defeated as he was by the Spaniards, repudiated by his own people, and living in circumstances of personal and public poverty. He looked for loans and assistance to his English friend Maxwell Hyslop, who with his brother Wellwood traded out of Jamaica to Cartagena and the mainland and followed the movement for independence with keen interest.[11] Maxwell was a true friend in need, a benefactor who came to the Liberator's rescue with loans and assistance, earning his undying gratitude, 'the services which you have rendered to Colombia and to me personally I shall never forget', he wrote years later. To his friend he was realistic about the prospects for the revolution. He admitted that if Morillo acted decisively and quickly, 'restoration of the Spanish government in South America appears inevitable'. And he had few illusions about popular opinion: 'While all thinking persons are, without exception, for independence, the mass of the people are still ignorant of their rights and unmindful of their interests.' South America will succumb unless a powerful nation comes to its aid. This is the opportunity for England, which has lost its trade to Venezuela and probably to New Granada, but which could regain it with little cost through offering the protection of its arms and its commerce.[12]

In the next few months Bolívar relied on Hyslop for cash, admitting that he was spent: 'I do not have a duro, for I have sold the little silver I brought with me.' A loan of a hundred pesos was followed by another request for the same amount.[13] Bolívar was spending not only on himself but also on fellow exiles, while his own needs were getting desperate. On 4 December he again requested a loan, to pay off his landlady who was harassing him for money. 'This wretched woman now demands more than a hundred pesos for extras, which are quite unjustified; but she has such a wicked and malicious tongue that I do not wish to be dragged before a magistrate for so little and be there provoked to violence by her insolence and insults. I don't have a *maravedí* and I beg you to let me have a hundred pesos to pay the woman off, which will make it 300 pesos that you have lent me.'[14]

Jamaica had worse terrors than landladies. While he changed lodgings, Bolívar was staying with Lieutenant-Colonel Páez and had a room at his house. On the night of 10 December, at about ten o'clock, an assassin crept into Bolívar's room, groped in the dark for the form sleeping in the hammock and plunged his knife into the neck of the victim, who struggled with his attacker until he received a second wound in the side, cutting off his cries and his life. The assassin was taken and found to be a black slave of Bolívar called Pio. The victim, however, was not Bolívar, but a compatriot, Félix Amestoy, formerly with Bolívar's Honour Guard who, while calling on the Liberator, had taken advantage of the empty hammock and fallen asleep. Bolívar's absence became the subject of various stories. In the legendary history of

Simón Bolívar, dramatic events often have an erotic subtext, and the Jamaican version has him pursuing a woman elsewhere. But who can tell? The murder and subsequent trial were reported in the Kingston press, and further details emerged. Two Spaniards, whose names he did not divulge, had offered Pio two thousand pesos to kill Bolívar and he had been plied with drink on the night. He confessed to the crime, was found guilty, executed and his head displayed in Kingston on a pole. According to the press this was the third attempt on the life of the Liberator by 'the lowest kind of Spaniards'.[15] Who were they? A trio of generals were in the frame of suspicion, Morillo, Moxó and La Torre, but O'Leary did not believe that Morillo would stoop so low, and Bolívar kept his thoughts to himself.

Jamaica was useful to Bolívar as a temporary refuge but was no base for a new invasion of Venezuela. Cartagena was a possibility and he still had support there, now headed by a dubious and malevolent ally, H. L. V. Ducoudray-Holstein, a Danish-born French mercenary, seconded by Luis Brión, a wealthy and amiable shipping merchant from Curaçao, Venezuelan by adoption and destined to be one of the most reliable of the Bolivarians. But Cartagena fell to Morillo on 6 December in a frenzy of death and disorder, a mirror image of the ultimate horrors of war. Bolívar left Jamaica on 18 December and, knowing of the fall of Cartagena, he sailed for Haiti, followed by a crowd of refugees from the stricken port. He landed at Aux Cayes and proceeded immediately to Port-au-Prince. Amidst myriad problems of managing men and materials, Bolívar always had time to woo and to win an attractive woman. Among the Venezuelan refugees was Carlos Soublette's pretty sister, Isabel, whose affections he had engaged in Cartagena and who now advanced further in his favour and joined the list of his lovers. Bolívar also approved of her brother, a distinguished young officer and one of the most loyal of the Bolivarians.

Alexandre Pétion, the *mulatto* president of Haiti, and a notable fighter for the independence of the former French colony, an independence triggered by violent slave revolution, welcomed Bolívar on 2 January 1816 and immediately raised his spirits. He gave his visitor heartening moral support for the expedition he was preparing and substantial material help in the form of six thousand rifles, munitions, supplies, naval transport and a sizeable sum of money. All this in return only for the promise that the Liberator would proclaim the abolition of slavery in the territory he liberated in Venezuela.[16] With the backing of a consortium of foreign merchants, and especially of loans from the English merchant Robert Sutherland, Bolívar assembled other refugees from Cartagena and prepared to renew the struggle.

The Caudillos

During Bolívar's absence from the mainland the revolution had not died. Resistance was kept alive by a number of bands under leaders who were to become indispensable to the patriot war effort: Pedro Zaraza in the upper *llanos*, José Antonio Páez in the western *llanos*, Manuel Cedeño in Caicara, José Tadeo Monagas in Cumaná, Jesús Berreto and Andrés Rojas in Maturín. These were the caudillos of the revolution, warlords whose power derived from access to land, men and resources, and whose armed bands were held together by the bond of patron and client, and propelled by the promise of constant booty.[17] The bands rose from the ruins of the second republic. The surviving patriots fled to the plains, jungles and forests of the east to escape royalist retribution. They then regrouped under a leader of their choice, partly for self-preservation, partly for the revolutionary cause.[18] For a guerrilla to surrender or to be captured was to walk into execution. In this sense resistance was the only option left. Groups converged and coalesced, until they found a supercaudillo. Armed with *púas* (lances), and taking their horses and cattle from the *llanos* of Barcelona and Cumaná, the guerrillas fought successfully against regular forces, attacking communications, ambushing detachments, harassing towns and then disappearing. They pinned down royalist forces in a number of different places and forced the Spaniards to maintain immobile garrisons.[19]

The guerrillas not only fought the royalists but also competed with each other. Leader rivalry in Venezuela obstructed operations, as caudillos struggled with each other for that supremacy that only military success and the ability to attract recruits could bring. No caudillo wanted to submit to another: each fought to remain independent, in a state of nature without a common power. Out of this internal war emerged the most powerful leaders: Monagas, Zaraza, Cedeño, Piar. This was in the east. Leadership in the western *llanos* demanded supreme physical talents, and it was this challenge that brought Páez to the fore:

> To command these men and dominate the situation was needed a partic-
> ular superiority and talent in using the lance with both hands, to fight on
> wild horses and to break them in during actual battle, to swim and to
> fight while swimming in swollen rivers, to lasso and kill wild beasts
> simply to get food, in short, to have the ability to dominate and overcome
> a thousand and more dangers which threaten in these conditions.[20]

Bolívar, too, possessed extraordinary natural talents, fortitude and endurance, and learned to compete with the caudillos on their own terms. His record of active service was in no way inferior to theirs. He conquered nature as well as men, overcoming the immense distances of America in marches which were as memorable as the battles. His severity was notorious and no one doubted his implacability. Yet Bolívar was never a caudillo, reliant on personal power alone. He always sought to institutionalize the revolution and to lead it to a political conclusion. The solution he favoured was a large nation state with a strong central government, totally dissimilar to the federal form of government and the decentralization of power preferred by the caudillos. Bolívar never possessed a true regional power base. The east had its own oligarchy, its own caudillos, who regarded themselves as allies rather than subordinates. The Apure was dominated by a number of great proprietors and then by Páez. Bolívar felt most at home in Caracas and the centre-north. There he had friends, followers and officers who had fought under him in New Granada, in the *Campaña Admirable*, and in other actions in central Venezuela. Bolívar could give orders to Urdaneta, Ribas and Campo as to trusted officers, assign them to one division or another, to this front or that. Professional officers had no problems with Bolívar: they saluted him for his culture, his character, his courage. It was the caudillos who challenged his leadership, jealous of their space. Moreover, from 1814 central Venezuela was occupied by the royal army, and Bolívar, who did not control the capital, had to assemble his power by a mixture of military and political success.

Few of the caudillos followed this example. The years 1813–17 were a time of trial for the revolution, when war on the enemy without was frustrated by the war of caudillos within. Yet the caudillos conformed to prevailing conditions more closely than did Bolívar, who lacked the resources they commanded. In the absence of a national army personal leadership was bound to be decisive, and without national objectives the structure of insurgency was inevitably informal. Anarchic and divisive though they were, the caudillos maintained a revolutionary presence during Bolívar's absence. As José de Austria observed: 'While they did not advance, neither could they be totally destroyed.'[21] Guerrilla warfare was the appropriate method, given the resources available, the nature of the war and the strength of the enemy. It was the counter-insurgency mounted by General Morillo that brought the caudillos out of their lairs, for it directly attacked the lives, property and vital interests of themselves and other Venezuelan leaders, and made war the only hope of security, 'caught as they were in the desperate alternative of dying or fighting'.[22] And so the rural guerrillas were mobilized again, not as a social or political force, but as military units under strong leaders who offered them booty.

Meanwhile in Haiti, where he was planning his new invasion into Venezuela, Bolívar had to resolve the question of leadership. A group of major caudillos was persuaded to recognize his authority for the expedition and until a congress could be held. The vote of the assembly was reinforced in the initial phase of the expedition at Margarita, whose caudillo, Arismendi, was a supporter of Bolívar's national authority, backed by Brión, paymaster and shipper. In a second assembly, held in the presence of Mariño, Piar and other caudillos, the leadership of Bolívar was confirmed, and a unanimous vote was given against the division of Venezuela into east and west: 'that the Republic of Venezuela shall be one and indivisible, that His Excellency, President and Captain-General Simón Bolívar is elected and recognized as its Supreme Head, and His Excellency General Santiago Mariño as his second-in-command'.[23] At the same time Bolívar agreed to legitimize the guerrilla chiefs by giving them rank and status in his army; the senior caudillos were made generals and colonels, and the others were given appropriate rank.

These rituals had only limited significance. One of the reasons why Bolívar did not dominate the caudillos was that he did not dominate the battlefield. To invade the mainland he thought he would need two thousand men and fourteen warships, but this was pure optimism. The first expedition from Haiti (31 March–17 July 1816) was strong in words but weak in resources, packed with officers and their women, and short on soldiers, some of whom were supplied by Pétion. The Caribbean was a large sea for small sailing vessels, which had to proceed carefully to avoid Spanish patrols, though the chief reason this fleet took a month to reach Margarita was Bolívar's insistence on going back for Josefina, her mother and sister when he heard that they had arrived at Aux Cayes. Reunited with his lover, Bolívar ignored the gawping and gossip among crew and soldiers. On Brión's advice he approached Margarita from the east via the Lesser Antilles, where his force might find a refuge or a base as necessary and liaise with the eastern resistance movements. In a brief and successful engagement with Spanish vessels Bolívar wisely stood back from the fray and left the fighting to his men.

He thought better of launching an invasion at Carúpano and eventually opted for Ocumare, east of Puerto Cabello, which he reached on 5 July, landing without Spanish resistance. He promptly issued a proclamation in which he made two statements, more important for their ideals than their effects, one to reconcile Spaniards to the revolution, the other to fulfil his obligation to Pétion. For his part, the war to the death had ended and Spaniards who surrendered would be pardoned. Moreover, he declared, in keeping with the demands of natural justice and policy, the slaves were now free, a freedom which he reported to Pétion as giving true meaning to the campaign for independence in South America.[24]

The military operation, however, went badly. Faulty intelligence, ineptitude of subordinates and failure of his forces to rendezvous promptly opened a gap between Soublette's unit which had struck inland and those who had remained at the port, leaving Soublette isolated and Bolívar, deceived by a treacherous aide, exposed to capture. The senior military agreed that a force should advance to the Aragua valleys but without Bolívar, who should embark and withdraw. Scenes of utter disorder were enacted during re-embarkation, setting the seal on a travesty of an invasion. There was a suspicion that Bolívar had been distracted by his mistress, whom he had brought along with him. He had to make yet another of his ignominious escapes by sea; after a hard voyage he reached Güiria on 16 August, dropping off Pepita and her family at St Thomas on the way. Although his commanders on the spot, Briceño Méndez, Soublette and Salom, loyal Bolivarians all, went out of their way to defend Bolívar's action and the patriots continued to fight well in the hinterland of Barcelona, his prestige was wounded by this new catastrophe at the hands of the Spaniards. Years later Ocumare was still on his mind and explained not as dereliction of duty but as a mistake of his subordinates and an escape from his enemies. But he was now actually weaker than the caudillos, some of whom had at least secured a foothold in the east.[25]

Mariño and Bermúdez, backed by troops of their own, were determined to deal with Bolívar, whom they called a deserter and traitor and regarded as inexpert in the art of war. A proclamation was published in Güiria (23 August 1816) deposing Bolívar and appointing Mariño as supreme chief, with Bermúdez second-in-command, the former in O'Leary's eyes a man devoted to 'licence and anarchy', the latter 'an uncultivated, rough and unstable' character.[26] The army split and civil war threatened the ranks of insurgency. The caudillos wanted to take Bolívar into custody and he barely escaped with his life, fleeing from Güiria to Haiti. The humiliation he suffered in 1816 owed something to his military errors, though he still had the backing of his own officers, including the tough warrior Arismendi and Gregor MacGregor, a Scottish adventurer highly rated by the patriot side, while in Haiti Pétion assured him of his moral and material support, and Sutherland continued to fund him. His Caribbean odyssey continued.

The war in these years, 1816–17, presented the Liberator with a serious strategic test, one that he did not immediately pass. The success of the Admirable Campaign, fought in classic style against a scattered enemy, had led him to underestimate the military problems he faced. At this point in the revolution it was impossible to win on the northern coast of Venezuela: it was too well defended as the royalist's richest and most fortified sector of the country. But he had still not learned this lesson or accepted the need for developing another front. As O'Leary writes, 'The fondness of Bolívar for Caracas, or the exaggerated idea he had of the patriotism of its inhabitants and the resources it could offer to whoever occupied it, caused many errors in his military career.'[27]

In the second invasion from Haiti, Bolívar landed at Barcelona on 31 December 1816 and inaugurated what he called 'the third period of the republic'. But the third period began more or less as the first two had ended, and his initial plan was to assemble an army to attack, not Guayana, where the enemy was exposed, but the royalist forces blocking the way to Caracas. He thus made himself utterly dependent upon the caudillos, who were already operating separately in various parts of the east. He wrote to one caudillo after another, calling on each to assemble around him in a great *proyecto de reunión*. He wrote to Piar, who had already marched on Guayana, instructing him to bring in his forces: 'Small divisions cannot achieve great objectives. The dispersion of our army, far from helping us, can destroy the Republic.'[28] He wrote to Mariño, Zaraza, Cedeño and Monagas, ordering, requesting, appealing for unity and obedience. But the caudillos did not suddenly change their ways; they stayed out, pursuing their separate objectives. The great army was an illusion, and Bolívar abandoned his hopes of occupying Caracas; he could not even hold Barcelona. He had to make his way to Guayana, still without an army of his own, still without a caudillo power base, the victim not only of his strategic predilections but of guerrilla anarchy.

Confrontation with Piar

The march into Guayana proved to be not a retreat but a decisive departure – to base the revolution deep in the hinterland, among the great plains of the Orinoco, impenetrable in the vastness, wide rivers and malarial swamps, a great barrier against defeat, a springboard for attack, and a source of wealth in their rich reserves of livestock. Now Bolívar was the master strategist. This was not an impromptu move, following in the tracks of Piar. The idea had been at the back of his mind since 1816; looking for a foothold on the mainland after leaving Haiti, he projected an expedition to Guayana but the idea was shelved through lack of resources and collaborators.[29] The delta of the Orinoco was four hundred miles across, splaying out channels up the river that only experienced pilots could navigate. Along its banks, through lush vegetation and tall trees bound to each other by the *bejuco* and festooned with brilliantly coloured flowers, could be seen still the ruins of villages devastated by Boves, in a region now open to republican gunboats and soldiers. To command Guayana made economic sense for the revolution, enabling Bolívar to gain substantial credit from his merchant friend Sutherland, who saw the advantage of exporting livestock from a guaranteed supply and an Orinoco dominated by patriot squadrons and privateers. This was an argument Bolívar employed to sell his authority to Páez, who had asked him why the *llaneros* of the Apure should transfer their allegiance from the caudillo they knew to the *patria* they had never heard of. Advantages were waiting:

The occupation of Guayana has improved our affairs. The possession of this important province has given us a great reputation and enhanced our standing to an extraordinary degree with foreigners, especially with the English, lords of the islands adjacent to this continent, who no sooner have they heard of the triumph of our arms than they have appeared with their vessels laden with merchandise and goods of all kinds. Several English merchants have come to conclude contracts with the government for rifles, gunpowder, shot, uniforms, and all kinds of war material, in exchange for the produce of our country, and some have already been signed.[30]

In this and following messages Bolívar gave his new ally a lesson in the achievements of the revolution, liberally mixed with flattery designed to keep Páez in line, news of the fate of dissident caudillos, volumes on infantry tactics along with some weapons, and in return asked Páez to send him 2,500 mules 'immediately, immediately, immediately', and a month later 'get them here as quickly as possible'.[31] Bolívar believed in wearing people down with words.

The Liberator crossed the wide Orinoco in a small canoe on the night of 30 April 1817 near Angostura and reached Piar's camp on 2 May, just ahead of his senior commanders, Arismendi, Bermúdez, Valdés, Zaraza and Soublette. Piar was now promoted to general but was challenged rather than appeased. He quickly made clear his independence, interpreting Bolívar's orders as he willed and making a point of killing Spanish prisoners. The war for Guayana was merciless. The first major target of Piar had been Angostura, 250 miles upriver from the sea, a handsome colonial town of whitewashed buildings and pleasant promenades on the left bank of the Orinoco, built on an elevated peninsular jutting into the river. But Angostura was too well defended.

He then attacked the missions of the Caroní River, a territory actively evangelized by Spanish Capuchins since 1724 and now the most cultivated part of Guayana, 'a model of good order and paternal government', a prime resource of the royalists and a subsistence for the patriot troops.[32] In early February 1817 this oasis of peace and prosperity, twenty-nine pueblos administered by Catalan missionaries, was caught in the crossfire between the two sides when it was invaded and occupied by Piar's troops with little resistance from the royalists. The friars were accused of having taken part in the defence of royalist Guayana against the patriot invaders. This was true in the sense that they had provided armed Indians, horses and supplies to the royal army; as Spanish nationals, subjects of the king of Spain, their benefactor, and surrounded by royalist forces, they could hardly do otherwise. But they were non-combatants and not personally involved. Of the forty-one priests in the Caroní missions, seven took flight, fourteen died in captivity and, on 7 May 1817, twenty captives were executed by machete and lance and their bodies burned.[33] The two republican officers directly responsible for the killings, allegedly misinterpreting an order from Bolívar who had denounced the friars as royalists, were never punished and the outrage was left to cast a shadow over the leadership of the Liberator. Piar himself disapproved of the atrocity; he had held the friars in his power from February to May, time in which to kill them had he wished. Bolívar arrived in Angostura on 2 May and was nominally in charge, though not yet fully in control. He considered the atrocity the work of 'madmen of the army . . . cruel savages'. Father José Félix Blanco, his administrator of the missions, declared that 'General Bolívar had nothing to do with the event'.[34] Someone at headquarters had authorized Colonel Jacinto Lara to take action, and it was he who had given the order to Captain Juan de Dios Monzón. O'Leary describes the outrage as a deplorable mistake, but Lara was on the staff of Bolívar and continued there, protected and promoted for his services to the Liberator.[35]

Now, before he re-established his authority in Guayana, Bolívar faced a rebellion of the caudillos. First Bermúdez and Valdés revolted against Mariño, then Mariño against Bolívar, and Piar against all authority. Mariño convoked a minicongress at Cariaco to establish a provisional government and make himself legitimate, urged on by the preposterous canon Cortés Madariaga, back from imprisonment in Spain and now a troublemaker no less to Bolívar than he had been to the Spaniards. On 9 May 1817 Mariño issued a proclamation to the peoples of Venezuela, a sign of his desire to be a national leader, not simply a regional caudillo. But a caudillo could not suddenly become a constitutionalist. This was where Mariño lost his credibility. Bermúdez and Valdés had already left him for Bolívar. Now General Urdaneta, Colonel Sucre and many other officers who had previously obeyed Mariño went to Guayana to place themselves under Bolívar's orders. The tide began to turn. With forces loyal to him personally, he was able to contribute to the military campaign and challenge Piar, who in April had won a crushing victory over superior royalist forces at San Félix, for leadership in Guayana. Bolívar's strategy was to neutralize Spanish power in Angostura and at the same time establish naval as well as military control over the Orinoco. On one occasion he was in danger of losing his life, or his liberty, when he dismounted to inspect his gunboats and was surprised by a Spanish detachment; he escaped by plunging into the river and swimming to safety. Military success in Guayana, naval control of the Orinoco and his own political sense enabled Bolívar to establish his absolute control of Angostura and Guayana, and to improve his prospects against the caudillos. It was at this point, when Bolívar was gathering power, that Piar chose to reject it.

Strong leadership at the top, freedom from rivals – these were not the only imperatives for Bolívar. He knew that the revolution also required a broader social base. To widen its constituency beyond white creoles, the popular sectors had to be brought into its ranks, a difficult decision and Bolívar was aware of its complexity. He spoke of 'this amazing chaos of *patriots, godos, self-seekers, whites, pardos, Venezuelans, Cundinamarquis, federalists, centralists, republicans, aristocrats, the good and the bad,* and the whole crowd of hierarchies into which each of these groups subdivide'.[36] The largest single group in Venezuelan society were the *pardos*, victims of discrimination by law and convention alike, emerging from colonial society ready for revolution. War gave them a kind of equality, new opportunities and new leaders; but war also denied them the richest prizes and showed them the limits of toleration. Bolívar scorned race prejudice; he fought for liberty and equality. This was the essence of independence: 'Legal equality is indispensable where physical inequality prevails.' The revolution would correct the imbalance imposed by nature and colonialism: previously 'the whites, by virtue of talent, merit and fortune, monopolized everything. The *pardos*, degraded to the most humiliating condition, had nothing. . . . But the revolution granted them every privilege, every right, every advantage.'[37] As a social phenomenon the war of independence can be seen as a competition between republican and royalist creoles for the allegiance of *pardos* and recruitment of slaves. In the Bolivarian model the revolution became a kind of coalition against Spain, a coalition of creoles, *pardos* and slaves. Not all the creole elite agreed with this. Coro and Maracaibo, centres of previous black rebellion, rejected Bolívar's coalition and resisted the revolution to the end. Bolívar knew he had to manage the coalition carefully, to include the *pardos* only as a subordinate partner and under creole control. They were not allowed autonomous leaders. This was why Bolívar had to confront and defeat the challenge from Manuel Piar.

In creole thinking Piar was a prototype of the racist demagogue. He was not a typical caudillo, for he did not possess an independent power base, either regional or economic. He had to rely on his military abilities alone, rising 'by my sword and good luck' to the rank of general-in-chief by decree of Bolívar himself.[38] He was a *pardo* from Curaçao and he made the *pardos* his constituency. According to a royalist chronicler, 'Piar was one of our most terrible enemies, adventurous, talented, and with great influence among the castes, to whom he belonged. He was thus one of the few Venezuelans who could inspire the greater part of the population.'[39] Bolívar, too, wanted to recruit coloureds, to free the slaves and incorporate the *pardos*, in order to tilt the balance of military forces toward the republic, but he did not propose to mobilize them politically.

Bolívar suffered much else from Piar, from his arrogance, ambition and insubordination. When in January 1817 a group of officers left Piar to join Bolívar, Piar demanded of his superior that he give them the severest punishment, the only lesson acknowledged by 'immoral, barbarous, and corrupt people like those. In such quarters clemency is seen as weakness; kindness is mistaken for lack of character and energy; all the virtues are reckoned for nothing. Your excellency ought to have known this.'[40] Bolívar endured these lessons in the law of the caudillo and made a point of repaying insults with reason, hinting that without political values the caudillos reverted to mere bandits: 'If we destroy ourselves through conflicts and anarchy, we will clear the republican ranks and they will rightly call us vagrants.'[41] But Piar was uncontrollable. He claimed the Orinoco campaign as his own theatre of war, Guayana and the missions as his private domain. A contest for supremacy turned into outright rebellion. According to General Morillo, there was evidence that Piar had an even more sinister plan than rebellion: 'Piar, a *mulatto* and the most important of the castes, has very close relations with Alexandre Pétion, a rebel *mulatto* who calls himself president of Haiti; together they propose to create a base in Guayana from which they can dominate America.'[42]

Piar appeared not to realize that the balance of power was turning against the caudillos, or perhaps this was what drove him. The victory over the royalists at Angostura – after a year-long siege and campaign in which blacks and Indians fought on both sides – confirmed Bolívar's power and placed the initiative with him. The time of decision had come in June 1817, following a period in which he had dealt with caudillos patiently, swallowing dissent, hostility, intrigues and arrogance from his subordinates. The posturing of the politicians at Cariaco and the behaviour of Piar in Guayana caused him to send a trusted officer, Pedro Briceño Méndez, for a clarifying talk with Piar. Briceño reported that Piar professed friendship and did not wish to disturb things; he was simply speaking of assigning Bolívar democratic institutions and creating a political authority alongside his military authority. Bolívar regarded the report as mealy-mouthed and he exploded. He was no longer operating from weakness, he said, as in Cartagena, Güiria and Carúpano; he was stronger than ever; three thousand men obeyed his every command and they would not tolerate factions. 'If I have been moderate up to now it is out of prudence, not weakness. . . . There is neither tyranny or anarchy here as long as I am alive with sword in hand.'[43] On 30 June he gave Piar a passport to leave for wherever he wished to go. But Piar was on his way to rebellion.

Bolívar decided the moment had come to challenge factionalism and dissidence in the east. In an extraordinary outburst, a marvellous exercise in sustained vituperation, he reversed his previous patience and denounced the rebel as one who claimed nobility against all the evidence of his *pardo* birth, a criminal, a man of violence, a thief, a ferocious despot, a mediocrity promoted beyond his merits, a monster who sought to provoke race war yet despised the coloureds he claimed to elevate. 'General Piar has broken the laws, has conspired against the system, has disobeyed the government, has resisted orders, has deserted the army, and has fled like a coward. So he has placed himself outside the law: his destruction is a duty and his destroyer a well doer.'[44]

In this mood he ordered Piar, 'with other caudillos and followers of his faction', to be hunted down.[45] Piar was captured, tried and sentenced to death as a deserter, a rebel and a traitor. The court was headed by Brión, the prosecution led by Soublette. Bolívar confirmed the sentence and had him publicly executed by a firing squad in the main square of Angostura 'for proclaiming the odious principles of race war . . . for inciting civil war, and for encouraging anarchy'.[46] The sentence may have been defective in terms of law, but Bolívar calculated carefully in executing Piar. Piar represented regionalism, personalism and Black revolution. Bolívar stood for centralism, constitutionalism and race harmony. He later claimed: 'The death of General Piar was a political necessity which saved the country, for otherwise he would have started a war of *pardos* against whites, leading to the extermination of the latter and the triumph of the Spaniards. General Mariño also deserved to die because of his dissidence, but he was not so dangerous and therefore policy could yield to humanity and even to an old friendship . . . never was there a death more useful, more politic, and at the same time more deserved.'[47]

The danger lay in *pardocracia*. Bolívar denounced Piar for inciting race war at a time when equality was already being granted to the coloured people: 'General Piar himself is an irrevocable proof of this equality.' The measured, gradual programme of reform under creole control was threatened by total subversion of the existing order, which could only lead to anarchy. While it was essential to widen the basis of the revolution, this did not involve destroying the creole leadership: 'Who are the authors of this revolution? Are they not the whites, the wealthy, the aristocracy and even the militia chiefs? What principles have these caudillos of the revolution proclaimed? The decrees of the republic are eternal monuments of justice and liberation . . . liberty even for the slaves who were previously the property of the same leaders, and independence in the widest sense of the word to replace the dependence in which we were bound.' Piar had sought to unleash a war against creoles 'simply because they had been born more or less white. According to Piar, a man's skin is a crime and carries with it the decree of life or death.'[48] The day after Piar's execution, Bolívar asked the soldiers of the liberating army: 'Have not our arms broken the chains of the slaves? Has not the odious distinction between classes and colours been abolished for ever? Have I not ordered national property to be distributed among you? Are you not equal, free, independent, happy and respected? Could Piar give you more? No. No. No.'[49]

The Tactics of Race

The problems of race and class were not so easily resolved. In spite of his initiative, Bolívar knew that he was taking risks and he had some misgivings, or at least he later expressed misgivings. In 1828, at Bucaramanga, he said:

> In the first years of Independence, we needed men who were above all brave, who could kill Spaniards and make themselves feared; blacks, *zambos*, *mulattos*, and whites, all were welcome as long as they fought bravely. No one could be rewarded with money, for there was none; the only way of maintaining ardour, rewarding exceptional actions and stimulating valour was by promotion, so that today men of every caste and colour are among the generals, leaders, and officers of our forces, though the majority of them have no other merit than brute strength. This was once useful to the Republic but now, in peacetime, is an obstacle to peace and tranquillity. But it was a necessary evil.[50]

From 1815–16, therefore, growing numbers of *pardos* were incorporated into the army of liberation; they were needed to fill the gaps in the patriot ranks left by creole casualties and desertions, and they themselves were imbued with greater expectations from wartime social mobility. From now on the traditional structure of the republican army was transformed, and while the creoles retained military and political control, the *pardos* had greater opportunities for advance to higher ranks and offices. Were they politically convinced by the cause of independence?

Bolívar campaigned to convince them, though not with complete success. In the early years of the revolution the balance of support among the black population had favoured the royalists. According to José Domingo Díaz, in December 1818 the royalist army in Venezuela numbered thirteen thousand men, of whom three thousand were Europeans and ten thousand Americans: 'Almost all the Americans in this brave army were Indians and *mulattos*, *zambos* and free blacks, but not slaves.'[51] Díaz was a royalist, of course, but there is no reason to doubt that his statement was more or less correct, though in the past the royalists had been more adroit – or more opportunist – than the republicans in assimilating slaves to their cause than he implied. O'Leary admitted that recruitment for the republican army was difficult. He explained the problem in terms of the social divide. The upper sector of society produced the republican officers, who were imbued with a sense of service and commitment:

> The lower classes, on the other hand, were the victims of the frequent incursions of the belligerents. Victory or defeat was all the same to them;

whoever was the victorious chief, he was sure to recruit his troops from them. The moral compensation of sooner or later winning independence, which sustained the upper class of society, was small consolation for the masses, who had few aspirations. Thus it became more difficult every day to find the necessary recruits to replace the casualties of the various units.[52]

War itself acted as a social dissolvent and divided the *pardos* against themselves, incorporating some into the officer corps and the upper sectors, and leaving the *pardo* masses at the bottom of society. Some royalists believed that the crown should take more advantage of these divisions and positively recruit from *pardo* ranks. But it remained Spanish policy basically to rely on Morillo's expeditionary force and the support of royalist creoles, in order to restore the colonial structure of society. To this extent Bolívar was right: the *pardos* had more to gain from the republican cause. But what had the slaves to gain?

Bolívar was a military leader who needed recruits, and during the war he tied emancipation to conscription, offering slaves manumission in return for military service. He began by announcing from the island of Margarita, fulfilling his commitment to Pétion: 'There will be no more slaves in Venezuela, except those who wish to remain so. All those who prefer liberty to repose will take up arms to defend their sacred rights and they will be citizens.' From the mainland, decrees of 2 June and 6 July 1816 then proclaimed the 'absolute' freedom of slaves on condition that they joined the republican forces. 'Nature, justice, and good policy demand the emancipation of the slaves: from now on there will be only one class of men in Venezuela, all will be citizens.'[53] The response was negative. Although Bolívar liberated his own slaves, few *hacendados* followed his example. Slave owners rarely volunteer to give up their property or abandon their investments, and the Venezuelan aristocracy were no exception. This was not their idea of republican revolution. So the decrees of 1816 were unavailing. The slaves themselves were hardly more enthusiastic. The Liberator believed that 'the slaves have lost even the desire to be free'. The truth was that the slaves were not interested in fighting the creoles' war – according to a republican officer: 'Very few were the slaves who wished to accept liberty in exchange for the burdens of war.'[54] Nevertheless, Bolívar's campaign was not in vain. It served to nullify rebellions of slaves; they no longer actively fought the republic as they had done in 1812–14, and they gradually receded from the war as an autonomous movement. It was clear that Morillo had nothing to offer them and that, whatever the republic stood for, Spain unequivocally stood for the status quo. Morillo was not averse to recruiting slaves when casualties forced him to do so, but their status hardly changed. As his army appeared more and more like a colonialist force, so it lost the popular following which Boves had won and which Bolívar now sought to divert towards the republic. And Bolívar wanted the support not only of the *pardos* and the slaves but also of a third marginalized group: the *llaneros*. That meant returning to the problem of subordination and recruiting their caudillo.

An Army for Liberation

The *Jefe Supremo* now took his campaign for supremacy a stage further. He could either continue to tolerate a rabble or create an army worthy of a liberator. The surest antidote to unrestrained caudillism was an effective army structure and a clear chain of command. With the authority and resources won from victory in Guayana, Bolívar initiated a series of army reforms designed to create a professional army modelled on military institutions in Europe. Bolívar had inherited from the colony a system of militias, useful for internal security but not for fighting a war. In the next few years combat units were improvised, and in 1815 he created his own *Guardia de Honor* of 450 men, which was subsequently incorporated into the main army. By the 1818 campaigning season this consisted of two divisions, four brigades and a variable number of battalions. The decree of 24 September 1817 marked the beginning of his campaign to replace personalism with professionalism. He created the General Staff 'for the organization and direction of the armies', a staff for the whole army and one for each division. The Staff was part of a career structure open to talent; it was also the source of command, instructions and orders downward to commanders, officers and troops.[55] He established courts martial at all levels of the army. And in an attempt to move beyond plunder he created a *tribunal de secuestros* to administer the confiscation of royalist estates, properties and possessions for the benefit not of individual caudillo bands but of 'the national treasury'.[56]

The caudillos became generals and regional commanders; their hordes became soldiers and subject to military discipline defined at the centre. Reform extended to recruitment. Commanders were given quotas and encouraged to seek troops beyond their original constituencies. Bolívar fought against regionalism and immobility, and projected a Venezuelan army with a national identity:

> The frequent desertion of soldiers from one division to another on the pretext of being natives of the province where their chosen division is operating, is a cause of disorder and insubordination in the army and encourages a spirit of regionalism which we have tried so hard to destroy. All Venezuelans ought to have the same interest in defending the territory

of the Republic where they have been born as their brothers, for Venezuela is no more than one single family composed of many individuals bound together by indissoluble ties and by identical interests.[57]

He urged the caudillos to help each other, ordering them to transfer men and supplies wherever necessary 'according to the development of the war'. New structures, impressive on paper, were not immediately effective. He did not succeed in integrating Venezuelan insurgency into a single army, and it remained a collection of local forces with a high turnover of troops through illness and desertion. But unity was his ideal. His object was to end dissidence, to harness regional resources and to inspire a national effort. In the course of 1817–19 he organized three military groups: the Army of the East, the Army of the West and the Army of the Centre under himself. To recruit and organize an army on the ground was his enduring task in these years and to create its logistical infrastructure a constant nightmare, but one from which he emerged with military credit. He could not hope to create an army of citizen soldiers attaining professional standards, but had to take what he could get, and this included bandits, guerrillas and more or less reluctant conscripts from all over Colombia, forming a series of armies of independence that were Bolivarian in the sense that he was their originator and supreme commander.[58]

Bolívar's problem was that he needed an army for all occasions, cavalry for warfare in the plains, infantry for fighting in the highlands and whatever artillery he could assemble. All these roles would usually be required in a single campaign, as the army proceeded from *llanos* to foothills to mountains, and the relative strength of each arm would be determined not wholly by tactical considerations but by what was available. Tactics, of course, were known, and Bolívar had a small library of military authorities teaching the drill of infantry movements, the deployment of supporting cavalry, and the use of effective fire power, and he had knowledgeable colleagues such as Sucre whose judgement he valued. But South America was not Europe; the terrain and its sheer size presented conditions beyond European experience. Improvisation rather than Napoleonic models was a key factor in Bolívar's military thinking. He had to be prepared to fight in plains and *páramos*, peaks and gorges, and to lead men reared in the tropics into icy altitudes without any chance to acclimatize. Once Bolívar had ordered his troops forward, within a basic structure of battalions, companies and squadrons, a battle would develop into a free-for-all and the result depended on a combination of manoeuvres and morale.

The Liberator's military reforms in the course of October–November 1817 were accompanied by political changes to assist him in the work of government.

Even without Piar's propaganda on behalf of 'democratization', Bolívar was aware of the need to institutionalize his authority as *Jefe Supremo*. He created a provisional council of state as an interim measure to supply the function of a legislative power until a constitution could be established after liberation. The council consisted of the chief military and civil officers, and existed to deal with matters of state, defence and justice. It was advisory only, and depended on the supreme chief for its meeting.[59] He also established a council of government, consisting of Juan Germán Roscio, Fernando Peñalver and Rafael Urdaneta, as an arm of the executive and to supply government in the case of the death of Bolívar.

Caudillos who collaborated were employed in specific assignments. After the execution of Piar, Mariño was isolated and his government collapsed. Bolívar could afford to wait for his voluntary submission. He sent Colonel Sucre, a model of the trained and professional soldier, on a mission of pacification to persuade Mariño's allies and subordinates to acknowledge the authority of the supreme chief. His charges against Mariño were expressed in precise terms: while Piar was a 'rebel', Mariño was a 'dissident', a threat to authority and unity, and Bolívar made it clear that he was determined 'to break up the faction of which you are caudillo'. In cool and caustic words he told Mariño: 'If you insist on resisting, you will no longer be a citizen of Venezuela but a public enemy. If you are determined to quit the service of the republic just say so and the government will have no problem in granting you leave to go.'[60] Bermúdez was appointed governor and military commandant of Cumaná, a province so impoverished by war that it was incapable of sustaining independent caudillism and had to be supplied from outside. Bolívar now approved of Bermúdez: 'He has a great reputation in his country, is well liked, obedient, and a keen defender of the government.'[61] Not everyone agreed.

Coercion of the caudillos was not complete. Bolívar's policy of using caudillos to control caudillos had only limited success. While he regarded Bermúdez as an agent of unification, others knew him as a savage and vindictive rival, a medium of discord, not peace, the arch-caudillo, who now happened to be on Bolívar's side. Mariño rejected the mission of Bermúdez and swore that 'no power on earth would remove him from his province'.[62] It was some time before Bolívar could pacify Mariño and persuade him to collaborate in an attack on the enemy; late in 1818 he appointed him general-in-chief of the Army of the East, with jurisdiction in the *llanos* of Barcelona, while other eastern districts were assigned to Bermúdez and Cedeño. But the struggle for leadership was not over. Having reconciled the easterners, Bolívar had still to win over the warlord of the west, José Antonio Páez.

Páez and the Llaneros: *A New Challenge*

In January 1817 General Morillo left New Granada for Venezuela, placed his forces astride the Andean provinces, and in August made his headquarters at Calabozo, the gateway to the plains. This was his preferred theatre of war, giving him access across the *llanos* to Guayana, Maturín and Cumaná, and positioning him to protect Caracas, Maracay and Valencia, and to defend himself against Páez in the Apure. As for Bolívar, he was now bursting with premature optimism, impatient to take the offensive. In July he told the still unliberated province of Caracas of great republican victories: 'From the wide plains of Casanare to the mouths of the great Orinoco, victory has led our steps. Twenty glorious actions have assured the fate of Venezuela.'[63] Bolívar himself held Guayana. Mariño had freed much of Cumaná. In Maturín General Rojas kept the republican cause alive. General Monagas engaged the royalists at Barcelona. And in the south-west, in the Apure valley, Páez fought as a republican caudillo of the *llaneros*. On the ground operations were not as conclusive or as promising as Bolívar depicted, but if Páez could be brought under his command, he would control a vast area from the Orinoco to the Andes.

Páez claimed that he commanded in the Apure 'with absolute independence and answerable to no human power'. In September 1816 in Trinidad de Arichuna he displaced Colonel Santander as commander-in-chief of the Army of the West, when he was chosen by a movement of chiefs and officers, seconded by a great many local people as 'the only one who could save them from the danger threatening on all sides' and inspire the defence of the republic against the royalist enemy.[64] This was the day when he was recognized as a caudillo, the supreme leader of the western *llanos*, anticipating a yet greater confrontation with Santander ten years later. He campaigned for over a year as an independent commander, yet when Bolívar sent a commission from Guayana to ask that Páez recognize him as 'supreme head of the republic', the caudillo did not hesitate; he agreed without even consulting his own officers, and insisted to his reluctant troops that they do the same.[65] So Páez submitted his authority to that of the Liberator, 'taking into account the military talents of Bolívar, the prestige of his name and his reputation abroad, and realizing above all the advantage to be derived from a supreme and central authority which would direct the different caudillos operating in various parts . . .'[66] On 31 December 1817 Bolívar left Angostura and, in a spectacular move by river and land, and hard marching by his troops across three hundred kilometres, took his force of three thousand to the Apure plains. There, at San Juan de Payara, Páez had his headquarters, while the royalists were stationed some fifty kilometres to the north at San Fernando de Apure. On 30 January

1818 Bolívar and Páez met for the first time, dismounting, embracing warmly and taking stock of each other.[67]

Páez, archetypal caudillo and leader in his own land, was a creole of modest origins, though he did not come from the margin of society. He was white, or could pass for white, son of a petty official, heir of the colonial bureaucracy, had fled into the *llanos* after a private affray in Barinas, and was promoted a cavalry captain in the army of the First Republic. Páez began life without basic reading and writing and was left with an enduring sense of inferiority. Officers in the British Legion noted his qualities as a *llanero* warrior but one of them also reported: 'When I served with him, Páez could neither read nor write, and until the English came to the *Llanos*, had never used a knife and fork, so rough and uncultured had been his former life; but when he began to meet the officers of the British Legion he copied their way of living and their dress, modelling himself as much as possible upon them, that is, as far as his lack of education allowed.'[68]

Observers noticed his sense of inferiority and silence in the presence of those he thought better educated than himself. During the war illiteracy was not a great handicap, though he had other weaknesses – being prone to epileptic fits when excited or crossed, and defective in his judgement of Bolívar and higher policy. Dressed in an ill-fitting green jacket, white pantaloons and a large cocked hat, he was slightly more presentable than his followers, described as 'all badly clad and some almost in a perfect state of nudity'. His power, like his dress, was informal, but he underwent recognizable preparations for leadership, learning *llanero* life the hard way on a cattle estate, and becoming more successful than others in fighting, looting and killing. Built like an ox, suspicious and cunning, accompanied always by a giant black bodyguard, his qualities of leadership attracted his first followers and plunder retained them.

His troops, or some of them, had previously fought for the enemy and were 'composed in large part of those ferocious and valiant *zambos*, *mulattos*, and blacks who had formed the army of Boves'.[69] But Páez had his own methods with the *llaneros*. Many of the Venezuelan officers he regarded as barbarians and assassins, claiming that unlike them he did not personally kill prisoners; his men certainly did, slicing their heads off with one blow of a sword, often to a round of applause. This was the force which he fashioned into an army of cavalry. This was the force Bolívar wanted for the army of independence. The republic offered the *llaneros* more than plunder. Páez promised a share of estates taken from the enemy, and Bolívar confirmed this policy in his decree of 1817, ordering land from national property to be distributed to the patriot troops.

The guerrilla war which Páez waged was a personal triumph; in the lands of the Arauca River and the plains of Apure he was supreme. But his force was not effectively linked to the independence movement, and while the Spaniards were harassed, they were not destroyed. Bolívar knew that he needed Páez and his army for the revolution. The two leaders came to terms. When Páez first met Bolívar in the *llanos* of San Juan de Payara he was struck by the contrast between his civilized manner and the wild surroundings, between his refined appearance and the barbarism of the *llaneros*. 'There could be seen in one place the two indispensable elements to make war: the intellectual force which plans and organizes and the material force which brings them to effect, qualities which assist each other and which are ineffective without the other.'[70] The caudillo's stereotypes were false and he was wrong in assuming that Bolívar was an intellectual only. In the next ten years the man of culture would march more miles and fight more battles than the warrior of the *llanos* would ever do.

In February 1818 Páez contributed a thousand cavalry to a joint force of over four thousand. The force included a group of British volunteers, among them the young Richard Vowell who had left Oxford with a reputation for extravagant living. Vowell came up with Bolívar, surrounded by his staff officers, on the road between the River Apure and the town of Calabozo. He saw a man of about thirty-five who looked more like forty, just below medium height but well proportioned and remarkably active. His features were thin and care-worn, expressing endurance under adversity, yet his manner remained elegant, 'surrounded as he was by men far his inferiors in birth and education'. He wore the helmet of a private dragoon and a plain jacket of blue cloth with red cuffs, coarse blue trousers and *alpargatas* on his feet. His officers were chiefly 'men of colour', except the two generals, Páez and Urdaneta, who were white. Summoned to meet the Liberator, 'we found him seated in a cotton net hammock, under some trees, and were received by him with the politeness of a man who had seen the world'; he had words of welcome for the newcomers from Europe, whom he expected to bring discipline, instruction and example to his officers and men.[71]

Bolívar moved north in February 1818 and after overrunning the royalist outpost at Guayabal forced Morillo to evacuate Calabozo, inflicting heavy casualties, capturing arms and supplies and offering to suspend the *guerra a muerte*.[72] But his optimism was premature. He allowed Morillo to evacuate Calabozo and, thwarted by battle fatigue among his troops and the disciplined fire of the Spanish infantry, failed to bring him to battle in the plains, where the patriots should have had cavalry advantage. He wanted to pursue the enemy northwards towards the coast, still beguiled by the lure of Caracas, but first he had to return to Calabozo to rest his troops and wait for Páez. There his army suffered mass desertions, most of them in the direction of Páez and, as he confessed: 'I cannot send more troops after them, for I do not trust these to return.' He needed Páez: 'Hurry, hurry, join me here, so we can seize the moment.'[73] But the caudillo was dragging his feet and instead continued to press the siege of San Fernando. There were good military reasons for this decision, beyond the prospect of booty. San Fernando was important in itself and for an opening to New Granada, while to pursue Morillo northward into the mountains was to take the patriot cavalry into territory where the Spanish infantry was superior.

The next stage of the campaign was not to Bolívar's advantage and according to his British officers his tactics were not of the best. With depleted forces he decided to make a stand at the Semen gorge, and in the battle of La Puerta (16 March 1818), scene of two previous defeats for the republicans, he was comprehensively defeated by Morillo, losing over a thousand infantry, much war material and his own papers, though not his reputation for personal courage in the field.[74] Still retreating, he was almost killed at Rincón de los Toros by a Spanish hit squad that penetrated the camp at night and, carelessly directed to the required spot by Colonel Santander on his rounds, surprised the general asleep; he escaped only with the help of his men though with a sprained ankle when a mule threw him. On 2 May Páez was defeated at Cojedes. Cumaná, too, was lost at this time.

There were political elements as well as tactical thinking in the caudillo's reluctance to advance northwards. He still played with the idea of an independent authority, and when a group of officers and *llaneros* at San Fernando de Apure attempted to install him as general-in-chief, he accepted, and it needed a steely response from Bolívar to crush this movement at birth. It was one thing to criticize his tactics, another to question his leadership. In his autobiography Páez tells the story as an innocent bystander, but this was not the impression of the young O'Leary, recently arrived in the Apure and now a direct observer of events. Bolívar was not a man to be embarrassed by his recent reverses and he did not hold back from reprimanding Páez. He made it clear that he took a serious view of the sedition of the ringleader, the Englishman Colonel Henry Wilson, whose arrest, imprisonment and dismissal he ordered: 'Military discipline, social principles, and the honour of the nation and the government demand exemplary punishment of such an execrable offence. Prompt punishment is the only way to curb indiscipline and military sedition, and to avoid anarchy.'[75] The episode was another piece in the fabric of his leadership. As for authority, he was secure enough to accept the law of the *llanos*, as O'Leary explained: 'In this, too, Bolívar had to acquiesce, because the troops of the Apure were more like the contingent of a confederate state than a division of the army. They wanted to return to their homes. . . . Páez, accustomed to exercise a despotic will and the enemy of all subordination, could not reconcile himself to an authority which he had so recently recognized. And Bolívar, for his part, was too shrewd and tactful to exasperate the violent and impetuous Páez.'[76]

Master of the grand strategy, Bolívar was not infallible in the tactics of war. The campaign in the *llanos* in 1818 taught him a lesson he might have been expected to know already: that Caracas and the coast, protected by mountainous terrain, could not be invaded from the south. Once again the republicans were forced back beyond the Orinoco. Bolívar returned to Angostura, a military camp, a river port to the sea, and a base from which to organize the republic and plan his next campaign. The presentation of his case to Venezuela, to the Americas and to the world was his daily preoccupation, and public relations his second nature. He established a weekly newspaper, *El Correo del Orinoco* to counterbalance the influence of the *Gaceta de Caracas*, now in the hands of the royalists and edited by José Domingo Díaz. The first of 128 numbers appeared on 27 June 1818 under the distinguished editorship of Francisco Antonio Zea, followed by Juan Germán Roscio and then by José Luis Ramos. While the editors were not mere figureheads, the input of Bolívar was obvious and decisive, and he kept a close eye on what he regarded as the intellectual preparation of the next offensive. In spite of his distrust of the idea of 'democratization', he took it for granted that there should be a legislative assembly and that 'while our soldiers fight, our citizens should exercise the valuable functions of sovereignty. . . . It is not enough to win battles, to eject our enemies, to have the whole world recognize our Independence, we need above all to be free, under the rule of liberal laws, deriving from the most sacred source which is *the will of the people*.'[77] So he proposed to the council of state the calling of a national congress and a law for the election of deputies, to meet on 1 January 1819. The organization of the army and the preparation of elections became his two most urgent tasks, taking him on long journeys out of Angostura, and dominating his correspondence with his generals and officials in the year 1818.

Among his political and military preoccupations, he still had time to think of Josefina Machado. In St Thomas his nephew Leandro Palacios was in touch with Pepita and through him an anxious Bolívar urged her to come to Angostura, at his expense and insistence, out of fear, apparently, of being mocked for her absence. Eventually Leandro was able to report that she was on her way, with her family in train, but by the time she reached Angostura, Bolívar had left on campaign in New Granada.[78] She tried to follow him but died on her way to him.

The years 1816–18, 'the third period of the republic', were among the most difficult in the life of Bolívar, when he had to resolve the three great problems of Spanish American independence: to defeat Spain in the field, to overcome insubordination in his own ranks and to fend off race war. Royalists, caudillos, *pardos*, these were the challenges, and none of them could be won in a day. To wage warfare in the *llanos* was a debatable strategy. In those empty plains

Bolívar could free masses of territory, but not masses of people. He was a shackled giant. With all his assets, a European education and three campaigns behind him, he was scarcely able to move the revolution forward an inch. The Spaniards occupied the centre-north, the economic and political core of Venezuela, its demographic heartland and the essence of the colonial system. This was what Bolívar craved. He had invaded in flanking movements from west and east, he had conquered the Orinoco and Guayana, he was advancing in the *llanos*. But he had still not taken Caracas. A new strategy of liberation was required and in the fertile mind of the Liberator it was already taking shape. In spite of appearances, Bolívar had reasons for optimism. He could see that the war in the *llanos*, overtly in General Morillo's favour, in fact had gained the Spaniard no strategic advance and had cost him personally a near-mortal wound. Morillo was wary of Bolívar: he thought him more dangerous in defeat than in victory. The Spaniard was pessimistic. He believed that the possession of Guayana and its resources gave Bolívar a decisive advantage and that the restoration of Spanish sovereignty in America would only be achieved by force after a great military victory by the royal army. Meanwhile, the forces of the Bolivarian alliance – the Liberators' own army augmented by insistent recruiting campaigns, plus the forces of Páez and other caudillos – amounted to some fourteen thousand troops, against the eleven thousand of Morillo, split between New Granada and Venezuela.[79]

Bolívar was ready to take on the world, or at least Spain and the Holy Alliance: 'The Republic of Venezuela, by divine and human right, is emancipated from the Spanish nation and constituted as an independent, free, and sovereign state.'[80] This was his judgement on the third age of the republic and his prophecy for the battles to come.

Chapter 6

NEW STRATEGY, NEW FRONT

The Angostura Address

In the first decade of revolution Bolívar's life acquired a rhythm of thought and action which he sustained with extraordinary consistency through periods otherwise marked by political disorder, military confusion and personal defeat. From the time of the first republic there was a pattern of advance, retreat, re-organize; this was repeated in the second republic with a further push, another defeat, another pause; then a third sequence of attack, rebuff and return, begin-ning in Haiti and ending in Guayana. In each stage there was a similar response to challenge: first analysis, then action. So the Cartagena Manifesto preceded the Admirable Campaign, and the Jamaica Letter the invasion of the mainland. Now, in 1819, as he contemplated the stalemate in Venezuela and pondered a new strategy, he prepared for further action with a further statement of belief.

His efforts to encourage elections throughout the liberated territories bore fruit at last and delegates began to make their way to Angostura. Bolívar returned from his military headquarters at San Juan de Payara, leaving command of the army to Páez, whom he promoted to major-general. During the journey back to Angostura along the upper Orinoco, its waters the home of snakes and alligators and its banks infested by mosquitoes, he reclined in his hammock during the heat of the day or on board the *flechera* or under the giant trees on the shores of the river in the cool of the evening. In a familiar posture, one hand on the collar of his jacket and his thumb on his upper lip, Bolívar dictated to his secretary the final version of the address on which he had been working since November and now planned to give to congress, together with the accompanying constitution for the republic, reaching for the ideas on which he had been brooding since their first expression in the Jamaica Letter.[1]

At ten thirty on the appointed day, 15 February 1819, twenty-six delegates, representatives of Margarita, Guayana, Cumaná, Barcelona, Caracas and

Barinas, took their seats in the modest hall of government house in Angostura to inaugurate the general congress. Bolívar and his staff officers arrived at the plain brick one-story building in the main square to a three-gun salute and military parade, and the delegates went out to greet him and conduct him to his place at the head of the assembly.[2] When he rose to present his constitution, the political peak of the revolution up to that time and the culmination of all his hopes, he spoke in a clear voice but one which betrayed his emotion. His audience, Venezuelan citizens and foreign guests, were also deeply moved, some to tears, as his angel tongue delivered a rare expression of reason and emotion.[3] He described an ideal democratic republic in the exact mould of the age of revolution: 'Venezuela, on breaking with Spain, has recovered her independence, her freedom, her equality, and her national sovereignty. By establishing a democratic republic she has abolished monarchy, distinction, nobility, prerogatives, and privileges. She has declared for the rights of man and freedom of action, thought, speech, and the press.'[4] These 'eminently liberal acts', as he called them, were possible because only in democracy was absolute liberty assured. But was this practicable? Democracy, he admitted, does not necessarily guarantee the power, prosperity and permanence of a state. The federal system in particular makes for weak and divided government. It may be appropriate for the people of North America, who were raised on liberty and political virtues, but 'it has never for a moment entered my mind to compare the position and character of two states as dissimilar as the Anglo-American and the Spanish American. It would be more difficult to apply to Venezuela the political system of the United States than it would be to apply to Spain that of England.'

Laws, remarked Montesquieu, should be suited to the people for whom they are made. Rousseau maintained even more explicitly that constitutions must take account of national character. Bolívar was no less insistent: constitutions must conform to the environment, character, history and resources of the people. 'This is the code we must consult, not the code of Washington.' Bolívar still sought something corresponding to Spanish American reality, not a North American imitation. Spanish American reality was revealed in two ways. The starting point was the multiracial character of society. Speaking of Venezuela, he observed: 'The diversity of social origin will require an infinitely firm hand and great tactfulness in order to manage this heterogeneous society, whose complex mechanism is easily impaired, separated, and disintegrated by the slightest controversy.' It was Bolívar's conviction that 'the fundamental principal of our political system depends directly and exclusively on the establishment and practice of equality in Venezuela. The wisdom of the ages proclaims that all men are born with equal rights to the benefits of society, but also that not all possess equal capabilities, virtue and talents.' So law must correct the disparity of intelligence and character imposed by nature. The logic of his own principles led him to conclude that the greater the social inequality, the greater the need for legal equality. Second, in seeking the institutions to secure true equality, legislators must consider political experience and capacity. While Greece, Rome, France, England and North America all had something to teach in matters of law and government, yet he reminded the delegates that the excellence of a government lies not in its theories or its forms, but in its being suited to the nature and character of the nation for which it is instituted. Bursting with ideas, he was neither dogmatic nor doctrinaire. In his speech the footprints of Montesquieu are plain, those of Rousseau fainter. Basically he was a pragmatist, as he had made clear in the Jamaica Letter: 'Do not adopt the best system of government, but the one that is most likely to work.'[5]

Rather than build upon French or North American models, Bolívar recommended British experience, though cautioning against slavish imitation and any adoption of monarchy. With these qualifications, the British constitution seemed the one most likely to bring about 'the greatest possible good' for those who adopted it. It recognized popular sovereignty, division and balance of powers, civil liberty, freedom of conscience and freedom of the press, and he recommended it as 'the most worthy to serve as a model for those who desire to enjoy the rights of man and all political happiness compatible with our fragile nature'. He began with a legislature modelled on the British parliament, with two chambers, one a house of elected representatives, the other a hereditary senate. The latter, he thought, would remain independent of popular and government pressures, and would protect the people against themselves. The senators would not be an aristocracy or a body of privilege, but an elite of virtue and wisdom produced not by electoral chance but by an enlightened education, specially designed for this vocation. Like the House of Lords in England, the Venezuelan senate would be 'a bulwark of liberty'. Yet the legislature, distinguished though it was, should not usurp power that properly belonged to the executive. Bolívar's executive, though elected, was powerful and centralized, virtually a king with the name of president. Again he looked to the British model, a strong executive at the head of government and the armed forces, but accountable to parliament, which had legislative functions and financial control. 'A perfect model for a kingdom, for an aristocracy, or for a democracy.' Give Venezuela such an executive power in the person of the president chosen by the people or their representatives, he advised, and you will have taken a great step towards national happiness. Add to this an independent judiciary and happiness would be complete, or almost complete, for Bolívar had a further proposal.

To the three classical powers Bolívar added a fourth of his own design, the *poder moral*, which would be responsible for training people in public spirit and political virtue. This idea was badly conceived and met with no response from his contemporaries, but it was typical of his search for a political education for his people, which he regarded as so important that it needed an institution to promote it. He believed that people were educable, if their natural inclinations and talents were respected; this was his experience in creating a multiracial army and his proof that his project was not a utopia.

Was not the whole Angostura project anti-democratic? Bolívar was ready with an answer. 'Absolute liberty invariably lapses into absolute power, and the mean between these two extremes is supreme social liberty. Abstract theories create the pernicious idea of unlimited freedom.' In his view stable government required 'moderation of the popular will and limitation of public authority'. He admitted that such a balance was 'difficult to define in practice', but could be achieved by education and experience in the administration of justice and the rule of law. On the subject of the British constitution – did he really understand it? – Bolívar parted company from the *philosophes*, among whom there was a strong bias against British political practice for its corruption and unrepresentative character, and from Rousseau too, who criticized the English system of government because parliament was independent of its constituents. The hereditary senate, one of the most controversial of all Bolívar's ideas, was an attempt to set a restraint on absolute democracy, which could be as tyrannical as any despot, but this transplanting of the English House of Lords to America – breaking his own 'American reality' principle – would simply have confirmed and prolonged the seigneurial social structure of Venezuela. The congress of Angostura adopted a constitution embodying many of Bolívar's ideas, though not the hereditary senate or the moral power. It elected Bolívar president of the Republic and Zea vice-president. But the new constitution was pure theory, for the war had still to be won. On the military front Bolívar had new opportunities and a new vision, an opportunity to realize his political ideals through organization, discipline and leadership.

Reinforcements and Reappraisal

In 1817 the Venezuelan representative in London, Luis López Méndez, was asked by Bolívar to recruit officers and sergeants to join the patriot army and navy, and from Grafton Street, Fitzroy Square, he began to negotiate with British officers to raise and lead regiments for service in Venezuela. In July he contracted with Colonel H.C. Wilson, in October with Colonel Gustavus Hippisley.[6] From this point, during the next five years, over six thousand volunteers left Britain and Ireland in fifty-three ships for service in South America, of whom at least 5,300 set foot there.[7] The Spanish ambassador protested to the Foreign Office that the entire population of England seemed to have joined expeditions to the Americas. British merchants were already playing a part in republican activities. They had provided assistance to Bolívar in Jamaica and helped to fund his expeditions from Haiti; in Guayana they traded hardware, arms and munitions in exchange for cattle and other exportable products, and the Hyslops described themselves as the commercial agents of General Bolívar as well as of New Granada. The official policy of the British government was to prohibit British subjects from taking part in the war between Spain and its colonies, as it was contrary to the government's policy of neutrality, and a decree of 13 May 1818 forbade the export of arms to Spanish America. Bolívar understood the limitations placed on Britain's freedom of action by its wide commitments and never pushed diplomacy too hard, preferring to seek specific gains and practical advantages. Circumstances favoured this approach.

In the aftermath of the Napoleonic wars there were numerous half-pay officers and unemployed soldiers ready to accept contracts as mercenaries for the wars of independence, and even more adventurers with no military experience seeking honourable causes and better opportunities in the Americas; there were surplus stores, arms and ammunition, which merchants were only too willing to sell, while public opinion generally favoured the cause of Spanish America rather than Spain. The Spanish embassy in London monitored every detail of the recruiting campaign of the Venezuelans and bombarded the Foreign Office with complaints; it was especially riled to see volunteers training daily in London. The British government was caught in a dilemma and in the event combined official disapproval of recruitment with toleration of the recruits' departure to Spanish America. In 1818 English envoys of Bolívar returned to organize yet further expeditions, to include soldiers as well as officers, the nucleus of the British Legion, together with ships, sailors and guns.

In one way or another, with the tolerance, connivance or indifference of the authorities, ships, men and arms, and entire regiments left British ports for South America in 1817–19, while volunteer officers and seamen also crossed the Atlantic to join the Venezuelan navy. Some fifty thousand rifles and muskets, hundreds of tons of lead and powder, artillery, lances, cutlasses, swords, sabres and pistols were sold to the republicans. The commercial aspect predominated, and in London there was perpetual conflict around López Méndez concerning money not paid by him and contracts not fulfilled by merchants. Eventually, the growing scale of the operation, the infraction of the law and the protests of Spain forced the British government to do something. The Foreign Enlistment Act of 1819 forbade British subjects to serve in the armies of South America and prohibited the export of arms to the insurgents; this prompted a scramble to get away and numerous vessels slipped out of Liverpool in the course of 1820. The British authorities went through the motions of enforcing the law but, favoured by public opinion, enlistment continued, as did the supply of arms.[8] Denounced in London by Spain, the legionaries were tracked in Venezuela by Spanish commanders. General Morillo tried to address them directly: 'You are serving under the command of a man in every respect insignificant, and have joined an horde of *banditti* who are famed for the exercise of the most barbarous cruelties, which are so averse to yor unational character, that you must abhorr them. He who retains the least spark of honour and justice cannot remain united with such a band of Ragamuffins.'[9] British soldiers rejected the overtures and the insults to Bolívar: 'Bolívar is as deserving of his country's gratitude and the admiration of the world as Washington himself – and like him he will be venerated whilst he lives, and his memory will be immortalized.'[10]

A tale of heroism and setbacks, this was the sequel to the recruiting drive, with disease, drunkenness and desertion reducing the ranks of fighting men who actually reached Bolívar's army. They soon found that 'campaigns in the immense plains of South America were no joke', and no way to wealth.[11] But the Liberator liked them, even if some of his officers looked askance. Wilson and Hippisley did not last long, but many of their forces persevered and the place of their commanders was taken by Colonel James Rooke and Thomas Ferriar who gave excellent service, as did Robert Pigott. Shiploads of troops landed at Angostura and were marched up country to join Colonel Rooke with Bolívar in the Apure, where he was planning a campaign into New Granada. Venezuelan commanders were divided in their opinions of the plan, but when it was Rooke's turn to speak he said he would follow the Liberator to Cape Horn if need be. Rooke's British unit, now called the British Legion, were there at the crossing of the Andes. The British soldiers soon became known as good marchers and when they were in the vanguard their pace was too fast for many; American troops incorporated into British units 'thought themselves above the other soldiers, and called themselves English, and swore in English by way of keeping up their title'.[12] Whatever their reputation, in the campaign of 1819 British troops made a difference. This was the belief of Bolívar, who used to say that the true Liberator was his recruiting agent in London, Luis López Méndez.[13]

A Second Front

From August 1818 Bolívar turned his mind towards the liberation of New Granada. In that month he sent General Santander to Casanare as governor and vanguard of a greater expedition. Casanare was a semi-desert, a poor and underpopulated province, but it was the sanctuary of New Granadan independence. It provided a nucleus of another army and it could become a base for an invasion of New Granada. Santander explored and exploited the weaknesses in the royalist position, the failure of leadership by the young Spanish commander, General José María Barreiro, demoralization and desertion by his troops, and renewal of resistance among the *llanero* guerrillas. Barreiro complained that his troops and officers were unpaid, the whole army on half rations and badly clothed; and creoles, who were in the royal army not for love of the king but for what they could get, were deserting in droves to the enemy. By May 1819 Santander was able to report to Bolívar that Casanare was clear of royalists, 'enthusiastic for its independence', and ready for its role in the campaign. 'Have no worries about Casanare.'[14]

It was a bold and difficult strategy, and in the scale of risks Bolívar had to weigh breakthrough against impasse. In Venezuela the revolution was at a standstill. In the Apure, it is true, Páez skilfully frustrated all Morillo's attempts to destroy him. Reinforcements were arriving to strengthen the patriot armies. Bolívar was optimistic, declared his troops comparable to 'the best in Europe', and believed that the military argument could now be won: 'There is no longer imbalance in weapons of destruction.'[15] But the republic found it impossible to crush the royalists. Its army needed action and victories, beyond skirmishes and sieges in the *llanos*. Could these not be attained more easily in New Granada?

The royalists in New Granada were more vulnerable, particularly exposed to a rapid invasion. Spanish rule – which meant in effect ten thousand troops, most of them Americans and disaffected and only two hundred reliable Spaniards – was spread over a vast area between Cartagena and Quito, and fully occupied with internal security and the problems of its own troops, 'sick, underpaid, ill supplied and divided'.[16] The government too was divided. Viceroy Francisco Montalvo's policy of conciliation was opposed at every turn by Morillo, whose hard line aroused the creoles, while his weakened army could not contain them. Montalvo's successor, the brutal Juan Sámano, inspired fear and loathing in equal measure. The royalist reconquest was cracking under the strain and paying for its years of oppression, racial abuse, forced recruitment, labour levies and financial exactions. These were self-inflicted blows before Bolívar had even struck.

Even so, there were risks for Bolívar. Success depended on the rapid penetration to the heart of Spanish power, and this too meant traversing great distances. And behind him Bolívar would leave a weak government and a number of semi-independent chieftains. Yet to switch the theatre of war from one country to another would have a magical effect and in itself constitute a rare moral victory. Bolívar could lure Morillo from Venezuela and, if the operation were successful, return to his homeland from a position of strength and with greater striking power. 'We will force Morillo either to evacuate

Venezuela in order to defend New Granada, or alternatively to allow the latter to be entirely lost.' This was his argument to Páez. And to New Granadans he proclaimed, 'The day of America has arrived and no human power can hold back the course of nature guided by the hand of Providence.'[17]

In March 1819 Bolívar once again left Angostura for the Apure, proceeding up the Orinoco accompanied by a battalion of three hundred Englishmen under Major John Mackintosh. In Arauca Páez had been conducting a perfect guerrilla campaign, luring the advancing forces of Morillo to the limits of their endurance. Now the Liberator himself took command in gruelling actions against Morillo. Páez again distinguished himself. At Las Queseras del Medio he led his cavalry in the *vuelvan caras* tactic, a spectacular about-turn from feigned retreat into lightning attack which cost Morillo heavy casualties. These inconclusive actions of Bolívar's final campaign in the *llanos*, a time of marching and fighting, crossing and recrossing the Arauca, avoiding defeats and grasping victories, proved to be a time of truth in the career of the Liberator. His colleagues were inspired by his mere routine. He arose at daybreak and visited the various units, advising and encouraging. He accompanied the army with his staff officers, dismounted at midday to wash and eat, then to issue orders and dictate his correspondence from his hammock, and so to continue the march until it was time to camp in woods or the open fields. The officers who accompanied him at that period recalled 'his incomparable activity and his vigilance, not only in regard to the fate of the Republic but also in regard to that of the very least of his soldiers'.[18] He was then thirty-five years old, at the height of his mental powers and as fit as he would ever be. He was also alert to dangers to his life, and not only on the battlefield, as his staff knew:

> Once, in the plains, he arrived with his staff at a *hato*, where he thought to remain till the next day. A girl, whose pretty figure had smitten him, held forth an inducement by offering to partake of his bed. Whether he suspected that all was not right, or that it was more convenient for the next day's journey to proceed a little farther, I forget. But he left the house. The girl, who was not a *patriot*, had dispatched a message to a Spanish outpost not far distant and, had he not decamped, he would have fallen into their hands.[19]

On 15 May he received news of Santander's success against the royalists in Casanare. This was the moment of decision. On 20 May he warned his commander that he was contemplating an operation in New Granada and that he should have all his forces ready to move in conjunction with other units as soon as he received orders: 'I don't yet know the precise day, nor have

I decided on the way to do it, so I am only telling you of the move in advance and stressing the need for absolute secrecy, without which nothing can be done. This is for your eyes and yours alone.'[20] Yet Morillo, briefed by his spies, had already guessed the Liberator's intentions and the direction he would take, and he regarded it as the most critical challenge he had yet faced.

Bolívar quickly decided that the day had come to open his second front, to make New Granada the fulcrum on which the revolution could turn, east to Venezuela and south to Quito and Peru. He announced the invasion – though not his real route – to his colleagues on 23 May in a council of war held in a ruined cabin in the deserted village of Setenta on the right bank of the Apure, where the only seats were the skulls of cattle bleached by the rain and sun of the plains.[21] Present were Soublette, Anzoátegui, Briceño Méndez, Cruz Carillo, Irribarren, Rangel, Rooke, Plaza and Manrique. All those there approved the plan, though among others there was some scepticism and Páez proved to be uncooperative. But the caudillos had little to lose. All the risks were Bolívar's. And what alternatives had he? Would it not be suicidal to remain and winter in the *llanos*, his forces exposed to the rains, consumed by yellow fever and malaria and open to desertion and dissolution? And he covered his back. In the following days he took the necessary steps to explain his plan to the government of Angostura, and to give precise instructions to Mariño, Bermúdez, Urdaneta and Brión. Nothing was left to chance. Bolívar was a consummate planner. But planning was not enough to bring in Páez. Bolívar cultivated him carefully and explained his plan at every step of the way. He instructed him to move on Cúcuta to cut the enemy's communications with Venezuela. Páez made excuses and refused. Bolívar requested three hundred horses out of the *llaneros'* sixteen hundred. Páez sent him two hundred 'skinny and mangy mares'.[22] Bolívar did not hide his disgust.

On 27 May 1819 the Liberator left the upper Apure to join with Santander and cross the Andes. Only then, in Guasdualito, did he publish the destination. He led his small army – four infantry battalions, three cavalry squadrons, 2,100 men in all – to one of the sublime actions of the war of liberation, when all the frustrations of recent years – the disunity, the insubordination, the poverty, the social and racial conflict – were suddenly overcome by great feats of will, courage and discipline. His senior officers, Soublette, Anzoátegui, Rooke, were ardent young men ready to follow Bolívar to the end, and all his junior officers were eager for action under his command. They crossed the Arauca and the savannahs of Casanare just as the season of torrential rain was beginning, the land a spate of streams, rivers, lakes and swamps, the soldiers splashing, swimming and rowing to move ahead. 'For seven days,' reported O'Leary, who was now Anzoátegui's aide-de-camp, 'the troops marched with water up to their waists, camping in whatever dry patches they could find, with only a blanket for protection, or rather to cover their weapons and ammunition.'[23] This was only the beginning, before a month's march through Casanare.

After the junction with Santander at Tame the joint army waded through further floods to Pore, a prelude to the ascent of the mighty cordillera. Men bred in the plains and tired from marching twenty miles a day through sodden terrain now had to endure the towering Andes, suffering exposure in the freezing rain, exhaustion as they struggled up mountain after mountain, and altitude sickness as they crossed at a height of thirteen thousand feet through the toughest of all the passes, the bleak Páramo de Pisba. The rain came down in sheets. 'The harshness of the mountain is incredible to anyone who has not felt it. . . . It hardly stops raining, day and night,' reported Bolívar. 'I almost despaired as I observed the difficulties that grew every day, and only grim determination to stick to my plan kept me going.'[24] There was another truth: only his own extraordinary leadership could explain why the army should follow him in these conditions. Men, animals and equipment were lost in great numbers; the cavalry, the pride of the army, were losing their mounts every day; to lie down was to suffer the sleep of death. A quarter of the British legion perished on the march, but one British wife marched on carrying her baby, born on the crossing.

On 6 July the exhausted survivors began to reach the other side of the mountains at the village of Socha, their uniforms in tatters, their boots worn through, many officers reduced to wearing *alpargatas*. Richard Vowell, who survived this test of endurance, reported: 'Those who had been possessed of shoes on leaving the *llanos*, had long since worn them out; and very many, even of the officers, had literally no trowsers, and were glad to cover themselves with pieces of blanket, or whatever they could procure.'[25] Local women were persuaded to strip off their clothes and give them to the men. There was no rest for Bolívar as he organized food and supplies, rounded up mules, brought in the sick and the stragglers, and reassured the New Granadans that the invaders were friends and fellow victims who sought nothing more than to 'establish them as a free and independent nation'.[26] It was a personal triumph for the Liberator; if the horrors of the crossing tested the spirit of the army, they also proved the character of Bolívar. 'Here is where this man rises above all men, showing extraordinary energy and resolution. In three days he remounts and arms the cavalry, assembles the artillery, and regroups the army; he sends out numerous patrols against the enemy, encourages the villages, and prepares to attack in all directions.'[27] A frank assessment; Santander, too, recognized that this man was superior.

From Bolívar's camp south of Socha a rare campaign scene survives. Among the reinforcements brought by Soublette came an English unit under the irrepressible Colonel Rooke, a veteran of Waterloo, who wasted no time in presenting himself and congratulating the Liberator on the state of his army. Invited to join Bolívar at his frugal breakfast, Rooke assured him this was the tastiest meal of his life, and to queries concerning his troops he answered, yes, they were fine and had suffered nothing on the Pisba pass. Anzoátegui came up, looking gloomy and ill-tempered as usual. 'What's new, Anzoátegui?' inquired Bolívar. 'As if anything could be new,' replied Anzoátegui, and asked if he had heard of the state of Rooke's dragoons. 'Yes, their colonel has just presented the most favourable reports and assures me that he suffered no losses on the *páramo*.' It soon emerged that in fact a quarter of the English troops and two officers had died on the crossing. 'I don't deny it,' exclaimed the incorrigible Rooke, 'but they deserved their fate, for these were the worst of my troops and we are better without them.' Bolívar could only smile at Rooke's protestations, but the ever disgruntled Anzoátegui was not amused.[28]

Boyacá

The campaign continued. Bolívar's genius had conceived the strategy, his leadership had brought them through, and now his inspiration took them forward, as he entered one of his greatest triumphs. On 25 July his army took the fight to the royalist force, rested and far superior in numbers, and at Pantano de Vargas earned victory from a hard day's battle, won by sheer courage against all the odds – the royalist forces had the advantage of the higher ground – by Rondón's *llanero* cavalry, the cool bravery of the few British troops, and the presence of Bolívar everywhere. Rooke was mortally wounded, O'Leary took a sabre cut across the head and there were casualties among other British officers, whose actions were recognized by Bolívar with the award of the Cross of Liberators the following day.[29]

Pausing only a few days to reorganize and recruit local patriots, vital assurance that liberation was a New Granadan enterprise as well as a foreign invasion, Bolívar moved forward again on 3 August, outmanoeuvring Barreiro, quietly occupying Tunja ahead of the royalists and then intercepting their retreat towards Bogotá at Boyacá. The young O'Leary, still active after his recent wound, was there to record the battle, and to see Bolívar, on 7 August, deliver the death blow to the royalists, attacking from each wing and with a decisive thrust through the centre. Santander's unit stormed the bridge, while Anzoátegui attacked the centre of the royalist position. Soublette attributed the victory above all to the intrepid Anzoátegui, who led his infantry battalions and a squadron of cavalry into the heart of the enemy.[30] But by now the enemy had lost heart. Isolated among a population alienated by their own actions, the royalists seemed to have no will to fight and simply turned and ran, demoralized by indecisive leadership against an army fired by its recent achievements.[31] Caught between these fierce attacks, Barreiro surrendered and with the remnants of his army was taken prisoner. It was all over in two hours. The liberators, two thousand against three thousand royalists, suffered thirteen dead and fifty-three wounded. A number of British officers were killed or severely wounded. Rooke's legion was rewarded with a new name, Batallón Albión, and all were honoured with the Star of the Order of Liberators.

The road to the capital, some seventy miles away, was now open. On 10 August, Bolívar entered Bogotá to find that the Spanish officials, authors of terror and fearful of retribution, had fled in panic to Cartagena. The hated Viceroy Sámano had departed so quickly – disguised as an Indian – that he had left a bag of money on his desk, to the great amusement of Bolívar. 'In the Casa de Moneda,' reported Soublette, 'we found more than half a million pesos, and in the stores enough arms and equipment to supply a large army.'[32]

The victory of Boyacá set the seal of success on Bolívar's authority and his strategy. He took pleasure and pride in the Boyacá campaign, 'my most complete victory'. His great act of faith was fulfilled. The heart of New Granada was liberated, the royalists were scattered and soon Spanish resistance was confined to Cartagena and Cúcuta. Morillo said it all. Boyacá was a decisive victory: if the patriots had lost they could have picked themselves up and tried again; when the Spaniards lost, they lost a division and a province never to be regained.[33] Official celebrations followed a month later. Bolívar, flanked by Santander and Anzoátegui, was received in a victory procession, with church bells, a Te Deum in the cathedral and a ceremony in the main square. Twenty young girls in white brought a crown of laurels to lay on the Liberator's brow, who in turn passed it to his two companions and then threw it to the soldiers. Bolívar remembered the script from his triumph in Caracas. One of the girls, Bernardina Ibáñez Arias, dark eyed, attractive and only sixteen, caught his attention and retained it even when others pursued her; the winner was Colonel Ambrosio Plaza, a young officer under Bolívar's command. Santander subsequently pleaded with Bolívar on behalf of the couple who wanted to marry and to have Plaza stationed locally. Bolívar asked, 'Well, is Plaza married or not? No doubt you will be pleased for it will increase the number of young Granadinos. I too, for I love the young couple.'[34] Six months later the story was still running.

Bolívar did not rest on his laurels but took immediate steps to preserve his prize from any counter-offensive that Morillo might launch. American troops were incorporated into the republican army. Soublette was sent with a strong division to occupy the valleys of Cúcuta and defend the frontier. Colonel Córdova was sent to drive the Spaniards out of Antioquia. Another unit was dispatched southwards to occupy Popayán. Beyond Popayán and in the highlands up to Quito the royalists still possessed a formidable stronghold. But the south, too, was already in Bolívar's sights. In a proclamation to his soldiers he included the promise, 'Soon over rich Peru the combined flags of Venezuela, New Granada, Argentina, and Chile will be flying, and Lima will shelter in her bosom as many liberators as are the glory of the New World.'[35] And at home nothing escaped his attention. From his own pocket he set up a pensions fund for the widows of victims of the Spanish occupation.

He then turned to the levers of political power. He was already president of the republic. Now he announced the kind of republic it would be – a republic of greater Colombia, formed from the union of New Granada and Venezuela. 'The union of New Granada and Venezuela in one Republic is the ardent wish of all good citizens and all foreign friends of the American cause.'[36] But he was aware that there might be resentment in New Granada against a perceived takeover by Venezuela, so he wanted a free and unanimous decision made in congress, and meanwhile he formed a provisional government for New Granada. On 20 September he appointed Santander, newly promoted to General of Division, at its head with the title of vice-president. A native of Cúcuta, son of a respectable creole family, product of a legal education and continuous service in the army, he had a good record, though in 1816 he had been rejected as leader by the *llaneros* in favour of Páez. He was a colleague, not a friend, distant from the Liberator's ideal, and their relationship was edgy. At twenty-seven he was a severe, humourless and touchy man, with a strong interest in money and a streak of vindictive cruelty. According to O'Leary, if Bolívar was the greatest man the South American revolution produced, and Sucre the most perfect, Santander was 'the most fortunate'.[37] He owed most of his promotion to Bolívar, partly by being in the right place at the right time, partly because he was an efficient administrator. Bolívar treated him with respect, and Santander reported to Bolívar as 'an obedient subject, impartial eulogist, loyal and accepted friend'.[38] Now his organizing talent as well as his loyalty was desperately needed: his first task was to mobilize New Granada for the continental war effort; the ultimate duty was to create a new nation. With Santander, Bolívar had to take the rough with the smooth. He soon had an example.

Bolívar had moved on since war to the death, and he treated the prisoners taken at Boyacá generously; repentant Americans could join his army or go home; Barreiro and his officers were kept in prison but in reasonable conditions, and he made it clear to the Spanish authorities that he wanted an exchange of prisoners. But no sooner had he left the capital than Santander had Barreiro and thirty-eight of his comrades, some of them Americans, shot in the main square. His reasons, as given to Bolívar, were specious, alleging the risk to security, the demands of the populace and the crimes against compa-triots committed by the prisoners. His covering letter was equally crass. 'At last I had to get rid of Barreiro and his thirty-eight companions. The sparks of danger made me mad and nothing good could come from keeping them in prison. . . . The records are well fixed, but it is essential that your reply covers me for all time.'[39] In fact he seems to have panicked and allowed his innate cruelty to get the better of his judgement. At midday on 11 October the pris-oners were led four abreast across the square dragging their chains. Barreiro was ordered to kneel and was shot in the back; his comrades suffered the same fate, as Santander watched on horseback from the entrance to government house. The latter then led a parade, with triumphant music, through the streets of the capital and ended the celebration with a ball at the palace.

The atrocity was ill received by many republicans, in both New Granada and Venezuela, and it was seen as an act of folly or inhumanity. Reading between the lines of Bolívar's response we can see a reproach but not a repri-mand: 'I hear with regret the perfidious behaviour of our war prisoners which has forced Your Excellency to have them executed when we were negotiating for an exchange. . . . Our enemies will not believe truly that our severity is an act of justice and not a reprisal and a gratuitous vengeance. But be that as it may, I thank Your Excellency for your zeal and activity in trying to save the Republic with that painful measure. Our reputation will certainly suffer.' Zea did not doubt it: 'The untimely reprisals of our good friend Santander have done us a lot of harm.'[40] Santander compounded his cruelty with hypocrisy, subsequently praising Bolívar's 'excessive' generosity to Spanish prisoners and resistance to the army's clamour for reprisals against royalist officers: 'The general insisted that they be treated decently and where possible he proposed an exchange of prisoners.'[41]

Tensions after Triumph

Bolívar took his leave of Bogotá on 20 September to resume command of the army, now gathering at Cúcuta. His route through the towns of Tunja, Leiva, Vélez, Socorro, San Gil, Bucaramanga and Pamplona became another triumphant procession of cheering crowds, votes of gratitude, floral tributes and young girls pressing laurels on his head, and also an opportunity to take stock of the situation. Then came two blows. Shortly after leaving Pamplona, news of the sudden and unaccountable death of General Anzoátegui, so recently his vigorous and trusted lieutenant in the north, affected him deeply as well as forcing him to readjust his command structure. A naturally gloomy man, Anzoátegui had been anxious to return home on leave, pining for his wife Teresa and two children, one a newly born he had never seen. His campaign friends were disconsolate. As for Bolívar, news from Angostura revived fears of insubordination and factions seeking to undermine his position, and he decided his presence was needed there. With tragedy behind and trouble ahead, the road to Angostura was not a triumph.

While Bolívar had loyal officers in his army, good colleagues in government, and trusted friends everywhere, he also had personal enemies who resented his policies and criticized his strategies, not necessarily on their merits but because they emanated from him, and he only needed to slacken the reins of control for opponents to emerge. His absence from Angostura gave such people space to operate, for caudillos to reach again for freedom and politicians for power. His enemies called the invasion of New Granada an abandonment of the interests of Venezuela, and some tried to force congress to declare him a deserter and an outlaw. In the east the caudillos were rearing their heads again. While Bolívar was on campaign, they were engaged in smaller operations, not always successful and rarely in agreement among themselves. Páez ignored specific instructions from Bolívar to move toward Cúcuta and cut the enemy communications with Venezuela.[42] Mariño failed to link up with Bermúdez. Urdaneta was obliged to arrest Arismendi for insubordination. And the caudillos now vented their hostility not directly on Bolívar but on the government in Angostura, especially the vice-president, Zea, who was civilian, a New Granadan, and a political moderate, qualities held in little respect by Venezuelan caudillos.[43] They forced Zea to resign, congress elected Arismendi in his place, and he in turn appointed Mariño general-in-chief, based at Maturín.

Thus in the course of September 1819, while Bolívar was receiving plaudits from New Granadan civilians, the military caudillos staged a comeback, expressing and exploiting Venezuelan nationalism in a way that was a warning for the future. But their victory was only temporary, for the news of Boyacá was already undermining the rebellion. Bolívar landed at Angostura on 11 December, and although it was three o'clock in the morning he was welcomed to cries of 'Viva Bolívar' and backslapping from the people, official respect and congratulations from the authorities, and firing of salvos from the riverboats. A congressional commission later went to his residence with a military band to escort him to the presidential seat.[44] Magnanimity was his method for dealing with the rebels; he was now powerful enough to forgive, if not to forget, and to post Arismendi and Bermúdez to military commands in the east. His glory was complete, politically as well as militarily.

He was now in a position to elaborate his constitutional ideas. 'The union of New Granada and Venezuela has been my only object since I first took up arms,' he told congress. 'Decree the political union of the two states and you will have fulfilled my most cherished desire and amply rewarded the army for its services.'[45] The project was seriously debated in two sessions, and by the Fundamental Law of 17 December 1819 the congress of Angostura formally created the Republic of Colombia, the name in honour of Christopher Columbus, the new state a union of the departments of Venezuela (formerly the captaincy-general of Venezuela), New Granada (formerly the viceroyalty of New Granada) and Quito (formerly the presidency of Quito), the latter still to be liberated. It was a bold project, which only the leadership and authority of Bolívar could have carried, but he was determined to procure it, because he believed that the revolution needed a large state, for the sake of its identity, its international status and his own power. Santander welcomed the union of the two peoples as an incalculable advantage, recognized Bolívar as the sole author and sent him his congratulations.[46] Bolívar did not need reminding that the project was 'illegal' and needed constitutional acceptance in New Granada, or Cundinamarca, as it was now called. He agreed with the decision of the congress of Angostura to convoke a constituent congress for this purpose, to meet in Cúcuta on 1 January 1821. No one thought of asking Venezuelans, New Granadans or *quiteños* whether they thought of themselves as Colombians.

Bolívar won election, without difficulty, as de facto president of Colombia, or Liberator President as congress insisted on a calling him, and Zea as vice-president. His next task was to end the war in Venezuela and prepare for a post-war settlement. Angostura had been a valuable base for the Liberator, but it was still full of political troublemakers and certainly not the place from which to conduct a continental war effort. At long distance he set in motion a number of strategic initiatives, in the north along the Caribbean coast and the lower Magdalena, and in the south towards Popayán, relying on subordinate commanders and local patriots. He instructed Padilla and Brión on maritime strategy. He kept his eye on Páez. And he showed his skill in talent spotting, promoting an accomplished administrator, Rafael Revenga, as minister of state. But the war needed his closer presence and authority.

In early March 1820 he returned to Bogotá, where he found the citizens still supportive and Santander preoccupied with war taxes and their impact. He then made a tour northward and based himself in the region of Cúcuta on the border between New Granada and Venezuela, where he enjoyed a welcome break between campaigns. O'Leary, who became an aide-de-camp to Bolívar about this time, observed his daily routine there.[47] He rose at six, inspected the horses in the stables, returned to his room, read until nine and then had breakfast. The rest of the morning was spent dealing with official business, listening to reports from his minister of war, private secretary and chief of staff, and dictating answers to letters in direct and concise language, striding up and down or seated in his hammock. His range and decisions were masterly: foreign affairs, recruitment, rifles, taxes, advice for his vice-presidents, arrangements for the constituent congress and always the next military moves. But his public image of confidence masked a cool, even cynical, awareness of the social obstacles to progress in Colombia, the failure of people to conform to the ideals he set out in his great speeches, the bad faith and worse behaviour among citizens, criticism and opposition from malcontents, envy and hatred from his enemies. In such a mood he wrote to Santander: 'The Spaniards have inspired terror in our national spirit. The more I think of it the more I am convinced that neither liberty, nor laws, nor the most brilliant enlightenment will make us law-abiding people, much less republicans and true patriots. Friend, we do not have blood in our veins but vice mixed with fear and error. What civic virtues!'[48]

But life was not all 'political philosophy', as he described outbursts of this kind. Amidst the public duties his thoughts strayed to women, the details embedded in the correspondence. He still hankered after Bernardina Ibañez and was irritated by her relationship with Ambrosio Plaza, wondering perhaps why she was wasting her time on the colonel when she could have the general, or more likely just anxious to press his suit. He asked Santander to have a word with her and let her know that 'I am tired of writing without any reply. Tell her that I too am single and like her more than does Plaza, for I have never been unfaithful.' The reply was not promising: 'She has hopes in Plaza and no hopes in the others, including you. Affairs of the heart are difficult to manage from a distance.'[49] Evidently she lingered in Bolívar's memory, but she was reluctant to give herself to a distant lover with a record of infidelity and a future in high power, and preferred the commitment of Plaza.

During business he thought and spoke rapidly, and expected his secretary to keep up with the flow – and accurately. His opinions of correspondents were not always for sending, and some he kept to himself. Santander had to be handled carefully and on an issue such as the liberation of slaves, to which Bolívar was dedicated, subjected to strong argument.[50] Páez was still awkward and had to be instructed in the duty of deference. Much of the business concerned petitions from officers and others wanting this and that. Some of the answers were amusing. 'Half of what he says is not true, but he is a good officer, so give him his promotion.' To one supplicant, a priest who had always been hostile to the cause of independence, he replied, 'Ask the king'. To a doctor who had exploited the anarchy in Bogotá between Sámano's flight and Bolívar's arrival to plunder some warehouses, and now asked for appointment as staff doctor with the rank of lieutenant colonel, he wrote in the margin of the petition, 'Be satisfied with what you have stolen'. In the afternoon he read until five and then took dinner. He was not averse to good meals and fine wines but at this time money was short and so were his rations, down to the simple fare of meat and vegetables, and water the only drink. After dinner he rode for a while with his aide or secretary, then conversed with his friends and visitors; in private, others noted, his conversation took on a mocking tone, and the sardonic remark was never far from his lips. He retired to his bedroom at nine. There, reclining in his hammock he read until eleven; in this period Montesquieu and Rousseau were his authors of choice and history his favourite subject. He also wrote articles for newspapers in Angostura or Bogotá.

Colonel Briceño Méndez, then minister of war, 'an intelligent, well-bred, and good-natured man', was close to him at this time, his calm and modest manner contrasting sharply with the fiery disposition of the Liberator, and known for his utter loyalty and lack of personal ambition. Colonel Bartolomé Salom, chief-of-staff, was another close and dependable colleague, a tireless worker for the Liberator, for whom nothing was too much trouble, and who asked and expected nothing for himself. Elsewhere O'Leary recorded other habits of the Liberator. He used to shave with both hands and so quickly that onlookers were afraid, though he kept up a conversation with them. He was also careless with firearms. He was a bad shot and would fire pistols carelessly in any direction without much regard for those nearby.[51]

In April and May, from San Cristóbal, Bolívar surveyed frontier defences and republican resources. He saw that in spite of the advance of liberation he could still not assemble enough troops and arms to fight a decisive war; Páez would not operate out of the *llanos*; and republican soldiers deserted in droves for lack of pay and food in a country that could not support them. Morillo, too, had his problems. He knew he had lost New Granada, his best division was crushed and his government in retreat. He continued to dominate Caracas and the coastal highlands, but amidst an economy in ruins he despaired, reporting, 'The people of this country are tired of war and disasters, and they will make the utmost effort to rally round the revolutionary government which is the one they want and the cause they love.'[52] At this point the Spanish commander, still reeling from the impact of Boyacá, was dealt a second blow and Bolívar received the boost he needed.

The Spanish liberal revolution of 1 January 1820, led by Colonel Rafael Riego and sanctioned by the army in Cadiz, anxious to avoid service in America, forced Ferdinand VII to abandon absolutism and accept the Constitution of 1812. The move deprived Morillo of reinforcements, weakened his absolute military authority and subverted his political position; he was ordered to negotiate with the patriots, offering peace on the basis of recognizing a constitutional government in Spain. The Spaniards, shackled by constitutional restraints and split between liberals and absolutists, soon found that Bolívar, victorious general, head of state and hero of liberated peoples, was no longer a rebel on the run but a tough negotiator, determined to make the most of his newly acquired superiority. 'It is the height of madness, and moreover ridiculous, to suggest that the republic of Colombia should submit itself to Spain. Do you believe that old and corrupt Spain can still dominate the New World?' he asked the Spaniards. And to Soublette he confided, 'They have everything to lose and nothing to gain. We have nothing to lose and want everything they possess: ... So we must offer only peace in return for Independence.'[53] He had to prevent the Spaniards from picking off republicans with false promises, and so he ordered all his subordinates, especially Páez, not to treat with agents of Morillo, for he was determined to keep the negotiations in his own hands and under his sole control. Meanwhile he manipulated the Spaniards while he won further ground. The caudillos were making some gains in the east. He himself was consolidating his position at Cúcuta and linking up with republican forces on the lower Magdalena. Cartagena was under siege by land and sea, and on the point of falling. The Indian caudillo, Juan de los Reyes Vargas deserted with his guerrilla band from the royalist side and became a valuable addition to the republican forces with the rank of colonel. By August Bolívar could negotiate with Morillo from a position of strength, but still he did not hurry. In October he was in Trujillo and ready to talk, but Morillo had his own reason for delay: to move up troops to back his negotiating position. Agreement was finally reached and commissioners signed a six-month armistice treaty on 25 November, each side agreeing to remain in the territory they then occupied and not to engage in offensive action. Humane rules of war and conditions for prisoners were agreed. Morillo wanted to greet Bolívar and the two leaders met on 27 November in Santa Ana, a village some nine miles north east of Trujillo. When O'Leary pointed out Bolívar to Morillo, the Spaniard asked, 'What, that little man in the blue frock-coat and forage cap riding a mule?'[54] They jumped to the ground and embraced, retired with their attendants to a meal prepared by the Spaniards, and the company spent the rest of the day celebrating and exchanging campaign stories. Years later Bolívar recalled that 'neither Morillo nor I were really taken in by these exchanges, conventional in style for negotiators'. But for the moment, ever generous of heart, he was moved to a new respect for his former enemies, 'now my new friends'.[55] He took to Morillo and his Spanish colleagues, accepted their liberal sentiments and expressions of admiration at face value, responded to their toasts to Colombian independence and was convinced that none of them wanted to continue the war. Morillo was moved that 'those who had previously been destined to mutual extermination for the first time saw themselves not merely as men but also as friends'.[56] Years later, in 1835, O'Leary and Soublette visited Morillo in La Coruña: 'When he heard that I was writing the life of his old rival, of whom he was a great admirer, he gave me many documents taken by the royalists on the battlefields of Venezuela.'[57]

The armistice was important for Venezuela, 'valuable for us, fatal for the Spaniards': it legitimized the struggle; it finally ended the war to the death; and it forced Spain to recognize the existence, if not the legality, of the new state of Colombia, whose president was Bolívar. As Bolívar saw it: 'The armistice is to our advantage because, with the establishment of uninterrupted communications and with our forces holding good positions in a continuous line of defence, we are in a superior situation to continue operations when the time comes; which, however, I believe will not be necessary, as the greatest advantage of the armistice will, to all appearances, be the end of the war.'[58] Even more important, perhaps, it caused Morillo to retire to Spain, leaving the less resolute General La Torre in command and the security forces dispirited. The news from the rest of the subcontinent was also encouraging. The United Provinces of the Río de la Plata were long independent of Spanish authority and free to dispute among themselves for an appropriate form of government. San Martín had defeated the Spaniards in Chile and was now leading a liberating expedition in Peru. Late in 1820 Guayaquil declared its independence, formed a new government and opened its port to foreign trade. The Liberator and his press publicized these news stories and took the propaganda war to the royalists.

Confident of the future in Venezuela, Bolívar was already thinking of more distant conquests. Quito was in his sights as a prime target, to restore its historical link with Bogotá, to complete the union of Colombia and to guard against a Spanish attack from Peru. He himself had unfinished business in the north, so from Bogotá he chose his most trusted general for the mission. Antonio José de Sucre, 'the most perfect by far' of republican commanders, was pure Bolivarian. As a young man, in 1813, he accompanied the expedition of Mariño and fought a number of important actions; but unlike his eastern colleagues he did not aspire to be an independent chieftain. He came from a wealthy Cumaná family and had received an education in Caracas. He was interested in the technology of warfare and became an expert in military engineering. 'He reduced everything to a method ... he was the scourge of disorder,' Bolívar later wrote of him.[59] He served as an officer in the Army of the East for four years, and came under the influence of Bolívar in 1817, accepting appointment to the Liberator's staff in preference to the factions of the east: 'I am resolved to obey you blindly and with pleasure.'[60] His obedience never faltered. When Vice-President Zea promoted him to the rank of brigadier general, without Bolívar's cognizance, Sucre explained later 'that he had never intended to accept promotion without General Bolívar's approval.'[61] Bolívar employed him as one of his armistice commissioners in

1820 and he now gave him a new role as his precursor in the south. In January 1821 Bolívar withdrew Sucre from his duties in Colombia and instructed him to lead an expeditionary force of a thousand to Guayaquil, to consolidate and to extend the revolution in the southern provinces and 'to incorporate them in the republic of Colombia'.[62] A few months before his appointment O'Leary saw Sucre for the first time in Cúcuta and asked Bolívar who the poor horseman was. 'He is one of the best officers in the army,' he replied. 'He combines the professional knowledge of Soublette, the good nature of Briceño, the talent of Santander, and the energy of Salom. Strange as it may seem, no one knows him or even suspects his abilities. I am determined to bring him into the light, convinced that one day he will be my rival.'[63]

Carabobo

The armistice did not last six months. On 28 January 1821 Maracaibo revolted against Spain and declared its independence with republican connivance. Bolívar sought to pacify La Torre with sophistries, arguing that Maracaibo had liberated itself, which it was entitled to do, and Colombian troops had therefore occupied a free nation, not subject to Spanish jurisdiction.[64] The Spaniard was no fool, neither was he a warmonger; he did not have the authority to accept Bolívar's ultimatum of war unless peace and independence were negotiated. Bolívar regarded the lull as a means of rearming and gaining ground. And in April he prepared to move, as a true liberator: 'This war will not be to the death, nor even a normal war. It will be a holy war, a struggle to disarm the enemy not to destroy him.'[65]

The Carabobo campaign was important not only for the defeat of the Spaniards but also for the further integration of the caudillos into a national army. Republican forces from the *llanos*, the Andes and Maracaibo, over-coming obstacles of distance, terrain and supplies, converged upon the valley of Aragua, while Bermúdez advanced towards Caracas from the east in a diversionary tactic. As divisional commanders, they led their troops out of their homelands to serve under a commander-in-chief whom they had so often repudiated in the past. To bring the republican army to its most effective position at the right time in the course of June 1821 – this marked the true progress in organization and discipline, the direct result of the military reforms of Bolívar. As the army advanced in search of its adversary, from his base at San Carlos Bolívar organized it into three divisions: the first commanded by General Páez, the second under General Cedeño, and the third in reserve commanded by Colonel Plaza. General Mariño served on the General Staff of the Liberator himself. Bolívar described this army as 'the greatest and finest ever to bear arms in Colombia on any battlefield'.[66] But these great troop movements had their price. Out of an anticipated 10,000, Bolívar took the field with only 6,400; the rest were in hospitals in Mérida, Trujillo and Barinas, victims of marches and malaria before the battle began. 'A bottomless sack,' was Bolívar's other description of the army. His soldiers inspired unease as well as pride, especially the *llaneros* and their leader Páez:

> These are men who have fought for a long time; they believe that they deserve much, yet they feel humiliated and frustrated, and they have lost hope of gathering the fruit of what they have won by their lances. They are resolute, ignorant *llaneros*, who have never regarded themselves the equals of other men with more knowledge and better appearance. I myself, their leader for so long, still do not know of how much they are capable. I treat them with great consideration; yet even this is not enough to inspire in them the confidence and frankness which should exist among comrades and compatriots. You can be sure that we are over an abyss, or rather a volcano that is about to erupt. I fear peace more than war.[67]

Post-war society – and its leaders – already cast a shadow, even in the year of victories.

O'Leary, who was on the staff, left an outline of the basic strategy on that day of triumph, 24 June 1821.[68] Avoiding a frontal attack, which the royalist general was expecting, Bolívar sent Páez and a force of Colombian infantry to the left along a narrow defile exposed to enemy fire, with instructions to gain possession of the heights and fall upon the right, and weakest, flank of the royalist army. Slashing their way through the undergrowth with machetes, the patriots gained the heights in heavy fighting and with heavy casualties; an attack from the leading Apure battalion had to be backed up with a bayonet charge by the British battalion, and support from two companies of the Tiradores. 'A small party of thirty of us,' reported a British officer, 'charged bayonets on the left flank, against above one hundred of the enemy; finding what was coming they retired in confusion.'[69] Once the heights had been won and the Colombian divisions were through the defile, they descended to the plain; the cavalry charged and put the royalists to flight and their infantry was also pushed back. The retreat was orderly, not a rout. Nevertheless, whole battalions surrendered and only one succeeded in reaching Puerto Cabello. The royalist commander, La Torre, subsequently thanked Bolívar for his humane treatment of royalist prisoners, a far cry from the war to the death.[70]

Both sides suffered heavy losses, the royalists over a thousand, the republicans many more than the two hundred reported by Bolívar; and the republicans lost the most in leaders and officers. General Cedeño fell in battle. Colonel Plaza, Bolívar's rival in love, lost his life and Bernardina the man of her choice. The

British Legion, going into battle 350 strong, lost eleven officers and ninety-five men. Bolívar singled them out as saviours of his country, renamed them the 'Batallón Carabobo' and decorated every survivor with the Order of the Liberators.[71] Páez was promoted to general-in-chief on the field. And Mariño was left as commander-in-chief of the army, while Bolívar and Páez set off for Caracas.

Pockets of royalist resistance were then overcome at Maracaibo and Coro; Cartagena, long the greatest fortress of Spain in America, surrendered on 1 October, Cumaná on 16 October; on 10 November Puerto Cabello surrendered and on 11 November Santa Marta fell to the republicans. Panama declared its independence as part of Colombia on 28 November, a strategic acquisition as Bolívar appreciated, preventing Spain from using the isthmus to supply its territories in Pacific South America. Thus the whole of the Caribbean coast was freed, and the Liberator's first objective secured. Now, Pasto in the south was the only province of New Granada in royalist control.

Bolívar entered Caracas on 29 June. The streets had been deserted until news of Carabobo had been confirmed, then suddenly everyone poured out to welcome the capital's most famous son, the Liberator, the *Padre de la Patria*, after an absence of seven years. Crowds besieged his house until midnight and all through the following days while he was busy organizing civil affairs and enforcing the surrender of La Guaira. On the way back to Valencia he could not resist visiting his San Mateo estate, the favourite of all his properties, home of his childhood and early adult life, and there reliving the ways of the plantation. 'Of the thousand slaves he possessed before the revolution he found only three, whom he immediately freed.'[72] Who knows what his assets were now? His private affairs were in disorder and he paid himself only modest sums from the state, declining to cash his real salaries. Like his army, he was seriously underpaid, a landed aristocrat but no longer wealthy. After a further brief visit to Caracas, he departed his homeland to take the revolution beyond its borders. He was not only a Venezuelan. He was president of Colombia and a liberator with further freedoms to win. He left his respected colleague Carlos Soublette as vice-president of Venezuela. But real power lay with Páez, leader of the *llaneros*, hero of Carabobo, one of the idols of Venezuela, who was inevitably given military command of the province. Bermúdez and Mariño were also appointed to high office, as the military caudillos entered their inheritance.

In the aftermath of Carabobo, Bolívar's satisfaction was tempered by his awareness of post-war political problems. He despaired of Venezuela: 'This is chaos; it is impossible to do anything good here, because the good men have disappeared and the bad have multiplied. Venezuela presents a picture of a people suddenly emerging from prolonged lethargy and no one knows what its condition is, what it ought to do, and what it is.'[73] One thing he knew: if Venezuela were to organize itself peacefully, it was essential to satisfy and to co-opt the caudillos. This he did in two ways: he gave them regional appointments and granted them land.[74]

On 16 July 1821 Bolívar issued a decree which in effect institutionalized caudillism. In the west he established two politico-military regions, one for Páez, the other for Mariño.[75] The eastern provinces he assigned to Bermúdez. Overtly all three were equal, and the country so divided into departments entered into the republic of Colombia on the same footing as other provinces. But from the start, the government of Páez enjoyed hegemony, and from regional caudillo Páez became a national hero, indisputable military and political leader of Venezuela. Established in the country's socio-economic centre around Caracas, commander of what remained of a disciplined army, the soldiers of the *llanos* of Apure, Páez was well placed to impose his authority over the other military caudillos, attentive to the oligarchy who surrounded him and the masses who idolized him. It was one of the supreme ironies of Bolívar's life that Caracas, his birthplace and first choice for liberation, was taken over by the man appointed by him and so given the means to assert his independence and to take Venezuela out of Colombia, Bolívar's own creation. Meanwhile, they had to cooperate, but their relationship continued to be one of convenience rather than trust. Having won the war in Venezuela, Bolívar had no alternative but to leave the new state to the caudillos while he moved on to supervise the constitutional settlement of Colombia and take the revolution to the south.

Bolívar's acceptance of the warlords in Venezuela exemplified the sense of realism and readiness to work with the inevitable that was a conspicuous quality of his leadership. In these years of glory from Angostura to Boyacá and onwards to Carabobo, many aspects of his authority were on display, as soldier, politician and statesman. Above all he had shown why people, even recalcitrants, would follow him through marches, battles, disputed constitutions and risky policies. Of all the makers of the revolution, he was the leader with the most powerful sense of purpose who could impose his will on others. His leadership had been tested and found solid. But he had never believed that revolution was the final goal or liberty an end in itself. He also wanted justice. In the closing words of his address to the congress of Angostura he professed a vision of a new world where the rule of law would prevail and equality and freedom triumph, and he commended two measures as his personal priorities: the absolute freedom of the slaves and the distribution of national property to the soldiers of the revolution. Social justice – this was the next challenge of the revolution.

Chapter 7

SOCIETY ACCORDING TO BOLÍVAR

Rousseau in Retreat

Leadership could win campaigns and deliver liberation, and in northern South America Bolívar was supreme leader. But the work of one man could not in itself transform society or reorder the economy. Bolívar might dominate events but not conditions. Amidst post-war turbulence he never ceased to identify needs, project policies or consider solutions. But people's lives were conditioned by the societies and economies in which they found themselves and which the war had not basically changed, except, perhaps, for the worse. Moreover, solutions were canvassed not only by Bolívar but by a multitude of politicians, interest groups and rivals, with whose opinions he more often than not disagreed. As peace loomed his forebodings grew.

The government of the republic moved from Angostura to Cúcuta in early 1821 and made preparations for a congress to endow the new state of Colombia with a constitution. After the death of the vice-president, Juan Germán Roscio, and of his successor, Luis Eduardo Azuola, Bolívar appointed Antonio Nariño, a known centralist and unitarist and recently returned from his prison exile in Spain, as provisional vice-president to preside over the congress, which met from 6 May to 14 October. Bolívar trusted Nariño; he was a soldier fit to govern a 'military republic' at a time when Colombia, 'far from being a social body is a military camp'.[1] The anti-centralists were also represented, those who saw federalism as more democratic, more republican, a greater guarantee of liberty and a firmer restraint on the executive. These were not only provincial opinions; some interests at the centre were also federalist, unwilling as they were to carry the weight and costs of the provinces, while civilian Cundinamarca had the further fear of domination by the Venezuelan military.

Bolívar's views on these matters were well known – strong central government was the only way to secure independence and the only way to constrain the social anarchy which independence released. Shortly before the battle of Carabobo, surrounded by soldiers who were already causing him some disquiet, he turned his gaze on the politicians in Cúcuta. He spoke with scorn of the 'delirium' of those who favoured federation: politicians and lawyers who believed that their opinion was the will of the people and who would go to such extremes that they would have to be banished from Colombia, as were the poets from Plato's republic:

> In fact in Colombia the people are the army, those who have actually liberated the country from the tyrants; these are the people who choose, the people who act, the people who determine. The rest of the population are inert, either malign or patriotic, with no right to be more than passive citizens. We will have to develop this policy, which certainly does not derive from Rousseau, otherwise these gentlemen will again be our ruin. They believe that Colombia is filled with simpletons huddled around the firesides of Bogotá, Tunja and Pamplona. They have not bothered to notice the Caribs of the Orinoco, the herdsmen of the Apure, the seamen of Maracaibo, the boatmen of the Magdalena, the bandits of Patía, the ungovernable people of Pasto, the Guajibos of Casanare, and all the savage hordes from Africa and America who roam like wild deer in the wilderness of Colombia. Don't you think, my dear Santander, that these legislators, ignorant rather than malicious and presumptuous rather than ambitious, are leading us on the road to anarchy, and from there to tyranny, and always to ruin? I am sure of it. And if the *llaneros* do not bring us down, the philosophers will.[2]

The Bolivarian message, dictated with typical irony, was consistent. Authority was needed to tame Colombians and to counteract their want of social homogeneity; those who opposed the message were a danger to the state and would have to be marginalized. He realized that this was a far cry from Rousseau, whose works were still among his favourite reading and to whom he nominally deferred. Bolívar was always concerned to protect his cultural image and to be known as a man of the Enlightenment, even as he retreated from some of the Enlightenment's basic ideas; the alternative would be obscurantism and a blow to his vanity. Who wants to appear illiberal? Who will abandon the mentors of a lifetime? So he continued to read and to quote Rousseau, a Bolivarian Rousseau, interpreted by him, not by American philosophers and legislators, who did not understand that liberalism had to acclimatize to American conditions. The liberalism of Bolívar was based not only on values but also on calculations. In making policy decisions he did not automatically reach for the political model of the Enlightenment but looked at specific situations.

Cúcuta appeared to give Bolívar the legal framework he sought but it fell short of the strong government he considered essential.[3] His own constitutional ideas from Angostura, the hereditary senate, the moral power, did not convince the legislators at Cúcuta, but he kept his peace and expressed his reservations discreetly. When the bells rang to celebrate the constitution he remarked, 'They are tolling for Colombia.' The Constitution of 12 July 1821 created a strongly centralist state, a greater Colombia, comprising Venezuela, New Granada and, potentially, Quito, united under a single government with its capital in Bogotá, and subdivided not into three regions but into a number of departments, headed by intendants, in effect the immediate agents of the executive. This was roughly what Bolívar wanted, but it was an elitist project imposed by the few on the many, who were not consulted, and it left questions of national identity unresolved.

Ultimate authority resided in the legislature, made up of a senate and house of representatives, chosen by electoral colleges voted in by those citizens who had the franchise; this was restricted to literates who had real property valued at a hundred pesos. The president, who was also commander-in-chief of the armed forces, was elected for four years, with the possibility of re-election for a second term. But his authority was limited except in the case of foreign invasion or domestic disorder, when he could assume complete power. Always ready with words, Bolívar remarked that 'the government of Colombia was either a gentle stream or a devastating torrent'. The constitution embodied the classic freedoms; the judicial power was absolutely independent of the executive and the judges were almost impossible to remove. It was also mildly reformist: it abolished the Indian tribute and gestured towards abolition of slavery, though what this meant in practice remained to be seen.

On 7 September congress elected Bolívar, the victor of Carabobo and the liberator of two countries, as first president of Colombia, with Santander as vice-president. Bolívar was sick of being denounced as a usurper, tyrant and despot, and he claimed no great administrative talent. So he disavowed any ambition to be president and had already suggested the nominations of Nariño, Urdaneta or Santander (in order of age); and 'if to my regret, they insist on nominating me, I will always be absent from the capital, or always ill'.[4] Against the insistence of his friends he protested that he was not qualified for government: 'You tell me that history will say great things about me. I believe that it will say nothing was greater than my renunciation of power and my absolute dedication to the arms that could save the government and the country. History will say, "Bolívar took over the government to free his countrymen, and when they were free he left them so that they would be ruled by law and not by his will." That is my answer.'[5]

But when he was informed that congress unanimously re-elected him to the presidency he travelled to Cúcuta to take office and to preside over a constitution that had already been ratified. He still protested that he was a soldier, not an administrator, and that his future lay on the battlefield not in a government office, which would be 'a torture chamber' for him. He accepted 'only out of obedience', and on condition that he be authorized to continue the campaign of liberation as head of the army, leaving government to the vice-president, Santander. In his speech to congress on taking office he reaffirmed his convictions: 'I am a son of war, the man whom combat has raised to government. . . . A man like me is a dangerous citizen for a popular government, a threat to national sovereignty.' And carried away perhaps by his own eloquence he beseeched them to address him not as Liberator, but as 'good citizen'.[6]

Already the politicians, the lawyers and the military were sharpening their knives. Congress passed a further law granting Bolívar extraordinary powers to secure the liberation of territories still held by Spain. As disunity reared its ugly head Bolívar was glad to leave the government of Colombia to the capable, if grim, Santander, as the law allowed and his ambition dictated, and to resume his career as Liberator. That was where glory lay. And the road to glory was still open. In mid-December 1821 he left Bogotá and began his march to the south, through unfamiliar country and routes new to him: Tocaima, La Plata, Pedregal, across the Cordillera Central to Calí, then down to Popayán and Taminango, a world away from Venezuela and the Caribbean.

Continuity and Change

As Bolívar rode southwards, the peoples he left behind began to gather the fruits of victory. They were not a sweet mixture. Officers secured estates. Soldiers claimed land. Landowners retained slaves. Slaves wanted freedom. Creoles sought offices. *Pardos* demanded equality. Liberation released a flood of incompatible interests.

The transition from colony to nation had implications beyond the political. The destruction of life and property, the emergence of new leaders, the militarization of society, these events were a shock to the old colonial order and to relations between social groups. Society could not be immune to the liberal and egalitarian ideas of the age, and to modes of thought which rejected discrimination and sought to reconcile social differences in the interests of nation building. Legal distinctions between racial groups were now abolished, and new constitutions declared all citizens equal before the law. But the law was not the only agent of change. Probably more important was the trend towards a class as distinct from a caste society, as wealth became the principal criterion of social distinctions and status derived from income rather than legal definition. Standard of living also defined the classes. Those who could afford foreign luxuries, enjoy sumptuous meals and drink wines imported from Chile or even France did not hide their wealth. Meanwhile Bolívar cared for war widows and left poor relief to charity.

Possession of land was a crucial issue in the war of independence and a prime source of wealth and power thereafter. Government office, of course, was of great interest to the creoles, and in general they replaced the Spaniards in top bureaucratic posts and found new opportunities in government and politics. But the urban elite was not a strong force in the new nations. The withdrawal of the Spaniards, the commercial dominance of foreign entrepreneurs and the political importance of the new power base – the *hacienda* – all combined to reduce the power and wealth of the urban elite and to diminish the role of the cities. Political power would now be exercised by those who had economic power, and this was based on land, an asset that remained firmly in the hands of a relatively small group of creoles who began to mobilize labour even more effectively than their colonial predecessors. In effect, Bolívar presided over a ruralization of power in which his immediate collaborators played a leading role.

In the course of the war the composition of the creole elite was modified, as soldiers, merchants and adventurers, who profited from the hostilities and from the decisions of the sequestration tribunals, managed to turn themselves into landed proprietors. In Venezuela, where the colonial aristocracy was reduced both in numbers and importance, the great estates passed into the hands of a new creole and *mestizo* oligarchy, the successful warlords of independence. Leaders such as Páez, who acquired property that should in many cases have been allocated to the troops, frustrated Bolívar's attempt to distribute confiscated and national land to the common soldiers, whom he regarded as the people in arms. But this moderate mobility did not affect the agrarian structure. Indeed this was now extended into new areas. In the *llanos* republican rulers promoted private property rights of big ranchers, deprived the nomadic plainsmen of communal usages, and reduced them to the status of rural labourers.

Control over labour was now virtually absolute. The slave trade, it is true, was abolished in 1810 or soon after, but slave emancipation and abolition of slavery was a slow and difficult process. A law of manumission in 1821 lacked conviction and was more concerned to compensate owners than to free slaves. Thus little was done. Indeed further black revolts in Venezuela in 1824–7 and in Ecuador in 1825–6 prejudiced circumstances for emancipation. An increased wave of agitation, and the attempted revolt of the *pardo* Admiral Padilla, led even Bolívar to speak of the 'natural enmity of the people of colour'. In the face of the class interest of the administrators of manumission and of the widespread refusal to pay the taxes necessary to compensate slave owners, manumission was restricted to a slow and partial system, in which scores rather than hundreds were freed each year.

Indians in a sense were emancipated, for they were now free citizens and released from the payment of tribute. In Colombia the Indians were a large minority, socially and culturally outside the national life; they had little interest in independence and took little part in the struggle, unless they were coerced into the armies of one side or the other. A few Indian groups were royalists, notably in the regions of Santa Marta and Pasto, where they responded to Spanish prompting. There were Indians who reportedly wept when they heard that the king was gone, sensing, perhaps, that they had lost a protector. Pockets of unconquered Indians simply wanted to be left alone. The degrading colonial practice of publicly whipping Indians as a punishment may have ended, but demands for personal services and expectation of obedience did not automatically end with independence.[7] After the war liberal legislators sought to make the Indians independent individualists, instead of protected subjects of the crown, to transfer community land to private ownership, preferably Indian ownership. Legislation in itself, of course, could not abolish Indian communities, which had their own mechanisms of survival. And community land was often protected in effect by the stagnation of commercial agriculture in the decades immediately after independence. But once demographic and market pressures increased, and Spanish America became more closely integrated into the international economy, then it would be found that the Indian communities had been stripped of their defences and abandoned to the encroachment of the *hacienda*.

While the prospects of blacks and Indians were little enhanced by independence, those of the mixed races were hardly better. In Venezuela the *pardos*, or *mulattos*, were the most numerous sector of society, about half of the population, and they came out of the war relatively stronger than other sectors. During the war in Venezuela population growth was reversed, declining from around 800,000 on the eve of independence to little more than 700,000 in 1825.[8] The white population diminished through casualties and emigration, and after the war the elite groups were at an even greater demographic disadvantage. The *pardos* now demanded freedom from traditional restraints which law and society imposed on them, and sought opportunities hitherto reserved for creoles. Many of Bolívar's officers were *pardos* and two of the most senior, Piar and Padilla, led revolts against him.[9] It was in the upper ranks of the *pardos* that frustration was most acute and the struggle for equality most insistent. Some of them were successful, and these gained access to education, offices and social status. The British consul in Maracaibo noted that 'The first officers, and leading men, civil and military, are of this class.'[10] An example of a successful *pardo* was Judas Tadeo Piñango, whom Sir Robert Ker Porter, the British consul in Caracas, described as 'an almost black – a sort of Sambo Indian', who married a white woman of Bogotá, reached the rank of General and became a member of the State Council.[11] Men of this rank came to have a vested interest in the revolution and were gravely suspicious of any constitutional change – towards monarchy, for example – that might revive their former status.

The racists of the time poured scorn on these developments. Level de Goda, a former royalist official, denounced the *pardo* leaders for constituting, in alliance with the traditional whites, a new elite that ruled independent Venezuela. The leader of this oligarchy was Páez, 'who is a *pardo* and an inveterate criminal'.[12] The son of Páez, who was at West Point, wrote home to say that he and his two brothers were being called '*mulatos*' in the United States, and his father was being called a '*mulato*' in the Philadelphia press – 'a terrible blow for me'.[13] Páez himself, in his writings at any rate, did not make a great thing about race or colour. He claimed to stand for equality: 'For the man of talent, whatever his origin, colour is neither here nor there, but simply a matter of chance.'[14] The social structure was another matter. Páez supported and conformed to the prevailing order, though this was hardly to the benefit of the *pardo* masses. He was as sensitive as any of the elite to the problems of law and order in Venezuela, and he was merciless to slave insubordination.

While there was a degree of social mobility in Venezuela, the mass of the *pardos* were not in a position to profit from it. In numbers alone they were indispensable to the creoles in the war of independence, and in the army they gained some promotion. They also gained legal equality, for republican laws abolished all external signs of discrimination and recognized only one class of citizens. But the new rulers confined voting rights and therefore full citizenship to property-owners, so that inequality came to be based not on law but on wealth. Equality before the law, assurance of civil rights, these were not enough for the *pardos*. As Bolívar pointed out, they wanted absolute equality of opportunities. And this was only the beginning. Next, he warned, they would demand political access, and, more than this, political power leading to rule over whites. Bolívar thought that this was inevitable, for the revolution stopped short of the *pardos* and the fruits of victory were reserved for others. There was a climate of unrest. Seeing the landed oligarchy advancing through independence while they were left behind, the *pardos* fought back and struggled for a further stage of revolution. In the 1820s the threat of *pardocracia* appeared real enough to Bolívar, and he believed that a war of races was a distinct possibility. In the late 1820s Valencia, Barcelona and Cumaná were scenes of *pardo* disaffection, evidence of a high degree of group consciousness and readiness to use violence. In 1827, when Bolívar was in Venezuela, there was an insurrection of blacks in Cumaná and Barcelona, where their numbers were increasing through immigration from Haiti; they received short shrift from the Liberator, though many survived to fight another day. In December 1830 a black was arrested for trying to subvert troops, saying 'that Venezuela ought to become a Second Hayti. That all the whites ought to be murdered, and that he had a strong band of blacks, who would aid them in the execution of this glorious task.'[15]

A substantial part of the *pardo* population worked in the rural sector. Some were already enlisted in plantation production and performed various tasks on the *hacienda*. But many had so far escaped peonage and did not form part of the labour force. Some worked in subsistence agriculture; many more found a life for themselves in the cattle economy of the *llanos*; and not a few survived on the margin of the agrarian sector, living by banditry and crime. Independence gave a new impetus to land concentration, as the victorious caudillos competed for *haciendas* in the centre north and powerful ranchers sought to establish yet greater private property rights in the *llanos*. Landowners observed a great mass of free and unemployed rural dwellers, and decided that the time had come to herd them into plantations and ranches, mobilize them for production and pay them minimal wages. Páez decreed a new 'law of landowners and ranchers in the *llanos*' (25 August 1828). This continued the policy of vindicating private property announced by the First Republic; it prohibited transit through estates without permission of owner or manager, and made rights over wild cattle depend on ownership of land.[16] Thus the *llaneros* were tamed and brought within the agrarian structure of the rest of the country, beyond the reach of the Liberator.

For the mass of the *pardos* independence was, if anything, a regression. Political mobilization ended with the end of the war. Social mobility had been a Spanish policy, against the protests of the creoles. Now the creoles were in power, the new elite. In the 1830s, in the aftermath of independence, the population of Venezuela was under 900,000, about half of whom were *pardos* and free blacks, over a quarter were whites, while slaves numbered about forty thousand. Among the whites there was a super-elite of some ten thousand people – landowners, rich merchants and their families and kinship groups – who constituted the privileged class, monopolizing power and institutions from the presidency down to the *cabildos*. Where they did not own land they controlled offices, and they prolonged the wartime establishment of higher military appointments which became mere sinecures. In default of legitimate ways of advance, disaffected *pardos* had recourse to protest and rebellion and became a danger to creole government, prone to manipulation by caudillos or recruitment by brigands. In the years around 1830, Bolívar's fears were realized, as black resentment erupted into sporadic violence in Venezuela. This was the volcano of which he spoke.

Bolivarian Society

Bolívar conceived the American revolution as more than a struggle for political independence. He saw it also as a great social movement, which would improve as well as liberate, and would respond to the radical as well as the liberal demands of the age. He sought strong government as an instrument of reform, capable of improving people's lives. Bolivarian reformism operated within existing structures and did not attempt to advance beyond what was politically possible. Nevertheless it set new goals for post-colonial society.

Bolívar was an abolitionist, though he was not the first in Venezuela. The republican conspiracy of Gual and España in 1797 proposed that 'slavery be immediately abolished as contrary to humanity', while linking abolition with service in the revolutionary militia and employment by the old master. The support of the Enlightenment was purely theoretical. From Montesquieu onwards the *philosophes* denounced slavery as useless and uneconomical as well as evil, but they did not make a crusade of abolition. No doubt Bolívar was also aware of contemporary movements in England and France, inspired as they were by humanitarian ideals and religious convictions. But his prime inspiration seems to have been an innate sense of justice. He regarded it as 'madness that a revolution for liberty should try to maintain slavery'. Yet his attempts to obtain legislation enforcing the absolute abolition of slavery throughout Colombia were not successful. He liberated his own slaves, first on condition of military service in 1814, when about fifteen accepted, then unconditionally in 1821 when over a hundred profited.[17] Few *hacendados* followed his example.

Bolívar continued to argue that the creole rulers and property-owners must accept the implications of the revolution, that the example of freedom was 'insistent and compelling', and that the republicans 'must triumph by the road of revolution and no other.'[18] But the delegates at Angostura were afraid to release ill-prepared slaves into free society, and contented themselves with a pious declaration on behalf of freedom for slaves while leaving the means to a future congress.[19] The policy of freedom in return for military service continued, but after 1819 proprietors tended to abandon wartime manumission, small though this had been. Yet the problem would not go away, and Bolívar realized that it was impossible to return to pre-war conditions, that it could no longer be a question of resisting slave expectations but of controlling and directing them. In 1820, when he was reinforcing the army after Boyacá, Bolívar ordered a reluctant Santander to recruit five thousand slaves in western New Granada. Santander argued that in Choco and Antioquia the slaves belonged not to the royalists but to '*familias afectas al sistema*', and that the mines depended on slave labour. Bolívar insisted: as president he had the power to call up slaves, who thereby gained their freedom; slaves were needed to fill the ranks and were fit for combat conditions. Invoking Montesquieu on the essential link between political liberty and civil liberty, he argued that left in a free society without freedom for themselves, the slaves would be dangerous and prone to rebellion:

> It is a political maxim drawn from history that any free government that commits the absurdity of maintaining slavery is punished by rebellion and in some cases by extermination, as in Haiti: . . . What is more appropriate or just in the acquisition of liberty than to fight for it? Is it right that only free men should die for the emancipation of the slaves? Is it not expedient that the slaves should acquire their rights on the battlefield, and that their dangerous numbers should be reduced by a process that is both effective and legitimate? In Venezuela we have seen the free population die and the slaves survive. I do not know whether this is politic, but I do know that unless we recruit slaves in Cundinamarca the same thing will happen again.[20]

Santander grudgingly complied, though there was opposition from mine-owners and agriculturalists in Cauca. Bolívar's stark statement subsequently disturbed liberal opinion, but he chose his words carefully and based his policy on existing law, which he himself had introduced for the benefit of slaves, and whose political philosophy he derived from Montesquieu. The Liberator was not a slave-driver and never a racist.

The congress of Cúcuta passed a complex law of manumission (21 July 1821), allowing for liberation of adult slaves, but it lacked teeth and depended for its operation on compensation financed from taxes, including death duties, levied on property-owners. These proved difficult to collect.[21] The Cúcuta law also provided for the freeing of all children subsequently born to slaves, on condition that each child worked for his mother's owner until the age of eighteen, thus postponing any real abolition; all slaves born after 1821 had to wait eighteen years to obtain freedom, a period extended to twenty-one years by the Venezuelan congress in 1830. And it soon emerged that even slaves opting for military service gained freedom only if their owners were indemnified from the manumission funds. Thus was Bolívar's vision mocked and liberation thwarted by fear of economic and social consequences, and by laws weighted in favour of proprietors. O'Leary observed that the law of 1821 'did not satisfy Bolívar, who at all times pleaded for the absolute and unconditional abolition of slavery'. He cited his message (14 July 1821) urging congress to go further: children henceforth born of slaves should be free and congress, 'authorized by its own laws, should decree the absolute freedom of all Colombians'.[22] But Bolívar alone could not realistically overcome the obstacles to abolition. His decree of 28 June 1827 reorganized the administration of the law and included humanitarian measures on behalf of slaves, but it did not basically improve the situation or bring abolition nearer. Some observers believed that in 1827 Bolívar came to an agreement with Venezuela's rulers not to insist on abolition.[23] But the last word of Bolívar on slavery is to be found not in a decree but in a constitution, that constitution which he regarded as Spanish America's last hope for peace and stability. The Bolivian Constitution declared the slaves free, and although in Bolivia itself the slave owners contrived to evade his intentions, his commitment to absolute abolition was uncompromising. Slavery, he declared, was the negation of all law, a violation of human dignity and of the sacred doctrine of equality, and an outrage to reason as well as to justice.[24] This was a policy based on values and more advanced than that of Páez and the landowners of Venezuela, where slavery was not abolished until 1854.

The Indians of Colombia and Peru, unlike the blacks and *pardos*, were not central to Bolívar's preoccupations, but he was affected by their condition and determined to improve it. His view of Indians in Venezuela was pragmatic, to say the least. He regarded them as good material for military recruitment. 'The more savage the Indians are the less they are missed for agriculture, industry, and so for society, yet their savagery does not prevent them making good soldiers. . . . In general the natives contribute nothing to production and this race has suffered less from the war than others.'[25] In most respects, however, his Indian policy conformed closely to the principles of contemporary liberalism, designed as it was to hispanicize Indians and individualize community land. But there was an element of improvisation in Bolívar's Indian policy which is difficult to reconcile with particular doctrines. The congress of Cúcuta issued a law (11 October 1821) abolishing the tribute and all unpaid labour services, and making the Indians subject to the same taxes as other citizens. Application of the law was delayed in Ecuador, for tribute from the Indian majority was regarded as too important for the war effort in Peru to be relinquished. In any case, Andean Indians did not automatically volunteer to relinquish the tribute or welcome its abolition. They often saw payment of tribute as proof of entitlement to land and a historic defence against attacks on their agrarian property, the yield of which enabled them to pay the tribute. This was not always understood in government circles: a complacent report from Ecuador in 1825 believed that 'the stupidity and degradation of the Indians has reached the point that they regard it as a mark of honour to pay tribute'.[26]

Bolívar decreed (20 May 1820) the restoration of all *resguardo* (reservation) land in Cundinamarca to the Indians and the distribution to each family of 'as much land as it can easily cultivate'; surplus land was to be leased out by auction and the income applied to payment of tribute and teachers' salaries. Indians were not to be employed without a formal wage, and priests in particular were warned to stop demanding parish fees, from which Indians were exempt, and other 'scandalous practices contrary to the spirit of religion'. In the following months he received a series of complaints from Indians that, far from benefiting from the decree, they were defrauded of their rightful property and banished to marginal lands. By a further decree of 12 February 1821, Bolívar confirmed his previous order, insisting on the restoration of *resguardos* to the Indians and the distribution to them of 'the richest and most fertile land'.[27] After that he could only rely on legislators and hope for the best. The Cúcuta law of 11 October 1821 ordered the liquidation of the *resguardo* system; it declared the Indians 'restored' to their rights, and assigned *resguardo* land hitherto held in common to individual families in full ownership; this was to be done within five years.[28] It was hoped that the Indians would become good property-owners, agriculturalists and taxpayers. But the state did not have the means or the will to supply the infrastructure of agrarian reform, and it succeeded only in disrupting Indian community labour and organization that had depended on communal ownership, and soon the *resguardos* came to be irretrievably alienated. The losers from this legislation were the Indians. The winners were the great landowners of the valleys of Caracas and Aragua, and those of New Granada, who managed to acquire much of this land for their own estates.

Bolívar sought to use his power in Peru from 1823 to inject further social and agrarian content into the revolution. His object here, as in Colombia, was to abolish the system of community landholding and to distribute the land to the Indians in individual ownership. There was a previous model for such legislation in a scheme inspired by the Spanish Cortes of 1812 and formulated by Viceroy Abascal in 1814.[29] The plan was not put into effect, but it was evidently drawn from the same stock of liberal thinking that animated Bolívar ten years later. His decree of 8 April 1824, issued in Trujillo, was intended primarily to promote agricultural production and raise revenue, but it also had social implications, for it assumed that production benefited from extension of private property. The decree ordered that all state lands be offered for sale at one third of the price of their real value. These were not to include lands in the possession of Indians, who were to be declared proprietors, with right to sell or alienate their lands in any way they wished. The Indian community lands were to be distributed among the landless occupants, especially to families, who were to be entitled to full legal ownership of their portions. Bolívar insisted that 'no Indian should remain without his own land'.

This attempt to turn the Indian peasantry into independent farmers was frustrated by landlords, *caciques* and officials, and in the following year at Cuzco Bolívar was obliged to issue a further decree (4 July 1825), reaffirming and clarifying the first. This restored Indian land, confiscated after the anti-colonial rebellion of 1814, ordered the distribution of community lands, regulated the method of distribution to include irrigation rights, and declared that the right freely to alienate their lands should not be exercised until after 1850, presumably in the belief that by then the Indians would have made sufficient progress to enable them to defend their interests.[30] Bolívar supplemented these decrees with other measures designed, in the name of equality, to free the Indians from longstanding discrimination and ill treatment at the hands of officials, *caciques*, parish priests and landowners, and in particular from labour services and domestic duties imposed without a free contract for paid labour.[31] He also abolished the tribute, but this was not uniformly observed, some arguing that this took from the Indian a traditional protection, others that the Indians lost by fiscal equality. Curiously, when Bolívar restored the Indian tribute by decree of 15 October 1828 he explained that 'the indigenous people themselves prefer and many have requested to be allowed to make a personal contribution, exempting them from the charges and fees levied on other citizens'.[32]

The Indian decrees of Bolívar were limited in scope and misguided in intent. As the great *haciendas* already occupied most of the best land in Peru, these measures simply made the Indians more vulnerable, for to give them land without capital, equipment and protection was to invite them to become indebted to more powerful landowners, to surrender their land in payment, and to end up in debt peonage. And as the communities crumbled, the *haciendas* were waiting to sweep up the fragments of Indian society: the new policy gave them an added supply of cheap labour, while the colonial labour and tenancy forms, perpetuated by the republican regime, guaranteed Indian society's subordination. Bolívar's policy was not informed by deep understanding of Indian problems, only by what he saw as an outside observer infused with liberal ideals and passionate sympathy. 'The poor Indians are truly in a state of lamentable depression. I intend to help them all I can, first as a matter of humanity, second because it is their right, and finally because doing good costs nothing and is worth much.'[33] But doing good was not enough, or not well defined, and the humanitarian instincts of the revolution were not in themselves beneficial to Andean communities.

Citizen Soldiers

If the war of independence was a struggle for power it was also a dispute over resources. Creoles and caudillos fought for land as well as liberty. Bolívar was the first to acknowledge this and to provide economic incentive as well as political access. It was also necessary to find a substitute for a salary. His decree of 3 September 1817 ordered the confiscation by the state of all property and land of the enemy, Americans as well as Spaniards, to be sold in public auction to the highest bidder or, failing that, to be rented out on behalf of the national treasury. The property was used not only as an immediate income for the patriot government, but also as a source of land grants to officers and soldiers of the republic according to rank, promotion being regarded as a gauge of service. The decree of 10 October 1817 ordered land grants ranging in value from 25,000 pesos for a general-in-chief to 500 for an ordinary soldier.[34] The intention, as Bolívar put it, was 'to make of every soldier a property-owning citizen'. In his Angostura Address he reminded legislators that this was one of his principal priorities, to reward 'those who have experienced the depths of cruelty in a terrible war, who have suffered the most painful deprivations and the most bitter torments' and asked congress to confirm his policy.[35]

The caudillos and the higher officers were the first to benefit. One of the earliest grants, by special request of Bolívar to the National Land Commission, was that to General Cedeño, to enable him to establish a *hacienda* in the *sabanas* of Palmar.[36] Even those out of favour were among the first recipients. The congress of Angostura in December 1819 confirmed the award of cacao *haciendas* in Güiria and Yaguarapo to Mariño and Arismendi. These were properties confiscated from Spaniards. The government also granted certain old properties belonging to Spaniards to Urdaneta, Bermúdez, Soublette and others, most of whom had entered the war of independence without any kind of property. From 1821 the caudillos were pressing their claims for specific *haciendas* and lands directly on to the executive, which usually preferred to pass the requests on to the land tribunals. According to Soublette, now vice-president of Venezuela, 'The military are among the strongest and most insistent claimants to confiscated property. They have fought successfully and undergone horrific deprivation ... and it will be impossible to ignore them much longer.'[37]

Bolívar's plans for the troops, however, were blatantly ignored when not actively frustrated by the combined action of legislators and officers. Congress decreed that soldiers be paid not in actual land but in *vales*, vouchers entitling the holder to receive national land at a vague post-war date. Ignorant and impoverished soldiers were easy prey: the vouchers were bought up by officers and civilian speculators at minimal prices, sometimes at less than 5 per cent of the legal amount; and in this way most of the soldiers were defrauded of their right to land. Bolívar protested that his intentions were being mocked and demanded that congress should implement the original law by assigning the troops not vouchers but land.[38] Slowly and with great reluctance the congress of Cúcuta took measures to end the practice of issuing vouchers instead of land grants but, to Bolívar's fury, insisted on extending the scheme to officials. The *llaneros* in particular remained unsatisfied, 'humiliated and frustrated and without hope of gathering the fruit of what they have won by their lances'.[39] In mid-1821 they were put on indefinite unpaid leave. Soon there was robbery and unrest in the Apure, while the successful landowners began to organize and extend their interests.

Páez was the most successful of all the caudillos. Yet Páez had used land as a medium of mobilization very early in the campaign. 'When General Páez occupied Apure in 1816 he found himself alone in enemy territory, without help or prospects and without even the support of public opinion. He was therefore forced to offer his troops a free share in the properties belonging to the government of Apure. This was one of the most effective ways of retaining the support of the troops and attracting new recruits, as they all stood the same chance of gaining.'[40] This policy did not materialize, for Páez proved to be more interested in his own acquisitions than in those of his men.

Even before the end of the war in Venezuela, Bolívar delegated to Páez 'the right to redistribute national properties', which he himself had received from congress as president of the republic, though as exercised by Páez it was confined to the army of Apure and the territory under his jurisdiction. These special prerogatives were delegated by Bolívar out of frustration over the failure of previous attempts to redistribute land among the military.[41] Before distribution, however, Páez acquired the best properties for himself. His holdings were not restricted to the *llanos*, but extended into the centre-north, the region of valuable commercial plantations and homeland of the traditional oligarchy, where he began to acquire a number of prime properties. In 1825 he made an overtly generous offer to the vice-president of Colombia to sell the government his own estates in Apure, together with their cattle and horses, so that the troops could be granted the land they had been promised in lieu of wages.[42] But this gesture was purely demagogic: it was designed to improve his reputation as a *patrón* and retain the loyalty of his troops, while reserving the right to buy back the debt vouchers, which were the first – and often the only – stage of a land grant. Congress rejected the offer and Páez himself was criticized for building a private fortune by 'scandalous speculation' in the land vouchers of his officers and men.[43] These were the tactics of many caudillos, who offered the troops sums of money (sometimes fifty or sixty pesos for vouchers worth a thousand) in exchange for these land certificates, a notorious abuse that extended throughout Venezuela and New Granada.

The project had never been conceived as agrarian reform. But even as a means of paying wages it failed. According to Pedro Briceño Méndez, secretary of Bolívar and minister of war: 'None of those who have received their payments in the form of certificates actually possess them; all of these, or the greater part of them, have passed into other hands, the hands of profiteers who have paid the infamous price I have mentioned [5 per cent of true value].'[44] A new elite of landowners, rewarded from sequestered property or public land, joined the colonial proprietors and in some cases replaced them. But the soldiers who had not received their due complained bitterly about the operations of the land commissions. From east to west there were accusations of favouritism, inertia, inefficiency and class prejudice in the distribution of land. Mothers, sons and widows presented claims and complaints against the land and property committees: 'More than a third of the houses and estates of Venezuela have been confiscated, but not to help those who most deserve it and who have the greatest right to compensation.'[45] The troops and their dependants received nothing; the caudillos everything. Far from changing the agrarian structure, independence produced yet greater land concentration. Bolívar's hopes for his citizen soldiers vanished into the valleys and plains of Colombia.

Bolívar was acutely conscious of the polarization of society and of the great tensions engendered by social and political discrimination. It was because of this that he feared the resentment and the claims of the masses, the increase of *pardocracia* and the danger of new social convulsions. His own policy was not revolutionary. The abolition of slavery and the distribution of land were reformist measures which would have modified but not transformed existing structures. In practice he was not able to proceed beyond the elite along the road of reform for fear of a reaction, in which independence itself might have been threatened. Aristocrat by birth and breeding, he differed from his class in his awareness of the limitations of the republican revolution. In 1828 he described with unique insight the state of slavery in which the Colombian lower class still lived, subject to local mayors and magnates, and denied the human rights to which they were entitled:

In Colombia there is an aristocracy of rank, office and wealth, equivalent by its influence, pretensions and pressure on the people, to the most despotic aristocracy of titles and birth in Europe. Included in the ranks of this aristocracy are the clergy, the religious, the educated, the lawyers, the military and the rich. For although they speak of liberty and constitutions, they want these only for themselves, not for the people, whom they wish to see continue under their oppression. They also want equality, but by this they mean equality with the upper classes, not the lower. In spite of all their liberalism, they prefer to regard the lower classes as their perpetual serfs.[46]

The polarization of society between an oligarchy of landed proprietors and their lesser allies on the one hand and the rural masses on the other was the future prospect of Colombia, and in his most pessimistic moods Bolívar doubted the ability of constitutions to make any difference. The rural masses and their masters were not, of course, the whole of Colombia, whose population of over one million also included urban artisans, miners and groups in the middle of society. And the rural population itself comprised tenant farmers as well as labourers, stockmen as well as peons, Indians as well as *mestizos*. Independence perhaps accentuated these distinctions in offering new opportunities for differentiation within existing society. But it did not offer basic mobility or decrease the divisions which Bolívar described. He remained convinced that if the new ruling classes did not accept reforms they would be threatened by a mass movement from below. The escape route was to reduce poverty through economic growth, an elusive goal for one man.

The Bolivarian Economy

The vital spark of Bolívar's glory could not fire the economy. Independence was a prize that had to be paid for. In 1825–6 military expenses were still absorbing three quarters of the state's revenue. The conflict was damaging and left many *haciendas* in ruins, targets for confiscation and plunder during the war and for personal vendettas afterwards.[47] Production suffered and cattle diminished as rival armies dragged off peons and raided herds; in the post-war years *hacendados*, survivors from colonial families or newcomers profiting from land grants, still suffered from rural insecurity and a legacy of crimes, vagrancy, banditry and slave rebellion. Loss of slaves meant loss of invested capital at a time when the owner was probably struggling to pay the interest on his mortgage and facing foreclosure. The demographic effects of war, the human costs of liberation, impressed many observers as catastrophic: people perished in fighting and atrocities, or fled, hid, or migrated, causing population shifts which the government could not track, probably less serious in New Granada, where demographic growth continued towards the 1.1 million calculated for 1825, than in Venezuela, which was said to have lost a third of its population in the conflict.[48] Conscription uprooted the work force from fields and mines and caused a flight of peons, Indians and slaves whenever recruiting gangs drew near.

News of the approach of Bolívar was as likely to cause people to disappear as to join the cheering.

The British consul at La Guaira concluded: 'The expulsion of the European Spaniards in 1823, the previous emigration from this country [Venezuela], added to the excesses committed by the contending parties, and consequent decrease of population, has, in many instances, left extensive and valuable estates abandoned, and others only partially cultivated.'[49] By 1821 many plantations had been invaded not only by warring parties but by tropical vegetation. To renew cultivation more labour and capital were needed than were available in these years, at a time, moreover, when international prices for tropical products, especially for coffee, were steeply declining. Local agriculture, on the other hand, was still productive. The plains of Bogotá were well cultivated: farmers obtained two harvests a year and, with a good system of irrigation, excellent crops of wheat, barley and lucerne were produced. But ploughs, harrows and other agricultural implements were primitive, and there was still a great dependence on imported hardware.[50]

The war in Peru left the country prostrate; farms and plantations the victims of military destruction and diversion of labour.[51] The traditional prop of the economy and Peru's major exportable assets, gold and silver, were also depressed; mining production was hit by disruption of communications and by severe shortage of labour, mercury, mules and capital. Between 1819 and 1825 an estimated 26.9 million dollars were shipped from Lima in British ships, representing payments for imports – consumer goods and war materials – and flight of capital to safer outlets.[52] Inevitably Peru could not earn enough to pay for imports of manufactured goods, at a time when excited British businessmen swarmed in to provide goods and services. Captain Basil Hall R.N. noticed the impact of recent changes when he dined in a Peruvian home in Huacho: 'A roll of English broad-cloth was resting on a French wine case, marked Medoc; on the table stood a bottle of champagne; the knives and forks were marked Sheffield, and the screen which divided the apartment was made of a piece of Glasgow printed cotton.'[53] The trade gap was temporarily bridged by foreign borrowing, itself a lesson in profligacy.

Bolívar's economic thought favoured development within a new liberal framework, but his policy was frustrated by post-war conditions and by powerful interest groups. A stagnant agriculture and inadequate revenue were his major difficulties. The prime source of economic liberalism was Adam Smith, who argued that existing restrictions resulted in the wrong distribution of resources, that is, away from agriculture. He therefore advocated free trade and a general programme of economic liberalism to remove restraints on land and labour. A more immediate impetus to Bolívar's economic ideas was given by his own observation of the colonial economy and his opposition to the

Spanish monopoly: 'Do you wish to know what our future was? We were mere consumers, confined to the cultivation of indigo, grain, coffee, sugar, cacao and cotton; raising cattle on the empty plains; hunting wild game in the wilderness; mining in the earth to produce gold for the insatiable greed of Spain.'[54]

Experience and enlightenment coincided to produce in Bolívar a belief in agricultural development, free trade and the benefits of foreign investment. He was satisfied with a primary export role for Spanish America and was not unduly concerned for the survival of artisan industries or the achievement of economic self-sufficiency. But he was not a slave to economic liberalism and was never doctrinaire. He envisaged a larger and more positive role for the state than classical liberalism allowed, and to this extent he showed his awareness of the particular problems of underdevelopment. In the case of Colombia these were aggravated by a decade of destruction and feeble administration; he decreed the death penalty for officials found guilty of peculation, but in a port like Cartagena, where evasion of customs duties was reduced to a fine art by experienced importers and underpaid officials, this was not likely to impress.[55]

More positively, Bolívar expected state action to improve the infrastructure, especially in improving communications between regions. He had travelled many thousands of miles through valleys, plains and *páramos* in these countries without roads and had shared the heroic marches of his armies before battle had even begun. There were no carriage highways in Colombia, only bridle roads. Transport was primitive: land conveyance was confined to mules, water transport to canoes and barges; in the whole country there were no carriages and Bogotá had only two gigs.[56] The Magdalena River, the major route from north to south, was held in the grip of its notorious boatmen, the *bogas*, whom foreigners found drunken and quarrelsome and Colombians regarded as a law unto themselves.[57] There were other hazards: the fifteen-year-old son of the British consul was carried off by an alligator while swimming in the Magdalena and his distraught mother suffered a miscarriage.[58] River travel from Barranquilla to Mompós could take fifteen days and over thirty from Mompós to Honda, the port of debarkation for the capital. A monopoly contract was conceded to John Bernard Elbers, a Colombian of German birth, to establish steamboats on the river, but failure to provide feeder roads and fuel stations and the technical deficiencies of the boats themselves combined to reduce operations, and in 1829 the contract was cancelled. In Guayaquil Bolívar committed the revenue of the salt monopoly for road building, and he decreed protection and tax breaks for the construction of a road from the port of Esmeraldas to the interior in which the government would invest.[59] But independence made little difference to the infrastructure and to conditions of life and work, and Bolívar learned that he had to leave Colombians to improve their own lives without the use of modern technology and little help from the state.

War and revolution added further burdens to an already feeble economy. Drift of labour, loss of animals, flight of capital, all reduced Venezuela and New Granada to new levels of depression and added to the problems of planners. From first steps with the congress of Cúcuta, republican legislation guaranteed freedom of agriculture, industry and commerce to operate without monopoly and corporative restrictions, and the government confined itself to providing the conditions within which private enterprise could operate. This was the theory. In practice, laissez-faire had to be modified and the Bolivarian economy accepted a model of moderate protectionism. Agriculture needed protection and encouragement, first to secure import substitution, then to produce a surplus for export. Exports of cacao, cotton, tobacco and hides from Cartagena and Santa Marta were basically stagnant and had to be supplemented by gold and silver to earn returns for imports. Venezuelan exports of cacao, coffee, cotton, indigo and hides were supplemented by more lucrative export of horses, mules and cattle, for which there was a market in the British Caribbean.[60]

Bolívar urged congress to prohibit the export of livestock in order to build up the national herds. He decreed the prohibition of the export of horses and mules.[61] And while he was in Cuzco he forbade the slaughter of *vicuñas* and authorized state subsidies for those who gathered them into herds.[62] Bolívar also wanted to free agriculture from the heavy duties imposed by the colonial regime, and he decreed the removal of tithes and export taxes. The congress of Cúcuta abolished internal customs barriers, the *alcabala* and entails. But the fiscal system tended to revert to its colonial state as more taxes were restored to finance the war effort and the post-war administration. The *alcabala* was revived in 1826, and its reduction from 5 to 4 per cent in 1828 was regarded as a concession designed to make Venezuelan exports more competitive.[63] The alcohol *estanco*, abolished in 1826, was re-established in 1828, and the colonial tobacco monopoly continued as a major revenue until its abolition in 1850. It was clear to Bolívar that the surplus from agriculture, above all in the export sector, was not being reinvested in production. The tobacco revenue in particular was used as an all-purpose fund to meet an endless series of expenses. Bolívar was concerned that none of the profits of tobacco was being ploughed back into production. As his finance minister Rafael Revenga observed: 'Far from thriving, the revenue will suffer if, instead of the income being used to promote production, as the Liberator has so often and urgently ordered, it is diverted to expenditure elsewhere.'[64]

In the absence of domestic accumulation, Bolívar looked abroad, and he made it known that foreign capital, entrepreneurs and immigrants were welcome in the new republics. Few of these, however, were attracted to agriculture, and capital tended to concentrate in abortive mining projects. Bolívar had liberal ideas on immigration, and there were many colonization and land company projects in New Granada and Venezuela, but these foundered on the greed of entrepreneurs, who sought quick profits, and the reluctance of European immigrants to come as labourers. Immigration policy contained glaring contradictions, not all of Bolívar's making. There was already a mass of landless peasants and *llaneros* in Colombia, but the state failed to implement adequately Bolívar's cherished scheme of land distribution. The landowning class, on the other hand, or some of it, received the further advantage of agricultural loans from the government.

Independence ended the Spanish colonial monopoly, but foreign trade continued to be subject to restrictions, and there was nothing approaching true free trade. Colombia was not ready to fill a significant role in the world economy, though it was still an exporter of gold. There was a flurry of British trade and investment in Colombia in the 1820s, and British loans to the government in 1820, 1822 and 1824 provided welcome foreign exchange and stimulated trade with Britain. But the boom ended in 1826 when Colombia defaulted and reverted to colonial trade trends, depending on meagre gold exports for foreign imports. In these conditions there was no basis for national development and Colombia divided into a number of regional economies, each more or less self-sufficient and providing a basic, if primitive, living for its inhabitants.[65] A similar tale could be told for Peru. A loan of £1.2 million was contracted in London in 1822, from which the Peruvian government would receive less than £900,000.[66] A further loan for £616,000 was contracted in 1825, but the government fell into arrears in the same year and suspended interest payments. These loans were simply used for meeting previous obligations to British merchants and for financing military and naval expenditure, and there was no surplus for investment in development.

The state's revenue depended on the income from trade. The congress of Cúcuta sought to establish an income tax, but lack of reliable statistics on taxpayers and the failings of revenue officials crippled this experiment from the start, and it was dropped in 1826.[67] So foreign trade had to take the strain. The tariff of 1826 imposed duties ranging from 7½ per cent to 36 per cent on most imports; this was primarily a revenue tariff but it also had a protective content to satisfy national economic interests, and state monopolies were protected by prohibition of the import of foreign tobacco and salt. By 1830 import duties were higher than at the end of the colonial regime. There were also some export duties for revenue purposes, though the country's export trade was hardly flourishing enough to sustain them. Colombia's production pattern remained the same: the principal items were coffee, cacao, tobacco, dyewoods and hides, with sugar and cotton on a smaller scale. The agriculturalists of northern New Granada, like those of coastal Venezuela, demanded and received protection for their plantation products. But the weaker wheat producers of the interior were not so protected against United States flour. And all agricultural production suffered from lack of investment capital, shortage of labour, poor communications and low prices on the international market. In the province of Neiva, through which Bolívar travelled on his way south in 1822, vast tracts of excellent land lay uncultivated for want of labour.[68] Bolívar soon realized that the economic problems of independence were more intractable than the military.

The manufacturing sector was even more vulnerable than agriculture and offered little resistance to British competition. Industries such as textiles could simply not compete with the flood of cheaper foreign goods. Manchester and Glasgow supplied Colombia with cotton goods, France with silks and wines, and luxury articles of any kind also came from abroad.[69] In Popayán the elites could buy foreign goods and drink wine imported from Chile through Guayaquil and brought inland on mules. Independence did not destroy national industries or entirely remove the protection afforded by isolation and local preference, so in the south and around Quito a traditional manufacture of carpets, course cotton cloths, *ruanas* and gloves survived. But outside of this, Colombian industry now entered a period of crisis: particular victims were the textiles of Socorro and the wool industry of Boyacá.[70] And the survival of the *alcabala* hardly improved the market conditions for national manufactures. The result was a further expansion of imports, while exports were confined to a moderate output of gold and silver from New Granada and a small trade in plantation products, chiefly cacao, tobacco and coffee. The trade gap was bridged by the illegal export of precious metals and by foreign borrowings, the latter procured in adverse conditions, badly employed and unreliably serviced. This eventually led to a limitation of imports by natural process.

In these conditions there was some reaction against the early optimism of free trade opinion towards ideas of protection and state intervention, as could be seen in the thought of Juan García del Río and José Rafael Revenga, though protection in itself could do little for Colombia without the growth of consumers and the development of labour, capital and skill. Revenga, the economist most closely associated with Bolívar, attributed the decadence of industry in Venezuela to what he called 'the excessive import of many articles which were previously produced by poor families here. . . . Foreign soap, for example, has destroyed the various soap factories which we formerly had in the interior. And now we even take candles from abroad, retailed at eight per real, and the few that are still made in this country actually import their wicks from abroad. . . . It is notorious that the more we rely on foreign interests to supply our needs, the more we diminish our national independence and our reliance now even extends to daily and vital needs.' Revenga appreciated that Venezuela was not in a position to industrialize: 'Our country is essentially agricultural; it will develop mining before manufactures; but it must strive to diminish its present dependence on foreign powers.'[71] Bolívar was not unaware of the protectionist argument, coming as it did from Páez in Venezuela, manufacturers in New Granada and the textile industry of Ecuador. To some extent he responded. The tendency of his tariff policy was upwards, though higher duties had a revenue as well as a protectionist purpose. And in 1829 he prohibited the import of certain foreign textiles.

Bolívar's thinking, however, showed little sign of that nationalist reaction to foreign penetration that later generations expressed. While he rejected the Spanish economic monopoly, he welcomed foreigners who subscribed to open trade, who brought much-needed manufactured goods and entrepreneurial skills, and who acquired an interest in preserving independence. Bolívar wanted yet feared British protection, sought yet dreaded dependency. With a British alliance the new republics could survive; without it they would perish. By accepting British dominance, he argued, they could then grow strong and break free from it. 'We must bind ourselves soul and body to the English, to preserve at least the forms and advantages of a legal and civil government, for to be governed by the Holy Alliance would mean a rule by conquerors and a military government.'[72] His language became even more deferential. 'Politically,' he wrote, 'alliance with Great Britain would be a greater victory than Ayacucho, and if we procured it you may be certain that our future happiness is assured. The advantages that will result for Colombia, if we ally ourselves with that mistress of the universe, are incalculable.'[73] It made sense, of course, for a young and weak state to acquire a protector – and a liberal protector – against the Holy Alliance, especially as Britain itself had no political pretensions in Spanish America. But while it was expressed in political terms, dependence could also have an economic application.

Bolívar was prepared to invite a greater British economic presence in Latin America than later generations would find acceptable: 'Here [Peru], I have sold the mines for two-and-a-half million pesos, and I expect to obtain far more from other sources. I have suggested to the Peruvian government that it sell in England all its mines, lands, properties and other government assets to cover the national debt, which is at least 20 million pesos.'[74] British participation in the post-independence economies was considered essential and beneficial to both sides. The alternative, in Bolívar's view, was isolation and stagnation. This is not to say that he was complacent. He certainly saw the flaws in the Venezuelan economy and deplored the incipient trend towards monoculture. He believed that it was necessary to diversify production and to expand the range of exports. Venezuela depended too much, he argued, on coffee, the price of which declined inexorably throughout the 1820s and, in his view, would never improve; it should be substituted for more marketable products such as indigo and cotton. 'We must diversify or perish,' he concluded.[75] Bolívar accepted the bias towards primary exports and simply sought to make them yield better results. There was a place for Spanish America in the age of Industrial Revolution, though it was necessarily a subordinate place, exchanging raw materials for manufactured goods and fulfilling a role conforming to its stage of development. The conclusions of the British consul-general in Lima, a familiar figure to Bolívar, were discouraging but realistic:

> In Peru there is an especial call for the encouragement of commercial intercourse with foreigners; it has no manufactures of the slightest consequence; it is not likely to have any conducted by natives for many years from not possessing any one of the essentials for their establishment, nor is it desirable to promote them. The introduction, therefore, of every description of foreign manufactures is particularly important; the inhabitants in general are too poor to purchase commodities at high prices; fair trade will be the sure means of their obtaining them at low rates.[76]

This was classic free trade theory. Bolívar could have written it.

Chapter 8

WAR AND LOVE IN THE ANDES

Mountain Barriers

The next two years, 1822–4, would be critical for Bolívar, the fulfilment or the failure of his hopes. He was determined to take the revolution south to Peru. This, he believed, was his mission, the magnet that drew him on. After the victory of Carabobo, Santander had issued a proclamation in which he described Bolívar as the '*hijo predilecto de la gloria*'.[1] A generous tribute, 'very elegant' acknowledged Bolívar, who was already imagining his future in the south: 'But take care, my friend, that you first let me have 4,000 or 5,000 men, so that Peru may give me two brothers of Boyacá and Carabobo. I won't go if glory does not follow me, for I have reached the point in life when I could either lose my way or follow the path of glory. I do not intend to throw away the achievement of eleven years with a humiliation, nor do I want San Martín to see me in any other role than that of the *chosen son*.'[2] Since then his strategic thinking had undergone various changes and, as 1822 began, he had still not finalized his chosen route.

Bolívar had originally planned to liberate Panama after Venezuela, and then move south by sea to Guayaquil. After the liberation of Cartagena, however, Panama achieved its own bloodless revolution and had declared for independence on 28 November 1821. But the principal reason behind Bolívar's decision to move directly southwards was the fear that San Martín might reach Ecuador first and claim it for Peru. On 9 October 1820 Guayaquil had risen, overthrown the Spanish authorities and established a revolutionary *junta*. The Fundamental Law of Colombia (17 December 1819) had declared Quito part of Colombia. By the doctrine of *uti possidetis*, whereby the new states inherited the colonial administrative boundaries, this was correct, for the presidency of Quito had been subject to the viceroy of New Granada since 1740. But law was not the only weapon: 'The principal object of Bolívar was to make Guayaquil recognize the government of Colombia, by choice or by force.'[3] At the beginning of 1821 Bolívar sent General Sucre to Guayaquil with a thousand men to support the revolution against the royalist forces under General Melchor Aymerich and to win the rest of Ecuador for Colombia.[4]

In the south Sucre was trapped in a political labyrinth, thwarted not only by the royalists, who closed the road to Quito, but also by warring factions within Guayaquil, divided as it was between those who wanted independence from Colombia as well as from Spain and those who demanded union with Peru. But if Sucre needed the insurgents of Guayaquil, these needed Sucre and Colombia, so without mention of the status of Guayaquil an alliance was signed in May 1821. Sucre could now defend the coast and perhaps move inland: he skilfully fended off a two-pronged royalist attack from Quito, defeating one division and forcing the other to withdraw. But he still did not have the power to thrust through the highlands to Quito and a rash attempt to do so met with near disaster; on this front he was glad to accept an armistice in November 1821. Protected by the cordillera on the west, Quito was also impregnable from the north where royalist enclaves closed the mountain passes to the revolution.

Bolívar left Bogotá on 13 December 1821 and made his way south to penetrate this fortress. His original plan was to embark at the Pacific port of Buenaventura with two thousand of his best troops, to assume personal command in Guayaquil, and to strike inland from there. But news that two Spanish frigates were cruising in those waters, while the republic had no sea power in the Pacific to protect his transports, caused him to abandon this idea. He decided instead to move his headquarters from Cali to Popayán and to attack Quito from the north, while Sucre led the second line of strategy from the coast. Across Bolívar's path lay the highland province of Pasto, its Catholic and conservative beliefs preserved intact through isolation, its royalism as impenetrable as its mountains, and its hatred of republicanism encouraged by an angry bishop.[5] The creoles of Pasto calculated that they were more likely to gain the regional power they sought from the monarchy than from the republic, while the Indians in the surrounding mountains trusted the colonial officials they knew more than unknown newcomers.[6]

The approach to this frontier of the revolution was not auspicious and the Colombian La Guardia Division had to overcome the environment before the enemy. Bolívar's troops had already marched, some from as far away as Valencia, by plains and *páramos*, across mountain passes and river gorges, through severe differences of climate before staggering into Popayán more dead than alive and severely decimated by disease and desertion. In early March they left Popayán only three thousand strong and began a nightmare trek across the hot, barren, and pestilential wastes of Patía, infested by guerrillas descended from the fugitive slaves and *mulatto* bandits of colonial times, before reaching Taminango and then the rugged cliffs and raging waters of the Juanambú River. At that point Bolívar had two thousand men left. Could Pasto itself be worse? But could it be avoided? In an Andean landscape of high mountains and open *páramo* intersected by deep ravines, the road through the Pasto plateau was the only route from Popayán to Quito.

Bolívar dreaded the encounter. He found the Spanish army, the Church and the people ranged against him, and he delayed action. First, he tried to recruit the bishop of Popayán, Salvador Jiménez, '*un hombre muy político*' who had great influence over the minds of the people. Bolívar argued that the prevailing assumption of opposition between an anti-religious republic and a Catholic monarchy was no longer valid, that the liberal revolution in Spain was harmful to religion, while in America bishops were already accepting the republican cause. 'Everything has changed and you also must change.'[7] But the bishop was not for conversion. Bolívar then procured forged papers from an obliging Santander, claiming that Spain had now acknowledged Colombian independence; after an elaborate process of deception he presented 'these lies', as he called them, to the Spanish commander in Pasto as an inducement to give up the struggle.[8] The Spaniard was not deceived. A direct appeal to the *pastusos* was no more successful. 'Have no fear of us or of any punishment or vengeance, for we will treat you as friends and brothers,' he told them.[9] But they despised talk of peace.

Combat was his only option. Retreat would be an admission of defeat. On 7 April Bolívar decided to attack the royalist position on the rocky heights of Cariaco, throwing in battalion after battalion of his infantry against fierce resistance; the Rifles* were at the heart of the fighting, advancing upwards with bayonets drawn; and for their heroism they received the distinction 'First of the Guard'. Sheer persistence dislodged the enemy, but at a terrible cost in dead (116) and wounded (341), according to their own reckoning. Bolívar described this as '*un triunfo muy glorioso*', but the 'victory' of Bombná was in fact an extravagance, with life held cheaper than glory. The most that can be said of the Pasto campaign is that it divided the Spanish war effort while Sucre was at last making progress towards Quito.[10] Bolívar's health had suffered and he had to be carried away on a litter. He decided to recross the Juanambú and await reinforcements from Popayán.

By the end of May Bolívar had overcome two of the arms opposing him, the military and the clerical, but he had not won the minds of the people. For this reason he leaned heavily on the Bishop of Popayán not to emigrate and abandon his flock but to stay in Colombia and 'lead the faithful on the road

---

*The 1st Rifles, the British unit that had fought for Bolívar since 1818.

to heaven'.[11] The Spanish commissioners negotiated a capitulation, by which Pasto was exempted from taxes and military service, and officials were confirmed in their posts. The Indians were also included in the settlement, though they replied that they only wanted to continue paying the tribute.

Sucre, meanwhile, reinforced by a division from Peru under Colonel Andrés Santa Cruz, crossed the cordillera in April 1822, marching his army high and hard through a land of volcanoes. He approached Quito, standing at 9,300 feet in the mountains. Instead of attacking from the south as expected, he outflanked the enemy on the left and positioned his forces north of the city, surprising and wrong-footing the Spaniards, and on the slopes of Mount Pichincha, 'its extinct volcano covered in eternal snows', his Colombian troops backed by the Albion battalion, 'with the bravery that has always distinguished this unit', defeated the Spaniards on 24 May 1822. The battle of Pichincha, the third major victory of the northern revolution, was won by smart tactics and dashing action, with the loss of two hundred men against four hundred of the enemy and the subsequent capture of over two thousand prisoners.[12]

While Sucre entered Quito and received the surrender of General Aymerich and the acclaim of the people, Bolívar accepted the grudging submission of Pasto. He was at pains to point out that 'the capitulation of Pasto is an exceptional achievement for us, because these men are extremely tenacious and obstinate; worse, their country is a network of precipices where you cannot move a step without falling'. The *pastusos* turned on their own side for capitulating, shot at the bishop, attacked the Spanish commander and challenged the Colombians to advance 'over their dead bodies'. There was tension in the air around the Liberator and he anticipated questions being asked: had Bomboná assisted Sucre, or had Pichincha assisted Bolívar? His concern was understandable. He had undertaken the most difficult of the two battles and the less glamorous, but he made his point too crudely with an inglorious suggestion that Sucre had enough glory without detracting from his own: 'Sucre had more troops than I, and fewer enemies; the country favoured him, owing to its inhabitants and the terrain; while we on the contrary were in a hell struggling with devils. The victory of Bomboná is more beautiful than that of Pichincha. Our loss in both cases was the same and the character of the enemy chiefs very different. General Sucre, on the day of the battle, won no more advantages than I did . . . we have taken the bastion of the south and he has taken the copy of our conquests.'[13] Bolívar left Pasto on 8 June and marched his army south through lands of indigenous communities to Quito. But he left behind a people more royalist than the king, and he had not heard the last of them.

On 15 June 1822 the Liberator entered Quito, a city of whites and *mestizos* in the midst of an Indian countryside. He was splendid in dress uniform, mounted on his white horse, Pastor, and ready to receive the cheers of the people. In the by now familiar ceremony, twelve young girls in white crowned him and Sucre with laurels, while another admirer, watching from a balcony, threw her own laurel. This was Bolívar's first sight of Manuela Sáenz, renewed that evening at the ball given in his honour, where the couple danced the night away. But he had other distractions, too. Leaving a reluctant Sucre as president of a new department of Quito, he had to concentrate on Guayaquil, one of the most intractable problems of his career and a cause of mounting tension between Colombia and Peru. He anticipated trouble from the independent *junta* and took the precaution of sending troops to Guayaquil under Salom. He went there in person at the beginning of July, travelling south from Quito through scenery alternately stark and lush, surveying a landscape of Indian townships and volcanic cones, and gazing in wonder at Mount Chimborazo, icy without, burning within, and, like the women of Ecuador, stealing his soul.

Bolívar climbed this mountain of 6,267 metres, following in the footsteps of La Condamine and Humboldt. There he underwent a strange transformation into a world of the spirit: he stood high above the earth and saw an apparition which showed him the history of the past and the thoughts of destiny. He remained in this delirium, possessed by the God of Colombia, until the mighty voice of Colombia aroused him. Then, in a state of heightened awareness, he described the experience in *Mi delirio sobre el Chimborazo*, a document late in appearing and published posthumously. Is the story true? Is this an authentic account of a real event? Or is it an exercise in literary imagination by Bolívar? Or a metaphor for the transfiguration of a new saviour on an American mountain, invented by an early devotee of the cult of Bolívar? For the majority of Bolivarian scholars the composition is authentic. To some it is a revelation of the real Bolívar. Yet it remains a mystery, and the lack of collaborative evidence and contemporary reference invites an agnostic response.[14]

Conference in Guayaquil

Guayaquil, now independent of the enemy, was a focus of interest from its friends. To which of its larger neighbours did it belong? San Martín wanted it for Peru, though he acknowledged its right to decide its own political future. Bolívar claimed it for Colombia on the ground that the presidency of Quito had belonged to the viceroyalty of New Granada, and he did not regard the matter as negotiable. He made his position absolutely clear in January 1822 when he abandoned his plan to take the Guayaquil route to Quito but not his claim to sovereignty over Guayaquil. 'I would have you know,' he informed the president of Guayaquil, 'that Guayaquil is part of the territory of Colombia;

that a province does not have the right to leave a union to which it belongs.'[15] Colombia wanted Quito, and Quito needed Guayaquil; economically the highlands had no other outlet to the sea. Bolívar had to use all his manipulative skills in dealing with petty politics and politicians in Guayaquil, divided into three factions, claimants for independence, for Peru, and for Colombia, but he also spoke frankly to them, playing on the need to save Guayaquil from mob rule: 'Alone you find yourself in a false, ambiguous, and absurd position. You are threatened with anarchy. I bring you salvation.' And on 13 July he decreed the formal incorporation of Guayaquil into Colombia, subsequently confirmed by 'vote' of the *guayaquileños*.[16] Taking into his own hands the civil and military government of the province, Bolívar now awaited the arrival of San Martín.

San Martín was five years older than Bolívar and came from a different milieu.[17] He was the son of Spanish parents, born in Yapeyú on 25 February 1778 in the remote Misiones province of the Río de la Plata, where his father was a military officer in the colonial service. His twenty-two years in the Spanish army, the last three on active service in the Peninsular War, gave him a combination of talents unique among all the liberators: military skill as a strategist and tactician, a knowledge of enlightened ideas, and an authority born of participation in some of the crucial events of modern history. But he was an American by birth and in 1812 he returned to Buenos Aires to join the struggle against Spain and, within a few years, to give that struggle a new strategy. This was based on the thesis that the South American revolution could not be secure until the heart of Spanish power in Peru had been destroyed, that Peru could not be invaded directly by land from northern Argentina, and that the way ahead was by a flanking movement across the Andes to Chile, then up the Pacific in a seaborne invasion of Peru. His *Plan Continental* was to establish a base in Mendoza, cross the Andes, defeat the Spaniards in Chile and then dispatch a further expedition to emancipate Peru. This he carried out with a genius for organization and planning, which perhaps only Bolívar could equal. San Martín went to Peru to wage a war not of conquest but of ideas, a war for the minds and hearts of Peruvians. Events seemed to vindicate his thesis of revolution without war. Lima and coastal Peru joined his cause, and on 28 July 1821 Peruvian independence was proclaimed. For the next year San Martín ruled as Protector, but he did not rule all Peru. In the sierra there was a powerful royalist army, and soon Peruvians began to dispute among themselves.

Political opposition to San Martín was growing. His closest associate, Bernardo de Monteagudo, was hated by many for his hard line against Spaniards. He also influenced the Protector's monarchism, which appealed to some Peruvians such as the marquis of Torre Tagle, but alienated many others.

The liberal wing of Peruvian politics had not spearheaded the independence movement, but now it sought to impose its views on the independent state. While they frustrated San Martín's political plans, the Peruvians also withheld the military help that he needed to end the war; indeed they resented his unemployed army and the financial burden which it imposed. And the viceregal forces remained intact. How could San Martín escape from this stalemate? How could he solve his political problems and end the military impasse? Leaving his ally Torre Tagle in executive command, he went to Guayaquil to confer with the liberator of the north. Yet an approach to Bolívar raised more problems than it solved. Bolívar was approaching the peak of his career: he too had liberated more than his native land and, while not without problems, he had recent victories and a successful army behind him. San Martín, on the other hand, was conscious that his position in Peru was weak. He had not won sufficient territory, his forces seemed to be losing the war, and the Spaniards had turned stubborn over negotiations. He could count on no further support from the Chileans, and the leadership in Buenos Aires was frankly hostile. Moreover, to visit Bolívar brought into question the whole basis of military collaboration; it exacerbated the issue of monarchy versus republic and introduced a new problem, the status of Guayaquil.

Guayaquil was a naval base, a shipbuilding centre, and a major port. Strategically and commercially it was indispensable to the revolution. At the end of 1821 San Martín had some bargaining power, for Bolívar was held up on his approach to Quito and needed the help of the division seconded by San Martín under the command of Colonel Andrés Santa Cruz. But Bolívar continued to treat Guayaquil as his own, and after the decisive victory at Pichincha in May 1822, which won Quito for the northern revolution, he entered Guayaquil in person with his army behind him. Bolívar approached the interview with San Martín, therefore, from a position of superior strength, which he never allowed him to forget. In the euphoria of Carabobo he had offered collaboration to the liberator of the south with the double-edged remark: 'I hope to heaven that the services of the Colombian army will not be necessary for the peoples of Peru.'[18]

Now, in June 1822, he offered to reciprocate the military help he had received from San Martín with 'even stronger aid to the government of Peru', and expressed his willingness to lead his army into Peru. But there was steel in his voice on the status of Guayaquil. He told the Protector that it was not for one part of a nation to dictate the national sovereignty but for the people as a whole: 'The interests of a small province must not interrupt the onward march of all South America.'[19] San Martín accepted the offer of assistance: 'Peru will gladly and gratefully receive all the troops you can spare to forward the campaign and end the war in Peru.'[20] He then made his way north. By now his position had been eroded. He had lost ground in Peru and he needed more from Bolívar than Bolívar needed from him. San Martín sought three things: the annexation of Guayaquil to Peru, the assistance of Colombian troops to bolster his own forces and defeat the Spaniards, and the acceptance of a monarchical constitution for the new states. As he approached Guayaquil it must have been obvious that he was the proposer, Bolívar the disposer. When his ship approached the harbour on the morning of 26 July, Bolívar was at first taken by surprise but then went on board and embraced his fellow liberator. It was the beginning of two days of public friendship.

The meetings were held on 26 and 27 July in private and there was no third person present.[21] So the Bolivarian version of the interview came from Bolívar himself.[22] This insisted that discussion was confined to political matters, that San Martín did not make an issue of the status of Guayaquil or request military aid, and that he did not procure Bolívar's agreement for a monarchy in Peru. According to San Martín's supporters, the Protector needed and requested the support of Bolívar's army to complete the destruction of royalist power in Peru, and to procure this he offered to serve under Bolívar's command. San Martín was deeply disappointed that Bolívar had pre-empted Guayaquil, but realist enough to see that nothing could be done to reverse the Colombian occupation. Bolívar also made it clear that there could be no European monarchy in America. So San Martín's basic aim was reduced to securing Bolívar's military support, in the form either of a large military force or of an army under Bolívar himself. But Bolívar rejected these proposals. He was ready to commit reinforcements but not his whole army, which he then needed for internal security in Colombia. So he regarded the offer and the request as excessive and he had serious doubts as to whether San Martín could deliver his side of the proposal. Would San Martín really take orders from a younger man and would San Martín's army accept such an arrangement? Moreover, he regarded San Martín's military policy as impractical and irresolute. So the interview was fruitless.

At the end of the meetings Guayaquil gave a ball for San Martín. While Bolívar was showing his prowess on the dance floor, San Martín remained aloof; he left at about two in the morning and returned to his ship to catch the tide, accompanied by Bolívar, who gave him a portrait of himself.[23] Behind the courtesies, San Martín left Guayaquil disillusioned, convinced that Bolívar either doubted the sincerity of his offer or was embarrassed by his presence in the revolution.[24] He believed that Bolívar was superficial, vain and ambitious, dominated by 'la pasión de mando'.[25] He also had the honesty to recognize that this was the man to win the war, a man who would crush anyone in his way, not only the Spaniards but if necessary San Martín himself.

The leader of the southern revolution decided to withdraw and leave the way open for Bolívar to conquer Peru for independence. As he said to his

1 The Young Bolívar, anonymous artist, Madrid, *c.* 1802.

2 Simón Bolívar, engraved by W. Holt, from an engraving by M.N. Bate, London 1823–8.

3 Simón Bolívar, miniature on ivory of 1828, after a painting by Roulin.

4 Simón Bolívar by José Gil de Castro, Lima, 1825.
'My portrait painted in Lima with great accuracy and likeness.'

5 Simón Bolívar, Libertador de Colombia, by José Gil de Castro, Lima 1827.

6 Daniel Florencio O'Leary by Antonio Meucci, nineteenth century.

7 Antonio José de Sucre.

8 Bolívar and the Patriot Forces crossing the Andes, 1819, by Tito Salas.

9 Francisco de Paula Santander.

10 Manuela Sáenz.

11 *Antiguo camino colonial entre Caracas y La Guaira* by Ferdinand Bellermann.

12 Chimborazo by Frederick Edwin Church, 1864.

friend Tomás Guido, 'There is not enough room in Peru for Bolívar and me.'[26] His decision was confirmed when he returned to Peru to find his position further eroded, his influence with the Peruvian ruling class weakened and his authority over his own army fading. On 20 September he resigned his command. The same night he left Lima and sailed the next day to Chile, thence to Europe and a long exile until his death in 1850. He was generous in defeat. He acknowledged that Peru could only be liberated by external aid, and that only Bolívar could do it. In 1826, when the liberation of Peru was complete, he wrote that 'the successes which I have gained in the war of independence are really inferior to those which General Bolívar has won for the general cause of America.'[27]

The Guayaquil interview, at which Bolívar had assured San Martín that he could contribute to the good of South America, was less dramatic for the Liberator than for the Protector.[28] Bolívar reported the meetings to Santander rather airily as 'compliments, talk, and goodbye'. San Martín 'did not mention any special purpose in coming, and he made no demands of Colombia'. He was not a democrat but favoured a monarchy imported from Europe. 'He impresses me as being very military in character, and he appears to be energetic, quick, and by no means dull. He has the type of correct ideas that would please you; but he did not strike me as being subtle enough to rise to the sublime.' Two put-downs for the price of one. Bolívar was satisfied with his success. 'There is now nothing more for me to do, my dear general, except to store in a safe place the treasure of my success, hiding it out of sight where no one can take it from me.'[29]

Defence of the Revolution

Victor of three campaigns, liberator of three countries, legal president of Colombia, de facto dictator of Guayaquil, Bolívar held all the cards; the future was his, in the south as well as in the north. For the next year he remained in Ecuador, waiting and resting. But moments of rest were few. In September 1822 he left Guayaquil in the capable hands of General Salom to visit the provinces of Cuenca and Loja. The news from Peru was not good. The new government rejected Bolívar's offer of assistance, and made life so difficult for the Colombian troops he had sent to Peru that they withdrew. Ecuador had a difficult neighbour to its south and needed protection; moreover, it still had to develop a sense of independent identity, and its military and bureaucracy were demanding to be paid. The budget of the new state was already a headache for him, and so were its politics: 'Pasto, Quito, Cuenca and Guayaquil are four powers, enemies of each other, all wanting to dominate, yet lacking the strength to do so, for their own internal politics tear them apart.'[30] Amidst these immediate preoccupations, the south was now reclaiming him and he had to resist calls to return home. 'I now belong to the Colombian family and not to the family of Bolívar; I no longer belong to Caracas alone, but to the whole nation. . . . The people of the south of Colombia have at their back Peru, which seeks to tempt them, and the royal army which seeks to conquer them.'[31] He could not abandon the south to its enemies within and without.

While he was in Loja news reached him of the rebellion of Pasto. A Spanish officer, Benito Boves, nephew of the infamous José Tomás Boves, escaped from Quito and in alliance with Agustín Agualongo, an Indian royalist officer, turned the area between the Guáitara and Juanambú rivers into a scene of rebellion and disorder. Bolívar ordered Sucre in with troops from the garrison in Quito. He was accompanied by José María Córdova, a young Colombian officer who was acquiring some notoriety in the wars of independence but whose bravery was flawed by an uncontrollable and capricious temper and more than a streak of cruelty. Nevertheless he appeared to enjoy the favour of the Liberator who overlooked his past violence and in Pasto promoted him to general of brigade.[32] Sucre's first action failed and he needed reinforcements before he could capture the rebel position at Taindala and turn the tide. He then advanced, overtook Boves at Yacuanquer, and routed the rebel forces. The next day he demanded the surrender of the city, but the *pastusos* refused to be defeated and stood their ground before finally giving way. Boves fled from the subsequent slaughter and the indiscriminate killing of soldiers and civilians. Agualongo and his Indian guerrillas continued to resist and to defy the republic until he was captured and shot in 1824.[33] But Bolívar had still not heard the last of Pasto.

Bolívar, after a stay in Ibarra, arrived in Pasto on 2 January 1823, to silence from an obstinate people. He made himself clear. All the inhabitants, except for two who had been forced to flee, had embraced the insurrection and were now punished with confiscation of their property and its redistribution to the officers and soldiers of the occupying forces.[34] He ordered General Salom to conscript into the army all the citizens of Pasto who had taken up arms against the republic. Then he appointed Colonel Juan José Flores governor of the province of Pasto and returned to Quito. Salom assembled the inhabitants in the public square and soldiers seized about a thousand of the men, who were immediately banished to Quito. Many perished on the way, many died in prison, and they all maintained a stubborn hatred of Colombia and were never reconciled to the cause of independence. Pasto itself was not pacified but left devastated and depopulated, ready for further rebellion, and in the mountains Indian guerrillas continued to resist. Bolívar saw the devotion to crown and Church in Pasto not merely as a local problem but as a running sore that could reinfect Colombia and attract the support of the Spaniards in Peru. Independence had to be indivisible. But within six months Pasto came back to haunt him and needed further punishment, this time five hundred deaths, but still the *pastusos* were there, challenging him to destroy them.

Colombia itself still caused the Liberator anxiety, and its fatal instinct towards division and federalism continued to repudiate his belief that large states were more effective than small states. There were many political permutations. Some liberals were centralists, convinced that strong government was needed to impose liberalism. Others were federalists, because they believed that federalism was more democratic. Some conservatives wanted maximum authority at the centre. Others backed regional interests against Santanderian liberalism in Bogotá. Bolívar was a law unto himself, at once liberal, conservative and centralist. 'We have two and a half million inhabitants scattered over vast spaces. One part is savage, the other slave, both enemies among themselves, and all corrupted by superstition and despotism. A happy contrast to set itself against all the nations of the world! This is our situation, this is Colombia. And still they wish to divide it.'[35] But he rejected Santander's request that he return to restore morale and deal with congress: he was on the campaign trail and nothing would drag him back from glory. 'You can tell everyone from me, I shall not keep the presidency if I am not allowed to exercise those extraordinary powers which congress voted me. I am absolutely convinced that the republic of Colombia cannot be governed with order and prosperity except by absolute power. . . . Colombia needs an army of occupation to keep it free.'[36]

On the way from Ibarra to Pasto he received ominous news from the government in Bogotá. The municipal authorities of Caracas had formally protested against the constitution, alleging that it did not represent the views of the electors chosen by the free will of the people. When the central government ordered the prosecution of those who had protested, the courts had declared that there was no case against them. Here were signs of an opposition party attacking the executive power of the centre, and duly reported by Santander who alleged that congress too was penetrated by these ideas of the Caracas faction, as he called the opposition. Bolívar, always alert to any threat from federalism, reacted strongly, voiced his disapproval of the innovators and urged the executive to prevent the legislators from making any changes in Colombia's fundamental code of laws. He himself made it plain to congress that he would not tolerate any revision of the constitution: 'The Constitution of Colombia is sacred for ten years and shall not be violated with impunity while I have any blood running through my veins and the liberators are under my orders.' He regarded Colombia as his personal creation, the core of his achievement, the source of his military strength. To Santander, in one of his most memorable letters, he made a striking restatement of his political principles, recalling his record of total commitment to the integrity of Colombia and its welfare. 'My policy has always been for stability, for strength, and for true liberty.' He had explained his views on government to the congress of Angostura, which accepted them in part, as did the congress of Cúcuta; he had sworn to the constitution, which was unalterable for ten years, indeed for a whole generation, in accordance with the 'Social Contract' of the world's first republican [Rousseau].

> The sovereignty of the people is not unlimited, because it is based on justice and constrained by the concept of perfect utility. This doctrine comes from the constitutional apostle of the day [Bentham]. How can the representatives of the people think they are authorized constantly to change the social organization? What will then become of the basis of the rights, properties, honour, and life of citizens? It would be better to live under a ruthless despotism, then at least their safety would have some protection from the same power that oppresses them. . . . I would rather abandon Colombia than accept any laws that undermined the magnifi- cent work of the Liberating Army. I ask you to present to the general congress my solemn promise not to recognize during my presidency any act of congress that revokes, changes, or modifies the fundamental laws of the Republic of Colombia.[37]

Bolívar won this round. In face of his frank speaking, congress backed off and indeed gave him a vote of thanks. O'Leary believed that at this point he had reached the peak of his influence in Colombia: 'There was nothing that was not within his powers.' But the resentment of the opposition and the determination of Bolívar would test those powers in the future.

Manuela Sáenz

The year 1822 was a memorable one for the Liberator, a year of punishing marches, hard battles, great victories, spectacular landscapes, new lands and political alarms from old adversaries. It was also a year in which he made two new acquaintances: an American hero, and a flamboyant mistress. San Martín soon departed from his life. The mistress was more enduring. Since the death of his young wife Bolívar had never remarried, though he had had a number of women.[38] In the case of Manuela Sáenz it seems to have been love, if not at first sight, one that became a lasting relationship. But at the beginning of the year his eyes, or at least his feelings, had been directed elsewhere, to a young woman in Bogotá who had once rejected him for another soldier and was still resisting his advances, or, as he described her, 'fastidious and lovely Bernardina', whom he implored to write to him. 'I think only of you and of those things that remind me of your attractions, and I can only imagine those. You are the only one in the world for me. Heavenly angel, you alone stir my senses and desires, my hopes for happiness, and all my longings. Modesty and discretion prevent me from saying all I want to say, but do not think that I do not love you. Write to me, who writes tirelessly to you. Adios. Your beloved.'[39] But within six months his passion was diverted.

Manuela Sáenz was not simply a pretty face looking over a balcony in Quito as the Liberator rode by. Born to María Joaquina de Aizpuru, the American mistress of Simón Sáenz, a Spanish businessman, she lost her mother while still young and emerged from a lax convent education a lively and independent girl with a talent for riding and shooting, and some sympathy for revolutionary ideas. She was soon the subject of rumours and legends, which followed her for the rest of her life and became traps for historians.[40] In 1817, at the age of twenty, she was married off to a wealthy English merchant, James Thorne, a worthy but dull man more than twenty years her senior, and accompanied him to royalist Lima where she lived from 1819 to 1820. She was attractive and shapely, her oval face, pearl complexion, dark eyes and flowing hair the epitome of South American beauty. Pleasure loving and irreverent, she was a lively figure in Lima society, a friend of the actress Rosita Campuzano who was reputed to be close to the Protector, and already determined to be a celebrity in her own right. She was also committed to the American revolution and, with the independence of Peru in 1821, to the cause of San Martín. Her services were recognized with the decoration known as the *Caballeresa del Sol* (Dame of the Order of the Sun). She was more devoted to politics and pleasure than to her husband and, accompanied by her father, she returned to Quito. There, at the age of twenty-five, she met her hero who became her friend, companion and lover. The relationship, begun at the victory ball, survived partings, distances, rows and their own passionate temperaments, and entered the Bolivarian story for all time.

But for Bolívar it began, as other affairs, as a post-campaign recreation. One conquest was not enough. Moving on to Guayaquil he was there captivated by the numerous women of the Garaycoa family, and his eyes fell especially on Joaquina, who greeted him in their home as *el glorioso* and he reciprocated by calling her *La Gloriosa*, sometimes *amable loca* or *loca gloriosa*. With La Gloriosa he conducted a romantic affair, showering her with his usual compliments, insisting that she was right to love him, for he loved her devotedly and she lived in his heart.[41] He wrote to her in family letters and personal messages, describing himself as 'the most wretched of your admirers', telling her not to be jealous during his absence, for the girls in the highlands were so modest that they fled at the sight of a soldier, and he describes his lodgings in Cuenca: 'The Church has conquered me. I live in an oratory. The nuns send me meals and the canons refreshments. The *Te Deum* is my song and prayer my nightly devotion. . . . When you see me again I shall be angelic.'[42] She calls him 'my dear sweet friend' and is always eager to hear from him. Pursuit and surrender? Or romantic yearnings?

Four years later he was still in touch with the family, now communicating with the married sister, Manuela, who tells him that La Gloriosa is ill with tertian fever: 'But you are the antidote for all ills; she took your letter and placed it on her brow, and imagined she was better.' By now it was Manuela who maintained a loving correspondence with him: 'My dear sweet friend, I wait impatiently for the happy day when I can embrace you.' And again, 'What fire of love burns in my breast for you, in fact we are all rivals in love for you.' 'La Gloriosa asks me to say so many things to you that I cannot express them; I too am carried away, for I hold within me the love of my Liberator.'[43] Their hero continued to write and to entertain Gloriosa with sweet nothings.[44] The sisters were disconsolate when he left the stage in 1830. Joaquina wrote to him, 'I am inspired by your goodness; I always hold you in my heart, there I see you, speak to you, hear you, embrace you, admire you.'[45]

With Manuela Sáenz, the relationship was sexual. Both were erotic creatures, and their feelings for each other when apart were the longings and loneliness of lovers. But it was a meeting of minds as well as emotions. Manuela, unlike his other lovers, was associated with his work and interested in his policies and, without accompanying him on the battlefield as legend has it, seems to have received more confidences from him than his passing fancies. No doubt she was an exhibitionist, determined to cut a public figure and challenge male culture. Always accompanied by two black servant girls, Jonatás and Nathán, she had her own entourage and caused a stir wherever she went. She provoked different reactions in Bolívar's staff: Sucre was a friend, O'Leary accepted her at headquarters as a part-time secretary and archivist, but there were some who hated her. She could be awkward and she guarded Bolívar's archive even against his own minister of war. The legends grew, as well as the scandal. The young French scientist Jean-Baptiste Boussingault, an erratic and mischievous observer, who seemed to have met her frequently in Peru in the mid 1820s, was fascinated by her:

At times she was like a great lady, at others a half-breed; she danced with equal grace the minuet or the *cachucha*. She was inseparable from a young and beautiful *mulata* slave, who was always dressed like a soldier, and encouraged Manuela's sensual and licentious tendencies. She was the shadow of her mistress, and possibly her lover, a vice very extensive in Peru. She performed dances that were highly lascivious. She had no lovers: her only love was Manuela.[46]

If the rumour of lesbianism were true, it was not something that affected her relations with Bolívar, who came to see her not only as a beautiful lover but as a brave and loyal – and jealous – woman, who would eventually help to save his life. The style of his words to her is extremely different from that of his dispatches, proclamations and decrees. In his letters he speaks the language of the heart.

The pain of parting was an essential theme of their relationship from the very beginning. She found it difficult to accept his absence in Pasto in January 1823, when she was touched by his concern for her interests but wanted him nearer: 'I have paid a lot for your victory at Yacuanquer. You will probably conclude that I am not patriotic in what I am saying. But I would rather triumph with you and without ten victories in Pasto. I often think how boring it must be for you in that village. Yet no matter how desperate it is for you it is not as desperate as it is for the best of your friends, who is Manuela.'[47] Separation, and her marital state, could bring doubts about their relationship in the mind of Bolívar. But separation was probably more deeply felt by Manuela who, active though she was, did not have the responsibilities of planning, commanding and fighting on many fronts to distract her. As he was preparing his campaign in Peru, he wanted his old tutor, Simón Rodríguez, to join him: 'Instead of a lover, I want a philosopher beside me, for at the moment I prefer Socrates to the lovely Aspasia.'[48] She was alarmed by any prolonged silence, as on the eve of the great march to Pasco, and would ask his staff for news: 'I have fallen into disfavour, everything is at an end,' she wrote to Captain Santana. 'The general no longer thinks of me, he has hardly written two letters in nineteen days. What's going on? You have always said you are my friend, so if I cannot ask you, who can I ask?'[49]

Later in 1823 James Thorne, faithful husband, was still left with an unfaithful wife. But she was not mercenary and seems to have resisted his money as well as his advances. On these she had no mercy. Mistress of Bolívar, secure in his love, passionate in her desire, she had no intention of returning to her husband, much less of accompanying him to England and enduring his English ways.

> Sir, you are an excellent person, an inimitable person, but my answer is still No, a thousand times No. . . . Do you think that it lowers my honour that this general is my lover and not my husband? I do not live by social rules, invented only to torment. So leave me alone, my dear Englishman. We will marry again when we are in heaven but not on earth. . . . You are boring, like your nation, which makes love without pleasure, conversation without grace, walks slowly, greets solemnly, stands up and sits down carefully, jokes without laughing. . . . Enough

banter. Seriously, with the truth and purity of an English woman, I say I will never return to you.

She later sent a copy of this letter to Bolívar, who was in Upper Peru at the time. He found her description of her husband 'sad and funny at the same time. . . . I don't want to steal a virtuous heart, but it is not my fault, and I don't know how to reconcile our love with our duty, or to cut the knot of my love with my lovely Manuela.'[50]

He wrestled with his conscience over their relationship and he did not hide his doubts, even trying to distance himself when he was travelling in Peru in 1825. 'I think of you and your fate at every moment and lament this horrible situation, for you to reconcile yourself with someone you don't love, and for me to leave the one I adore. . . . When you were mine I loved you more for your lovely nature than for your physical beauty. . . . Now, to separate is to tear our lives apart. In future you will be alone, though at the side of your husband, and I will be alone in the middle of the world. Our only consolation will be the glory of having won through.'[51] He does not sound very convinced, or convincing. From Potosí he is anxious for her welfare, an errant wife in a traditional society, and he advises her to go to Arequipa where he has friends who would look after her. Absence only increases her passion for him, which she preserves for her peace of mind and declares it is for ever.[52]

Separated by a vast distance, he valued her letters, and when their locations were reversed – he in Lima and she in Bolivia – he implored her to wait for him 'at all costs, do you hear, do you understand?' He begged her not to go to London or anywhere else: 'I want to see you, to touch you, feel you, taste you, to join you to me in complete union. . . . Learn to love me and don't go away, not even with God himself. To the only woman, as you say to me. Your own.'[53] She too found distances and silences unbearable. Her love is greater than his, she declares: 'You had a little love for me and the long separation killed it. But I, who had a great passion for you, have kept it to preserve my peace and happiness.'[54] Four years after their first meeting his letters to her were as passionate as ever. Writing to her on his journey from Quito to Bogotá in 1826 he laments that he has not the time to write the long letters in small writing that she prefers.

You are all love. I too am consumed by this burning fever that devours us like two children. At my age I suffer the sickness that I ought to have forgotten long ago. You alone hold me in this state. You ask me to tell you that *I love no one else.* Oh, no, *I love no one else, and never will.* The altar you occupy will not be profaned by any other idol or image, not even by God himself. You have made me an idolater of human beauty, of

Manuela. Believe me: I love you and you alone and no one else. Don't kill yourself, live for me and for yourself: live to console the unfortunate and to console your lover who longs *to see you.*[55]

In April 1828 they were still exchanging tender letters and she could still amuse as well as move him. From Bucaramanga he told her he was coming straight back to Bogotá, missing out Venezuela and Cartagena, and that they would see each other soon: 'Doesn't that make you pleased with him who loves you with all his soul?'[56] And in July, when she was criticized by some for her public role, he sent a lover's plea: 'Your love renews a life that is expiring. I cannot live without you, my Manuela, I cannot freely give you up. I do not have as much strength as you, not enough not to see you: I see you even at a distance. Come, come, come.' And on his last journey he lamented their cruel separation and declared his never-ending love.[57] The course of true love ran too swiftly for Bolívar.

Into Peru

Peru in 1823 was a challenge to Bolívar, its government an object of contempt. Once San Martín had left there was no great liberator with whom he could negotiate. The creoles were uncommitted, the aristocracy unreliable. Such was José de la Riva Agüero, in February appointed president with the rank of grand marshal: 'Congress thus awarded political power and the highest military rank to the caudillo who had provoked the military revolt against congress and who had not fought in a single campaign or a single battle.'[58] Unwilling to liberate itself, Peru was reluctant to be liberated by others. This prospect caused greater resentment than the Spanish presence had ever done, and Peruvian nationalism first expressed itself not against Spaniards but against Americans. Yet Peruvians themselves had a cross to bear. Two years of war had undermined their already fragile economy, lowered their subsistence level and diminished their resistance to disease, to malaria, dysentery, and typhoid, and to the severe climatic changes of the time.[59] Peruvians in 1822 were in no condition to support a further scourge of war.

Bolívar felt the full force of Andean xenophobia before he even entered Peru. After the liberation of Quito he was anxious to pursue the enemy in the south and he offered aid to the Peruvian leaders, but the offer was rejected and he himself was villified in the Lima press. 'The members of the government,' he remarked, 'are more jealous of us than they are afraid of the Spaniards.' Bolívar believed that he had the right to intervene in Peru without invitation in defence of the American revolution: 'The enemy will come here if I do not go there to forestall him; moreover, enemy territory should be regarded not as foreign territory but as conquerable territory.'[60] Yet he hesitated to go, conscious of the instability he would leave behind and the chaos that lay ahead: 'The desire to end the war in America drives me to Peru, and the love of my reputation holds me back at the same time.'[61]

In March 1823 he agreed to assign six thousand troops to Peru, and in April he sent his chosen precursor to establish liaison with the Peruvian government and command the Colombian advance division. But in Peru Sucre was isolated, frustrated by factionalism. In June a royalist force seized Lima, and Sucre barely managed to evacuate the city and save the army. 'The anarchy was indescribable. I curse the moment I came to Lima. What a task you have landed me with!' he complained.[62] The government fled to Callao, where congress deposed Riva Agüero and appointed Sucre to supreme command. But Riva Agüero refused to accept dismissal. To the relief of Sucre, he withdrew to Trujillo, followed by a group of congressmen; there he raised an army and dissolved congress. The latter reconstituted itself in Lima, now evacuated by the royalists, and appointed a new president, Torre Tagle, whom Riva Agüero refused to recognize and who literally bought a following with money from the public treasury.[63]

Peru was now split into two zones, occupied in the south by Spain and divided in the north by civil war. It was the extreme inconvenience of this anarchy which drove the Peruvian ruling class to seek Bolívar's assistance. He had his own problems within the world of revolution, disaster in Peru, bad news from Pasto, murmurs in Bogotá, shortage of troops:

> An interesting situation. I won't call it critical, for the word is overused, nor dangerous, for it could also have advantages. My mind fluctuates between hope and anxiety. Mounted on the slopes of Pichincha, my view extends from the mouth of the Orinoco to the peak of Potosí; this great field of war and politics absorbs my mind and each of its extremes calls my attention imperiously, and like God I would wish to be in all of them. . . . The worst is that I am not in any part, because to attend to the *pastusos* is to be away from glory and away from the field of battle. What bitterness. Only my patriotism keeps me going.[64]

In the event, for the sake of the continental revolution, he had to go to Peru. On 3 August he finally received permission from the congress of Colombia to do so. He sailed from Guayaquil on 7 August on board the *Chimborazo*. The name would not leave him. During the voyage there was a fire on board owing to the negligence of the cook, but Bolívar retained his usual sangfroid and the passage continued amid much ribaldry.[65]

To arrive in Peru is not to enter a scene of gold and silver. Lima is not a gateway to the sun, but a grey wasteland of coastal desert giving way to gloomy hills beyond. Bolívar's mood was no lighter. Although he regarded the long march from Caracas to Lima as a continuous process of liberation, and journey's end as simply another revolution in waiting, in fact Peru was a new phase of his life, a people whom he would find strange, a landscape full of dangers, a political scene more difficult than he had ever known. Peru was different. And for Peru, Colombia was different: Bolívar was a Venezuelan, and his army invaders.

Yet Lima gave him a frenzied welcome when he arrived on 1 September 1823 and he was immediately invested with supreme military and political authority. Manuela Sáenz followed soon afterwards. His spirits picked up. 'Lima is a large pleasant city which was once rich. It seems very patriotic. The men appear to be loyal to me and say they are ready to make sacrifices. The ladies are very pleasant and very pretty. There is a ball being given today where I shall see them all.' He tried to be optimistic: 'The men respect me and the women love me. That is all very nice. They hold many pleasures for those that can pay for them. . . . The food is excellent, the theatre fair but adorned by beautiful eyes and attractive figures . . . carriages, horses, excursions, bull-fights, Te Deums . . . nothing is lacking but money.'[66] Bolívar had a roving eye but in Lima it rested on Manuela, and their love was still young. She stayed at home with her complaisant husband and visited her lover at night. Other formalities were also observed; in deference to what was socially acceptable she was not able to visit him on his sickbed at Pativilca.

Politically Peru was hideous to behold, the site of four separate patriot forces – Peruvian, Argentine, Chilean and Colombian – a semi-rebellious navy, and a large royalist army.[67] It had a congress, two presidents and a dictator. The legitimate president, Torre Tagle, resented his now empty title. And the ruling class rediscovered its suspicions of foreigners. Bolívar knew that his own presence was a liability: 'This is not Colombia, and I am not Peruvian. I shall always be a foreigner to Peruvian people and I shall always arouse the jealousy and distrust of these gentlemen. . . . I have already regretted that I ever came here.'[68] He was forced to act as a military governor, yet he had little to govern. Argentina and Chile were anxious to withdraw their support. In the south the Peruvian army under Santa Cruz disintegrated before it even engaged the enemy. The guerrillas of the central zone, Peruvians before all else and torn in their allegiance between Riva Agüero and Bolívar, were reduced to a few disorganized bands. And in the north, ex-President Riva Agüero, displaying more energy against Colombia that he had ever done against Spain, opened negotiations with the royalists rather than submit to Bolívar. His intentions are disputed. Did he hope to establish an independent monarchy? Did he plan a joint campaign with the royalists to drive out the Colombians? Bolívar had no doubt that he was 'a usurper, rebel and traitor'. Traitor or not, Riva Agüero was hopelessly wrong, for he could not negotiate successfully with Spain from a position of weakness. In any case his troops rose against him in November 1823 and submitted to Bolívar, and Riva Agüero was allowed to depart for Europe. Bolívar was more disillusioned by the day: 'I face the storm for the good of Colombia. . . . Chileans and Argentines can no longer be relied upon. And these Peruvians are the most miserable kind of men for this war.'[69] 'Discord, misery, discontent and egoism reigned everywhere,' he recalled, 'and Peru no longer existed.' Santander might be his life line: 'In the middle of the Andes, breathing the poisonous air called the *soroche*, upon the snow, and with llamas at my side, I write you this letter. It will surely be frozen, if the condor does not carry it away and warm it in the sun.'[70] Peru was hopeless; only Colombia could win liberation, and he needed more Colombian troops.

On his way back to Lima from Trujillo the pressures of Peru caught up with him, and on 1 January 1824 in the harbour of Pativilca, a small village north of Lima, he collapsed with a high temperature and was carried ashore. For seven days he fought for his life with no professional aid and few medicines against an illness which he described in terms of rheumatism, gastric fever and renal colic, aggravated by recent journeys in the high sierra, but which could also have been food poisoning or even early symptoms of tuberculosis. He had to remain in Pativilca for two months, weak and emaciated, hardly recognizable, 'very spent and very old', he admitted, his slightest movement an agony. His mood veered between defeatism and defiance. His view of Ecuadorians and Peruvians, never high, plunged further. 'Of all the Colombians, the *quiteños* are the worst. The Venezuelans are saints compared with these villains. The *quiteños* and the Peruvians are the same thing: infamously vicious and utterly depraved. The whites have the same character as the Indians, and the Indians are all cunning, thieving, cheating, treacherous, totally devoid of any moral principles.'[71] These were the views of a foreigner who did not understand strangers and had evidently not heard of José Olaya, Indian messenger and 'martyr of the patriot cause'. They were also the outpourings of a sick man, who wanted to renounce his public destiny and his command in the south and return to Bogotá.

As conflicting thoughts passed through his mind, resignation was one of them and the example of San Martín. But Bolívar tended to speak in two voices. One, to Santander from whom he was demanding troops, insisted that he would resign the presidency of Colombia and leave the country; it would simply need a single attack from the Spanish forces and his tiny army would be pushed out of Peru and with it would go his own reputation. The other, to

Sucre and his commanders, was remarkably cool. He did not make a great deal of his illness or spread alarm and despondency, but gave every sign of keeping control and taking the fight to the Spaniards. His pessimism fought with his ambition. He continued to organize the revolution, dictating letters – a total of forty-two in these painful weeks – and issuing orders from his sickbed. It was a superb performance in the face of real danger, for the royalists in 1824 reoccupied most of Peru, including Lima and Callao, and independence seemed a lost cause.

He desperately needed more troops, Colombian and Peruvian. He complained to Torre Tagle that the Peruvian troops had no interest in the war: 'All the Peruvian troops that are not kept shut up within a fortress are sure to desert . . . no sooner are they left to sleep in the open or taken on long marches than they desert to a man.'[72] Yet Torre Tagle himself was the greatest security risk, and it was an error of judgement for Bolívar to entrust him with the task of negotiating with the Spanish command in order to gain time. This weak and confused opportunist wanted more than negotiations with the Spaniards, and was in fact preparing to change sides yet again. On 5 February 1824 Argentine and Chilean troops in Callao mutinied for arrears of pay, and receiving no satisfaction from the Peruvian government they handed over the fortress to the royalists. On 29 February, with the connivance of Torre Tagle and other turncoats, the enemy occupied Lima once again with an army of Spaniards, creoles, blacks and Indians, a warning and a lesson to white waverers. Torre Tagle, the principal officials and over three hundred officers of the Peruvian army promptly went over to the royalists, as they had previously passed from the royalists to the patriots, always anxious to be on the strongest side.[73] 'Peru is a chamber of horrors,' exclaimed Bolívar. In his five months in Peru he had witnessed one disaster after another: the loss of the army of Santa Cruz, the treason of Riva Agüero, the desertion of the Chileans, the uprising of the Peruvian fleet, the surrender of Callao and the loss of Lima. He seemed to have reached the end of the road. In a mood of deep introspection he wrote one of his most emotive and elusive letters:

Until now I have fought for liberty: in future I will fight for my glory, no matter what it costs. My glory now consists in ruling no more and in thinking of nothing but myself; I have always had this intention but it increases progressively by the day. My years, my ill health, and my disillusion with all the dreams of youth prevent me from taking any other way. The revulsion I feel is such that I do not wish to see or to eat with anyone. The presence of another person kills me: I live among the trees of this miserable place on the coast of Peru and I have become a misanthrope overnight. But you must understand that I am not depressed, and this loathing for people and society does not come from a physical cause or from any personal trouble, but from a conviction deep within me. Ambition, says Rousseau, guides men when they reach the age of forty, and I have reached that age. But my ambition has died. I have nothing to hope for and everything to fear. Observe the breakdown in human affairs. At all times the works of men have been ephemeral but in our day they are like the emerging embryo that dies before it even develops. On all sides I hear the sounds of disaster. My era is one of catastrophes. Everything comes to life and dies before my eyes as though struck by lightning. Everything passes, and I would be a fool to flatter myself that I can stand firm in the midst of so many upheavals, in the midst of so much destruction, in the midst of the moral subversion of the world. No, my friend, that cannot be! Since death has not decided to take me under its protective wings, I must hurry to hide my head in the midst of oblivion and silence, before I am struck by blows from heaven and reduced to dust, to ashes, to nothingness. It would be madness on my part to watch the storm and fail to take shelter. . . . Everyone falls, struck by disgrace or disaster. Can I remain standing? Impossible. I too must fall.[74]

A dark night for Bolívar, his thoughts apparently lost in a maze of words but emitting one clear message: he had a will to survive and did not intend to succumb. In Pativilca an innate ability to pick himself up reasserted itself and rescued him from despair. Within weeks he was his old self, impervious to the disasters around him. The Colombian envoy to Peru, Joaquín Mosquera, travelling nearby, was alerted by an Indian that the Liberator was lying mortally ill in Pativilca. He saw him in his garden, slumped on an old bench too ill to rise, his head bound in a scarf, looking skinny and decrepit. Mosquera asked him how the Colombian army could survive; what would he do? 'Triumph!' was the reply. 'In three months I shall have an army ready to attack. I shall climb the cordilleras and defeat the Spanish.' The timing was premature but the determination real: 'Tell our comrades how you left me lying on this inhospitable shore, where I fight with shattered arms to achieve the independence of Peru and the safety of Colombia.'[75] Now everything depended on the Liberator, and his Colombian army was the last line of defence, if he could persuade an exasperated Santander to send more arms and men. But Santander was dragging his feet over Peru. It needed all the Liberator's tact and powers of persuasion to get him to square congress and send him aid. Times had changed since Bolívar's departure. Bogotá now had more lawyers, professors and journalists, and a ruling class prone towards liberal opinions that did not know or appreciate the distant Bolívar, or accept his constant demands for troops and money for projects that were not Colombian. So Santander was caught between a reluctant congress and an exigent Liberator, who seemed to regard him as a ready source of funds for his own campaigns. There was a critical moment of confrontation, from which both drew back and started again.

By decree of 10 February 1824 the Peruvian congress appointed Bolívar Dictator 'for the salvation of the country' and suspended the constitution. O'Leary recorded the event in a memorable passage:

> The situation of Peru when this decree was issued was very different from what it was when San Martín disembarked four years previously. At that time the support for independence was general throughout Peru, and enthusiasm for the liberators matched the resources placed at their disposal. San Martín had only to come, see, and conquer; he came, he saw, and he could have conquered. But the task was perhaps beyond him, or at least he believed so; he hesitated and finally abandoned it. When congress entrusted to Bolívar the salvation of the republic, it handed him a corpse.[76]

O'Leary exaggerated the degree of support which the Peruvians had given San Martín, but otherwise there was truth in his invidious comparison. San Martín had sought to win the minds and hearts of Peruvians. Bolívar, on the other hand, saw a 'Peru divided into three parties: first, anti-Colombian patriots; second, Spanish loyalists; third, loyalists of Torre Tagle and Riva Agüero. The rest of the unarmed masses has no commitment at all.'[77] And he perceived more acutely than San Martín that Peruvians were indifferent to one cause or the other, that each sector of this highly stratified society sought only to retain its own immediate advantage, that in these circumstances only power could persuade, and only a military victory by an American army could liberate Peru. 'We are the only ones who feel these disasters, for they are of little concern to the Peruvians. They have no hope at all, so they will do everything by sheer strength, like men who expect nothing from our sacrifices. But if we lose Peru, adios Colombia. So, for the good of Colombia, I am going to ride out the storm.'[78]

Bolívar did not go further and ask why this should be so. Why were the Peruvian elite, at first apparently ready to resist Spain, no longer committed to independence? One answer is that they had been alienated by the brutal expulsion of Spanish families and confiscation of their properties, people with whom they had many ties of family, friendship and business. After 1822 many creoles, led by Riva Agüero and Torre Tagle, rediscovered their cultural ties with Spain, their social affinity with the Spanish regime and their hostility to brutish Colombians.[79] A further explanation may have been that the elite were convinced that independence would bring a lax regime with a liberal policy towards Indians and blacks and that their security would be better protected by Spanish viceroys and generals than by Bolívar and his republicans.

Bolívar's friends and colleagues were convinced that it was madness to accept the dictatorship of Peru and advised him to withdraw. But his position was strong and legitimate, even if it did create a dilemma. The congress of Angostura had made him president of Venezuela in 1819. The congress of Cúcuta appointed him president of Colombia in 1821 with special powers to absent himself on military duty. Quito acclaimed him and accepted its incorporation into the Republic of Colombia. Now, his Peruvian dictatorship too came sanctioned by a congress. Appointed by others, Bolívar then trusted his own genius and vision. After recuperating at Pativilca, he began to organize resistance, to stop the rot, to improve morale. Civil affairs he placed in the hands of a single minister, José Sánchez Carrión, an able Peruvian and known patriot, who collaborated closely with Bolívar and was responsible for the renewal and creation of civil institutions, social policies and the administration of law in the liberated territories, giving added meaning to the concept of dictatorship. The Liberator's own task was to assemble an army, to procure more troops from Colombia, more recruits from Peru, and to find the money to pay for men and supplies. While still convalescing at Pativilca he had sent a long set of instructions to Sucre, the work of a professional commander at the top of his form. He gave an expert description of the landscape of battle, the challenges of the terrain and climate, the resources available to the army on the move. He laid down rules for training, the need for route marches to make their army as quick as the enemy's and capable of reacting to decisions for advance or retreat. He emphasized the different deployment of cavalry and infantry, the need for provisions and animals, the welfare of troops, not forgetting the provision of hospitals. He considered too the disposition of the enemy and the critical question of whether to prepare for attack or defence.[80] However debilitating his illness, Pativilca was a place of convalescence which gave him two months to think and plan his decisive campaign.

At the beginning of March he established his headquarters at Trujillo and in April moved to Huamachuco. He had to make the highlands, not the coast, his theatre of war, in order to take the fight to the enemy: the sierra was the royalist power base and the last chance for Spain. He made northern Peru the supply base of the revolution. He confiscated royalist property, cajoled money out of the Church, imposed taxes. It was now that Peruvians made their contribution to the cause of independence with men, money and supplies. Bolívar's indispensable assistant in the task of recruiting and organizing was the faithful Sucre, 'the right arm of the Liberator and the mainstay of the army', who established workshops for arms and horseshoes, placed orders in Trujillo for uniforms, prepared maps, reconnoitred the routes. Between them they created and trained a new army of liberation. Santander did not let him down entirely over Colombian troops. Reinforcements arrived from Panama and Guayaquil, among them an Irish contingent led by Colonel Francis Burdett O'Connor, who showed a talent for logistics that impressed Bolívar and who was appointed chief-of-staff to coordinate personnel and supplies in the patriot forces. Another Irishman, Arthur Sandes, a veteran of the Peninsular War, had joined Bolívar in Venezuela and had reached the rank of colonel by the time of the Peruvian campaign and was afterwards promoted to general.[81] By April 1824 the patriot army was eight thousand strong, composed of a majority of Colombians under the command of General Jacinto Lara and Colonel Córdova, heavily reinforced by Peruvian recruits under Marshal La Mar, against a Spanish army of sixteen thousand dispersed between Peru and Upper Peru and consisting of Indians and *cholos*, officered by Spaniards and Peruvians. The patriot army enjoyed two distinct assets. It possessed an incomparable cavalry, composed of the *gauchos* of Argentina, the *huasos* of Chile and the *llaneros* of Venezuela and Colombia. And it was paid, if not well (half a dollar a week) at least regularly; on this Bolívar insisted.

The liberators had a further advantage – the enemy's disarray. For the Spaniards too were subverted by Peru, and they too suffered demoralization and disunity. At the end of 1823 this was not apparent. While Americans fought and failed each other, the royalists consolidated their position. In the north General Canterac commanded an army almost eight thousand strong based on Huancayo. Viceroy La Serna had a thousand men in Cuzco. In Arequipa the army of the south under General Valdés comprised some three thousand. And behind them, in Upper Peru, General Olañeta had a force of four thousand men. These formidable armies were poised to concentrate and move on the Colombians. It was vital that they acted quickly, to anticipate Bolívar's own build-up, and to avoid the unpopularity which a parasite army of occupation incurred in a lengthy campaign. But at this point the Spanish position was undermined from within. On 1 October 1823 Ferdinand VII, released from constitutional bondage by a French army, abolished the constitution and restored abolutism, provoking in Peru a royalist split between former constitutionalists, La Serna, Canterac and Valdés, and absolutist Olañeta. But this was a struggle for power rather than a conflict of principles.[82] At the end of 1823 Olañeta defected, withdrew his military collaboration and established in Upper Peru a crudely conservative regime; with a cry for king and religion, he ousted the constitutional administration and packed the government with his relations and supporters. The royalist hinterland, hitherto one of the viceroy's most valuable assets, suddenly became a liability. The army of General Valdés was drawn off in a vain attempt to reduce Olañeta. And this diversion prevented the royalists from striking at the

Colombians in February or March, when the latter were just beginning to regroup and were extremely vulnerable, inferior in numbers, weapons and resources.

Bolívar had long pondered his strategy. Should he attack, anticipating his prospects? Or should he defend, wasting his resources? The problem required all his judgement, skill and experience. Delay in receiving intelligence of enemy movements, combined with problems in his own camp, prevented Bolívar from answering this question immediately and from exploiting La Serna's embarrassment to the full. But once he was aware of the situation he moved, confident that he had nothing to lose and everything to gain by taking the offensive. 'I am consumed by the demon of war, determined to finish this struggle, one way or the other.'[83]

Junín and Ayacucho

In May 1824 the Liberator led his army forward and upward to Pasco in one of the classic marches of the war of independence, 'over the most rugged districts, of the most mountainous country in the world, presenting at every step difficulties which in Europe would be considered perfectly insurmountable'.[84] As the troops struggled through the labyrinth of valleys and mountains across the cordillera in lands untouched by roads and still occupied by Indian communities, they were tortured by altitude sickness, radiation from the minerals, hazards of the terrain and night temperatures below freezing. Infantry and cavalry had to pick their way in single file along precipitous tracks. They were followed by columns of Indians carrying supplies and equipment, and in the rear driving a three-hundred mule train and herds of cattle as reserve provisions.

The leadership of Bolívar and the planning of Sucre came together in perfect collaboration in this their most decisive campaign. By the beginning of August, high in the sierra at Cerro de Pasco, the liberators had assembled an army of almost nine thousand; there were men from Caracas, Panama, Quito, Lima, Chile and Buenos Aires, many of them veterans of Maipú, Boyacá, Carabobo and Pichincha. With an inspired sense of occasion, Bolívar reviewed and addressed his troops: 'Soldiers! You are going to free an entire world from slavery, the freedom of the New World is the hope of the universe, you are invincible.' The ranks resounded with cheers.[85] At last, on 6 August, they engaged Canterac on the plateau of Junín, and Bolívar's proven skill in manoeuvring his army into a favourable position was again on display. It was a sharp and furious battle in which not a single shot was fired; the breathless silence was broken only by the clash of swords and lances and the stamping of the horses. And it was the patriots' superior cavalry and longer lances that won the day and forced the royalists into flight. 'The charges of our *llaneros*,' wrote O'Connor, 'made the earth tremble.'[86] Bolívar slept that night on the battlefield, where 259 of the enemy were killed for the loss of forty-five patriots dead and ninety-nine wounded.

Victory gave the liberators strategic command of the fruitful valley of Jauja, though the Spanish army was still largely intact and its spirit unquelled. Bolívar had to take steps to raise his own forces to maximum strength and he commissioned Sucre to bring in the lost, the stragglers and the convalescents, a task which he performed correctly but then complained that it had caused him to lose face among his colleagues, and he requested leave to retire. Bolívar knew Sucre as a vain and touchy individual and his reply was tactful but firm: 'If you think I wanted to insult you then you must have taken leave of your senses. I entrusted the assignment to you believing you could do it better than me, and it was proof of my esteem not of your humiliation. This excessive sensitivity and attention to the gossip of little people is unworthy of you. Glory consists in being great and useful.' Sucre had second thoughts, and Bolívar subsequently went out of his way to commend the post-Junín exertions of Sucre on behalf of the wounded and the missing, describing him as '*el general del soldado*'.[87]

Leaving Sucre as commander-in-chief of the army, with discretion to engage the enemy, Bolívar moved in early October, first to Huancayo, where Manuela awaited him, then to the coast, organizing civil administration as he went, and in December he liberated Lima and received a hero's welcome. But even after victories Bolívar was never allowed undiluted pleasure. First Sucre, then Santander. In Huancayo, news reached him from Bogotá that congress had passed a law (28 July 1824) revoking Bolívar's extraordinary powers and transferring them to Santander, giving as their reason that Bolívar had accepted the dictatorship of Peru. Another dispatch from Santander ordered Bolívar to give Sucre command of the Colombian troops.

The Liberator was enraged by these gratuitous insults but stifled his injured pride, and when he reached the coast he dictated friendly letters to Santander repaying meanness with generosity: he gave news of the successes, thanked him for the troops he had sent, assured him that Sucre already commanded the army and, at Ayacucho, had just won 'the most brilliant victory of the American war'.[88] He played down the loyal protests of Sucre and senior officers and held back from Bogotá their angry petition. There is no doubt that he could have led a revolt against this petty decision, inspired as it was by Santander, but he immediately delegated to Sucre command of the Colombian army. As O'Leary wrote, 'Bolívar thus gave an example of obedience to the law of his country, when a single word or sign on his part would have been sufficient to gain the wholehearted support of the army and the people of Colombia.'[89] But he did not forget the outrage to his leadership or overlook the intervention of Santander; after years of close contact Bolívar ended his private correspondence with the vice-president. And he remained dictator of Peru.

Meanwhile in the sierra La Serna fought back quickly. Leading the joint forces of Canterac and Valdés, an army of 9,300 with superior weapons and resources, he advanced on Sucre and sought to encircle him, while Sucre manoeuvred his six thousand men out of distance, both sides moving as though choreographed for a spectacle. As a general Sucre was supreme, brave, talented and indefatigable, alert to the details as well as the big picture. He wrote his own dispatches, controlled the espionage, reconnoitred, visited the outposts at all hours, made sure the rations were delivered. He was qualified to lead the last great victory. On 8 December 1824, on the plain of Ayacucho encircled by mountains and itself over ten thousand feet above sea level, the two armies finally confronted each other. Sucre's advice to his men was terse: 'Upon your efforts depends the fate of South America.' Their own fate was also at stake: royalist Indians who had already harassed the patriots now waited in the wings to cut them down in the event of their defeat and flight. Lieutenant-Colonel Medina of the Colombian army was killed by the Indians of Huando on his way to Lima with Sucre's dispatch of the battle.[90] But in the battle itself it was the royalists who were defeated, as much, perhaps, by the hopelessness of their cause as by the tactics of Sucre. This last great battle of the American war, fought high in the Andes by troops in brightly coloured uniforms, was a strange anticlimax and casualties were not heavy (sixty-seven on the patriot side), though off the field of battle the Rifles were decimated defending the patriots' baggage train. Viceroy La Serna was taken prisoner, and on 9 December General Canterac conceded unconditional surrender, on terms that provided for the surrender of all remaining royalist forces in Peru. 'The battle for Peru is complete: its independence and the peace of America have been established on this battleground.'[91] The royalists could conceivably have concentrated all their remaining forces in Peru and Upper Peru and fought yet again. But what were their prospects? They had no hope of reinforcements from Spain, and this perhaps was the most demoralizing knowledge of all.

Military victory in Peru enabled Bolívar to clarify his political position. He sent his resignation from the presidency to the congress of Colombia; this stunned the assembly into silence, followed by applause for the Liberator, and rejection of his resignation. He ordered the congress of Peru to assemble on 10 February 1825, when he presented his resignation and congratulated Peru on no longer having a dictator. But Peruvians loved a victor and would not let him go: congress immediately conferred on him supreme political and military authority until it next met in 1826. By remaining cool and reasonable

Bolívar retained his panoply of power. At the same time he reminded Santander of his place in the hierarchy of the revolution: 'It is an honour that two of my friends and assistants have emerged as two prodigies. . . . I am the man of difficulties, you are the man of law, and Sucre is the man of war.'[92] The meaning was clear: I am supreme, the one who solves the great problems. I command, you administer.

On Christmas Day Bolívar proclaimed the great victory: 'Soldiers! The good cause, the cause of the rights of man, has won with your arms the terrible struggle against the oppressors.' And on 27 December, declaring that 'this glorious victory is due exclusively to the skill, bravery, and heroism of General in Chief Antonio José de Sucre, the other Generals, Commanders, officers and troops', he decreed honours for the victors and appointed Sucre Grand Marshal, a Peruvian rank beyond the control of the small minds in Bogotá.[93] He was generous in his recognition of the role of Sucre and wrote a paper on his life and achievement, concluding, 'The battle of Ayacucho is the summit of American glory and the work of General Sucre. . . . Posterity will represent Sucre with one foot on Pichincha and the other on Potosí.'[94] Soon the grand marshal took the war to Upper Peru and Potosí, though it would be another year, after a lengthy and costly siege, before Callao, the port of Lima, capitulated on 23 January 1826.

'These were glorious days in the life of the Liberator,' O'Leary remarked of the time after Ayacucho, when Colombia and Peru competed in their praises and even his enemies suspended their calumnies.[95] Bolívar spent the early part of 1825 in civil administration, applying republican principles of liberty and equality, reforming political, legal, and economic institutions, and establishing a system of schools on the Lancaster model. The Peruvian Congress awarded him one million pesos, which he accepted only on condition it was diverted to charitable works in Venezuela. In Peru he lived like a prince in a country house outside Lima. La Magdalena was his palace, Manuela his lover, Peruvians his admirers, poets his flatterers. Interests and lobbyists came to press their claims, women to enjoy his company, messengers to bring and collect his mail. He loved it all. He was the centre of the world, seduced though not satiated by success. What more could he want? Action and glory in the whole of Latin America, wherever danger led? But his own revolution still called.

In April he left Lima for Arequipa with a travelling office of political and military aides, and a mobile library including works by Helvetius, Montesquieu, Napoleon, De Pradt and Bentham. But he left Manuela with a heavy heart, accepting the claims of her marriage. Amidst the banquets and balls celebrating his visit he still had time to make his mark as a reforming minister and a dispenser of justice and good government. He also reminded the bishop of his duty to preach republican, not monarchical, principles, so that people would know that religion did not deprive them of their natural rights.[96] His civil regime in Peru, however, would have needed an army of Bolivarian bureaucrats to make it work, and in their absence many of the projected reforms were not carried out. As he crossed the cordillera to Cuzco his progress was retarded not only by the effects of the *soroche* at an altitude of over three thousand metres but by the isolation of the highland departments from the coast; in an effort to improve communications he ordered the construction of three highways into Cuzco and Puno and outlined their routes, but the project was neglected once he had left.

The ancient capital of the Incas, for Bolívar a monument to a noble history and historic injustice, gave him another hero's welcome, unsurpassed in ceremonial and generosity, and in turn was the object of enlightened policies towards education, social reform and Indian welfare, in particular the termination of forced service and other inequalities.[97] Observers might have drawn two conclusions from Bolívar's programme in Cuzco. Where vested interests were strong enough to resist innovation – for example the landed elite's use of Indian labour – the reforms were ignored or diluted. But where traditional institutions, no longer enjoying the prestige and resources of former times, were the targets, modernization could be made to succeed. Thus the republican concept of liberty as opposed to obedience, and state action as distinct from charity, undermined the convents of Cuzco when Bolívar issued decrees for the care of orphans, a state school for boys and a new school for girls, funded from property and income taken from the convents.[98] In Bolívar's view of the world there were losers as well as winners. And from the sierra his view of Peru was now more benign. After two years of turmoil he wrote to his close friend Fernando de Peñalver: 'At present this country is more peaceful than Colombia, and it has admirable respect and gratitude for its liberators.'[99] He also had time to criticize an ode written by the Ecuadorian poet José Joaquín Olmedo, and to advise him to take Alexander Pope as his model, whose translation of the *Iliad* the Liberator seems to have known.[100]

From Cuzco and its historic sites he travelled south through further landmarks of the Inca empire to Puno and Lake Titicaca, and in early August he set out on his final journey of liberation. General Sucre came to meet him in Zepita and together they crossed the Desaguadero into Upper Peru.

Chapter 9

THE MAN OF PROBLEMS

Across the Desaguadero

Liberation was a rolling enterprise. One conquest succeeded another from Venezuela onwards, and a further target was always in sight. In these serial campaigns Bolívar could use his talents for big thinking and detailed improvisation, and exercise an indomitable will. Under his direction, the revolution moved on, fifteen years of slow but sure advance against the Spanish empire. Yet there was a limit to the boundaries of liberation, an end to the enemy armies. The last victory stopped the charge forward, and as the liberators reined in and looked around they saw not Spaniards but Americans. The scene changed from liberation to reconstruction. State building too was within the Liberator's competence, and another stage for glory, but the enemies were new and their challenges different. It was a cruel fate that in the world he had created no one was his equal, anyone his critic. In describing himself to Santander as '*el hombre de las dificultades*', he forecast the course of the year 1826, the end of the revolution and the beginning of post-war problems, his problems.

The last Spanish army of occupation took its stand in Upper Peru. It had beaten off attempts by Buenos Aires to export the May Revolution, the liberal doctrines of which did not appeal to creoles reluctant to subvert a society in which they were vastly outnumbered by Indians. Resistance was kept alive by *mestizo* guerrilla bands who fought not so much for national independence as for freedom from outside control, whether Spanish or Argentine; before 1819 they had not even heard of Bolívar.[1] The Indians, unlike creoles and *mestizos*, took sides not for individual motives but in conformity with traditional allegiances, whether these were royalist or guerrilla chieftains, and their preference was to avoid the war, from which they had nothing to gain. While the peninsular leaders were fighting Bolívar in Lower Peru, the Spanish forces were left under the command of tough creole officers who supported the

Spanish cause. The majority of the creole elite also supported that cause, or at least did not challenge it. When, in 1823, General Santa Cruz, a *mestizo* from La Paz and himself a former royalist, invaded Upper Peru, he sensed the lack of support for liberation and, surrounded by royalist forces, he quickly retreated.

The leader of Upper Peru's conservatives was Pedro Antonio Olañeta, a commander more royalist than the viceroy, more absolutist than the king, and enemy of all liberals, whether Spanish generals or republican leaders. He repudiated Viceroy La Serna and declared that he would die for king and religion. His rebellion split the Spanish front and forced the creole elite of Upper Peru to make some awkward decisions. Opportunism rather than convictions ruled their choice. Convinced that Spain's last bastion in America was doomed, they sought an alternative regime that would preserve their interests, their landed property, their control of Indian labour. So they sought a form of autonomy for Upper Peru. Did this mean Olañeta, self-appointed spokesman for absolute monarchy? Or did it mean Bolívar, who would bring a liberal republic? The answer would be given in battle.

After Ayacucho, Bolívar assigned the liberation of Upper Peru to Sucre. The grand marshal soon swept up the debris of Spanish rule in the sierra, entered Cuzco on 24 December 1824, and then crossed the Desaguadero to advance cautiously into Upper Peru, simultaneously negotiating with Olañeta and occupying territory. Olañeta's forces now began to desert in great numbers, responding to Sucre's call to join the liberating army. The creoles too had to make up their minds between loyalty to a distant king or acknowledgement of the immediate power of Bolívar and Sucre. Olañeta decided on the king. But the majority of the creoles opted for the winning side and virtually inherited a revolution they had not made. Cochabamba, La Paz and other towns declared their allegiance. Finally, cornered and isolated, Olañeta was mortally wounded at the battle of Tumusla (1 April 1825) and his forces defeated. This was the last battle of the South American revolution, and in its wake Sucre occupied Potosí, the treasury of Spain for three hundred years, as Bolívar called it.

What was Upper Peru? A nation? A people? A province? Sucre issued at La Paz a decree (9 February 1825) proclaiming the virtual independence of Upper Peru. The army, he insisted, had come to liberate, not to govern. Upper Peru could no longer continue its previous dependence on Buenos Aires, for the latter did not possess a government legally representing these provinces; the ultimate solution would have to be based upon a decision of the provinces and an agreement between Peru and Buenos Aires. Meanwhile, Upper Peru would continue under the authority of the commander of the liberating army until a general assembly decided the form of government. Sucre believed, with some justification, that this decree represented the political thinking of his leader. But Bolívar, the professional liberator, disapproved of the initiative and reminded Sucre that he was the commander of an army, not the disposer of political rights, and that in any case he had violated the principle of *uti possidetis*, by which the new states succeeded to the territorial jurisdiction of the major administrative units of the colonial period.[2] While he was still in Lima he shared his thoughts with Santander.

> Upper Peru belongs by right to the Río de la Plata; in fact to Spain; by wish of its people, who want a separate state, to independence; and by claim to Peru, who previously owned it and wants it now. . . . To give it to the Río de la Plata would be to deliver it into anarchy. To give it to Peru would be to violate the international law which we have established. To create a new republic, as the inhabitants demand, would be an innovation which I do not care to undertake, for only an American assembly can decide that.[3]

In fact, three months later, when he had presumably forgiven Sucre for usurping his role, he confirmed the decree of 9 February. His reasons were compelling: he knew that neither Argentina nor Peru would agree on the other procuring this territory; he himself did not want to enlarge the power of either country by awarding them a valuable mining zone; and he took account of opinion in Upper Peru itself.

What did the Bolivarian revolution mean for its newest recruit? Was it really Bolivarian? A 'representative' assembly met on 10 July 1825 in Chuquisaca, the city of four names.[4] In a country of well over one million people there were forty-eight delegates, elected by a restricted and complex franchise that included literacy and property tests, and a large province such as Santa Cruz, penalized by its mass illiteracy, could send only two deputies. At least thirty of the deputies were graduates of the University of Chuquisaca, in whose halls the assembly met. And only two – guerrillas both – had actually fought in the war. Thus the creole aristocracy came into their inheritance, replacing Spaniards in a social hierarchy – *caballeros, cholos, indios* – which endured for many generations to come. The assembly was a meeting of the local elite, men such as Casimiro Olañeta, nephew of the general, who had been first royalists, then *olañetistas*, and for independence only at the last minute, and who now represented not a nation but a ruling group. For them independence meant control of policy and patronage; only in Upper Peru could they expect to rule, and they were determined that only they should rule there. The assembly declared independence on 6 August, and the new republic adopted the name of Bolívar, later changed to Bolivia, and appointed the Liberator to supreme executive power. The deputies also requested him to draw up a constitution for Bolivia. He was on his way from Cuzco to Puno when he received these decisions and in August he hastened to greet a new country.

When Bolívar was approaching Bolivia, Sucre came to meet him north of the Desaguadero. Alighting from his horse to salute the Liberator his sword fell from his scabbard. In the evening he remarked to O'Leary that it was a bad omen. The next day one of his servants was insolent. He drew his sword and was striking him with the flat of it when it broke. 'That's a worse omen,' said O'Leary, 'now your misfortunes begin.' 'I was thinking so myself,' replied Sucre.[5] Misfortunes there would be, but the immediate future looked good. At least the Liberator thought so. The wonders of nature in the southern Andes raised Bolívar's spirits and, as he passed under the arches erected in his honour along the mountain routes, he spoke to his staff of his envy of the Emperor Napoleon's passing over the Alps in triumph. He received a triumphant welcome in La Paz, where he arrived on 18 August. Presented with a crown of gold studded with diamonds, he handed it to Sucre: 'This reward belongs to the victor, the hero of Ayacucho.'[6] La Paz, in turn, received some of the benefits of Bolívar's liberal thinking in reforms of administrative and clerical abuses, not all of them immediately welcome. He left La Paz on 20 September, crossing the altiplano towards Oruro, and after a succession of mountains each appearing higher than the last, finally reached Potosí. There he was handsomely received by its prefect, General William Miller, English veteran of the army of the Andes, in a series of colourful entertainments and Indian parades.[7] He was also pestered by two Argentine agents wanting the assistance of Colombian forces for a war with Brazil, a project which was not in Colombia's interests or Bolívar's gift but which he acknowledged with diplomatic tact. An English visitor to Potosí at this time, Captain Joseph Andrews, travelling on behalf of the Chilean and Peruvian Mining Association, found the Liberator looking tense, careworn and tired, with an anxious brow, penetrating eyes and rapid speech, but he was also very approachable, with a 'cordial, downright, English shake of the hand'.[8]

Bolívar, whose health was long supposed to be precarious, was never deterred by altitudes or averse to triumphs. After a hard climb by mule and the final stage on foot, accompanied by Sucre and his staff, he reached the summit of the great silver mountain, an icon of imperial wealth and power and supreme trophy of the revolution. In the chill winds of the mountain top they unfurled the flags of independence, Colombia, Peru and Argentina, and drank to the American revolution. It was a historic event for all there, especially the Liberator himself. As he looked northwards across the bleak *páramo* and beyond the Cordillera Central, he saw in his mind's eye the narrative of his odyssey, from the shores of the Orinoco and the coasts of the Caribbean, across the great plains of Venezuela, the peaks and valleys of Colombia and

Ecuador, to the awesome landscapes of Peru. At that moment fifteen years of marches and battles, failures and successes, bitterness and pleasure, fifteen years of glory passed across his mind.[9]

An emotional moment, but not one to be prolonged. Following his usual practice – to conquer, to pronounce, and to depart – he left a protesting Sucre to govern Bolivia and returned to Lima to further his political life. If legend is to be believed he also left a fleeting lover, María Costa, wife of an Argentine general, and in due course a secret offspring, José Antonio, who claimed to be the son of Simón Bolívar.[10] His journey took him to Chuquisaca, where he dashed off a decree prohibiting the circulation of obscene publications, 'so conducive to immorality', deferred the next meeting of the general assembly to 25 May 1826, and delegated supreme authority to Sucre.[11] Then on to Cochabamba and Arica, where he embarked in the *Chimborazo* on 2 February 1826 and arrived at Chorrillos on the night of 7 February; from there it was a short journey north to Lima and his residence of La Magdalena. On 10 February he made a public entry into Lima amid cheering crowds, flags and triumphant arches, a welcome rarely extended to their own.

He had already begun to collect his documents, his drafts, his thoughts for the constitution that would bear his name. Now, in a mood of great elation, he began to place them on paper. 'The Bolivian Republic has a special delight for me. First, there is its name, and then all its advantages, without a single drawback; it appears destined to be fashioned by hand. The more I think of the destiny of this country, the more it seems a small marvel.'[12] He took great pride in the commission: 'If I receive no other public honours, to give my name to an entire people fills my soul and my heart to overflowing.'[13] The task of legislating for the management of free people, as he put it, was hard and difficult and he gave it everything he had. It was finished and dispatched on 12 May, committed not to the postal service but to Colonel William Ferguson and Captain Belford Hinton Wilson, who completed the journey of eighteen hundred miles in an epic ride of twenty-one days to deliver the constitution to Sucre in Chuquisaca.[14] On 18 May Peru recognized the independence of Bolivia.

The Bolivarian Enlightenment

As the revolution advanced into its final stages, Bolívar was haunted by America's need for strong government, and it was in this frame of mind that he drafted the Bolivian constitution.[15] It was the culmination of his political thought, 'his great idea', written in his maturity, when the war was over and the peace waiting to be established. His lifelong search for a balance between tyranny and anarchy now moved unerringly towards authority. He told the

British consul in Lima 'that his heart always beats in favour of liberty, but that his head leans towards aristocracy ... if the principles of liberty are too rapidly introduced anarchy and the destruction of the white inhabitants will be the inevitable consequences'.[16] As O'Leary explained, 'He sought a system capable of controlling revolutions, not theories which might foment them; the fatal spirit of ill-conceived democracy which had already produced so many evils in America had to be curbed if its effects were to be avoided.'[17]

The new constitution preserved the division of powers – legislative, executive and judicial – and to these he added an elective power, by which groups of citizens in each province chose an elector, and the electing body then chose representatives and nominated mayors and justices. The legislative power was divided into three bodies – tribunes, senators and censors – all elected. The tribunes initiated finance and major policy issues; the senators were guardians of law and ecclesiastical patronage; and the censors were responsible for the preservation of civil liberties, culture, and the constitution – an awkward revival of his previous notion of a 'moral power'. The president was appointed by the legislature for life and had the right to appoint his successor; this Bolívar regarded as 'the most sublime inspiration of republican ideas', the president being 'the sun which, fixed in its orbit, imparts life to the universe'.[18] The president appointed the vice-president, who held the office of prime minister and would succeed the president in office. Thus 'elections would be avoided, which are the greatest scourge of republics and produce only anarchy'. This was the measure of his disillusion seven years after 1819 when, at Angostura, he had declared: 'The continuation of authority in the same individual has frequently meant the end of democratic governments. Repeated elections are essential in proper systems of government.'

The constitution, insisted Bolívar with justification, was a liberal document. It provided for civil rights – liberty, equality, security and property – and for a strong, independent judicial power. Equality too was enshrined. The constitution abolished social privileges and declared the slaves free 'from the day the constitution was published'. Bolívar was alive to the problems latent in the concept of liberty. Liberty in America was no longer freedom from the Spanish monarchy but from the republican state, and it needed a firm base. 'God has destined man to freedom,' he proclaimed in his presentation. With its origin secure in divine power it also needed a rule of limitation; this he found in the demands of public interest and security. But this was not a theoretical liberty alone: the Liberator sought an applied liberty and one that influenced the life of society. This was the basic justification for the strong and uncompromising institutions that the constitution created.

Some observers were genuinely impressed. The British consul believed that it was 'founded apparently on the basis of the British constitution', allowing 'useful liberty' but 'obviating any mischievous excess of popular power'.[19] In London, Bolívar's friend Sir Robert Wilson made the point that criticism of the constitution in North America was not surprising in a state where slavery was so firmly rooted, but it was increasingly favoured by enlightened opinion.[20] Bolívar himself claimed that the constitutional restraints on the president were 'the closest ever known', restricted as he was by his ministers, who in turn were responsible to the censors and scrutinized by the legislators. He warned Bolivians against 'two monstrous enemies who will attack you at once. *Tyranny* and *anarchy* constitute an immense ocean of oppression encircling a tiny island of freedom.' Their salvation would be the institutions and the liberties enshrined in his constitution.

The constitution, however, was branded by its executive power, by the life-president with the right to choose his successor.[21] Sucre, a man with his own opinions and not easily influenced, supported the constitution and the life-presidency, but he knew that it was controversial: 'I believe you should be here in person to present the constitution, for the essential article of the life-president raises thousands of difficulties, and I doubt whether it will get through.'[22] In other words there were opponents in congress and some of them presented reasonable arguments, fearing that a life-presidency would become a republican monarch and degenerate into a hereditary one. Sucre himself, knowing he was the designated appointee, suggested that the first president be elected by popular vote and not merely by that of congress.[23] In the event the article was accepted without amendment. There was another keen debate on giving the vote to Indians, for the constitution excluded illiterates. It was argued that if sovereignty resided in the people and two thirds of Bolivians were Indians, then these could not in justice be excluded; others pointed out that qualifications could be improved by education, and others that ignorance precluded political participation. A compromise was reached when congress agreed that the requirement of literacy should be postponed until 1835.[24] On religion there was no compromise. Bolívar wanted to exclude all reference to the subject but congress insisted on defining the Catholic religion as the exclusive religion of the republic.

Many Americans, conservatives as well as liberals, were outraged by the idea of a president for life. No doubt Bolívar's experience of the frightening anarchy of Peru and the obstacles to stability in Bolivia help to explain his preference for a life-president. But the fact remains that he was anxious to export the constitution to other American countries. Five editions were quickly printed in South America, and he sent copies to his friends, colleagues and enemies throughout Colombia. Páez was on the list. There was a London edition aimed at his favourite power, which he hoped to recruit to his cause. He regarded the Constitution as 'the ark of the covenant, an alliance between

Europe and America, between soldier and civilian, between democracy and aristocracy, between imperialism and republicanism'.[25] And in recommending it to a wider audience he claimed that 'in it are combined all the advantages of federalism, all the strength of centralized government, all the stability of monarchical regimes'.[26] Indeed, the life-presidency was a source of particular pride and he considered it superior to hereditary monarchy, for the president appointed his successor, who was thus a ruler by merit and not by hereditary right. According to O'Leary, far from endangering freedom, the Bolivian Constitution was a great defence and guarantor of freedom, freedom from anarchy and revolution. This could be seen in the address accompanying the constitution: 'The one who wrote it fought for the cause of liberty from his study with extraordinary eloquence, after having been its most renowned champion on the field of battle.'[27]

Bolívar had a strongly personal view of power and always found it necessary to exercise his individual will, not only in military campaigns but also in state building. An active government had to be strong and free from constraints. He personally always wanted freedom to escape the narrow bounds of institutional control and to impose his will, in the field or in government house, and for this he needed absolute power. The Bolivian Constitution should also be judged in terms of function. Bolívar never saw liberty as an end in itself. For him there was always a further question: freedom for what? He did not regard the role of government as purely passive, defending rights, preserving privileges, exercising patronage. Government existed to maximize human happiness, and its function was to make policy as well as to satisfy interests. He was not the last to learn that new countries had a special need of strong government as an effective instrument of reform. In his own mind he had no doubt that his constitution was liberal and reformist, 'more liberal and more durable than that of Colombia', containing as it did the unconditional abolition of slavery and the revocation of all privileges. Bolivia could be a model of the Bolivarian state. In a remote corner of the Andes, far from their native Venezuela, Bolívar and Sucre began a historic enterprise of state building, starting if not from a *tabula rasa*, at least from their own agenda.

Bolívar considered Sucre the only man capable and worthy of exercising the life-presidency. But Sucre did not want the presidency for life and when, in 1826, the Bolivian congress adopted the constitution and elected Sucre to the office (28 October), he undertook to hold it only until 1828. His dearest wish was to return to Quito and marry his betrothed, Mariana Carcelán y Larrea, marquesa de Solanda. Instead, he stuck to his task and made his regime in Bolivia a model of enlightened absolutism, a quest for economic development and social reform that was a mirror image of Bolívar's ideas. Such at least was his policy, if not achievement. The obstacles to change were many and powerful, and Bolívar himself had encountered them in other parts of South America. The creoles were conservative, their economic horizons bounded by stagnant *haciendas*, rentier values and public office; their habits indifferent to entrepreneurial activities; their social outlook wedded to a profound and immobile inequality. Dominating congress they modified some of the ecclesiastical and electoral details of the constitution in an illiberal sense. Warfare had dealt another blow to an already defective economy, and flight of Indian labour and white capital had brought mining and agriculture almost to a standstill. To construct a national economy Sucre had to lay his hands on more revenue, so his first task was to devise a more equitable and productive tax system. In 1826 congress abolished the *alcabala* and reduced other taxes on vital consumer goods. This was self-interest. The real test was direct taxation. Bolívar himself abolished the Indian tribute by decree of 22 December 1825. It was replaced by an income tax and property tax, a revolutionary departure from the fiscal privilege long enjoyed by whites and assimilated *mestizos*. These interests stubbornly resisted the new policy and fought an unscrupulous campaign to revive the colonial tax system. In Cochabamba census officials were harassed by *el pueblo bajo*, who locked their doors long enough to enable the occupants to escape out the back.[28] In July 1826 the Indian tribute was restored, and the income and property taxes were abolished in December. Within a year, therefore, the country had returned to the colonial tax structure with its built-in discrimination and inequality. As Sucre pointed out, the oppressed classes were themselves divided against each other: 'The *cholos* do not wish to be classed as Indians, and even the Indians have distinctions among themselves.'[29]

Yet Bolivia had one asset, its silver, if only this could be realized. The industry needed large injections of capital to expand operations, procure machinery and undertake drainage. For this it had to look abroad, which meant looking to the London money market, where the El Dorado of Potosí stirred the imagination and blunted the mind. By decree of 2 August 1825 Bolívar ordered that all abandoned and unworked mines revert to the state for renting out or auction. The British consul estimated that mines to the value of five million pesos thus became public property.[30] The new law, operating in peacetime conditions, was sufficient to produce a modest rise in silver production from 1825, and coin production also improved. General Miller, prefect of the department of Potosí, reported that from 1810 to 1825 the mint coined an annual average of no more than half a million dollars; but during the first five months after liberation it coined upwards of a million.[31]

More spectacular results were anticipated from foreign investment. In London a mania of speculation led to the formation of twenty-six mining associations in 1824–5 for exploiting Spanish American mines.[32] Of these the Potosí, La Paz and Peruvian Mining Association assembled the most capital and attracted most support; it had six members of parliament on its board and James Paroissien as its agent. The company's representatives were welcomed in Bolivia and authorized to purchase mines and associated installations, with full protection of the law and many fiscal privileges. But in London ignorant and improvident speculation was followed by a resounding crash; when, in December 1825, the money market collapsed, the vital flow of capital was cut and the company was unable to meet its obligations in South America. This brought mining operations to an abrupt halt; an official embargo was placed on machinery, equipment and supplies at the port of Arica; and the company was forced into liquidation, the victim of inadequate capital, extravagance of the company's agents, lack of skilled labour, and inferior technology. Basically the English expected too much for too little.[33] The collapse of the Potosí Mining Association ended prospects of major improvement in Bolivian silver production. The government was thus starved of revenue for investment in economic and social reforms, in roads, public works and schools. The country was desperately bankrupt, without the basic necessity for development: a port of entry and exit independent of other powers. The government unsuccessfully tried to buy Arica from Peru. It then sought to make a viable port of Cobija, renamed by Bolívar Puerto de La Mar. But in spite of possessing competitive tariffs, this was an unlikely outlet for overseas trade: it was five hundred miles from Potosí, on the edge of the Atacama desert, and lacked roads, people and water.[34]

Like their counterparts in Peru, the Bolivian aristocracy monopolized the few assets the country possessed, and they continued to exert an inexorable control over land and labour. The Indians of Bolivia formed 80 per cent of the population at the beginning of the nineteenth century.[35] On the eve of independence they were still subject to the *mita, repartimiento*, tribute, parish charges and tithes, *pongueaje* and other personal services, and agricultural labour on the land of the whites. Community Indians were perhaps even worse off than those of the *haciendas*, for they were forced to give personal services to a multiplicity of authorities and officials. Independence brought some improvement of status. The *mita* was abolished and, unlike the tribute, it did not reappear. In August 1825 at La Paz, Bolívar proclaimed the policy which he had already attempted to apply in Peru. He abolished personal service, declaring equality among all citizens. But the creoles did not cooperate, and the Indians were slow to respond, distrusting these measures as traps set by the cruel whites to ensnare them still more. Results were therefore negligible. 'Prejudices and timidity on their own part, and the interest of those who still keep up the delusion, in order to profit by the gratuitous labours of others, will combine to counteract the most benevolent views of the patriotic government.'[36] The Indians of Bolivia continued to be exploited by whites, contrary to the spirit of the new laws, and more and more became dependent on the *hacendados* for plots of land, the rent of which had to be paid in services on the master's estate and in his house.

Bolívar decreed a measure of agrarian change in 1825: the object was to distribute state land in Bolivia, preferably among 'the natives and those who have offered and suffered much for the cause of independence'.[37] But as rural misery was even worse in Bolivia than in Colombia, the scene of his first experiment, he decreed that land should be distributed to everyone in need, not simply to army veterans: 'Every individual without discrimination of age or sex shall receive a *fanegada* of land in the fertile areas and two *fanegadas* in the poorer land which lacks irrigation', the only condition being that the recipients should begin cultivation within a year. But these reforms were sabotaged by the Bolivian ruling class, who regarded a free and landed peasantry as a threat to their dependent labour supply. On 20 September 1827 the Bolivian congress issued a law suspending the Bolivarian decrees concerning distribution of land to the Indians 'until the prefects of the departments concerned report on the number of Indians and the amounts of lands remaining over, in order that each one can be assigned what he needs according to the locality'. This was another way of saying no, the official word of Bolivia's rulers on agrarian change.

Bolívar's anti-slavery policy was also unpopular. In 1825 the general assembly of Bolivia voted Bolívar a million dollars as a reward for his services; he accepted the grant 'only upon condition that the money should be employed in purchasing the liberty of about one thousand black slaves existing in Bolivia'.[38] The response was negative. But in 1826 he returned to the attack in his constitution that declared Bolivians to be 'all those who until now have been slaves and who are thereby in fact freed by the publication of this constitution; a special law shall determine the amount to be paid as indemnity to their former owners'. The deputies pretended to comply, but in fact they substantially modified Bolívar's text; the new version declared former slaves free citizens 'but they cannot abandon the house of their former owners except in the form which a special law will determine'.[39] The principal objects of concern were labour and recompense, for although large-scale plantation agriculture was not practised in Bolivia, slaves were used on estates and in domestic service, principally in the region of La Paz, and they represented an investment that owners were not prepared to lose. 'The only indemnity they seek,' reported Sucre, 'is that slaves should be forced to work in their existing *haciendas* as peons.' He seemed to think that this was '*muy generoso*', not a sentiment that Bolívar would have shared.[40] The contrivance was characteristic of abolition throughout Spanish America; slavery was replaced not by freedom but by servile labour.

The attempt by Bolívar and Sucre to transform Bolivia into a liberal and prosperous state failed. Bolívar's utopia of political literacy also vanished. Education was an opportunity but also a problem. The Liberator decreed the establishment of primary schools and orphanages and diverted clerical revenues obtained through his ecclesiastical reforms for their funding. But he also appointed Simón Rodríguez, the former teacher for whom he still retained an unaccountable admiration, as director of public education and supervisor of charitable institutions. Sucre, pining all the while for his fiancée in Quito, found that in addition to other duties he had inherited a mad professor and his crazy projects. Soon he was groaning at the folly of Don Samuel, as he called him, who was appointing hordes of teachers without the means to pay them, and establishing shelters for beggars with more officials than inmates. Rodríguez claimed independence to do what he liked, insulting locals as ignorant brutes, throwing his weight around and stirring up trouble. Sucre, though wary of offending Bolívar, was eventually relieved to accept the resignation of this loose cannon. Sucre was conscious of the defects of what he called the 'colonial education' they had received, which left Americans inexpert in the art of government and at a disadvantage in dealing with Europeans. His own policy of school expansion was not entirely fruitless, but education still suffered from a shortfall in funding and a shortage of teachers and books.[41]

Bolivia brought out the flaws in Bolivarian modernization. The attack on ecclesiastical privilege and the egalitarian direction of tax reform directly threatened the main interest groups of traditional society, the clergy and the landowners, which the new state simply did not have the power to confront.[42] The result was fiscal failure and another obstacle to economic growth. The experiment proved that the prospects of this new Andean republic, without assets of man or nature, were as bleak as the landscape of its windswept altiplano. But its rulers were determined to keep what little they had, and if this was nationalism then Sucre soon felt its impact. The continued presence of Colombian troops brought to the surface latent passions against foreigners, passions which resentful Argentines and Peruvians, deprived of what they regarded as their colonial inheritance, did their utmost to inflame. Sucre reported to Bolívar: 'The *porteños* and the Peruvians are very active in stirring up resentment in the country against the Colombian troops.' And Bolívar eventually advised him: 'If I were you I would not remain in the south, because in the final analysis we suffer from the defect of being Venezuelans, just as we have been Colombians in Peru.'[43] Anxious still to re-annex these provinces, Peru lost no opportunity of exploiting anti-Colombian feelings, and in 1827–8 combined subversion within and attack from without. On 18 April 1828 a rebellion in Chuquisaca led by an Argentine sergeant and two Peruvians, seconded by an invasion from Peru, was the beginning of the end for the Bolivarian enlightenment in Bolivia. Sucre was severely wounded in the right arm confronting the first rebels, and on 7 July the government was forced to sign an agreement for the expulsion of all foreigners from the Bolivian army and the immediate withdrawal of Colombian troops. The irony did not escape Sucre: a survivor of the war, he was now a casualty of the peace.[44] He resigned the presidency, pessimistic of Bolivia's capacity to become a viable nation, and in August he left for home, anxious to be with his new wife who had married him by proxy in Quito on 20 April while he was lying wounded in Chuquisaca. In Bolivia he left a companion, Rosalía Cortés, and a two-year-old son.

The Lost Purity of his Principles

The euphoria of liberation did not endure. It was galling for Peruvians to witness Chileans and Argentines enter their country in the guise of liberators, and Colombians too outstayed their welcome. During the war the Indian guerrilla leader Ninavilca described the Colombians as a 'mob of thieves', despoilers of Peruvian resources, and they were no more popular now than then.[45] Peruvians came to detest Bolívar's dictatorship, and they did not respond favourably to his idea of a confederation of the Andes.

Bolívar felt the full force of Peruvian nationalism after his return from the south in 1826, though he did not give it credit for what it was, attributing opposition to selfish interests hurt by his radical reforms of the administration.[46] The capitulation of Callao on 23 January 1826 completed his work as liberator and he could now glory in the fact that, of its once great American empire, Spain retained only the two islands of Cuba and Puerto Rico. He had earned some leave and was now free to return to Colombia with his army. Yet he stayed. The government was headed first by General La Mar, then by General Santa Cruz, but Bolívar continued to be the power behind the administration. Peruvians were increasingly restless at his presence and he became the target of conspiratorial attack, congressional opposition and widespread criticism in the country. The conspiracy he crushed, congress he browbeat, and criticism he brushed off, confident of his Colombian troops.

But he could do little about economic or social life. The traditional prop of the economy and Peru's major exportable assets, gold and silver, were suffering from post-war depression; mining production was hit by disruption of communications and by severe shortage of labour, mercury, mules and capital. The Commercial Code of 6 June 1826, though prefaced by liberal clichés, was in fact highly restrictive.[47] It suppressed internal customs and reduced *alcabalas*, but it placed a basic 30 per cent duty on all foreign imports, and imports such as liquor, certain texiles, sugar and other items competing with national production bore an 80 per cent protective tariff, subsequently raised to 90 per cent. Peru did not possess institutions capable of enforcing these excessive duties along its extensive coastline. The tariff, therefore, fulfilled neither its revenue nor protection functions; the treasury suffered from contraband, the economy from stagnation, and foreign merchants from bureaucratic corruption and delay.

The allocation of scarce national resources was conducted according to the values and structures inherited from colonial society. The social structure underwent only marginal change. Those Spaniards who survived independence and remained were integrated into the Peruvian oligarchy to form an upper class of land and office, monopolists of wealth, power and privilege. The *mestizos* and free *pardos* of the coast were confined to the service sector and local workshops, and advancement was a slow process. Bolívar's experience in Peru convinced him that 'many of the higher classes had imbibed the prejudices and vices of their late Spanish rulers, and had followed their example in oppressing the lower orders'.[48] In a world of greed and inequality that he was powerless to change, the Liberator remained incorruptible. By 1826 he was paying fifteen thousand pesos a year out of his own presidential salary to worthy causes and needy people, in his mind an argument for retaining the presidency of Colombia and also for curtailing government extravagance that threatened his income.[49]

Slavery was reduced but not abolished.[50] San Martín had confirmed the abolition of the slave trade and attempted to abolish slavery itself through a policy of compensation to owners and in return for military service. But slave owners opposed even this moderate programme; for them slaves were an investment as well as a work force and slavery survived independence virtually intact, just as the rest of their property did, and the gap between the plantations of the coast and Indian labour in the sierra remained unbridgeable. When Bolívar's constitution was adopted in Peru in 1826 the clause emancipating the slaves was omitted, the government regarding it as unrealistic: 'The grounds for this belief are that the manumission of the slaves who are the only cultivators of the soil, would be followed by their desertion from the estates on which they were employed; and that the landholders would hence be exposed to have their lands left waste, as it has been found impossible heretofore to induce the natives to leave the mountainous district for the purpose of working as labourers in the low lands.'[51] The policy of the two liberators sprang from liberal minds and humanitarian convictions, but was also evidence of the constraints operating in a society dominated by a landowning elite. In theory Bolívar was a dictator in Peru but he could not do as he pleased and this was not his country. Where property was concerned he had to leave many decisions to the local ruling class. It was 1855 before Peru abolished slavery.

Peru was Bolívar's nemesis. A great prize in anticipation, it became a battle-ground of his hopes and achievements. The Peruvian ruling class was torn between resentment of Bolívar's dictatorship and fear of anarchy, social unrest and slave rebellion if he should leave. Bolívar exploited this ambiguity; he decided to impose the Bolivian Constitution on Peru, in the expectation, perhaps, of being elected life-president. Peru brought out the worst in Bolívar, at once flattering and frustrating his taste for glory and leadership. Even his devoted aide noted that these were 'the days of the lost purity and innocence of his principles'. He attributed the change to his conversations with José María Pando, an able *limeño* and recent convert to independence, whom he had appointed his minister of finance, regarding him as incorruptible and intelligent, superior even to Revenga. Pando praised the Bolivian Constitution unreservedly as adaptable to any government and told Bolívar what he wanted to hear, that it was a work of genius and perfection.[52]

It is true that Peru was not an end in itself for Bolívar. He wanted a confed-eration of the Andean countries, Colombia, Peru, and Bolivia, and he knew that this would be more easily organized if each component had the same constitution, and if he himself exercised a powerful influence. But this too was a serious miscalculation. He was tempted to spend more time in Peru than was good for either him or Peruvians. Treated as a supreme guide and philoso-pher, visited by admirers, and loved by Manuela, the lord of La Magdalena liked the luxury and revelled in the role. Life would not be true without a conspiracy or two against him, but he brushed them off without too much thought. On 16 August 1826 the electoral college of Lima, with some help from the Liberator, adopted the Bolivian Constitution and nominated Bolívar president for life. A life-president, backed by a foreign army – is this what Peruvians understood by liberation? It could not be. Bolívar recovered his political sense, influenced by events in Colombia as much as in Peru. He refused to accept the presidency and prepared to return to Bogotá, leaving a disconsolate Manuela and a party of pleading ladies in Lima, and an elite that suddenly rediscovered the insecurity of life without the Liberator. He also left the Colombian army, creating hostility by its mere presence. The country he abandoned was subject to unbearable tensions, torn between ambitious mili-tary and self-seeking creoles, parasites both on the Indians and castes. According to Pando, Peru was 'incapable of governing herself and unwilling to be governed'.[53] Was there any way ahead for Spanish America? Did Bolívar have anything further to offer?

An Ever Greater America

Spanish America was at once receptive and indifferent to nationalist projects. Bolívar understood their significance. As a doctrine, dividing the world into nations, describing their character and interests, and testing their existence in terms of language, race, culture and religion, nationalism frequently appears in his writings. As an organized political movement, designed to further the aims and interests of a nation and ensure that the nation constitutes a sovereign state, nationalism was at the heart of his revolution. In its more active sense nationalism is frequently a response to foreign pressure, political, economic, or cultural, which is perceived as a threat to national identity and interests. Spanish Americans found their identity first in reaction to the imperial pressure of the Bourbon state, then in the long war against Spain, and subsequently in conflicts with their neighbours and relations with foreign states. One of the first objectives of nationalism is independence, that is, the creation of a sovereign state in which the nation is dominant. This was partially achieved in Spanish America in the years 1810–30. Bolívar was coming to believe that it was the revolution's only achievement: 'I am ashamed to admit it, but independence is the only benefit we have gained, at the cost of everything else.'[54] A second object of nationalism is national unity, the incorporation within the frontiers of the new state of all groups considered to belong to the nation. There is in some cases a third objective, to build a nation within an independent state, by extending down to the people as a whole the belief in the existence of the nation, hitherto held only by a minority.[55] The Liberator was aware of the need for national unity and national awareness among the people, but his policy was not completely successful in achieving them.

Bolívar saw the revolution as a struggle for independence, and independence as the creation of a nation. In his early political thought Venezuela and New Granada, inheriting colonial administrative divisions, were described as incipient nations, and the nation state as the basis of stable government, towards which 'a national spirit' was required to nurture the citizen's allegiance. Patriotism, the love of the *patria*, obedience to the new states, these concepts were taken for granted by Bolívar, for, as he said to Venezuelans in 1818, 'You are all Venezuelans, children of the same *patria*, members of the same society, citizens of the same Republic.'[56] Spanish America was already dividing into different states, conforming not only to colonial boundaries but also to national feelings. He admitted he was a foreigner in Peru, that Colombians were not Peruvians, that Venezuelans were not popular among Bolivians. In the Jamaica Letter he agreed with De Pradt in dividing America into fifteen or seventeen independent states.[57]

From the very beginning of the revolution, however, Bolívar's sense of national identity transcended individual nations to embrace a greater America. He was supreme among the Americanists, a small minority among the creole elites that included the distinguished names of Francisco de Miranda and Andrés Bello. He had long desired the creation of the great state of Colombia, embracing Venezuela, New Granada and Ecuador. In 1813 he argued that 'union under one supreme government will give us strength and make us formidable to everyone'.[58] But this vision was not confined to Colombia: he believed that the union of Venezuela and New Granada would inspire a greater Spanish American unity. These ideas, of course, operated at different levels of planning and possibility.[59] He made it clear from the beginning that he did not see America as a single nation; unity of this kind would be impossible, and a single government for all America would need the power of God to marshal all its resources and people. At its highest level, his thought envisaged a league, or confederation, of Spanish American nations. The enemy of federalism within a nation, he was an advocate of continental federalism, a structure for Spanish American unity.

The union would be articulated by a congress in Panama, where plenipotentiaries of the liberated countries would coordinate American policy towards the rest of the world and simultaneously constitute an organ of conciliation among the American nations, a kind of supranational legislature. On this inspiring theme his imagination knew no bounds. In the Jamaica Letter in 1815 he had already envisaged the meeting of an international congress: 'How sublime it would be if the Isthmus of Panama could be for us what the Isthmus of Corinth was for the Greeks!'[60] In 1822 he declared: 'The great day of America has not yet dawned. We have expelled our oppressors, broken the tables of their tyrannical laws and founded legitimate institutions. But we still need to establish the basis of the social compact, which ought to form of this world a nation of republics.'[61] Whatever he meant by 'a nation of republics', he advocated supranational unity of some kind. If this were secured, he asked, 'who will resist America reunited in heart, subject to one law, and guided by the torch of liberty?'

The American congress on which he had set his mind opened sessions in Panama. Bolívar deliberately excluded the United States, in deference to British susceptibilities among other reasons, Brazil as a monarchy, and Haiti, like the United States, as 'foreigners to us and heterogeneous in character', that is to say, different in language, history, and culture.[62] It was only later that the United States and Brazil were invited to attend. But he also invited Britain, convinced as he was that 'our American federation cannot survive without English protection'.[63] In his invitation to the governments of America, dated 7 December 1824 and recalling his invitation of 1822 to the governments of

Mexico, Peru, Chile and Argentina, he spoke of giving the American republics a fundamental political basis to secure their future by means of 'a sublime authority' directing the policy of their governments. He foresaw the day of the meeting as 'immortal in the international history of America'.[64] In a paper written in 1826 he recorded his maximum agenda for the congress to be held in Panama.[65] The new, independent and equal nations would be united under a common law regulating their international relations and guaranteeing their survival through a permanent congress. Spain would make peace out of respect for England, and the Holy Alliance would grant its recognition. The league would have powers of mediation on internal and external disputes, and should intervene in cases of internal anarchy or external aggression. Social and racial discrimination would cease to have significance, and the slave trade must be abolished. America would become the centre of Britain's relations with Europe and Asia. The British should be given rights of South American citizens, and South Americans should emulate the British and embrace their moral code.

The republics were not inspired by similar sentiments. Attendance was agonizingly slow, delegates flinching at the pestilential climate of the Isthmus, and some arriving too late. At the meeting in Panama on 22 June 1826 the only delegates present were those from Mexico, Central America, Colombia and Peru. Britain was represented by an observer, Edward Dawkins, who found the deputies 'much less republican than I expected'.[66] The United States observers did not reach the meeting. The congress resolved on 'union, league and perpetual confederation' of the states represented and set up a tribunal to arbitrate boundary disputes, to be backed by an army of the confederation.[67] In the event, only Colombia ratified these agreements, and the creation of a South American league was no nearer. Trust and collaboration did not come naturally to the new nations. Bolívar observed these events from Lima, refusing to put any pressure on the delegates. He was not impressed. The project did not meet his expectations and he became diffident about its prospects. Yet he had introduced some real issues into American collaboration – issues of security, foreign aid, and social reform – for which future statesmen would receive the credit. He himself played down the significance of the whole enterprise. 'I called the Congress of Panama in order to cause a stir, to make the name of Colombia and the other South American republics resonate in the world. . . . I never believed that it would produce an American Alliance, comparable to the Holy Alliance formed at the Congress of Vienna.'[68] He referred to the congress as a vain boast, a theatrical show. He had not lost faith in the principles of international cooperation in America, but was aware of the divisive interests involved. 'I see the Congress of the Isthmus as a theatrical performance, and like Solon I believe the measures promulgated there to be snares for the weak and supports for the strong.'[69]

In 1826 as anarchy and infirmity appeared to consume the new states, and the Panama congress failed to inspire great confidence, some of his Peruvian advisers were urging a true federation, to include Peru, Bolivia and Colombia. Bolívar, ever convinced that bigger meant stronger, was attracted to the idea, envisaging an Andean union in which each state would adopt a version of the Bolivian Constitution, and that there would be a federal president (himself), vice president and congress.[70] He worked on the idea, 'the most perfect possible union in federal form', but it proved to be a purely theoretical structure and did not get beyond the desks of the planners, testimony only to the Liberator's anxiety over the state of America in these years.

Peru was not alone in its instability. The insidious anarchy of Colombia, the result of 'an excess of ill-applied liberalism', as well as agitation in Venezuela, required Bolívar's personal attention. He appreciated that, for the moment at least, he must abandon his cosmopolitanism for a more national role. He left Peru for Colombia in September 1826, and in October wrote to General Santa Cruz, for whom he had planned a central role in the Andean union, an eloquent declaration of faith in national interests:

> I have too many problems in my native land, which I have long neglected for other countries in America. Now that I see that the evils have gone too far and that Venezuela is the victim of my very achievements, I have no desire to incur the slur of ingratitude to the land of my birth. . . . I would avise you to relinquish American plans and pursue a purely Peruvian programme, indeed a programme designed exclusively in the interests of Peru. . . . I intend to do all the good I can for Venezuela without attempting anything further. Let you and your colleagues, therefore, do the same for Peru. Our native land must take preference above everything, as its elements have shaped our being. . . . Are there any more sacred claims upon love and devotion? Yes, General, let each serve his native land and let all other things be secondary to this duty.[71]

Leaving aside Bolívar's more extreme flights of fancy, therefore, it is evident that his ideas of confederation and congress assumed the existence of individual nations and simply sought to give them collective security. His ideal of a great Colombia was not a denial of national identity but an affirmation of it. He was merely trying to establish the appropriate size of a viable nation, as he made clear as early as 1813: 'If we establish two independent authorities, one in the east and the other in the west, we will create two different nations which, because of their inability to maintain themselves as such, or even more to take their place among other nations, will look ridiculous. Only a Venezuela united with New Granada could form a nation that would inspire in others the proper consideration due to her. How can we think of dividing her into two?'[72] Bolívar thus sought unity as a means to national strength and economic viability. In the first place, unity would ensure peace and well-being as opposed to the anarchy of local caudillo rule: 'I do not want these mini-governments. That's what the hooligans want, to make revolutions and more revolutions. Not me. I am resolved to die amidst the ruins of Colombia, fighting for its fundamental law and for absolute unity.'[73] Secondly, unity would earn greater respect from other nations, from the United States and from Britain. In Bolívar's view foreign indifference and contempt for Latin American independence was a consequence of the proliferation of tiny sovereignties, squabbling among themselves: 'Sections, mere fragments, which, though large in area, possess neither population nor resources, cannot inspire interest or confidence among those who might wish to establish relations with them.'[74] Colombia, then, was Bolívar's nation state, the embodiment of national unity. And its institutions compared well with those of the rest of independent America, 'with its absolute and dissolute governments, its heroes, its *trigarantes*, emperors, directors, protectors, delegates, regents, admirals, etc.'[75] Colombia was his favourite child. 'Union, union, union,' he proclaimed.

When all else failed, his hopes rested on England. Towards the United States he was cool and guarded, but not overtly hostile, and he respected its revolutionary and republican credentials. Britain, however, engaged his sympathy as well as his admiration. These sentiments went back to his early years in the struggle. During his exile in Jamaica he wanted British support for independence, offering commercial advantages and even territory – admittedly only Panama and Nicaragua, which were not in his gift – in exchange for aid.[76] Basically he doubted the capacity of the people of South America to defend themselves and to democratize their societies; they needed a tutor and protector. He was impressed by the liberal credentials of Britain, a constitutional model for those who wanted freedom and stability. And the ascending power of England since the Napoleonic wars had never ceased to fascinate him. But the authors of British policy were not all-powerful, and Canning, succeeding Castlereagh in the Foreign Office in September 1822, soon found that his own powers were constricted. In October he appointed consuls to the new states, and although he believed that recognition was inevitable, it was December 1824 before he won from the British cabinet a decision to recognize Colombia. Bolívar recorded his sense of loss on the death of Canning: 'America will never forget that Mr Canning caused her rights to be respected. . . . Humanity was interested in the existence of this illustrious man, who with caution and wisdom was realizing that which the French Revolution illusively promised, and which America is successfully carrying into effect.'[77]

However, more important than British recognition was British power. As the historian of Anglo-American relations in Spanish America observed, 'It was inevitable that the greatest naval, industrial and financial power in the world should count for more with the infant Spanish American states than did the United States.'[78] Bolívar put his finger on the essential contribution of Britain to Latin American independence: the interposition of the British fleet between Europe and America. 'Do not fear the Allies, for the ditch is large and the English fleet still larger.' There was no alternative to cooperation with Britain; it was necessary for survival. As for the risks, they were minimal, for Spanish America would become strong under British protection and thus able to escape dependence. He did not hide his contempt for hostile liberal and nationalist opinion: this is my policy, he insisted, and I will take responsibility for it.[79] His scheme for Spanish American union depended on British support and 'cannot be achieved unless the English protect it body and soul'. 'English power is on a rising curve, unhappy are those who oppose it, or even fail to ally themselves with her. The whole of America together is not equal to a British fleet; the entire Holy Alliance is powerless against her liberal principles combined with immense resources.'[80] In his 'Thought on the Congress of Panama' of 1826 he spoke of 'the union of the new states with the British Empire', which would create 'the most extensive, most extraordinary, and most powerful league ever to have appeared on earth'.[81] In addition to gaining commercial resources and gateways, Britain could contribute to the social well-being of Spanish America. Through Britain, Spanish America could further its own progress, including social reform, fortified by British 'character and customs' which would become models for Americans in the future.

Thoughts from a fertile mind, fruit of the wish rather than the deed, and a despairing attempt to shore up a world that was slipping away. British policy-makers, on the other hand, were content to rest their relations with Bolívar's America on their consuls, their naval stations and their merchants.

A Deal with the Devil

With each year that passed Bolívar became more conscious of the racial divisions in American society and the propensity of its people to anarchy:

> I am convinced to the very marrow of my bones that America can only be ruled by an able despotism. . . . We are the vile offspring of the preda-tory Spaniards who came to America to bleed her white and to breed with their victims. Later the illegitimate offspring of these unions joined

with the offspring of slaves transported from Africa. With such racial mixture and such a moral record, can we afford to place laws above leaders and principles above men?[82]

From La Magdalena he warned Santander against the liberal ideologues, 'the vilest and most cowardly of men', slavish copiers of the Spanish liberals, who will reduce us to another Haiti and unleash a liberty they cannot control. 'Where is there an army of occupation to impose order? Africa? – we shall have more and more of Africa. I do not say this lightly, for anyone with a white skin who escapes will be lucky.' Eventually the call from Colombia became compelling. Santander was insistent and always moralizing: overtly supportive, he had his own liberal agenda and needed Bolívar to back him in his conflict with the rebellious Páez and what he regarded as the threat of civil war. There was usually an insinuation in his message: 'As president of the Republic, its Liberator, the father of the *patria*, the soldier of liberty, and the first subject of the constitution and its laws, you will understand the situation and know which course to take to save Colombia, your own offspring.'[83]

In November 1826 Bolívar returned from Peru to a divided nation, where Santanderian liberalism, federalism and his own conservative constitution all competed for support. As he approached the borderlands, he did not disguise his dismay at the state of Colombia. 'The south of Colombia has received me with much show and rejoicing, but their speeches are laments, their words sighs, and everyone complains of everything; it sounds like the wailing of purgatory.' The republican system had failed its citizens; taxes were too high, incomes too low, while the bureaucracy was swollen with useless officials. The Colombian utopia was finished. He was expected to do something. But what?

The south hates the north, the coast hates the highlands, Venezuela hates Cundinamarca; Cundinamarca suffers from the disorders in Venezuela. The army is discontented and outraged by the regulations imposed on it. The precious freedom of the press has become a scandal, breaking all restraint and enraging every opinion. And in the midst of all this disturbance *pardocracia* flourishes. None of this is my fault, or the army's. The legislators and the philosophers are to blame. I have fought the laws of Spain; I am not going to fight now for republican laws which are no better, indeed more absurd.[84]

The further north he travelled the more convinced he became that strong central government was the only answer, and that was to be found in his Bolivian Constitution.

His return after five years was an event to celebrate. Santander led a party of senior colleagues – war minister Soublette, foreign secretary Revenga – south as far as Tocaima to greet him. Later, approaching Bogotá on 14 November, another delegation met him containing a familiar type, an official mouthing liberal criticisms of laws broken and rights infringed, which stung the Liberator into an angry rejoinder: 'This day is set aside to celebrate the glories of the liberating army, not to discuss violations of laws.' He wheeled away and entered Bogotá in a rain as cold as his feelings, observing with distaste the liberal graffiti no doubt inspired by Santander. The atmosphere improved at an official reception in Government House, where the greeting from Santander was formally friendly and his own reply generous. This was in keeping with their correspondence during the past three years, exchanging two or three letters every month, discussing matters of state, issues of politics, financial problems, and military movements and promotions. Bolívar always took care to inform Santander of his next move, checked with anything that congress would need to know, and even had time to discuss intellectual ideas. He was invariably open and reasonable, Santander always polite and respectful. Yet beneath the routine lay unspoken tensions, unspoken at least to each other. Soon the tensions would snap.

In Bogotá the Liberator briefly assumed control of the administrative machine and performed some brisk repairs. He did not disguise his disapproval of what he regarded as Santander's indiscriminate liberalism, his financial ineptitude and the divisive effects on the nation, and he wasted no opportunity to promote his Bolivian Constitution. But in the event he altered little, apart from trying 'to bring the expenditure of the country within its income'.[85] Time was against him. He was now recalled beyond Bogotá to Venezuela, where Páez was in revolt. In March congress had re-elected Bolívar president for a second four-year term beginning on 2 January 1827, and Santander as vice-president. Bolívar now exercised the presidency with extraordinary powers, leaving Santander to take charge in Bogotá.

There were many ironies in Bolívar's life, none more painful than this: that his own Venezuela, the first to conceive Colombia, should be the first to challenge it. Venezuelan separatism had a long history. Opposition between Venezuela and New Granada was manifest as early as 1815; it produced resistance to Bolívar and his officers in New Granada, and contributed to the success of the Spanish counter-revolution of 1815–16. In 1819 national conflict was responsible for the deposition of New Granadan Zea as vice-president of Venezuela by the congress of Angostura and his replacement by Arismendi. Once Colombia was constituted these tensions persisted. The great distances separating Venezuela, Cundinamarca and Quito, the mountain ranges, the poor communications, the heterogeneous mass of the population, *pardos* of Venezuela, *mestizos* of New Granada, Indians of Ecuador, all made it impossible to unite greater Colombia or to inform it with 'national character and national feeling'.[86] There was no impetus to economic integration: the economics of Venezuela and New Granada were separate and independent, and while both had serious problems these were not such as could be resolved by unification. Venezuelans complained that they did not receive a fair share of national expenditure. But the real discrimination was of another kind.

The relative inaccessibility of Bogotá, remote from the periphery in time and space, deprived the Venezuelans of adequate representation in the capital, while the constitution also denied them discretionary power over their internal affairs and forced them to refer everything to Bogotá for decision, with consequent delay and opportunity for bribery and corruption. The first freedom fighters were now subject to new restraints, governed by a new metropolis. Venezuelans came to regard the New Granadans as foreign masters, a view given credence by the advantages that these gained from the fact of being at the centre of offices and opportunities. The centralization of the republic in Cundinamarca ushered Bogotá into a boom period, during which it became the site of an expanding bureaucracy, new public works, fiscal favouritism, population growth. Bogotá thus advanced from a primitive outpost of empire to a civilized capital.[87] Even so it still reproduced the features of many South American towns of handsome ecclesiastical buildings surrounded by undistinguished one-storey dwellings. The Venezuelan military criticized what they regarded as a new colonialism: while they had fought for victory corrupt politicians in Bogotá enjoyed the fruits. In Bogotá lawyers and officials, a traditional and powerful elite, also had their point of view, resenting the Venezuelan dominance of the army and the burden of the military budget.[88] To some degree, therefore, relations between Venezuela and Bogotá suffered from antagonism between military commanders and civil officials. But national feelings, recognized by Bolívar, also played their part. People were primarily Venezuelans, New Granadans, *quiteños*, and they found their national home in their own country, where they developed a higher degree of communication with each other than with outsiders. War nurtured nationality. The armies brought together men of different *patrias*, often in uneasy proximity, close observers of their differences and rivalries. National prejudices were born and stereotypes created, revealed in the language of the time, and sometimes in that of Bolívar: Venezuelans were *pardos* or *militares*, New Granadans *mestizos* or *curiales*, Ecuadorians *indios*. Americans did not naturally like each other.

José Antonio Páez, commandant-general of the department of Venezuela, spoke for many Venezuelans when he expressed resentment. He represented a military, and to some extent a popular, constituency in opposition to Intendant

Juan de Escolona and his masters in Bogotá. It was unrealistic to appoint Escalona, a known enemy of Páez, to administer Venezuela and then to replace Páez as head of the army.[89] A major caudillo could not be treated like this. Bolívar understood the problem, but Santander did not. The *llanero* warrior had now acquired a huge fortune and vast landed wealth, not only in the *llanos* but also in the centre-north where he forged an alliance with the established elite of that region. There he acquired a new power base and was successful in reassuring the landowners, merchants and office-holders of Caracas that he stood for order and stability; they in turn tamed their chosen caudillo and converted him to new economic priorities, identifying with the hegemony of the northern *hacendados* and the exporting sector. Bolívar did not take fright at these developments, regarding Páez as an asset for a country such as Venezuela: 'I believe that Venezuela could very well be governed by Páez, with a good secretary and a good adviser like General Briceño Méndez, and with the help of 4,000 men of the army which went to Peru. . . . I want Briceño Méndez to go to Caracas to marry my niece and become adviser to Páez. . . . General Páez, together with Briceño Méndez, will rule the region to perfection, as Páez is feared by all the factious elements and the others are not important.'[90] Yet the problem was more complex. Páez as a medium of authority was useful. Páez as a national leader was dangerous. He was leading the Venezuelan oligarchy in a separatist movement which would place their country under the control of the national elite, ruled from Caracas and not from Bogotá, and monopolizing its own resources. This was an alliance of landowners and military caudillos on behalf of a conservative and independent Venezuela. But a movement against Colombia was a movement against Bolívar and this demanded a response from him. Santander was badgering him to take action against 'a chief whose authority came from rebellion and force'.

Páez had few political ideas of his own, and his greatest passions were gambling and cock-fighting, but he was trying hard to improve himself and to learn how to read and write and to use a knife and fork. He was ready to take advice, not, however, from Briceño Méndez or other Bolivarians, but from a faction in Caracas which Bolívar called 'the demagogues'. These included Mariño, his second-in-command, a master of intrigue and inveterate opponent of Bolívar, Dr Miguel Peña, his civil adviser, an able if unprincipled politician who had already crossed swords with Santander; and Colonel Francisco Carabaño, a military colleague sullenly resentful of Bolívar. These were the nucleus of a separatist or federalist faction, of which observers believed Páez to be 'rather an instrument than a leader'.[91] Whatever the truth of this, Páez was encouraged in his inferiority complex: he came to believe that he had not received the power and recognition he deserved. His exasperation with legislators and politicians focused especially on those in Bogotá, civilians whom he regarded as oppressors of the 'poor military'. The military were predominantly Venezuelan. And Venezuela was the source of an alarming idea.

In 1825 Páez urged Bolívar to take greater, even monarchical, powers, and make himself a Napoleon of South America to save the *patria*.[92] He transmitted his letter by a special agent, Antonio Leocadio Guzmán – destined to be a leading liberal politician in independent Venezuela – on the pretext that he distrusted the postal system, but really in order to create a stir and publicize a political move. Bolívar rejected the idea out of hand. He saw it as emanating from the 'demagogues' in Caracas. He was insulted by the assumption that he was motivated by vulgar ambition, and embarrassed by the damage it would do to his reputation. He gave Páez a simple lesson in French history, pointing out that Colombia was not France and that he was not Napoleon. 'The title of Liberator is superior to any that human pride can bestow. . . . I tell you frankly that this plan is not good for you, for me, or for the country.' Instead he recommended his Bolivian Constitution, which combined authority and liberty, was a mean between federalism and monarchy, and deserved to be publicized.[93]

His sister, María Antonia, aware of trends in Caracas, advised him to beware of anyone who offered him a crown, an infamous proposal: 'Tell them you will be Liberator or nothing, that is your true title, one that will preserve your hard-won glory.'[94] Sucre, who never claimed to be a democrat, agreed with María Antonia that he should be Liberator or nothing, and warned Bolívar against the bad faith of those in Caracas who urged the Napoleonic project; prudence and patriotism alike would demand that he reject the idea: 'If you had children I might think differently, but without heirs the project would destabilize the country and on your death its authors would compete to succeed you.' The Bolivian Constitution, he advised, resolved all the problems, providing strong government in a free and independent nation.[95] Santander was even more dismissive of Páez and his idea, which he described as insulting to Bolívar, anarchical and unpopular and, as Bolívar was not eternal, likely to leave a succession problem. He reserved his opinion on some of the details of the Bolivian Constitution, particularly the life presidency, but meanwhile agreed that it was 'liberal, popular, strong, and vigorous'.[96] An insincere letter, even by Santander's standards. His true thoughts were contained in an autobiographical memoir he subsequently wrote, where he described the life-president as 'more powerful than the monarchy of England or France'. The whole constitution, he thought, was complicated, absurd and destabilizing, and showed how far Bolívar had moved from the legislator of Angostura. He had remained silent out of respect for Bolívar's reputation and on the assumption that the constitution was appropriate only for Bolivia.[97] Santander objected to any talk of a life presidency for Colombia, as he had ambitions of his own to succeed Bolívar at the end of the latter's presidency – under the existing Colombian constitution – in 1831.

In April 1826 Páez was relieved of his command and summoned to Bogotá for impeachment by congress on charges of illegal and arbitrary conduct in conscripting civilians for the militia in Caracas. The object, as Santander explained, was 'to make the first chiefs of the republic understand that their services and heroism are not a licence to abuse the citizens'.[98] But Páez resisted. Backed by the *llaneros*, and prompted by the Venezuelan military and the extreme federalists around him, he hoisted the banner of revolt on 30 April, first in Valencia, then in the department of Venezuela. The cry was raised – independence for Venezuela. There was much support for Páez, though not universal support, for the sense of national identity was not sufficiently developed to appeal to everyone. His action, in fact, was divisive. Other caudillos reacted variously. Mariño aligned himself with Páez; Bermúdez rejected him and offered to crush the rebellion. In Zulia General Urdaneta awaited orders from Bogotá and remained a loyal Bolivarian. Like many of the military, however, he derived satisfaction from Páez's opposition to Congress, as it reinforced pressure on Bolívar to establish a stronger government. The Liberator was now the focus of the personalism that he so abhorred. The British consul in Maracaibo reported, after an interview with Urdaneta, that the military 'remain constant in their attachment and obedience to their Chiefs, rather than to the Constitution and to Congress, and hope much from the return of the President'. According to the same source, the military were disillusioned with a government 'monopolized by General Santander and by a faction of shopkeepers in Bogotá. . . . My impression is that there are very few military men in the country that would not cheerfully cry out tomorrow, "Long live King Bolívar".[99]

Bolívar sent O'Leary on a mission of pacification. The Irishman found Páez at Achaguas, capital of Apure, in a friend's house, seated on a stool, playing a violin, 'his only audience a blind Negro'. He was reminded irresistibly of Nero. Otherwise he was not impressed. After ten futile days he left with Páez's final answer ringing in his ears: 'I hope the president will not force me to be his enemy and destroy Colombia with civil war.'[100] O'Leary was convinced that the rebellion had no roots '*en el alma popular*', that Páez was an instrument of faction and swayed by those around him, and was now worried that he had started something he could not control.[101]

The rebellion of Páez placed Bolívar in a dilemma. He did not approve of military rebellion against civil power. Yet in this case he had more sympathy with Páez than with Santander and the legislators, believing that Páez and the military were victims of the excessive liberalism of civilian politicians. These sought to 'destroy their liberators', and they made a great mistake in summoning Páez before congress. He also knew that they were being unrealistic in trying to deprive a caudillo of his military command. Bolívar did not wish to become personally involved, for if he failed he risked his own authority. As the news from Bogotá reached him in Lima he read it with increasing irritation; his instinctive reaction was to identify military discontent, socio-racial agitation, and caudillo affinity to both, as the factors behind rebellion of the warlords, and he would have wished to wash his hands of the whole madness. 'These two men [Páez and Padilla] have elements of power in their blood; therefore, it is useless for me to oppose them because my own blood means nothing to the people.'[102]

It was in this mood that he wrote his dramatic analysis of the racial origins and the moral history of Americans, and expressed his preference for 'an able despotism'. Given the social and racial formation of Americans, he asked, 'Can we place laws above heroes and principles above men?'[103] Bolívar here recognized the force of personalism and the power of the strongman, and gave it a structural explanation. It was in this context too that he wrote to Páez, admitting the danger of demoralizing the army and destabilizing the regions: 'Each province has taken power and authority to itself; each one wishes to be the centre of the nation. We shall not speak of the democrats and fanatics. And we shall say nothing of the coloureds, for to enter the bottomless abyss of these problems is to bury reason as in the house of death. . . . A great volcano lies at our feet and its stirrings are not poetic or imaginary but very real.' And he asked, 'Who shall reconcile minds? Who shall restrain the oppressed classes? Slavery will break its yoke, each shade of colour will seek mastery, and the rest will fight on to victory or death. Latent hatreds between the different classes will break out again, each opinion will want to be sovereign.' What then was the solution? 'The Congress of Panama, an organization that should have been admirable if only it had been effective, is no different from that mad Greek who from a rock sought to direct sailing vessels. Its power will be a shadow and its decrees mere advice, no more.' The answer lay in his Bolivian Constitution, which could be adapted to individual states within a confederation. Meanwhile, the government had to maintain law and order 'by means of the press, the pulpit, and the bayonet'.[104] Bolívar conceded nothing to Bogotá. While Santander spoke the language of constitutional outrage and denounced the perfidy of Páez, Bolívar mocked him and ridiculed the intransigents in Bogotá. 'Our sacred pact was pure and intact, preserved in spotless virginity; now it has been violated, broken, and stained, and of no use to anyone. Congress arranged the divorce and Páez concluded it. We need a new contract, and another hymn to celebrate a new marriage, and then we can forget the infidelities.'[105] Behind the irony he was selling the Bolivian Constitution.

The conflict between centralism and federalism also contained a racial problem, or so Bolívar believed. He was aware that there were strong objections to the choice of Bogotá as capital, not least the fact of its remoteness. But he argued that there was no alternative, 'for though Caracas appeared to be the more natural spot, from being more populous and influential, yet the province was chiefly composed of people of colour who were jealous of and opposed to the white inhabitants, and it was desirable consequently for the general tranquillity to diminish rather than augment the influence of Caracas'.[106] From the same facts the Venezuelan ruling class drew precisely the opposite conclusion. They wanted proximate power, even home rule, for Venezuela, 'a very energetic and concentrated system in consequence of its containing a great diversity of colour'.[107] Racial tension and *pardo* ambition required close supervision and control, and the unspoken conclusion was that the elite could not but support Páez because he was virtually the only leader who could control the popular classes.

Bolívar moved into Venezuela in late 1826 to confront the rebellion of Páez. He warned the caudillo, as a master warns his pupil, of his previous encounters with personalism: 'General Castillo opposed me and lost; General Piar opposed me and lost; General Mariño opposed me and lost; General Torre Tagle opposed me and lost. It would seem that Providence condemns my personal enemies, whether American or Spanish, to perdition. But see how far Generals Sucre, Santander, and Santa Cruz have gone.'[108] Military preparations were made for war against the rebels, Briceño Méndez occupied Puerto Cabello, and the Liberator's language became tougher. He also made it crystal clear to Páez that he went as president and not as a mere citizen of Venezuela, pointing out that his was the only legitimate sovereignty in Venezuela, whereas Páez's command 'came from the municipalities and was born in violence; none of this is glorious, my dear general'. Although he mobilized, he did not want violence. From Coro he warned, 'I have come from Peru to save you from the crime of civil war.'[109] Conciliation was also favoured by the majority opinion in both countries. There was little alternative. Bolívar was aware of the danger of trying to use force against Páez, 'since almost all the principal military commands throughout Colombia are filled by natives of Caracas'.[110] So he compromised; to avoid civil war he had no choice. On 1 January 1827 he received Páez's submission – but at a price, namely, total amnesty for all the rebels, guarantees of security in their offices and property, and promises of constitutional reform. After months of political turbulence and inner turmoil, the year 1826 ended with some respite for Bolívar, accompanied by signs that Colombia's problems were far from over.

Chapter 10

THE MAGIC OF HIS PRESTIGE

Adios Venezuela

Bolívar loved his native city from a distance, though he was not always home-sick for it, 'for the earthquakes there are intolerable and the people more so'.[1] But on 4 January 1827, accompanied by Páez, he entered Caracas to a hero's welcome and the triumphal arches, garlands, songs, ceremonies and celebra-tions that recalled happier times. Fifteen young women in white presented him with two laurel crowns, 'one for his triumph over the tyrants, the other for his triumph in preventing civil war', laurels which he promptly diverted, one to Páez and the other in dedication to Colombia. And in a scene orchestrated by the Liberator himself he presented Páez with his sword, and sat through the reply: 'Fellow countrymen, the sword of Bolívar is in my hands. For you and for him I will march with it to eternity.'[2] It was to be a double-edged weapon.

Bolívar was privately critical of Páez, but he flattered him in public, had him live in the same house and seemed to be preparing Venezuela for separate acceptance of his Bolivian Constitution and entry into the confederation of the Andes. From January to June 1827 Bolívar governed Venezuela in person. He proceeded on the assumption that Venezuelans – Spanish Americans – were not fit for democracy. Abject, superstitious and ignorant as they were, they did not understand the practice of good government, having been deprived of it by their Spanish oppressors. 'Instead of liberty, we find insub-ordination and licentiousness; under the name of patriotism, intrigue and treachery; venality in the place of public virtue, whilst personal revenge is covered by the cloak of justice.'[3] Therefore he found nothing alarming in a strong executive, if that was what Páez could provide. He confirmed the caudillo in his command with the title of Superior Chief of Venezuela, a title which did not exist in the constitution and which Bolívar produced to recog-nize the facts of the case and legitimize a caudillo. Páez would never obey Bogotá, but he might obey Bolívar. Yet Páez's political role was determined not only by Bolívar. He was recognized as a valuable leader by the Caracas landowners, merchants and others of the coalition that he kept together on a platform of peace and security and on the awareness of a mutual need. He was also appreciated by his cronies, Mariño, Peña and others, who were promptly appointed by Bolívar to the various offices they craved.[4] All this, pleasing to the Caracas faction, incurred the most scathing criticism of Santander and his supporters for leniency towards Páez and unconstitutional tendencies. Ironically, Bolívar himself had serious doubts about Páez, whom he saw as an insincere and authoritarian figure, doing well in his own business deals, yet incapable of independent judgement or even of writing his own letters:

> General Páez is the most ambitious and vain man in the world: he has no desire to obey, only to command; it pains him to see me above him in the political hierarchy of Colombia; he does not even recognize his own incompetence, so blinded is he by pride and ignorance, always the instrument of his advisers. I regard him as the most dangerous man for Colombia, for he has means of action, determination, and prestige among the *llaneros*, and whenever he wishes he can secure the support of the people and of the blacks and *zambos*.[5]

The conclusion of the British consul in Caracas was unequivocal. The mass of the people in Venezuela wanted a change in the form of government. The traditional aristocracy, army and clergy wanted a hereditary prince. The republicans and reformers favoured the Bolivian Constitution. The intellectuals and lawyers wanted an independent federated state. The popular sectors mainly wanted a quiet life from whatever form of government, though some preferred a complete revolution to bring the coloureds to power and would be happy to promote 'the extinction of the whites'. General opinion would favour a supreme government for Venezuela, federated with Colombia, Quito, Peru and Bolivia, and the whole under the immediate auspices and protection of the Liberator, as supreme president. The amnesty and settlement granted by Bolívar to Páez and his party had given 'universal satisfaction' in Venezuela. But Ker Porter himself did not doubt that Colombia needed a dictatorship, free from the vice-president and his adherents, that Bolívar alone could save the country and that he would give the people 'that form of government he judges best suited to their present moral state'. A partial view, perhaps, but one which probably reflected the views of the Liberator.[6]

Bolívar spent his working life receiving bad news, and in 1826–27 the news was always bad. The Bolivian Constitution had few supporters outside Bolivia. And political opinion in Bogotá derided the projected federation of the Andes as unrealistic and unacceptable to the component parts. As Santander himself remarked, with ironic understatement, 'It seems to me rather impractical.'[7] Relations with Santander deteriorated further, as the vice-president criticized Bolívar's Venezuelan settlement and alleged ambition for dictatorship, while the *santanderistas* campaigned against the Liberator in the liberal press. Bolívar denounced Santander's financial administration and his handling of the British loan: 'Public confidence, love for law, and respect for state officials have vanished. Dissatisfaction is general.'[8] He cultivated his own Bolivarians in opposition to the so-called constitutionalists. His relations with Santander, damaged since 1824, now plunged beyond repair as he renounced their friendship and stopped writing. 'I can no longer stand the faithless ingratitude of Santander; I have today informed him that I will no longer write to him, for I do not wish to reply to him or to call him friend.'[9] Santander replied that it was better to bring the break into the open than to hide behind a pretence. He maintained a position of public respect and private hatred, advising Bolívar to return to Bogotá and submit himself to the constitution, and in any case to get rid of Páez.[10] Soon he dropped all pretence and demanded Bolívar's removal from the presidency. And the public now knew that their president and vice-president were enemies.

The news from Peru was also bad. The Colombian division mutinied against its Venezuelan officers and, under orders from its commander Colonel José Bustamante, a New Granadan, arrested officers of Venezuelan descent, claiming to act in defence of the constitution. The rebels then sailed for Colombia. With the departure of the army Bolivarian Peru fell apart. Bolívar's constitution was thrown out; a new president, Santa Cruz, was elected, and among the turncoats was the 'incorruptible' Pando. Guayaquil looked likely to secede to Peru, with Santa Cruz's encouragement and Bustamante's connivance. Santander was implicated in the mutiny and did not hide his support of Bustamante. In Bogotá he had the bells rung in celebration and went out on the streets to enjoy the cheers of the masses. Bolívar was furious, convinced that Santander had actively instigated the Peruvian crash. He had one trustworthy ally. In Lima, Manuela rode in her uniform to the barracks and appealed to the troops to remember their loyalty to the Liberator, but was promptly imprisoned for her pains and ordered out of Peru; making her way to Guayaquil, she managed to reach Quito with Bolívar's archives secure in her possession.

Bolívar was still in Caracas, trying to stem the tides of destitution and despair. The country was bankrupt, the army unpaid, soldiers were rampaging, officials starving. In Barcelona blacks and slaves were stirring and social unrest was a daily menace. He set to work on customs duties, education, hospitals and the conditions of slaves. But it was a losing battle: 'We Americans, reared in a system of slavery, do not understand living according to simple laws or liberal principles. I am determined to do my utmost. To save my country I once declared war to the death. . . . To save it again I shall make war on the rebels even if I must fall to their knives.'[11] Even in the midst of political turmoil he never abandoned his interest in education and civilized values. Although he himself was not a university graduate, he took a close interest in the affairs of the University of Caracas. He supported José María Vargas, a respected medical doctor who had studied at the University of Edinburgh, for appointment as Rector, against those who wanted to invoke the law against the appointment of Doctors of Medicine, and a few days before leaving Caracas he personally approved the reform of the university's statutes.[12]

Appreciated in Caracas and suspect in Bogotá, he was in a quandary, despairing that what he established with his hands others trampled underfoot. He delayed, until he heard that Bustamante had invaded the region of Guayaquil and raised the stakes for war between Colombia and Peru. Then he knew he had to go south, at least as far as Bogotá, and he said goodbye to Caracas for the last time in his life. He sailed from La Guaira on 4 July 1827 and a week later was handsomely entertained in Cartagena by General José Prudencio Padilla before sailing up the Magdalena from Barranca by steamboat. As he approached the Colombian capital, each side waged a war of words and of nerves, Santander challenging him to advance no further, Bolívar, keeping his army at his side, determined to take over the executive power. Santander described the approach to Bogotá by Bolívar and his commander, Urdaneta, as an army marching against a rebel city, ready to punish the government and constitutionalists as traitors to be sacrificed to Bolívar's vengeance and ambition.[13]

Before Congress on 10 September Bolívar was sworn into office and called for the convocation of the national assembly. The ceremony was held in the church of Santo Domingo with members of congress seated in a double circle of chairs. Mary English, wife of a British merchant, was present near the front with a good view of the proceedings. She saw the Liberator emerge from the street to music and the peal of bells, and walk slowly up the middle of the church with a steady step but an awkward gait, like a person affected by long riding and, though she may not have known, by painful haemorrhoids, from which he had long suffered. He looked tired and not in good health, but he repeated the form of oath firmly and made a speech. At Government House the meeting with Santander was cold and they did not shake hands, but formal speeches were made. Afterwards Bolívar caught sight of the lovely Mrs English, previously wooed and lost by Colonel Patrick Campbell, the British consul-general, and seems to have recovered his spirits sitting next to her and flattering her with his attentions. She saw him a number of times, at balls, the races, and her home, and was impressed by his beautiful manners, affable nature, intellectual face, and the 'perfect symmetry and beauty' of his ankles. He gave her an engraving of himself.[14] But in the midst of his political and social life his thoughts were with Manuela and he wanted her with him now more than ever.

On 18 November a severe earthquake shook Bogotá, causing damage to many churches, convents and houses, including that of Colonel Campbell. But political life continued, as did the stand-off between president and vice-president. For Bolívar the political future looked bleak. The repudiation of his system in Peru ended any idea of a federation of the Andes. General Flores ejected Bustamante from Guayaquil and established a government favourable to Bolívar, but Flores was now a power in Quito, another question mark against Colombian unity. The Bolivian Constitution was becoming a liability. 'Throw it in the fire if you don't want it,' Bolívar said, 'I don't have an author's vanity in matters of human concern.'[15] He seemed not to realize why politicians would never agree to a life-presidency. It deprived them of the major political prize for the foreseeable future, their prime ambition snatched from them. Meanwhile he governed through the extraordinary powers the existing constitution allowed him, and so was branded a dictator by the liberals. But it was not in his nature to resign. He was not about to abandon sixteen years of struggle and throw away the achievements of successive liberations to satisfy politicians whom he despised.

Quest for Strong Government

For the next three years Bolívar was living on what O'Leary called 'the magic of his prestige'.[16] Deprived of the political security he sought for himself and the institutions he wanted for Colombia, he was vulnerable to hostility and disrespect for his views and policies. Although he continued to speak of liberation, tyranny and victories, the battles were not the same. In 1827–8 every day was a day of politics, a time of tension, a scene of conflict between president and vice-president. Amidst the growing anarchy, when the independence of the great magnates and the restlessness of the masses threatened to destroy the young republic, rival policies were canvassed. Bolívar spoke compulsively of the need for 'strong government'. 'I can see the certain destruction of Colombia unless the government is given an enormous power, capable of subduing the anarchy which will raise a thousand seditious heads.'[17] He believed that the constitution did not conform to the social structure or the needs of the people: 'We have made the legislative alone the sovereign body, whereas it should only have a share of sovereignty. We have made the executive subordinate to the legislative, which has been given a far greater share in administration than the nation's true interests require.'[18] The right to initiate legislation had been given exclusively to the legislative, which also had the power to prevail over the executive veto. Moreover, the constitution gave the judicial power excessive independence, and the executive no means of intervening when necessary; it had even given the civil courts absolute control in military cases, thus destroying discipline and undermining the confidence of the army. These defects would have to be remedied by a new constitutional congress; meanwhile he himself tried to supply the deficiencies of the constitution and to give Colombia the 'strong government' which it needed. Liberals were outraged. Santander regarded the new regime as conservative and militarist, a threat to all the liberal achievements of the last six years, and he now veered towards outright federalism. Some of his associates overreacted and went into hiding, fearing for their lives.

Bolívar was not a lone leader. He had friends and allies among the military, and officers such as Urdaneta who had been with him from the beginning did not waver. In the cabinet he had the support of Soublette and most of the other ministers, and in congress many politicians preferred him to Santander or any other option. And his domestic life improved. Manuela joined him in Bogotá in early January 1828, accompanied from Quito by a few Bolivarian officers and a cavalry unit, the archives still in tow. She took up residence with him at the Villa Quinta on the outskirts of the city and managed his private life.

How did Bolívar look, as he approached the climax of his career? In February 1828 the French doctor and artist François Desirée Roulin sketched a description and profile of Bolívar which became the model of many paintings and statues of the Liberator.[19] He was not an easy subject. Another distinguished artist for whom he sat, José María Espinosa, commented that it was difficult to get him to sit still, and he frequently looked across to the window and out into the street. They all wanted to see him in repose, when he would withdraw into a mood of solitude, melancholy and nostalgia. But he could not turn this on at will. Roulin, a specialist in anatomy as well as art, described Bolívar as slightly below medium height, slim and graceful, with a nervous and irritable temperament, restless in his movements, impatient and superior in his demeanour. In his youth his complexion had been very white in the way of a Venezuelan of Spanish descent, but his skin had become brown, burned by the sun and fifteen years of travel and campaigns. His walk was brisk rather than stately, but when standing he frequently crossed his arms and assumed statuesque poses, especially in serious moments. He had a well-shaped head, regular features but with a large forehead, angular face, pointed chin and prominent cheekbones. By now he was always clean-shaven, without a beard. His hair was wavy, curled in a parting on top and combed towards the front. He had a good profile, with a noble brow, straight nose, small mouth and thick, arched eyebrows, giving an impression at once alert and perceptive. His eyes were large, black, lively and deep. He spoke rapidly and incisively, did not waste words and adjusted his speech to the occasion, was sometimes indiscreet in conversation, original and intelligent in correspondence, serious and confident in speeches. His replies to questions or requests were short and quick, and he could be brusque with anyone who irritated him. Judging by Roulin's assessment, the Liberator's looks at the age of forty-six had not yet declined and his health was still holding up. We know from O'Leary that his eyesight was good and his sense of hearing exceptionally keen. We can conclude, too, that his mind was as strong as ever and reason still his guide.

Peace of mind, however, was becoming rarer, and his political preoccupations were compounded by personal anxieties. Now, his own future troubled him, as he sought to realize his last remaining asset, the Aroa copper mines. His agent in London, Andrés Bello, struggled dutifully with disputes over ownership and occupancy, and his failure to complete the sale worsened the already fragile relationship between the Liberator and his former tutor.[20] In London Bello lived on the edge of poverty; as secretary of the Colombian legation his salary was meagre and often in arrears, and as one who had received his first diplomatic office in 1810 he deserved better. He was a diffident man and could not understand why Bolívar failed to help him. Bolívar, admirer though he was of Bello, found it difficult to promote him, partly because he was out of touch with the scholar and probably did not appreciate his true curriculum vitae of these years, partly because by 1828 he was not in a position to ignore the government of Santander and make any appointment he pleased. Moreover, Bello did not help his own cause. In his poem *Alocución a la Poesía*, which developed into an account of the wars of independence, Bello used words not designed to wound but whose faint praise was calculated to offend a leader as sensitive of his reputation as the Liberator. Worse still, he saw fit to praise Manuel Piar, Bolívar's bête noire, whose execution the Liberator now went out of his way to defend as 'a political necessity and a measure of security, and as a precaution against a war of the blacks against the whites'.[21] He regarded his war record as above reproach, and at a time when his political enemies were sharpening their knives, he expected respect from his friends, and Bello was not exempt. Distance and necessity had reduced these two giants of the revolution to mutual incomprehension.

The Road to Ocaña and Power

In September 1827 congress voted that a Grand National Convention meet, not in 1831 as foreseen by the congress of Cúcuta, but on 2 March 1828 in Ocaña, to review and revise the constitution of Colombia. From Caracas

Bolívar himself had proclaimed the urgent necessity of such a convention; it was 'the cry of Colombia', to save its people from anarchy and, although he did not say it outright, to adopt the Bolivian Constitution.[22] The prospect divided Colombians into three parties. One for strong central government, giving more power to the executive and with a vice-president in each department, would preserve the integrity of the union; this was Bolívar's position, and for that reason commanded considerable, though not universal, support.[23] A second party, supported by Santander and the constitutionalists, wanted federalism though there was no agreement over what administrative divisions should be federated. A third party wanted Venezuela, New Granada and Quito to be independent states.

The congress of Ocaña, thought Bolívar, was 'Colombia's last chance', but ill-starred from the start it never looked equal to its role. He expected that 'the spirit of party will dictate interests, not laws; it will be the final triumph of the demagogy of the rabble. These are my deepest fears . . . but I am not prepared to go under and bury my glory in the ruins of Colombia.'[24] The election campaign itself made things worse for Bolívar. He could not compete with the propaganda of Santander who stood as a candidate and campaigned with the constitutionalists in open opposition to Bolívar, on a federal platform and assisted by a sympathetic press.[25] Bolívar scrupulously kept the government out of the political fray, though that did not prevent Bolivarian partisans in the military intimidating their opponents. When the returns were known it was clear that Santander and a majority of his candidates had been elected. Bolívar cried fraud, yet conceded that Santander was 'the idol of the people'. The British minister agreed that Santander, whom he described as 'an habitual gamester who paid his bills out of the treasury', had a considerable following, assembled from clients who owed their appointments and privileges to him over a long period of power. But Santander also had the support of many lawyers, who resented Bolívar's 'military faction' and viewed with alarm the possibility of a strong centralized state blocking their access to power.[26] Amidst these concerns the news from Venezuela was an almost welcome distraction.

Spain was striving to revive its presence in the Orinoco and royalist vessels from Puerto Rico were increasing their activities along the coast, exploiting unrest among the black population inland. Bolívar told Páez that he was coming to help him, but also took the opportunity to preach the virtues of unity: 'Without union, adios to the republic, adios to General Páez, and adios to your friend, Bolívar.'[27] He left Bogotá on 16 March 1828, travelling the familiar route from Tunja to Cúcuta, but on the way he received news that a royalist revolt in Coro had been crushed and Venezuelan commanders had suppressed guerrilla-inspired revolts in the rest of the country. Hardly had he rejoiced in these events when he received news of another revolt, this time in Cartagena, where blacks and *pardos* of the coast were being recruited for a race war. He abruptly changed his route towards Cartagena and paused in Bucaramanga.

José Prudencio Padilla, a survivor of Trafalgar, naval veteran of the war against Spain and hero of the battle of Lake Maracaibo in 1823, proclaimed himself commandant-general and intendant of Cartagena, and sought to raise the people of the coast against Bolívar and 'tyranny'.[28] Padilla was a *pardo*, or, as O'Leary put it, a *'mulatto*, ferocious and sanguinary'; he appealed to the *pardos*, who were a majority of the population in the Magdalena department, and whom he defined as 'my class', as opposed to the whites, whom he scorned as enemies of freedom and equality and threatened with the sword.[29] Padilla had already come to the attention of Bolívar, ever aware of racism from whatever side it came. While he could not fault him for loyalty to the revolution, he had some reservations about his social and political ambitions: 'Equality before the law is not enough for the people in their present mood. They want absolute equality as a public and a social right. Next they will demand *pardocracia*, that they, the *pardos*, should rule. This is a very natural inclination which will ultimately lead to the extermination of the privileged class.'[30] Cartagena was a dilemma for Bolívar. General Mariano Montilla, commander-in-chief of the Magdalena department and a committed Bolivarian, was from the white elite and lacked a mass following. Padilla, denied top office and agitating for equality, was a *pardo*, popular among his people. On 2 March 1828 Padilla addressed a group of *pardo* officers and let it be known that he was leading the people to protect their freedom. Montilla then moved smartly, ordered all military units out of Cartagena and lured Padilla into mobilizing his followers and declaring himself military commander of the department. But the rebel had gone too far, placed himself outside the law, and in the event failed to receive the support he expected. While Montilla restored security to Cartagena, Padilla fled to Ocaña, hoping for protection from Santander. O'Leary interviewed him there and reported to Bolívar: 'Your Excellency has formed a very exaggerated idea of events in Cartagena. The steps which Padillo took there and his behaviour with me show without any doubt that he has no party at all.' O'Leary advised against putting Padilla on trial in Cartagena, for although he had been abandoned by the people and the army when his actions were unlawful, he might be regarded with sympathy if he were to become a victim.[31]

O'Leary had a point. Conditions were not on Padilla's side. Another Bolivarian officer, Joaquín Posada Gutiérrez, observed:

> In our coastal provinces, especially Cartagena, there are educated and sensible *pardos*. As they enjoy complete equality in possession of political

and civil rights, they are well aware of their true interests. They know that knowledge and merit are the best qualifications for preferment, and that they can earn by lawful means due promotion to social positions, working and living honourably. This has a moderating influence on the rest. It is true that among the ignorant blacks of the fields and the lower classes in the towns there exists a certain hostility towards us, but this is directed more towards social status than towards colour, for they have the same aversion to the upper-class *pardos*.[32]

It was these depressed *pardos* whom Padilla tried to revolutionize. His enemies, of course, were indignant. Posada Gutiérrez expressed the hope that time and goodwill would assuage these racial tensions, 'for which we whites are not responsible'. Others were less complacent: 'The *zambo* General Padilla will meet the same fate as Piar, because from his many declarations it is clear that his object has been to kill all the whites and to make this another Santo Domingo.'[33] There was a further danger to Bolívar. Politically the movement was linked to Santander and offered Bolívar's enemy another political base, in an important port and fortress in the Caribbean. Bolívar's own view was that Padilla should be tried according to the law as an example to others; he had him arrested in Ocaña for trial in Cartagena. But Montilla, apparently taking the same line as O'Leary, sent him to Bogotá.

Manuela was much agitated by events in Cartagena, which she linked with Bolívar's opponents everywhere, especially those whose names began with a 'P'. 'God, let them die all these scoundrels called Paula, Padilla, Páez, it will be a great day for Colombia when they all go, these and others . . . that will be more humane, that ten die to save millions.'[34] She and Bolívar exchanged letters of love and humour and arguments, and he reassured her with a promise that he would not go to Venezuela or Cartagena but return to Bogotá very soon.[35]

Bolívar remained at Bucaramanga, some ninety miles south of Ocaña, a convenient place to communicate with O'Leary and the delegates and remain in contact with Cartagena and Bogotá. Among his staff at Bucaramanga was the French officer Louis Peru de Lacroix, veteran of Napoleonic campaigns and of Bolívar's army from 1823, who for three months observed the lifestyle of the Liberator and chronicled his opinions and recollections. He described his daily routine: he usually went out riding, at a fast pace, but he also liked to go swimming, jogging, and to lie reading in a hammock. His preferred meals were vegetables and fruit rather than meat, he liked wine in moderation, and prepared his own salads; he did not smoke and disliked anyone smoking in his presence. By now he had lost his former passion for dancing. He was in a mood for musing about the past and the present. He wondered about his place in history. Bolívar noticed that his minister, the historian José Manuel Restrepo, was receiving a good press for a recent publication, *Historia de la revolución de Colombia*, which was generous in its praise for the Liberator, too generous he thought; it held back on criticism 'because I am alive and have power and he is dependent on me'. He read the book avidly and concluded: 'We no longer live in times when national histories are written by a privileged historiographer who gains credibility, without scrutiny, for whatever he says. The people alone have the right to write their annals and judge their great men. So let the Colombian people judge me; that is what I want, what I will appreciate, what I believe will make my glory, not the judgement of my Minister of the Interior.'[36] He reflected too on Napoleon, though discreetly and not for publication. Urged on no doubt by the Frenchman, he was persuaded to admit that he admired the universal acclaim the emperor received from his countrymen and the glory that awaited a liberator who could emulate him.[37] Excited by political news or by passages in Restrepo's book, he was cool in emergencies. He made a practice of attending mass together with his staff, and he disapproved of anyone sitting cross-legged in church. On one occasion the church was suddenly emptied by alarm – false in the event – at an earth tremor, leaving only the priest at the altar and Bolívar in the choir; when everyone returned he was observed sitting quietly reading, not a missal but a secular periodical.[38] News from Ocaña, however, could raise his temper.

Santander went out of his way to welcome the delegates and pay for their lodgings, but in the event he did not command a majority. When the convention opened on 9 April there were found to be twenty-three *santanderistas*, twenty-one Bolivarians, and eighteen independents and moderates; of the 108 delegates elected, forty-four were absent. Most delegates agreed on the need for constitutional reform, though not on the details. But while the Bolivarians were determined to behave correctly, free of party spirit, the '*anarquists*' formed a tight group, eating and living together, and coordinating their tactics, all targeted on weakening the executive. 'I see this as the beginning of the end,' said Bolívar. 'Only a miracle can bring good rather than bad from the Grand Convention.'[39] The arguments went on for eight weeks. Santander stood for defence of the law against the danger of dictatorship, moving beyond mere liberalism to 'federation, as the only recourse left to us to save our national liberties'. O'Leary, who was Bolívar's personal observer at the convention and detested Santander, 'a mediocre man with average ability, a lot of effrontery, and no morality', recorded that from the rostrum he declaimed, 'I have the heart of a tiger.' Too true, commented O'Leary, if by that he means supreme conceit, a thick skin, ferocious nature, and other vices.[40] Santander reciprocated the hatred and described O'Leary as Bolívar's spy at Ocaña, whose duty was to report on the work of the deputies and carry out the orders of his master.

Bolívar was rapidly losing what little hope he had in the convention and was strongly critical of its factionalism and hostility to Bolivarian policies. He was outraged when the delegates endorsed the rebellion of Padilla, who in addition to racial incitement had sought to rally Cartagena against Bolívar in favour of Santander and the constitution of Cúcuta, 'an abominable act', which aroused two of Bolívar's prime susceptibilities, Santander and *pardocracia*.[41] Turmoil increased and prevented the adoption of constitutional reform. The Santanderists proposed retaining the existing constitution with article 128 deleted, the article which granted the president extraordinary powers in time of crisis. At this point Bolívar's supporters deserted the convention to prevent a quorum, and the convention disbanded on 11 June with nothing accomplished. Bolívar had thwarted Santander but did not see where to go next. It was at this time that he began speaking of the possibility of dividing the republic into three or four states and granting self-government to each, an idea born of despair and arousing incredulity among his followers.[42] Could he be serious?

The rebellion of Padilla, thought the British consul, had the 'effect of rallying all the people of property and influence round the person of General Bolívar, as the only one capable of now restoring the tranquillity of Colombia'.[43] As the convention of Ocaña broke up in deadlock, Bolívar left Bucaramanga in a rare mood of vacillation, convinced that whatever he did he would be condemned by some as a constitutionalist, by others as a dictator. Meanwhile, on 13 June in Bogotá the intendant and *cabildo* called an open meeting of the great and the good. These reviewed the dangers threatening the republic from within and without, repudiated the convention of Ocaña, and asked Bolívar to return and take exclusive possession of 'supreme authority with absolute power'.[44] In the course of three hours, five hundred supporting signatures, 'including those of the archbishop and of the principal people', were collected. Bolívar paused to think, but not for long. He agreed and rode on. He entered the capital to a saviour's welcome, attended a mass of thanksgiving in the cathedral and was escorted to government house. He assumed supreme power with apparently wide support, or at least the support of an open plebiscite, mobilized by local authorities in thirty-one towns throughout the country.[45] In Popayán the intendant Tomás Cipriano de Mosquera called a *cabildo abierto* to acknowledge the Liberator as *jefe supremo* of the nation, specifically excluding the military from attending.[46] General Urdaneta told the British minister that the Bolivarians had been inactive for too long and it was necessary to convince the world that 'Colombia would never permit itself to be ruled by a small faction of demagogues whose measures tended to deluge the country in blood for their own self-interest and to satiate their personal hatreds'.[47] Then the bad news began to arrive. Bolívar heard of the rebellion of troops in Chuquisaca and the assault on Sucre on 18 April 1828.[48] Peru was now openly belligerent, to the north as well as the south of its frontiers and Guayaquil was in danger. The Liberator could be forgiven for believing that foreign policy alone demanded a strong government in Colombia and a firm response to aggression. Looking ahead, exactions of men and money for the Peruvian war would not be popular, and only decisive action would carry the policy.

Supreme power was made absolute by the Organic Decree of 27 August 1828.[49] The Liberator President, as he was now called, justified the decree as flowing from 'the essential rights which the people always preserve to free themselves from the ravages of anarchy', and which they had now placed in his hands to exercise until a national assembly could be convoked. The decree was a measure to institutionalize his power, proof 'of my most ardent desire to unburden myself of the intolerable weight of unlimited authority and to see the Republic reconstituted by its representatives'.[50] But his options were reduced by two events: the attempt on his life and the invasion by Peru. So the power of the Liberator President was a personal power, exercised by decrees that had the force of law and through appointments that were under his control. The Organic Decree eliminated the office of vice-president and Santander was appointed minister to the United States, an appointment which he was ready to accept though he made no move to leave. Bolívar established a council of state, with an advisory function only, consisting of all five ministers, regional representatives, and military and clerical personnel. He had always believed in the separation of the judicial power but not in its total independence, which in practice had hindered legitimate government; therefore, in increasing the influence of the executive in law enforcement as well as law-making through a series of judicial changes, he was not abandoning his principles. He had long regarded the military as vulnerable to civilian liberals, and he now confirmed and even extended the traditional military *fuero* inherited from Spain, and in the interests of defence it was reasonable to increase the size of the armed forces. None of these measures made the presidency a military dictatorship. He regarded the regime as temporary, until the assembly of a congress on 2 January 1830.[51] In other respects Bolívar still revealed liberal instincts. His government had already declared its opposition to any attempt to by-pass the prohibition of the slave trade. A decree of 5 January 1828 prohibited trade in slaves for domestic service and freed those thus enslaved since 1821.[52]

What was the truth of the supreme power? Was it the final proof of Bolívar's loss of political purity and the erosion of his principles? Interpretations of his rule in 1828–30 have been influenced by his previous reputation as well as subsequent actions. It is contrasted with the great avowals of liberty, equality and even occasionally of democracy, and therefore judged as a decline from his own standards. Alternatively it has been seen as the culmination of his absolutist tendencies already present in the Bolivian Constitution, with its life president, and in the extraordinary powers he had invoked under the Colombian constitution. Yet it was not a deviation. Bolívar had always been ill at ease with democracy, which in Spanish America was too close to anarchy for his liking. And from the beginning he had advocated strong government: as early as the Jamaica Letter he was speculating that Colombia might have an executive, though not hereditary, power elected for life. Moreover, his political thought and policy statements record a remarkable continuity in his commitment to liberal republicanism. Even at Angostura, when he recommended to the legislators the study of the British constitution, he did so not in servile imitation of monarchy but in defence of republicanism. 'When I speak of the British government I refer only to its republican features; and indeed, can a political system be called a pure monarchy when it recognizes popular sovereignty, division and balance of powers, civil liberty, freedom of conscience and of the press, and all that is sublime in politics? Can there be greater freedom in any other form of republic? Can more be expected of any social order?'[53]

The essential features of independence and freedom, his permanent objectives, were best guaranteed by strong government and, if necessary, until they could be secured in a constitution, by his personal rule. Yet the policy and practice of his personal rule have been exaggerated. Even when he exercised absolute power in 1828–30 Bolívar did not rule like a caudillo or a despot; his rule responded to no particular social or regional interest, his use of patronage was not extravagant, and his respect for the rule of law did not desert him. It is true that there were some Bolivarians who were extremists, some who genuinely frightened liberals, ultras who tried to stir up social unrest by appealing to popular passions, even to religious instincts, and this 'by men who normally believe nothing'.[54] But there were others, such as the interior minister Restrepo, who were politically moderate and were qualified for office whatever the regime. And there was one to raise eyebrows.

While Bolívar resided in the presidential palace of San Carlos, Manuela had taken a house nearby in the Plazuela de San Carlos, where she lived her own life, riding out by day in military uniform and entertaining in the evening with the help of port wine and the adulation of visitors. On 24 July, Bolívar's birthday, she gave a party at his villa outside Bogotá where she suggested that an effigy be made of Santander; this was then positioned sitting on a bench and shot in the back by a detachment of Grenadiers. Bolívar was not present, but according to General Córdova, who reported the scandal to him, there was much talk of a kind embarrassing to his reputation and critical of a lady who 'meddles in government affairs'. Bolívar's reply revealed some embarrassment but not too much; he dismissed the incident as vulgar nonsense and not criminal. He would suspend the commanding officer of the Grenadiers and send the men to serve elsewhere. 'As for the lovable Loca, what can I say? You have known her from way back. I have tried to leave her, but one can do nothing against a resistance such as hers; nevertheless, as soon as this episode is past, I intend to make the most determined effort to send her to her country, or wherever she will go. But let me say that she has never meddled except in pleading [for favours for others?]. So do not worry. I am not weak, nor do I fear to be told the truth.'[55] Within weeks he was begging her to come to him and revive his spirits with her love. 'I see you even when I am parted from you. Come, come, come quickly.' Bolívar would not offend his soldiers, but equally he would never betray Manuela.

The Assassins

Bolívar was not a dictator by nature, and he did not regard absolute power as a permanent settlement, much less as a step towards monarchy. In practice he did not substantially extend his extraordinary powers. There was a decree on conspiracy (20 February 1828) already in existence, but it was not effectively applied, even against opponents who were denouncing 'the execrable triumvirate of Bolívar, Urdaneta, and Castillo'.[56] Bolívar himself was first in the firing line. Extremists targeted him in the early months of the regime and plotted to remove him. The conspiracy was not a caudillo-type action, much less a mass revolt, but a projected coup designed to overthrow Bolívar, whom the conspirators identified as the supreme enemy of freedom. They consulted Santander, who agreed on the criminality of Bolívar but declined to participate in violence; when specifically sounded he expressed his disapproval, though he did not rule out some future collaboration in a peaceful movement.[57] The conspirators were army officers, together with a number of professors and students 'allegedly liberals', meeting in a so-called Philological Society.[58] They were young men, of a generation for whom the revolution of 1810 was past history and Bolívar a man who had not moved on. The leader was Pedro Carujo, a twenty-six-year-old Venezuelan staff officer with literary aspirations, aided by Ramón Guerra, chief of the general staff in Bogotá, and Luis Vargas Tejada, a liberal politician; the civilian coodinator was Florentino González, an admirer and subsequently husband of Bernardina Ibáñez, whom Bolívar had pursued in the years after Boyacá. Although the leaders had ideas of extending the movement to the provinces, the conspiracy had little resonance in the country; as Santander himself admitted, the army and the people were with Bolívar.

The conspirators were opportunists, and after a false start they decided to murder Bolívar on the night of Thursday 25 September 1828 as he slept in the palace of San Carlos. There were rumours of trouble, but Bolívar did not take them seriously. He had sent for Manuela earlier in the evening and remarked to her that there was going to be a revolution. She too was casual: 'There may be ten as far as you are concerned, for all the notice you take.' 'Don't worry,' he replied, 'nothing is going to happen.' She read to him while he was taking a bath, and then he retired and slept soundly, with only his sword and pistols to hand. At midnight, thirty conspirators attacked in three groups: one, headed by Carujo and Agustín Horment, a Navarrese, planned to attack the presidential palace and kill Bolívar; a second would attack the barracks of the Vargas Battalion and free Padilla from jail; and a third would attack the Grenadiers in their barracks. At the entrance to the palace the conspirators killed the three sentries and the guard dogs and made their way indoors, wounding Andrés Ibarra, one of Bolívar's aides, on the way. Wakened by the commotion, Bolívar was for confronting the intruders, sword in hand, but Manuela saw the danger and persuaded him to dress and escape from the window, holding him back until some passers-by had gone. Then he jumped from the balcony and ran four or five blocks away, followed by one of his servants who, seeing his master turn with a pistol ready, announced himself, 'Soy Trinidad, mi general!'[59]

The door burst open and Manuela, armed with a sword, confronted Carujo, who marched her roughly through the palace in a vain search for Bolívar, and beat her in frustration when her directions proved false. She ministered to Ibarra and tried to warn off Colonel Ferguson, who rushed in to help. A survivor of many campaigns, he was shot and killed by Carujo. José Palacio, Bolívar's mayordomo, was only saved because at the time he was ill in another bedroom. At the Vargas barracks Padilla was freed and his guard killed, but the battalion reacted quickly and put the aggressors to flight. The Grenadiers repulsed the third group. Urdaneta took command, restored order and dispatched squads to find Bolívar and capture the conspirators. Bolívar had spent three hours shivering under the Bridge of Carmen in the murky waters of the small San Agustín River, listening to rival shouts for Santander and for Bolívar. When he heard 'Viva el Libertador' and no reply he judged it safe to emerge from his vile refuge at three o'clock in the morning. Exposure to danger and the elements had left the Liberator drained and convinced that Manuela was truly 'la libertadora del Libertador'. As for the emotional scars, he would carry them for the rest of his life.[60]

The next day Santander, Padilla and several others were arrested. General Urdaneta, the presiding judge of the trials, was a known enemy of Santander. He was for a hard line, convinced that this was a wider conspiracy, inspired by Santander, 'el alma del negocio', and that he himself was one of seven others targeted for assassination. 'My line is that it's either them or us.'[61] Of the fifty-nine named as principal participants, eight were acquitted, fourteen condemned to death, five sentenced to internal exile, three escaped and the rest were imprisoned or barred from teaching. Padilla, Guerra, Horment and ten others were found guilty of conspiracy and executed. Padilla, rebel if not conspirator, faced the firing squad shouting 'cobardes' and refusing a blindfold. Carujo bargained for his life by testifying against Santander and others, but was still sentenced to death, and only saved by a pardon from the council of ministers; after arguing his way through various prisons he escaped in August 1829 and was eventually amnestied by Páez, a lucky exit from a supposedly ruthless dictatorship. A wider net was cast against the fringe conspirators, but the response to what had been an act of extreme violence at the heart of government was hardly a bloodbath. Removal of teaching licences and academic degrees, the imposition of travel restrictions and the prohibition of secret societies completed the official action. Santander was convicted of giving counsel and aid to the conspirators, though no direct evidence of participation was presented. Urdaneta was convinced of his guilt and sentenced him to be executed, but the council of ministers was not satisfied with the proof and on the wider grounds of public interest recommended that the sentence be commuted to banishment.[62] On this advice, which he said he bitterly resented but may have welcomed as a reprieve for himself, Bolívar spared the life of his enemy.

The conspiracy against Bolívar's life was a shock to his glory, an affront to his pride. Now he underwent an inner struggle, conscious of the resentment of the pardos. Piar, Padilla and others had died for the crime of rebellion, so why should Santander, a public enemy whose conduct could only lead to anarchy, escape? 'Those of the same class as Piar and Padilla will say, and justifiably, that I have shown weakness only in favour of this infamous white, whose services do not compare with those of these famous patriots.'[63] Santander added his own gloss. 'We do not know the real reason why Bolívar commuted the death sentence,' he wrote. 'He has said that his glory demanded it. The only thing we can say with certainty is that public opinion pronounced strongly in favour of Santander and against the terror inspiring the government.'[64] In many other cases, however, Bolívar also advised clemency. Eventually he was exasperated by the whole protracted process: 'I've got conspiracy up to the eyeballs,' he said. After it was over, to escape from 'this chamber of horrors', he took a break in the country, spending a few weeks in the Indian villages of Chia north of Bogotá, one of his favourite places for relaxation. Urdaneta too went through tortuous procedures to get to the truth and became convinced that Santander was guilty of having advance knowledge of the conspiracy and not denouncing it, and therefore of high treason. Santander left Colombia in 1829 for exile in Europe and the United States, returning in 1832 to serve as the first elected president of New Granada.

The Liberator President had the support of office-holders in Church and state, most of the military, the higher ranks of the caudillos, and Bolivarians in all sectors. Urdaneta, minister of war and army commander, was closely associated with the regime from the beginning. Sucre had no doubts that more authority was needed at the centre; in his view the people were disillusioned with written guarantees and theoretical liberty, and only wanted protection for their persons and property by a strong government. A year later he added: 'I will always be sorry that in order to obtain this internal peace and stability you have not made use of your dictatorial power to give Colombia a constitution, which would have been sustained by the army.... What the people want is peace and guarantees; as for the rest, I do not believe that they dispute for principles or political theories, which have caused so much damage to their right of property and security.'[65] Páez stood firm against the 'enemy' *convencionistas* as they returned from Ocaña; he recognized the regime promptly and considered it the best solution against the factionalism of the military and the mischief of the liberals, of whom there were more than a few in Venezuela. He expressed some reservations on religious policy, alleging that Venezuela was less clerical than Bogotá and confined religion to doctrine not jurisdiction, and he advised the Liberator to proceed 'with all the discretion demanded by the age of enlightenment'.[66] To receive a lecture on the Enlightenment from Páez of all people must have tried the patience, and the credulity, of Bolívar. Politically, the President and caudillo both wanted the same thing, strong government and stability. But Páez also wanted the independence of Venezuela, though peacefully and without another revolution, because, as Soublette reported, 'He does not have the will to start another revolution, nor does he dare to break his often-repeated oaths of allegiance to you.'[67] Bolívar seemed to accept that Venezuela, with its military fiefdoms so unlike the rest of Colombia, might have to go its own way. He recognized that Colombia suffered from its size and its geography: the centre was too remote from the outlying districts, government authority was dissipated by distance, and distance increased by the terrain. 'There is no prefect, no governor, who does not invest himself with supreme authority, principally as a matter of absolute necessity. It might be said that each department is a government, distinct from the national, modified by local conditions or circumstances peculiar to the area, or even personal in nature.'[68] These were the conditions that bred independent regions and their caudillos. Ecuador, too, was sensitive to over-centralization, and the presidency allowed Flores, like Páez, some immunity from the strictest degree of absolutism demanded by Bogotá.

Foundations of the Faith

Bolívar's rejection of the liberal state was not simply a reaction to the attempt on his life but expressed a consistent policy that had always governed his attitude to religion. At the beginning of his final presidency he explained his principle of government to Páez as a return to tradition: 'I plan to base my reforms on the solid foundation of religion and, as far as is compatible with our circumstances, to seek the simplest, the most secure and the most effective traditional laws.'[69] His mindset was secularist and he was instinctively suspicious of the Church. But he was too political to allow his basic objectives to be jeopardized by gratuitous anti-clericalism, much less by overt freethinking. He conformed to the Catholic religion and went to church services. It would be unrealistic to expect absolute statements of belief or to conclude from their absence that he was irreligious. Other indications, mostly indirect, are better guides. He attended mass, for some periods frequently, he disapproved of casual behaviour in church, he was scornful of some priests, respectful of others, expecting serious standards from clergy and faithful. Whenever he rebuked the clergy it was for specific actions. The earthquake of 1812 was openly exploited by priests who preached against the republic, in Bolívar's view 'sacrilegiously abusing the sanctity of their office' on behalf of the royalist cause.[70]

While royalist clergy angered him, he also had reason to be grateful for the support of many priests who rallied the faithful to the republican cause with words and deeds. Juan Fernández de Sotomayor, parish priest of Mompós and future bishop of Cartagena, in 1814 published the *Catecismo o instrucción popular* in which he denounced the Spanish colonial regime as unjust and the priests who supported it as enemies of religion; this was 'a just and holy war', which would liberate New Granada from slavery and lead to freedom and independence.[71] Bolívar never acknowledged the contribution of clerical propagandists for independence, preachers who were able to reach an audience beyond his speeches and proclamations. He would have liked to disestablish the Church, but in a deeply Catholic society he had to move carefully. In his message to the constituent congress of Bolivia he explained that his Bolivian Constitution excluded religion from any public role, and he came close to saying that religion was a purely private concern, a matter of conscience, not of politics. He specifically declined to provide for an established Church or a state religion: 'The sacred precepts and dogmas are useful, enlightening and metaphysical in their nature; we should profess them but this is a moral duty, not a political one.'[72] The state should guarantee freedom of religion, without prescribing any particular religion. Bolívar thus defended a view of toleration familiar to modern religionists, in which faith exists on its own strength and merits without the support of legal sanctions. He never subscribed to Rousseau's idea of a civil religion, designed for its social and political utility and intended to take the place of existing churches. Bolívar was a man of ideas but he was also a realist. This realism did not desert him during the presidential regime, and he sought to maintain a balance between the views of conservatives and liberals.

Bolívar had long admired Jeremy Bentham and regarded his republican system inspired by utility as appropriate for Americans. In 1822 he reassured Bentham that 'the name of the preceptor of legislation is never pronounced, even in these savage regions of America, without veneration, nor without gratitude'. Utilitarianism offered Spanish America a new philosophical framework that would give republicanism a moral legitimacy after the collapse of royal government. Seeking an alternative authority to absolutism and religion, liberals seized upon utilitarianism as a modern philosophy capable of giving them the intellectual credibility they wanted. The doctrine of utility became Bolívar's working philosophy.[73] He acknowledged his enthusiasm for Bentham and expected the philosopher to adopt him 'as one of his disciples, as, in consequence of being initiated in his doctrines, I have defended liberty, till it has been made the sovereign rule of Colombia'.[74] For his part, Bentham had misgivings concerning the killing of prisoners by Bolívar, of which he claimed to have hearsay evidence in 1820. He seems to have decided not to raise the issue, which he could see was provocative, and there the matter rested.[75] In 1823 Bentham wrote twice to Bolívar, advising him on government and, among other things, of the most appropriate way of appointing diplomatic envoys or, as he put it, an 'Ambonational mode of Agency'. In August 1825 he sent Bolívar various copies of his books, including his *Constitutional Code* and *Codification Proposal*, and a long letter on his current life and labour. He advised him to avoid the English practice of rewarding government officials with excessive salaries, commending Bolívar's own exemplary sacrifices in the public service, and he recommended the greatest happiness principle as the best antidote available to governments to avoid assassination projects, of which the Liberator had more than once been a target. He recalled their meeting in his garden in 1810, expressed his confidence in Bolívar and admiration for his achievements, and ended with the hope that he would soon be able to rest on his laurels and dedicate himself exclusively to the arts of peace.[76] The books did not arrive but the letter impressed Bolívar who in reply voiced his enthusiasm for the thought of Bentham, which he described as 'marvellously developed' to dispel evil and ignorance.[77]

In republican Colombia the works of Bentham came under attack from the clergy and other conservatives, and the materialism, scepticism and anti-clericalism of the English philosopher were declared harmful to the Catholic religion. Bolívar was forced into painful decisions, not all of his own desiring and hardly justified in terms of the works' contents. Convinced by now that the constitution and laws of Colombia were excessively liberal and that they threatened the dissolution of society and the state, and pressed by conservatives on the specific issue of Bentham, Bolívar had to take sides. In 1825 Santander had decreed that the universities should teach legislation according to the principles of Bentham.[78] Now this policy was abandoned. A decree of March 1828 prohibited the teaching of Bentham's *Tratados de Legislación Civil y Penal* in the universities of Colombia. The attempt to assassinate Bolívar in September 1828 and the involvement of university personnel in the conspiracy further convinced him that university students were being dangerously indoctrinated. To Archbishop Méndez of Caracas he wrote that 'deviation from sound principles has produced the madness which agitates the country and needs to be corrected by the voice of pastors inculcating respect, obedience, and virtue'.[79] His government issued a circular on public education (20 October 1828) denouncing the study of 'principles of legislation by authors like Bentham and the others, whose works contain not only enlightening ideas but also many that are hostile to religion and morality and public order'. These courses should be replaced by, among others, the study of Latin, Roman and Canon Law, and the Roman Catholic religion and its history.[80] The selection of Bentham as a pernicious influence is difficult to explain, for there was nothing in his works justifying assassination of a head of state, and other authors of the Enlightenment were available for those who wanted them. An English traveller in Bogotá noticed that young men 'of good families and liberal education' repudiated religion in favour of the works of Voltaire, Rousseau 'and other freethinkers'.[81] As it was, the episode left a cloud over the Liberator's reputation.

During a visit to London in July 1830, Santander had dinner with Bentham, then aged eighty-two, and enjoyed what he described as an agreeable evening at his house, when Colombia, Bolívar and English politics were all discussed. In a subsequent letter Bentham asked Santander for the name of the author of '*cette belle Constitution Bolivienne*', which had evidently impressed him. An innocent question and a tendentious reply. Santander could not resist the chance to besmirch Bolívar's reputation and brand him as an enemy of liberal and republican institutions: 'This monstrous constitution has been the real apple of discord dividing and ruining Colombia, Peru and Bolivia.' As 'the tyrant' Bolívar fell from grace in the mind of Bentham, so the 'distinguished' Santander rose in his estimation. Santander did not allow the opportunity to pass: 'Instead of giving us peace, tranquillity, and freedom he bequeaths hatreds, and resentments, and passions. . . . Alas, the same sword which overthrew Spanish domination, has destroyed the liberties of the Colombian people.'[82] Bolívar knew the script.

Religious orders benefited from Bolívar's rule, but only in the sense that they were allowed the right to exist. Liberal legislation by the congress of Cúcuta had suppressed *conventos menores* (small monasteries with fewer than eight members). Bolívar's decree of July 1828 restored these religious houses in general, but did not apply to those now in use as schools or hospitals, neither did it restore their revenues. Another decree in the same month suspended the law of 1826 that made the age of twenty-five the minimum for taking religious vows, but again the renewed right was not absolute, for in future members of religous orders would have to give five years to pastoral service in Indian missions.[83] Other measures were taken in defence of miscellaneous clerical practices, such as protecting *censos*, restoring the position of military chaplains and prohibiting attacks on the Catholic religion. These measures, even in conjunction, could not be regarded as any more extreme than the liberalism they replaced, or as evidence of Bolívar's supposed conversion to clericalism. In any case, he was unrepentant. The Organic Decree explicitly listed protection of the Roman Catholic religion as a function of the national authorities: 'The government will sustain and protect the Catholic, Apostolic, Roman religion as the religion of Colombians.'[84] And as a postscript to his policy he later added: 'Allow me in my last act to recommend to you [congress in January 1830] that you protect the holy religion that we profess, deep source of the blessings of heaven.'[85] But these were formal and general statements without great policy impact. His colleagues and associates were not all clericalists. O'Leary recorded that many of Bolívar's friends disapproved of his decree restoring the convents to the friars and he used to reply, 'It is necessary to oppose religious fanaticism to the fanaticism of the demagogues.'[86] Liberals may have opposed, but not the common people and from Popayán, admittedly a traditionally Catholic department, Tomás Mosquera reported that suspending the law suppressing convents had been well received by the *gentes de pueblo*.[87]

Clerical interests were not allowed to prevail over matters of political or economic importance. A decree of December 1828 exempted from payment of tithes any grain crops introduced in future on plantations of coffee, cacao and indigo, and landowners in highland Ecuador were allowed by decree of August 1829 to make interest payments to creditors (usually ecclesiastical) in kind. Bolívar was not likely to object to the provision of freedom of conscience and private worship allowed to non-Catholics in international treaties, such as that with Britain in 1826 and the Netherlands in 1829. He continued to insist that the republic would exercise the right of presentation to ecclesiastical benefices, as the Spanish and republican practice had always been, despite ultramontanist arguments that this required papal agreement. So episcopal appointments continued to be made by the state, though lesser appointments were left to the bishops. And Quito's bishop was raised to archbishop without waiting for papal confirmation.

Meanwhile the policy of the Church towards republicanism had been changing, in America, if not in Rome.[88] Disillusioned with the policies of Spain and impressed by the achievements of the revolution, royalist prelates opened their eyes to the republic and, from about 1820, one by one they converted to the cause of independence. Rafael Lasso de la Vega, bishop of Mérida, a creole born in Panama who had once excommunicated rebel leaders, now disavowed the divine right of kings, basing his republicanism on the right of the people to choose their government. A long interview with Bolívar convinced him that the Catholic religion was safer in the hands of the Liberator than in those of a liberal Spanish *cortes*. He began to work for the reconstruction of the Church in an independent Colombia, becoming one of the firmest allies of Bolívar and his first link with Rome. When he was appointed bishop of Quito in 1829, the Liberator told him of his great pleasure at his appointment 'to care for the faithful who clamour to have a bishop worthy to be called prince of the Church and above all father of the poor'.[89] During this time of crisis and division for religion, the Church in America received little help from Rome, where opposition to independence was reinforced by its experience of revolution in Europe and was expressed in a series of hostile encyclicals.[90] Bolívar remained cool. A fighter for independence from Spain, he never sought independence from Rome. Like the bishops he could live with Roman intransigence and continue to seek collaboration. In Angostura in 1817 he committed himself 'as head of a Christian people' to preserve unity with the Roman Church.[91] In 1822, in the turmoil of Pasto, he pleaded with the Spanish bishop of Popayán not to abandon Colombia in its hour of need, bereft as it was of priests and guidance:

> As long as His Holiness does not recognize the political and religious existence of the Colombian nation, our Church has all the more need of its bishops to alleviate its orphan status. A violent separation of this hemisphere can only diminish the universality of the Roman Church, and responsibility for this terrible separation will fall especially on those who, in a position to maintain the unity of the Roman Church, have contributed by their negative conduct, to accelerate the ills that will ruin the Church and cause the eternal death of its souls.

Bolívar admired Bishop Jiménez de Enciso, a man with a sharp mind who listened carefully, spoke sensibly, was 'already a good Colombian' and could represent the republican cause with the same fervour with which he had served Ferdinand VII. He recommended him to Santander as a friend worth cultivating in Bogotá.[92] And in the following year the bishop did in fact recommend the cause of independence to Pius VII.

Bolívar wanted to re-establish relations with the Holy See and eventually, in 1827, his representatives gained from Pope Leo XII recognition of bishops for Colombia and Bolivia. In welcoming the appointment of archbishops and bishops for the sees of Bogotá, Caracas, Santa Marta, Antioquia, Quito, Cuenca and Charcas, Bolívar gave a banquet in Bogotá in October 1827 at which he pronounced a toast to the new prelates and to the renewed unity with the Church of Rome, 'the fount of heaven'. 'The descendants of Saint Peter have always been our fathers, but war had left us orphans like a lamb bleating in vain for its lost mother. Now she has given us pastors worthy of the Church and of the Republic. [The new bishops] will be our guides, models of religion and of political virtues.'[93] The Vatican continued to regard Bolívar with reserve, to give priority to Spain, and to concede nothing to American independence. Yet, in 1829 Bolívar assured Pius VIII of his 'adhesion to the head of the Catholic Church, and respect and veneration for the sacred person of Your Holiness'.[94] Bolívar could give Rome a lesson in Christian sentiments as well as in political judgement.

Bolívar's government of 1828–30 was not a clerical reaction and he himself did not undergo a reconversion. He had not previously been excessively anti-clerical and he had never been completely detached from religion. His mind and his policies were still pragmatic and secular, still consistent with his past. In 1828 he wrote to the priest Justiniano Gutiérrez, thanking him for his concern over his safety on the night of 25 September:

Let me recommend my friend, Dr Molano, who is going to Guaduas to see to his community, encouraged by the restoration of religion and the monastic orders. These contribute so much to the civilization of this country, and moreover work unceasingly to prevent the propagation of principles that are destroying us and which in the end not only succeed in destroying religion but also people's lives. This happened in the French Revolution, when the most passionate philosophers had to repent of the very thing they had previously professed. So it was that Abbé Raynal died stricken by remorse, and many others like him, because without a sense of religion morality has no foundation.[95]

None of these sentiments amounted to religious absolutism and none were new to Bolívar's thinking.

The Limits of Revolution

Since May 1826 the Bolivarian revolution had faltered, apparently lost in a maze of complexities. In the Bolivian Constitution and accompanying message Bolívar reached the crest of his creativity. From then on it was defence all the way, verbal in reply to opposition, active in response to attack. What had gone wrong? We could, of course, accept his own explanation: blame the enemies who rejected his policies, criticize the friends who stood silent. 'It will be the Colombians who will go down to posterity covered in ignominy, not me.'[96] But the events of 1826–8 point to a deeper problem, beyond accusations, involving the whole strategy of independence.

From Angostura to Potosí, Bolívar directed the revolution: he conceived policy, decided strategy and controlled the way forward. He took the revolution so far ahead of its base that he put it beyond his own control and it became impossible to preserve the model of government he had designed: strong, central authority guaranteeing freedom within order and equality within reason. The Colombian army was there to impose a minimum of order, and he was supported too by the Bolivarians, a group of officers and administrators bound to him out of respect for his ideas and loyalty to his person. But the army could not be everywhere, and his Bolivarians, though posted to strategic positions, were not the equal of their leader and some, such as Urdaneta, were more Bolivarian than Bolívar himself. There was only one Bolivarian capable of ruling a state, and on the outer perimeter of the revolution even Sucre was vulnerable. In the Bolivarian scheme of things, Peru was essential to liberation because it shielded a Spanish army, but strategically it was a revolution too far; his political lines became stretched, his military power dispersed. Bolívar was aware of these dangers. World history had long recorded the trend: rulers who became overambitious, armies that marched too far, empires that outgrew their strength, conquests too expensive to defend. He knew that he would not be received with instant obedience everywhere, that equality for some meant disadvantage for others. He had planted the seeds of his ideas, but not all the ground was fertile and some of the growths were poisonous. None of this was news to him. Virtually every flaw in his world was seen, and often foreseen, by Bolívar himself. Was it humanly possible to do more?

The Bolivian Constitution was his ultimate solution, his final expression of hope but, as he suspected, only Sucre was capable of fulfilling it and ruling in his absence. If Sucre were rejected, what then? There were no other proconsuls in line. As he dragged his Bolivian Constitution around from country to country it became a weight in his baggage that he could not unload. The life presidency in particular was a stumbling block: it closed the route to success for all other candidates; it denied politicians the perquisites of power and their clients the fruits of office. In closing options to his opponents he opened the door to greater destruction. He was left with Colombia, the core of his revolution. Colombia was under control, but after an absence of five years followed by two years of conflict and controversy, it was not entirely in *his* control, and even Colombia's borderlands suffered from surrounding disorder. Bolívar stood for the continuation of Colombia under his supreme authority, exercised first through the extraordinary powers which the constitution allowed him, then by the absolute power finally conferred by popular acclaim. But could the Colombian union hold? The politics of the revolution surged on and marooned its maker. As Venezuela seceded and the exodus spread, he looked increasingly isolated. 'Colombia,' it has been aptly said, 'was a republic with only one citizen.'[97]

Chapter 11

JOURNEY OF DISILLUSION

Rebels and Invaders

There were few choices now, only further trials by battle. If 1828 was a bad year worse were to come. The chronology, the policies and the itineraries of the time are complex, and the observer has to track Bolívar closely to follow his mind and movements. But the logic of events is clear. In 1829 the juxta-position of external shock and internal revolt produced a classic state of crisis, a turning point when things were on a knife-edge. Attack from Peru encour-aged dissidents in Colombia, these challenged the regime, and the exodus from the doomed state began. Bolívar was struggling in that fatal year. The war on nature which he had proclaimed in Caracas during the earthquake of 1812 came back to haunt him. Now his own health was crumbling and he could not defy it. Yet he was not a helpless victim of events. His legendary instincts survived: if there was a fire, quench it, if there was a revolt, stifle it, and always look for a political deal. As new rivals rose to scourge Bolívar and old enemies renewed their attack, he remained cool under pressure, mobilized the Bolivarians, posted his generals, stationed his forces and continued to negotiate with his enemies. So 1829 was not totally bleak; there were breaks in the clouds and brief flashes of hope. But as the year drew to a close, despair was the prevailing mood.

Bolívar was aware of the crisis and spoke of it. The historian is tempted to believe that Bolívar's own diagnosis was correct: the Colombians are to blame, not me. Every political measure, the liberal regime in Colombia, the presi-dency with extraordinary powers, absolutism by acclaim, received only partial or temporary support, and that because of the prestige of the Liberator. Even his cherished Bolivian Constitution, he believed, 'would not last longer than a slice of bread'.[1] Nothing else endured. The irreducible fact remained, that the source of the Liberator's legitimacy was his own personal qualities. The dilemma was still unresolved. Bolívar ruled alone, the only stable thing in a world in turmoil. That was the world he blamed, and his analysis had its merits. Without Bolívar the revolution would have split into numerous fiefdoms, the caudillos the ultimate authorities. Only he had the perseverance for a national revolution and political union. Moreover, Bolívar raised legitimate questions concerning the appropriate extent of liberty and the freedom of opposition groups to subvert the very state that guaranteed their existence. Absolute freedom placed its defenders in a classic liberal dilemma when they supported dangerous and illiberal extremists. Did not a duly constituted government have the right to protect itself from those proclaiming its destruction in the name of freedom? For liberals were not lambs. They too claimed absolute power. For the likes of Santander, to be free meant to govern other people. Possession of government, that was the touchstone of their liberalism. To paraphrase Alberdi, who observed a similar trend in Argentina, it never occurred to Colombian liberals to respect the views of others when they were in disagreement with their own. Liberals of this kind were soon at Bolívar's throat. He needed his honour guard as a body guard.

The attempt on Bolívar's life in September 1828 had repercussions in southern Colombia. Colonel José María Obando declared against Bolívar in Popayán late in October, with the same intention as the assassins in Bogotá but with more resources, for he seized gold meant for the mint and looted rich estates. The illegitimate son of an upper-class Popayán family, he had fought as a guerrilla leader under royalist colours from 1819 to 1822, switched sides, and served as a republican officer from 1822 to 1828. He was a bloodthirsty enemy wherever he fought, a classic caudillo who, while proclaiming the usual slogans, 'long live liberty, death to tyrants', would have had no compunction about killing Bolívar and defending his own lair in southern Colombia. He promoted his career by a mixture of force and fraud, Hobbes's two cardinal virtues in war. He unleashed a force of blacks and Indians to terrorize the Popayán countryside before he launched his four hundred against the seven hundred badly led troops of the Bolivarian commander, Tomás C. Mosquera; he triumphed in the battle of La Ladera on 11 November 1828, and captured two thousand rifles with ammunition. While Mosquera abandoned his troops and fled, Obando predictably massacred his prisoners for, as Posada Gutiérrez explained, 'In the Cauca wars no quarter is normally given, and the murder of defenceless men who have surrendered is not regarded as criminal, a custom which is still prevalent among the revolutionaries of our own day.'[2] He assigned Colonel José Hilario López to take charge of 'our noble revolution' in Popayán and moved south to Pasto, his natural habitat, where he recruited Indians by claiming that he was fighting 'for the King of Spain and the Catholic religion'; he also made contact with the Peruvian enemies of

Colombia and assured La Mar that Bolívar, 'the Sultan of Colombia', was finished and 'we are resolved only to deal with his ashes'.[3]

Bolívar distrusted 'these infernal regions', as he called them. He had hated Pasto since his first bloody battle there in 1822, and its subsequent rebellions infuriated him beyond measure. In 1825 he advocated that 'the *pastusos* should be liquidated and their women and children transported to another part of the country, leaving Pasto for occupation as a military colony. Otherwise the *pastusos* will return to haunt Colombia at the slightest disturbance for the next hundred years'.[4] Meanwhile they were useful fodder for his foes. López was a native of Popayán and after joining the republican cause spent some years in prison for his pains. He opposed Bolívar's government and in most respects was a mirror image of Obando, whose tutelage he followed with enthusiasm. Meanwhile, Obando cultivated his power base in Pasto, and there he remained, a warlord in waiting.

Bolívar heard of the Cauca rebellion on 22 November, while he was in Chía; he left his rural retreat to return to Bogotá and face the problems he was coming to dread. He had to take action quickly for the danger of liaison between Peru and the rebels was too great to ignore. As an immediate response he sent General Córdova with fifteen hundred troops, while he prepared to follow personally to confront the threats from the south. He left a council of ministers to rule in his absence and on 24 December decreed that elections for delegates to a constituent congress be held in July 1829. Reminding the public that the government established by his Organic Decree of 27 August was 'strictly provisional', he laid down that the congress would convene in Bogotá on 2 January 1830 to decide on a permanent constitution for Colombia 'in keeping with the enlightened ideas of the age and the customs and needs of the people'.[5] Then on 28 December he moved south in the wake of Córdova. Now time seemed shorter, distance longer, as the effort and pain of marching and riding increased.

Córdova arrived in Popayán and recaptured the city in late December, then harassed López and the rebel troops towards Pasto. Delighted to be released on to a larger stage, Córdova began to anticipate his prospects. In Popayán he derided Mosquera for his weak defence against the fewer troops of Obando and created an enemy who would not forget the insults.[6] He also began to develop ideas at variance with those of the Liberator, who did not need sermons from a military subordinate advising him to resign or accept a constitution. Anxious to push forward towards Peru and to avoid having to fight his way through the punishing passes he recalled from 1822, Bolívar decided to negotiate with the rebel Obando. He recruited two priests to make an offer of amnesty to those rebels who laid down their arms, while Obando sent two commissioners to represent his views. They met on 2 March at the bridge over the Río de Mayo, close to Berruecos. Bolívar took a risk in entrusting himself without his own troops to the mercies of Obando and riding with him overnight. The hind travelled with the panther, but his nerve held and he reached a deal. On 9 March he reported to Urdaneta, 'At last we are in Pasto, and not badly received by the people and Obando, who will be a good friend in time according to all the signs he is showing now.'[7] In fact it was not quite like that. Obando accepted Bolívar's terms, safe passage for his armies through Popayán and Pasto and southwards through Ecuador, but charged a high price: promotion for himself to the rank of general and exemption of Pasto from conscription for a year. Bolívar then heard of Sucre's victory over the Peruvians at Tarqui and realized he had conceded too much. As for Obando, a man without shame, he now appeared reconciled and replaced outright abuse of Bolívar with cringing messages of regret and promises of good behaviour.[8]

Bolívar made serious charges against the Peruvian government, specifically its involvement in the rebellion of the Colombian Third Division, intervention in Bolivia, occupation of Colombian border territory and failure to pay its debt for Colombian aid. He refused to receive the Peruvian minister, whom he suspected of connivance with the liberal opposition, and came out with fighting words, reminiscent of his old style, declaring that war was inevitable and was the responsibility of Peru. 'Colombians of the south, arm yourselves, hasten to the frontiers of Peru, and wait there for the hour of vengeance. My presence among you will be the signal for combat.'[9] For their part the ruling class of Peru had never been entirely comfortable with Bolívar's settlement. They regarded themselves as the experts on managing life and labour in Peru, controlling Indians in the sierra and blacks on the coast. Their generals had their eyes on the frontiers, which they regarded as insecure or an affront to historic claims, and they had never reconciled themselves to the loss of Guayaquil. In 1828 General Agustín Gamarra stationed an army on the Bolivian border, while collaborators in Chuquisaca raised a mutiny among the garrison on 18 April and badly wounded Sucre. Gamarra invaded at the end of April, and forced Sucre to resign and take his Colombian troops home. In the north General La Mar, now President of Peru, moved to invade Colombia by land while a naval force blockaded Guayaquil. General Juan José Flores, a fighter in the war of independence who subsequently preferred to serve Bolívar in his adopted country, Ecuador, regarded these actions as a declaration of war, and took measures to defend Guayaquil and the Ecuadorian provinces bordering Peru. Bolívar appointed O'Leary as a peace commissioner in the south to negotiate a truce and raise the question of the boundary between Peru and Colombia. Bolívar wanted war with Peru but needed time to mobilize and move an army from Colombia to Guayaquil and the southern border.

O'Leary and Flores arrived in Guayaquil on 13 September, overtly to talk peace and negotiate a settlement of the debt and the boundary, in fact to buy time to make war. Flores needed five thousand troops and two months to mobilize them. O'Leary argued that a military victory would be the best preparation for peace negotiations. Sucre joined them on 19 September on route from Bolivia, still nursing a wounded arm, and briefed them on the situation in Peru and Bolivia. President La Mar, whom Bolívar described scathingly as a coward, barbarian and traitor, was making warlike noises, and moving the Peruvian army towards the Colombian border, while a squadron under Admiral George Martin Guise, an English naval officer, menaced Guayaquil by sea to install a blockade.

Sucre then left for Quito, where he arrived on 30 September, relieved to be with Mariana after five years' separation; he looked older, he was carrying a wound and he was alarmed by the signs of enforced mobilization in Ecuador, which increased his determination to retire from public life. But war was approaching. For the moment La Mar remained with the army in northern Peru, 'talking much, doing nothing'. In early November O'Leary informed Bolívar that Flores had gone to Riobamba to raise an army, leaving an Englishman, General John Illingsworth, or Illingrot as he was known locally, in command at Guayaquil. The Englishman responded vigorously to Guise's shelling and his counter-fire killed the admiral, 'a brave and excellent seaman', commented O'Leary.[10] The fleet then broke off the attack and Guayaquil was spared a sacking. War with Peru was an economic problem for all concerned. On his journey to Quito in September Sucre reported: 'I have heard repeated clamours against the war with Peru, because it is the source of the parlous state of this country and of its overwhelming poverty, forced exactions of mules, horses, potatoes, wheat, cattle, and then the inexorable conscription, not only of vagrants and single men but also of fathers of families.'[11] His own family was heavily taxed for the war, adding to his rancour and his personal financial difficulties.

The threats to Bolívar's scheme of things brought out evident tensions between the senior Bolivarians, as they came together in Guayaquil, their personalities colliding and clashing. Who was top? Whose service record was best? Who had the ear of the Liberator? Sucre was cool and superior, no mere sycophant, recently wounded in action, ready to throw it all in from a position of leadership, and known to be a touchy individual. Flores was a Venezuelan *pardo*, conscious of Bolívar's patronage, more of an opportunist, driven by ambition, and not Sucre's best friend. Both had married into the Quito aristocracy, but Sucre came from a superior family to start with. O'Leary was third in ranking order, a foreigner, the ever loyal servant, by now accepted by Bolívar as a confidant as well as an aide, and able to report on the other two with candour. In his *Detached Recollections* he was generous in his appraisal of Sucre, 'the best general of Colombia, a man of talent and good sense, superior to most public men', while Flores, 'a bastard of singular merit', rated a lesser entry.[12] There could also be policy differences. Sucre was less warlike towards Peru than the other two and was convinced that war would prejudice any progress towards stability in Colombia. O'Leary was hard line on most issues. The future of the Bolivarian cause exercised all their minds. There was probably, too, a lot of barrack-room talk and gossip, and private views about Bolívar that did not diminish their loyalty but were more critical than they expressed in public.

These exchanges, formal and informal, seem to have been reflected in the writings of O'Leary. In *Detached Recollections* he wrote of Sucre, 'He was once an idolater of General Bolívar and continued so until he was wounded in Chuquisaca. Ever afterwards he abused him and accused him of being the author of the disasters which Colombia suffered.' In October 1828, following the trio's discussions in Guayaquil, he wrote to Bolívar that he got on well with Flores, who was also 'a great friend of yours', though he could not say the same of Sucre, who was criticizing official policy of commandeering resources for the army. 'General Sucre *was* my friend, but I do not have or wish to have any friendship with one who tries to recruit supporters for himself by unseemly means. I thought of writing him a strong letter, but then preferred not to clash with him direct, so as to be able to mediate between him and Flores should dissensions occur between them. The behaviour of Sucre should hasten Your Excellency's coming; now more than ever your presence is needed in these departments.'[13] A curious intervention by the Irishman, reflecting the Bolivarian tensions of the time. Later, during the crisis of Colombia, when the Liberator's hand was weakening, O'Leary asked not to be placed under the command of Sucre on the north-east frontier but to operate independently, though deferring to Bolívar's decision.[14]

Bolívar had already decided that the south needed his presence to resist the threats to external and internal security, and also evidently to reduce jealousies and clarify ranking among his senior colleagues. Before leaving Bogotá he sent a special envoy to Sucre in Quito, bearing a message of welcome and relief: 'These papers contain your appointment as absolute chief of the south. All my powers, for good and evil, I delegate to you. Whether you make war or peace, save or lose the south, you are the arbiter of its destinies. I have placed all my hopes in you.'[15] Bolívar had long experience of his colleagues' sensitivities. He knew the appointment would irritate Sucre, who was anti-war and anxious to retire, and arouse jealousy in others, especially Flores, who was pro-war and eager to command, and he advised Sucre to read the special dispatch to Flores and O'Leary, 'so that they may know I have given Simón Bolívar's being to you. Yes, my dear Sucre, you are one with me, except in your goodness and my luck.' And to Flores he insisted, 'I do not deprive you of the slightest glory, for there is no glory to be won in these unhappy times. I give you this successor to spare you a disaster, and advise you to bow to circumstances, like the rest of us.'[16]

Sucre bowed once more to his fate and planned how best to confront the Peruvians. He had to decide between a strike against their ally Obando lurking on the Pasto frontier and a campaign in the south against the main enemy. Then he had to avoid the rain and floods surrounding Guayaquil, and chose a site suitable for battle and for supplies. He designed his campaign expertly around the plain of Tarqui, stationing Flores and his army at Cuenca and withdrawing Illingsworth from Guayaquil to conduct guerrilla operations from Daule to the north. Sucre joined the Colombian army at Cuenca on 27 January, and on 21 February at Tarqui led his force of fifteen hundred and a cavalry squadron against five thousand enemy infantry.[17] Some of the latent tensions among Bolívar's commanders surfaced at Tarqui, and at one point in the battle O'Leary was caught between obeying Sucre or Flores in ordering his battalion to advance.[18] After two hours of fighting, the Peruvians suffered fifteen hundred killed and a thousand more in wounded prisoners and fugitives. Another victory for Sucre and another exemplary peace: in accordance with his strict ideas of justice rather than retribution, he simply insisted in the Convention of Girón (28 February) that a treaty would be made after the Peruvian troops had evacuated Colombian territory. Sucre left the army under the command of Flores and returned to Quito, reporting to Bolívar that the campaign, and indeed the war, was over. He was tired and the only reward he wanted was to be relieved of his command and all public office. 'A campaign of thirty days by the army of the south has swept away the two-year menace from Peru, and a battle of two hours was sufficient for our 1,500 troops to overcome all the forces of Peru.'[19] His inner thoughts were not so sanguine. The Tarqui campaign had confirmed his worst fears for the political stability of Colombia and his alarm at the growing indiscipline among the military, convictions which strengthened his affiliation with the Liberator in a search for strong government.[20]

Bolívar received Sucre's request for retirement as he neared Pasto. He too feared for Colombia as he faced another crisis, and in a mood of pessimism he wrote in his inimitable style a new political paper as a press release and for circulation to his collaborators. 'There is no good faith in America, nor among the nations of America. Treaties are scraps of paper; constitutions, mere books; elections, battles; freedom, anarchy; and life, a torment.' Where had Americans gone wrong? 'You fell in love with freedom, and were dazzled by her potent charms. But, since freedom is as dangerous as beauty in women, whom all seduce and desire out of love or vanity, you have not kept her as innocent and pure as when she descended from Heaven. Power, the born enemy of human rights, has excited personal ambition in all classes of the state.'[21]

Sombre Thoughts from Guayaquil

In Pasto, having reached a deal with Obando, Bolívar learned of Sucre's victory at Tarqui and his request for retirement. He knew it would be premature to demobilize, for he did not trust the Peruvians and he was not convinced that he had heard the last from Pasto. In April he rode on to Quito to meet Sucre. After a separation of over three years, it was an emotional meeting. He granted Sucre's wish to be relieved of office and respected the family's desire to be left in peace while they awaited their first child. But the south still needed a firm hand, for his suspicions of the Peruvians soon proved to be correct: they ignored the Girón convention, failed to evacuate Guayaquil and preferred the way of war. He summoned Córdova's division from Popayán but took command personally; there was only one Sucre and Bolívar did not regard Flores or Córdova as qualified to succeed him. O'Leary was sent to report on the south to ministers in Bogotá.

Bolívar decided to remain in Ecuador while the situation was insecure and in June made his way to Guayaquil, still the leader and still a warrior. In the event he did not have to fight. Gamarra overthrew La Mar's government in early June and exiled La Mar to Guatemala, where he died, unlamented by Bolívar, who described him as 'a man in a donkey-skin, with the claws of a tiger and an insatiable lust for American blood'.[22] Bolívar unsettled the Peruvians in his menacing mood as he led his forces expertly towards their defences. They concluded that war with Colombia was too costly to justify, and a major battle with Bolívar something to avoid: better to come to terms. Comissioners arranged an armistice in Piura, signed by Gamarra on 10 July; Peru would return Guayaquil to Colombia after Bolívar signed the armistice. The peace treaty was eventually signed on 22 September. On 21 July Bolívar entered Guayaquil, to demonstrations of joy from the people and no doubt a warm welcome from the young women of the Garaycoa family. Sucre warned him not to trust the 'perfidious' Gamarra, but the peace seemed to hold. Mariana gave birth to a daughter, Teresita, on 10 July, which Sucre reported to Bolívar almost with apologies that he did not have a son to serve his country as a soldier. He himself no longer wanted a military command but neither was he prepared to leave Colombia to the mercy of the liberals, and he presented himself for election to the constituent congress. As the news came in from his generals and friends throughout Colombia, the Liberator faced challenges of his own.

In Guayaquil Bolívar fell seriously ill, suffering from symptoms that he described as a liver complaint but in fact were a worsening of his not yet diagnosed tubercular condition. Colombia's demons returned to torment him and he saw a great anarch stalking the land. Days of disillusion stretched ahead. He returned to a decision made more than once in recent years, that the time had come to resign his office and retire from public affairs. His collaborators had heard the refrain before and this time Sucre responded with some dismay and impatience, for it left present policies and future prospects in suspense. To abandon the country in the current crisis when he is most needed, Sucre reproached him, would be regarded as desertion and leave a stain on his career:

> A time may come to silence your slanderers; but the best action now and one which every reasonable person would approve is to constitute the country and to set its affairs on a stable and solid course. Nothing else is worthy of you. To retire when so many dangers threaten the country, simply to prove your disinterestedness, is a measure foreign to your character; and, frankly speaking, it will be looked upon by the world as a mere trick, so that in the subsequent conflict of parties, when a thousand knives may tear the *patria* apart, you might be called back as the saviour and the conciliator.[23]

With Sucre around Bolívar would never want for straight talking. In August, weary of power and disillusioned with constitutions, Bolívar floated an idea to O'Leary for passing to the legislators in Bogotá. The proposal was that he should be a roving presence, alongside the president, a kind of troubleshooter and enforcer in one, bringing peace and freedom to Colombia and further glory to himself. 'By God, O'Leary, for Colombia and for me, propose this idea and suggest it to the legislators and to everyone.'[24] Was he joking? It was hard to tell with Bolívar.

Irony, however, was his forte. To Mosquera he bemoaned the current popularity of federalism, but if that was what the people wanted let them have it. 'They don't want a monarchy, or life-presidency, much less an aristocracy. So why don't they try anarchy, a noisy and happy ocean to drown in? It is very popular and could well be the best solution, because it conforms to my own maxim, *the Sovereign has to be infallible.*'[25] 'People have no right to crucify me,' he added, 'and if it were only the cross I would patiently suffer it as the last of my agonies. Jesus Christ endured 33 years of this mortal life; my own has lasted over 46, and the worst is that I am not an impassive God; if I were I could bear it for all eternity.'

In Guayaquil he had to take to his bed from 2 to 13 August, and then he remained weak. By the end of August he obtained a country house on a small island on the River Guayas, about a mile from the city, and claimed he was making a good recovery.[26] However, unable to accept that a hitherto active life should be reduced to apathy and inertia, he opened his mind to O'Leary, revealing his personal and political anxieties in one of his frankest letters, reminiscent of his historic statements.[27] Now he was serious. He presented himself after twenty years' continuous service as physically finished, prematurely old, having nothing left to offer and – with pathetic optimism – 'with only four to six years to live'. As for political prospects, some were good: they had defeated Peru and vanquished the anarchists at home. But what would happen when the present administrators had passed their prime and his own authority was no more? The sheer size of Colombia demanded a prompt answer to prevent the threatened catastrophe, and he could foresee only two, neither of them good for the country:

> Royal authority or general confederation are the only forms suitable for ruling this vast region. I cannot even conceive of the possibility of establishing a kingdom in a country which is essentially democratic. The lower and most numerous classes claim their prerogatives, to which they have incontestable rights. Equality before the law is indispensable where physical inequality exists, in order that the injustices of nature can, in some measure, be corrected. Moreover, who would be king in Colombia? No one, as I see it.

Warning of the consequences of monarchy – a new form of tyranny, expensive government, a new aristocracy – he scornfully dismissed this 'chimera'. And he still had no time for the federal form of government. 'Such a system is no more than organized anarchy, or, at best a law that implicitly decrees the obligation to dissolve and ruin the state with all its members. It would be better, I think, for South America to adopt the Koran rather than the United States' form of government, although the latter is the best in the world.' Colombia is so large and its people so ignorant that its institutions need more power than is offered by the European model, but in fact they are hardly sufficient to rule a single province:

> The Constituent Congress must choose one of two courses, the only ones available in the present situation: 1) The separation of New Granada and Venezuela. 2) The creation of a strong life-term government. . . . Colombia must forget her illusions and make her decisions, for I cannot rule any longer. These are the facts and we must face the difficulties. What will Congress do to appoint my successor? Will he be New Granadan or Venezuelan? An army man or a civilian? . . . Are the military always to rule by the sword? Will not the civilian population complain of

the despotism of the soldiers? I admit that the existing Republic cannot be governed except by the sword, and at the same time I must agree that the military spirit is incompatible with civilian rule. Congress will be forced to return to the question of dividing the country, because whoever they select their choice of a president will always be questioned.

There remained no other way for Colombia but to organize, as best it could, a centralized system duly proportionate to the size of its territory and the character of its inhabitants.

At the end of September 1829, the peace treaty with Peru concluded, Bolívar left Guayaquil and rode slowly north, thinking back on his letter to O'Leary and still pondering his future. 'I am serious in what I said to you, though I leave it unsaid, I mean secret.' On the journey his preoccupations grew. O'Leary was in Medellín quelling a rebellion when he received the fateful letter of 13 September. Bolívar's melancholy saddened him and he implored his leader not to give up; in spite of all the traitors in the years since 1826 there had been many loyal followers, and he still had widespread support among the people. O'Leary was determined to crush the remnants of rebellion in the gold fields of the Chocó, 'for we have to cut the throats of all those infamous blacks'.[28]

Monarchist Friends, Republican Enemies

When O'Leary arrived in Bogotá at the end of April 1829 he found two women in the news: Manuela, who was living an active social life and attracting foreign diplomats to her parties, and La Nicolasa, Santander's mistress, who in the aftermath of her lover's disgrace was agitating to be expelled on her own account and leave as a martyr rather than an adulterous partner of the former vice-president.[29] More ominously he discovered that the government was actively pursuing a plan to establish a monarchy and was involved in discussions on the project with the French and British representatives. He kept Bolívar informed of these developments as well as of the gossip. Some ministers told him that republican institutions had failed the country, that the attempt to assassinate Bolívar had shocked everyone, and that a radical change was necessary. 'They told me that there was no idea of consulting General Bolívar until affairs were in a more advanced state, as they dreaded that he would discountenance the plan.' Páez had been consulted and was hostile to the idea, but he recommended delay for the present. Briceño Méndez and Soublette were both strongly opposed, predicting that it would simply give Bolívar's enemies in Venezuela a pretext for revolution. Montilla was also of the opinion that the time was not opportune. Liberals, of course, were outraged. But the ministers rashly persisted in the enterprise, and Urdaneta was one of the strongest supporters. It was not intended that Bolívar be crowned or retired, but would remain head of government with the title of Liberator, and after his death a foreign prince would succeed. O'Leary never understood whether the idea of monarchy originated in Bogotá or had been imported, but by early September he was reporting that the project was now taken for granted in Bogotá with no observable opposition. He himself seems to have been persuaded by the arguments in favour of a monarchy: it would provide stability and security, appeal to the military and ecclesiastical elites, confound the liberals and reassure foreign investors. According to Posada Gutiérrez, 'The members of the council of ministers were those who principally adopted the project and submitted it to public discussion in the press,' and, he added, 'without previous consultation with the Liberator.'[30]

Consultation there had been, though it was muted and inconclusive. In April 1829, while he was in Quito, Bolívar revived a suggestion he had previously promoted, that Colombia would benefit from the protection of Britain; such a possibility had been a recurring idea in his thinking on American unity and now he recommended it to his cabinet. A single pebble stirred a great lake. The ministers brought the French and British representatives into the discussion. On 8 April 1829 Restrepo informed Bolívar that the ministers were discussing a project for a constitution in preparation for the constituent congress and concluded that Spanish America needed a change of constitutional system: 'The hereditary succession is necessary and everything follows from that. There are difficulties but they are not insuperable, counting on your support and that of the army.' On 6 May Bolívar replied: 'I entirely agree that it is absolutely necessary to change the constitutional system of Spanish America, so that it consolidates itself; and I also believe that although there are difficulties, they are not insurmountable.'[31] Restrepo took the discussion a stage further, introducing the notion of importing a foreign prince: 'I am glad you agree with the necessity to change constitutional forms. . . . There is a slight difficulty concerning the dynasty which will succeed you in office, the family of which must perpetuate the crown by succession. . . . It seems that we, your friends, should bring forward the scheme and that you should appear outwardly a stranger to it, though without opposing it.' He also mentioned that the constituent congress would have to agree to the change, no doubt another 'slight difficulty'.[32]

In July the news that Bolívar had decided to retire from office perplexed the ministers. How could they proceed without his cooperation? They assumed they had it. They must have a clear line from him.[33] Bolívar admitted to the British chargé d'affaires, Patrick Campbell, that Campbell's reference to the new project to nominate a European prince as his successor did not take him entirely by surprise, because something of this had been communicated to him, though obscurely and cautiously, 'for they know my way of thinking'. But his words to Campbell were guarded and his attitude essentially diplomatic. He was not personally involved, for he was determined to resign at the next congress. He pointed out the countless difficulties and disadvantages of such a plan, the reaction of England if a Bourbon were selected. 'Would not all the new American states, and the United States, which seem destined by Providence to plague America with miseries in the name of Liberty, be opposed to such a plan?' Everyone would become the enemy of poor Colombia.[34] But he reserved his final opinion, reluctant to throw away an idea he had often floated himself. In his letter to O'Leary a month later he was specific: 'I cannot even conceive of the possibility of establishing a kingdom in a country which is essentially democratic.'[35]

Communications were not so dire in Colombia that discussions of this kind could be kept secret. In any case Restrepo and his colleagues were committed to transparency. When the firebrand General José María Córdova heard of the monarchy project, he left Popayán for Antioquia, his native province, proclaiming liberty and denouncing Bolívar. He had been under suspicion since April when his enemy Mosquera reported that he was intriguing with the officers under his command and criticizing Bolívar and his policies.[36] O'Leary stopped in Pasto on his way to Bogotá and spoke to Córdova, who had been a friend of his since Angostura days; Córdova denied that he had any intentions hostile to the Liberator but was simply speaking to colleagues, including Obando, on the prospects for Colombian unity after Bolívar. O'Leary regarded Córdova – and the regime in Pasto – as a security risk and from June his warnings to the Liberator became more urgent, at a time when the government in Bogotá was weak and only the 'terror' imposed by General Urdaneta maintained law and order.[37] In September, in a rambling manifesto, Córdova denounced Bolívar for his absolutism: he had deceived the people of Colombia, thrown out the rights of man, terrorized the convention of Ocaña and betrayed the constitution. The rebel urged the people of Colombia to save nineteen years of sacrifice from a new slavery.[38] He proclaimed that Bolívar expected to rule as though 'he disposed of the Republic as outright owner, bound by no legitimate authority', and that it was his duty to reject the absolute rule of Bolívar and restore the constitution of Cúcuta. News of Córdova's rebellion reached Bogotá on the night of 25 September, the anniversary of the attempt to assassinate the Liberator. The streets were strangely deserted, either because of people's memory of that event or from a sense of impending crisis. In the early evening O'Leary took a walk in the centre of town and saw very few people, though the weather was fine. Then the news from Medellín arrived and everything changed. The troops were put under arms, and the next day the minister of war, Urdaneta, ordered O'Leary, now a general, to lead an operational division of seven hundred troops to attack the rebels and re-establish order.

Córdova's rebellion, small-scale in itself, shook Bolívar as he learned that his former protégé in arms had become 'a missionary of division and rebellion, and was seeking the help of Páez and the collaboration of the British consul in Bogotá'. To Sucre he wrote, 'He is saying among other things that you want to make yourself king of Peru! How's that? As for me, I am everything, everything bad; yet they still want me to continue ruling. We will always be guilty simply by our birth: whites and Venezuelans. Charged with these crimes we can never rule in these regions.'[39] He issued instructions to Urdaneta for troop dispositions to encircle the rebellion and prevent it infecting other parts of Colombia. And he prepared to move north. His mood now wavered between optimism and despair. Congress would just have to do what it thought best. He accepted that, for as he remarked to Sucre, 'I too am a liberal; no one will believe it but it is true.'

O'Leary brought Córdova to battle at Santuario, east of Medellín. As he approached with his troops on 17 October the rebel recognized him and came up to talk, but O'Leary brought the conversation to a close when Córdoba sought to 'seduce' his *antioqueño* followers. In the ensuing action, a matter of two hours, the rebel troops were no match for the regulars; Córdova fought bravely but was wounded and lay on the floor of a house where he sought refuge and which O'Leary ordered to be stormed. Colonel Rupert Hand, an Irish veteran of the British Legion and a man with a violent past, found Córdova prostrate on the floor and coolly killed him with two thrusts of his sword. O'Leary did not give these details to Bolívar, though he seems to have been present and even to have spoken to 'the poor devil'. He reported the death of Córdova as a duty to avenge Bolívar and defend his own honour.[40] He reminded Bolívar that he had warned him against the rebel some time before and that his judgement had been ignored; Córdova was a fool and a failure, with only his bravery to recommend him.[41] Pity had no place in the revolution, and if the incident disturbed O'Leary as Hand's commanding officer it did not show or prevent him from appointing the perpetrator to a further operation in the Chocó. In 1831, at the instigation of Obando, Hand was arrested and tried for murder; he was sentenced to death but escaped from prison to Venezuela, where he avoided extradition and became the first Professor of English in the University of Caracas.[42]

In the aftermath of the Córdova rebellion the question remained: had Bolívar succumbed to temptation? Did he wish to become king, or collaborate with a monarchy? When they knew of the rebel's defeat, ministers returned to the monarchy project and officially informed the French and British agents of their intention to alter the form of government. It was now time to advise Bolívar of what had taken place, and the foreign secretary wrote to him on the subject. From Popayán Bolívar replied, protesting in strong terms that his colleagues had gone too far. On 22 November 1829 he wrote to the council of ministers that their negotiations had contravened government policy, which was to call congress; 'they had usurped the high functions of the congress summoned to consider the organization of a national government', and he warned them, 'You should now suspend all negotiations with the governments of France and England.' In private letters to Urdaneta he spoke more tactfully, but still insisted that 'we have got too involved and should go no further, leaving congress to do its duty'. And in congress it will be 'easier to appoint a president than a prince'.[43] This was consistent with his responses throughout the affair, when his motive was to steer constitutional change towards his favourite goal of stronger government, monocracy perhaps, but not specifically monarchy. His 'Glance at Spanish America', to which Restrepo appealed, expressed no preference for monarchy. The rebuke caused a sensation in Bogotá. The ministers sent in their resignations, protesting that they had merely acted according to his instructions. But his only explicit instructions had been to solicit the protection of some European power, as he considered that the country could not maintain itself as a nation without some such support.[44]

During these months of 1829 Bolívar's leadership was tested on two fronts. Following hard on his military campaign in the south he was faced with political confusion in the rest of Colombia, including a project of monarchy not of his making. Any leader who has to think through a decision or a policy, turning one way then another, considering one option then its opposite, changing course in the process of decision-making, will understand that this was not ambivalence, or duplicity, or inconsistency, but a reasonable way of reaching conclusions and taking action. Such was Bolívar's procedure in 1829, as it had been in other crises of his life. He now closed the subject, appointed a new cabinet and suspended negotiations with Bresson and Campbell. He saw that political liberalism and its advocates were still in fighting mood, and that it was dangerous even to mention the word monarchy in the Colombia of his time.

The Exodus

The insurrection of Córdova encouraged the opposition in Venezuela. Páez abandoned vacillation and moved purposefully to take his country out of the union. From the moment the news arrived at Caracas on 28 October, Bolívar's enemies surrounded Páez, exaggerated the news, exploited the controversy over monarchy, and pressed their caudillo to lose no time in revolutionizing Venezuela. At this critical date, his judgement perhaps impaired by his isolation and his illness, Bolívar presented the politicians and caudillos with a needless advantage. Unreconciled to a purely personalist solution, he decided to consult the people. On 16 October 1829, the Ministry of the Interior issued Bolívar's circular letter of 31 August 1829 authorizing, indeed ordering, that public meetings be held where the citizens could give their opinion on a new form of government and the future organization of Colombia.[45] This was for congress to determine, but the elected deputies were to attend congress not as free agents but as delegates mandated by written instructions. So Bolívar sought the will of the people and undertook to be bound by it, for good or for ill.[46] But were the people free to express their will? Would not the caudillos control or coerce the assemblies? Bolívar's closest friends and advisers had grave reservations about this procedure. From Quito Sucre warned that it was alienating reasonable and substantial citizens and encouraging radicals, and advised him to reduce it to the simple right of petition; otherwise the right to give binding instructions 'will revive local pretensions'.[47]

Indeed the separatists immediately exploited these meetings to secure the opinions they wanted. Representation could not in itself frustrate the local warlords. In Caracas the public meeting of the people on 25 November 1829 was preceded on the night before by a meeting of four hundred leading citizens and landowners in the house of the caudillo Arismendi, with other generals present. The gathering pronounced, with only two dissenting voices – Revenga and Intendant Clementi – for the independence of Venezuela and against Bolívar, a lead which was followed by the public meeting in the Franciscan church the following day.[48] Another example of pressure was given in a complaint from the town of Escuque to General Páez against the procedures adopted by the military commander of the district of Trujillo, Colonel Cegarra:

Even the popular assemblies have been the occasion of his [Cegarra's] insolence, since he has insisted that the citizens sign not what has been said and agreed in their meetings, but various papers which he himself has written in his own home, threatening with violence those who refused to obey. Is this freedom, Sir? Can a people speak freely when at the very time of their assembly they see a squadron of cavalry and a company of fusiliers forming up in the main square? If the papers which Sr Cegarra wanted us to sign had contained fair and reasoned complaints, then our approval might have been sought at an opportune moment. But to require us to subscribe to a lot of insults, abuse, and insolence against General Bolívar does not seem proper, for we have always believed that we could reject his authority yet treat him with respect.[49]

Spectacles of this kind revealed the scale of the task facing Bolívar. Most of the towns and districts of Venezuela pronounced for independence from Colombia, and in favour of Páez against Bolívar, whom they called a tyrant and worse. Worse, apparently, than their local tyrants, the majority of whom wanted independence. 'The untrammelled expression of popular desires' so ardently sought by Bolívar turned into a torrent of abuse and defiance, and the constituent congress of Colombia promised little better. In November 1829 the Venezuelans were already speaking the language of withdrawal from Colombia, arguing that, 'Venezuela ought not to remain united to New Granada and Quito, because the laws which are appropriate for those countries are not suitable for ours, which is completely different in customs, climate and products; and because government applied over a great area loses its strength and energy.'[50] On 1 December Páez told Bolívar, 'Venezuelans have a heartfelt hatred for the union with Bogotá, and they are resolved to make whatever sacrifice it needs to secure separation.' He would hold his hand for the moment, but he expected Bolívar to recognize that 'separation is inevitable' and to recommend it to the forthcoming constituent congress, otherwise he could not answer for the consequences. A bitter experience for the Liberator to listen to arrogance from a crass caudillo! He was in despair at 'the horrible news' coming out of Venezuela and the infamy of his native country, which did not even give him the option of resigning voluntarily. 'I have never suffered so much as now, and I long for the desperate moment when this shameful life may end.'[51]

As Bolívar approached the end of his political career in Colombia, he knew that Venezuela and the caudillos had repudiated him. Bermúdez issued a strident proclamation calling Venezuela to arms against the 'despot', the promoter of monarchy, the enemy of the republic. Mariño, who claimed to know 'the virtues, the views, the particular interests of every inhabitant of Cumaná', was outraged when Bolívar refused to employ him in the east.[52] Páez wanted an independent Venezuela, and independence meant opposing Bolívar. Caudillism now advanced because it concided with Venezuelan nationalism, and this was an expression of interests as well as of identity. The Venezuelan caudillos had begun as local leaders with access to limited resources. War gave them the opportunity to improve their personal fortunes and expand their bases of power. Peace brought them even greater rewards, and these they were determined to keep. The caudillos abandoned Colombia because they were Venezuelans and because they were resolved to retain Venezuelan resources for themselves and their clients. Caudillism and nationalism reinforced each other. The greatest victim was Bolívar.

The constituent congress of Venezuela assembled in Valencia on 6 May 1830. From his headquarters at San Carlos, Páez sent a message: 'My sword, my lance and all my military triumphs are subject to the decisions of the law, in respect and obedience.'[53] It was a double-edged remark, reminding legislators that, in spite of his claim to be 'a simple citizen', with his *llaneros* behind him and the oligarchy of wealth and office at his side, he was the supreme power in the land. This congress founded the sovereign and independent republic of Venezuela, in which Páez retained the dual authority of president and army commander. As for Bolívar, he was deeply disillusioned: 'The tyrants of my country have taken it from me and I am banished; now I have no homeland for which to sacrifice myself.'[54]

Venezuela was the first to go, but not the last. Ecuador too sought its own national identity. The country's political experience was less violent than Venezuela's, whose *pardos* and *mestizos* were more ambitious than the passive and apolitical Indians of Ecuador, and whose upper classes were more active than the Quito aristocracy. But Ecuador too had its grievances. The liberal economic policy of Colombia did not give sufficient protection to Ecuador's industry, already damaged by war and disruption of export routes. The country had also suffered from heavy conscription and the exaction of forced loans and supplies; Ecuador sustained a substantial part of the final war effort in Peru, and Bolívar milked the Ecuadorian economy dry to pay for the Colombian army in 1828–9. The large agricultural estates yielded little more than subsistence production, and the only commercial output was that of cacao, together with some shipbuilding and repairing at Guayaquil.[55] These problems were neglected by the Bogotá government, which provided no tax relief, no protection and no subsidy for Ecuador. And its liberalism provoked the latent conservatism of Ecuador's ruling class, one of whose demands was for the retention of Indian tribute and black slavery. Ecuadoreans were underrepresented in the central government and its offices, and at home they had a sense of being colonized by new imperialists. For the foreign liberators stayed on as a virtual army of occupation, and Ecuadorean civil and military institutions were staffed by soldiers and bureaucrats from other parts of Colombia. On 13 May 1830 the southern departments of Colombia seceded from the union and declared the independent state of Ecuador under the presidency of General Juan José Flores, a Venezuelan *mulatto* made respectable by his marriage. In due course, accepting the political fragmentation that seemed inevitable, the constituent congress agreed to divide Colombia into three states. The former New Granada was left to bear alone the name of Colombia.

Farewell to Power, Salute to Glory

The constituent congress called by Bolívar for 2 January 1830 slowly began to assemble in the following weeks as delegates made their way from distant provinces; across mountains, hills and plains, these regional leaders converged on Bogotá to listen to the supreme leader of the union. The gathering was small, exclusive and conservative; lawyers and the military were strongly represented, the regions less so.[56] Bolívar arrived on 15 January, outwardly a shadow of the man who had entered Bogotá after Boyacá, his face drawn, his hair thin, his movements laboured, but inwardly no less lucid in his ideas and determined in his actions. He convened congress on 20 January and after mass in the cathedral the delegates gathered in the Assembly Hall; they had different expectations of the days ahead but all minds were focused on the Liberator. He was soon in action. Sucre was elected president of the congress and the bishop of Santa Marta, José María Esteves, vice-president. The hand of Bolívar was evident here. But manipulated or not, these nominations now represented his ideal of Church and State: Sucre as his heir apparent, and a bishop to speak for 'the holy religion we profess'. In his message to the '*Congreso Admirable*', as he called it, he reviewed the recent problems of Colombia, defended his responses to disturbances within and attacks from without, and hoped that from this grim picture they would learn lessons for the future.[57] Then, in words with bitter undertones, he submitted his resignation, admonishing congress not to try and re-elect him, for he had no wish to vote himself into power, and there were others who were above suspicion and worthy of the office of president:

> Only I am branded with aspirations to tyranny. Spare me, I beg you, the disgrace that awaits me if I continue to fulfil a destiny that can never be free of the censure of ambition. . . . Do as you will with the presidency, which I respectfully abdicate into your hands. From this day forth, I am but a citizen-in-arms, ready to defend the country and obey the government. My public duties are finished for ever. I formally and solemnly deliver to you the supreme authority conferred upon me by votes of the nation.

And he closed with one of his starkest confessions: 'I am ashamed to admit it, but independence is the only benefit we have gained, at the cost of everything else.'

Bolívar had reached the end of his constitutional projects. He could not totally let go, and in the following weeks he was besieged from one side and another, his mind a turmoil of conflicting ideas, clutching at the slimmest of hopes that something might be rescued from the constitutional ruins of

Colombia. But there was nothing left, and no one to equal him. As Bolívar lost his strength of body and powers of leadership, he still remained the one outstanding figure in a gallery of mediocrities. He was now concerned above all to defend his record and refute his enemies. A kingdom was never his intention. Power was gone. Glory alone remained, and this he was determined to protect. He instructed José Fernández Madrid, the Colombian agent in London, to answer the slanders that were being spread:[58]

First, I have never sought to establish the Bolivian constitution in Colombia; nor was it I who did so in Peru. The people and the ministers did this of their own accord.

Second, every act of treachery, duplicity, or deceit attributed to me is complete slander. Whatever I have done or said has been with seriousness and without any dissimulation.

Third, you should totally deny any cruelty toward the patriots, and declare that if at any time I dealt cruelly with the Spaniards, it was in reprisal.

Fourth, you can deny any act of self-interest on my part, and make it clear that I have dealt generously with most of my enemies.

Fifth, you can assert that during the war I took no step dictated by prudence or reason that can be attributed to cowardice.[59] My every action was prompted by calculation, and even more by daring.

The committee named by congress to frame a reply to Bolívar's message postponed a decision on his resignation until a new constitution and new leaders were in place. Bolívar appointed a provisional president, Domingo Caicedo, and left for the latter's country house in Fucha on the western outskirts of the city to recover his health. Among his visitors was the Bolivarian officer Posada Gutiérrez, who recorded his impressions of an evening walk through the meadows:

He [Bolívar] walked slowly and wearily, and his voice was so low that he had to strain to make himself heard; he preferred to walk by the banks of a brook that winds silently through the picturesque countryside, and with arms crossed he stopped to watch the stream, an image of life. 'How long,' he said to me, 'will this water take before it dissolves into the immense ocean, as man decomposes in the grave and merges into the earth from which he came? Much of it will evaporate and disappear, like human glory, like fame. Isn't it true, Colonel?'.... And then in a trembling voice he exclaimed, 'My glory! My glory! Why do they take it from me? Why do they slander me?'[60]

Meanwhile the politicians continued to agitate, stirring the ashes of Bolívar's rule. The weeks spent by congress debating the new constitution allowed more political activity to flare up, factionalism to flourish, conflicting ideas to descend upon Bolívar, and new uncertainties to disturb his mind and spirit and trouble the Bolivarians. Did Congress want him, or not? Did the people want him, or not? And if not him, who? There was even time for him to have a row, and reconciliation, with Urdaneta, one of his oldest colleagues. But none of this was surprising. How could a world leader suddenly disappear into a soundproof cell? How could he stifle the clamour of critics, or prevent politicians making politics? By the end of April he knew that Colombian liberals still hated him, that his friends were divided, and that his leadership was irretrievably ended. He shook off all doubts and doubters, and on 27 April he informed congress yet again that he renounced the presidency and intended to leave the country: 'Be assured that the good of the *patria* demands of me the sacrifice of leaving for ever the country that gave me life, so that my presence in Colombia will not stand in the way of the happiness of my fellow citizens.'[61]

While preparing the new constitution congress was also facing the challenge from Páez, who had declared Venezuela an independent and sovereign state. But the Venezuelans could not even secede gracefully. O'Leary, whose troops were stationed on the north-east frontier, repudiated an 'insolent' challenge from Mariño, who had dared him to take a step beyond Táchira.[62] The Venezuelans cut off the pensions of the dependants of military and civil personnel serving outside Venezuela, specifically including the pensions granted by Bolívar out of his own salaries.[63] They held off the Colombian commissioners, Sucre and Bishop Esteves, and kept them waiting in Cúcuta, outside Venezuelan territory, until mid-April for Venezuelan negotiators to arrive, and then conceded nothing. The Colombian congress now realized that Venezuelan independence was not negotiable, and soon it also knew that Páez was insisting on Bolívar's expulsion from Colombia as a condition of any settlement.[64] When congress finally accepted Bolívar's resignation it appointed the New Granadan liberal politician Joaquín Mosquera as President.

Bolívar now wanted to leave Colombia. The immediate problem was money. Could he afford it? He was not a wealthy man. His landed wealth had been eroded by wartime sequestrations. His major asset, the Aroa copper mines, had become a major headache, 'a mortal agony' in his final years. In 1824 with the help of his sister María Antonia he had rented them to an English company, which yielded some returns, but not enough. Since 1826 his agents in London had been trying to sell them, but they had still not succeeded by 1830.[65] Congress confirmed the 30,000 pesos yearly for life which he had been granted in 1823, but payment was never absolutely secure and he had always used what he did receive to fund Bolivarian social security. He had already begun to sell his few possessions and prepare for his journey: his silver table service raised 2,500 pesos; jewels, horses and other possessions brought in 17,000 pesos.[66] He began his journey with only a few thousand pesos in ready cash, and anxious about the mines.

The mob was out in the streets, rejoicing at the departure of Bolívar, burning his portraits and shouting for Santander. He still had friends and fighters on his side. Sucre was one of them: 'In his principles,' recorded O'Leary, 'he was liberal, but no republican. The last words he ever said to me were: "Tell the Liberator to concentrate all the troops he can dispose of and not allow himself to be dictated to by anyone. Tell him that now is the time to save the country and, if he thinks that the monarchic form is what Colombia wants, let him say it and he shall not need men who will support him." '[67] But in Bogotá it was tense. The Venezuelan troops, 600 Granaderos and 180 Húsares de Apure, finally rebelled against their unpopularity in Colombia and left for home ahead of Bolívar, silently marching out of the capital, followed by the 'daughters of the regiment'.[68] Life became precarious for him. He departed on 8 May to an emotional farewell from the leading people. An escort of ministers, diplomats, military and civilian friends, and foreign residents escorted him for some miles out of the city.

Journey's End

Three days after arriving in Bogotá on 5 May, Sucre became alarmed at the demonstrations against Bolívar and rushed to his residence, but Bolívar had already left for Cartagena and exile.

> When I came to your house to accompany you, you had already left. Perhaps this was just as well, since I was spared the grief of a painful farewell. In this hour, my heart oppressed, I do not know what to say to you. Words cannot express the feeling for you in my soul. You know, for you have known me for many years, and you know that it is not your power but your friendship that inspired in me the tenderest affection for you. . . . Be happy wherever you may be, and wherever you are you may count on the services and the gratitude of your faithful and devoted, Sucre.

Bolívar received Sucre's letter as he neared Cartagena. He replied on 26 May, sad but more restrained: 'Your esteemed undated letter, in which you take leave of me, has filled me with emotion; if it pained you to write it, what of me, for I am leaving not only a friend but also my country. . . . Words fail the heart in circumstances like these, but accept my sincerest wishes for your well being and happiness.'[69] Sucre was the most important man in Colombia after Bolívar, and he was hated by the same people for the same reasons. In Bolivia he was rejected as a foreigner. In Peru he was commander of a Colombian army. In Venezuela he represented union with a foreign state. In Colombia he was an opponent of dissolution and defender of the Venezuelan military. The *Congreso Admirable* was not so admirable for Sucre: it passed a law making forty the minimum age for president and thus ruling out Sucre for the next five years. He departed for Quito a marked man.

In Bogotá Bolívar bade a fond farewell to Manuela and, still saddened by the separation, cruel for her as well as for him, wrote to her as he began his journey north: 'I love you, my love, but I will love you even more if you show great prudence, now more than ever. Take care how you go, for if you do not ruin us both, you will ruin yourself. Your ever faithful lover, Bolívar.'[70] She did not follow his advice, demonstrating actively on his behalf. Meanwhile, in Honda, waiting for transport down the Magdalena, his mind veered between bitterness and resignation. On a visit to the mines of Santa Ana, he asked Posada Gutiérrez, 'Why do you think I am here?' 'Fate, my General,' replied his friend. 'What fate?' he asked vehemently. 'No, I am here because I refused to deliver the Republic to the College of San Bartolomé.'[71] And as he rested at the Padilla ravine, an oasis in the *llanos* of Mariquita, with the cordillera in the background and the distant murmur of the River Gualí flowing into the Magdalena, he was overcome by the splendour of nature and exclaimed, 'What grandeur, what magnificence! God can be seen, felt, and touched! How can men deny it?' At the mines, the scene of Robert Stephenson's recent labours, he was moved when the miners and their English colleagues formed up to greet him with the cry, 'Viva el Libertador!', a generous tribute to a fallen idol. He travelled north down the Magdalena, its waters a poignant reminder of early triumphs, and after a stop in Turbaco reached Cartagena by the end of June. No one was absolutely sure where he was going: Jamaica, Europe, England? Plans changed and rumours abounded.

In Cartagena he received a generous reception, and a crushing blow. On 1 July at nine in the evening two carriages drew up and General Montilla burst out: 'General, Sucre has been treacherously murdered in the mountains of Berruecos!' Bolívar hit his brow with his hand in despair: 'Holy God, they have shed the blood of Abel.' He asked to be left alone with his thoughts. Pacing the house and patio, he could not settle, sunk deep in depression for Sucre and for Colombia.[72] Details began to come in. On his way home to Quito to join his wife, Sucre had passed along the mountain road of Berruecos, on route to

Pasto, the land of political bandits and serial rebels, trusting his luck without escort or security; there, on 4 June, he was shot down and his body left lying in a swamp. He was thirty-five. Accusations and recriminations began, and responsibility was soon being attributed to the authorities of Cauca. The author of the crime seemed to be Obando, the hired gunmen were Apolinar Morillo and José Erazo; the former in due course was condemned and executed for having fired the fatal shot.[73] In Bolívar's world Sucre was his spiritual and political heir. His death was the end of the revolution. He wrote to Mariana of the great loss to her, to Colombia, and to America, and of his own 'deepest and inexpressible sorrow for the death of a friend to whom I owe eternal gratitude for his loyalty, esteem, and services'.[74] He now wanted to see Colombia's Carthage, that lair of the monsters of Cauca, destroyed to avenge Sucre, 'the most innocent of men', whose death was being described in Europe as 'the blackest and most indelible stain on the history of the New World'.[75]

In Cartagena hope struggled with despair, as news from outside continued to obsess him. On 5 September his former commander and minister, Rafael Urdaneta, led a revolt in Bogotá against President Mosquera, on a platform of Bolívar back to power and Colombia united. Bolívar, conscious of 'the bronze barrier of legality' could not accept, and though he warned Urdaneta of the loss of his reputation if he broke the electoral law, he played with the idea of helping Urdaneta in some way. 'If they give me an army, I shall accept it. If they send me to Venezuela, I shall go.'[76] But it was hopeless. 'Although the best party, the party of national integrity, is the strongest . . . I have my doubts about the final re-establishment of order.'[77] He could not accept office from a mutiny, he told his former minister Estanislao Vergara: 'Believe me, I have never looked on insurrections with a good eye; and of late I have deplored even our own against the Spaniards. . . . All my reasons are based on one: *I have no hope of salvation for the* patria.'[78] By the end of October he evidently felt that the 'restoration of Colombia' was beyond anyone's reach; 'between Venezuela here, assassins in the south, and demagogues everywhere' a final crash appeared inevitable, but he felt that the people were still with him.[79]

The man of a thousand places was now isolated in a corner of Colombia, deprived of calm and comfort. The heat and humidity of Cartagena became intolerable, as he waited impatiently for money to finance his exile, money that never came, either from the Aroa mines, still unsold, or from estates that no longer yielded. José Palacios and a few friends moved him to Soledad in October 1830, where Wilson reported him 'very ill, very wasted', hardly able to walk across the room and low in spirits. Then they took him to Barranquilla. Reduced to 'a living skeleton' as he put it, he was barely able to take a few paces indoors and unable to climb the stairs. He could hardly keep food down. He longed for a little sherry and a glass of beer, or his favourite vegetables, but there were none to be had in the market, and who could he ask? Amidst coughing and struggling for breath, he could still dictate letters, and the news from outside refused to leave him alone. In a lengthy letter to Urdaneta he deplored the state of his health and the condition of helplessness to which he was reduced. He advised his old comrade to take care in the struggle for power, for it would only be resolved by the survival of the 'the most ferocious', and he wondered whether it was worth expending life and authority for a situation that was irremediable. 'The situation of America is so extraordinary and monstrous that no one should flatter himself that he can keep power for long.'[80]

By now he was reconciled to almost anything. His favourite cause of Union was now finished and he gave his blessing to General Flores, head of the now independent Ecuador. As with Urdaneta, he spoke to him frankly and with a weary realism. In America public opinion means the will of the masses, and power the audacity of a few leaders. He only had one thing to ask Flores: to use his power to punish Pasto and avenge the death of Sucre, in Bolívar's eyes a man without blemish. And as soon as you feel you are on the way down, get out with honour:

> You know that I have ruled for twenty years, and from these I have derived only a few certainties: (1) America is ungovernable, for us; (2) Those who serve a revolution plough the sea; (3) The only thing one can do in America is to emigrate; (4) This country will fall inevitably into the hands of the unbridled masses and then pass almost imperceptibly into the hands of petty tyrants, of all colours and races; (5) Once we have been devoured by every crime and extinguished by utter ferocity, the Europeans will not even regard us as worth conquering; (6) If it were possible for any part of the world to revert to primitive chaos, it would be America in her final hour.[81]

He knew that the Bolivarians were anxious. Men who had served him in good times and bad and depended on him for advice and decisions were now staring into a future without a guide, uncertain what to do next, and not quite trusting each other once the vital link in the chain of allegiance was broken. O'Leary looked to him for advice, but Bolívar had to tell him he was powerless and had nothing to offer; his health was hopeless, his cough unceasing. He could only suggest that he should stick with Urdaneta.[82]

Joaquín Mier, a wealthy Spaniard, sent Bolívar an invitation to rest in his country house, three miles from Santa Marta, and provided a vessel, the brig *Manuel*, to take him along the coast. He arrived in Santa Marta on the evening of 1 December and was carried ashore in a sedan chair. A French doctor, Alexandre Prospère Révérend, and a United States navy surgeon, George

MacNight, examined him and, though differing in detail, both pointed to a serious lung condition; modern medicine would diagnose tuberculosis.[83] On 6 December José Palacios, his long-serving *mayordomo*, carried him to a carriage that took him to Mier's villa, San Pedro Alejandrino. Close to him in this retreat were Belford Hinton Wilson, his nephew Fernando, and José Palacios, while General Montilla was his liaison with the outside world, and his French doctor remained in constant attendance. The loyal O'Leary was on duty elsewhere, and in nearby rooms noisy army officers were playing cards. Up to 8 December he was still dictating advice to Urdaneta, seeking to resolve the differences among the Bolivarians.[84] By the tenth his physical condition was deteriorating badly, with chest pains and drowsiness. Yet his mind remained clear, and he listened attentively to the bishop of Santa Marta, José María Esteves, who advised him of his terminal condition and his immortal soul. He had to decide what his next move should be: a great leap in the dark or the final step on the Christian journey? He recoiled. Am I so ill? he asked. 'How will I get out of this labyrinth?'

Bolívar died in the Catholic faith, supported by Bishop Esteves and a priest from a nearby Indian village. He made his confession and received the last rites, answering the responses clearly and firmly. There is speculation concerning his state of mind at this point, much of it sceptical. If he appeared to hesitate, it was probably a desire to stop time, the dread of the finality of the holy viaticum. What he said in confession we do not know. But the rites of extreme unction and the reception of communion are sacraments that invite commitment and it would be fair to conclude that he meant what he did. Then he confirmed his will, in a form of words commonly used at the time, but no less credible because of that. He stated that he believed in the Holy Trinity, in the Father, the Son, and the Holy Spirit, three persons in one God, and in all the other mysteries of the Roman Catholic Church, 'in whose faith and belief I have lived and profess I shall live until I die, as a true Catholic and Christian'.[85] He declared he possessed no other goods than the mines of Aroa and some jewellery. He left eight thousand pesos to José Palacios, 'in consideration of his loyal service'. And he bequeathed the residue of all his goods, assets, and incomes to his heirs, his sisters, María Antonia and Juana, and the children of his deceased brother, Juan Vicente. He instructed his executors to return the sword that Sucre had given him to his widow, 'as a token of the love I have always cherished for the Grand Marshal', and to give his thanks to General Robert Wilson 'for the good conduct of his son Colonel Belford Wilson who so faithfully remained with me to the last moments of my life'. He expressed his wish to be buried in his birthplace, the city of Caracas.

As the end day approached, he issued his final valediction to the people of Colombia in a proclamation dated 10 December 1830:

People of Colombia:

You have witnessed my efforts to establish liberty where tyranny once reigned. I have worked unselfishly, sacrificing my fortune and my peace of mind. I resigned my command when I became convinced that you distrusted my detachment. My enemies exploited your credulity and destroyed what is most sacred to me – my reputation and my love of liberty. I have been the victim of my persecutors, who have brought me to the brink of the grave. I forgive them.

As I depart from your midst, my regard for you tells me that I should make known my last wishes. I aspire to no other glory than the consolidation of Colombia. You must all work for the supreme good of the Union: the people, by obeying the present government in order to save themselves from anarchy; the ministers of religion, by addressing their supplications to heaven; and the military, by defending social guarantees with the sword. Colombians! My last wishes are for the happiness of our native land. If my death will help to end factions to consolidate the Union, I shall go to my grave in peace.[86]

He was not long in dying. His final days were uncomfortable and restless, as he moved from bed to hammock and back again and fought for breath. 'Let's go! Let's go!' he said, as in a dream. 'People in this land do not want me. Come boys! Take my luggage on board the frigate.'[87] At the end the doctor advised the waiting company and they gathered round his bed. He died at the age of forty-seven shortly after one o'clock on the afternoon of 17 December 1830, 'his last moments – the last embers of an expiring volcano – the dust of the Andes still on his garments.'[88]

Manuela received the fatal news from Peru de Lacroix, whom she had sent from Bogotá to keep her informed. She outlived her lover by twenty-six years, none of them very happy, at first a wandering victim of spite and hostility from their enemies, and to some extent of her own temperament. She finally settled in Paita, a small port in northern Peru. In the 1840s she passed to O'Leary a box of Bolívar's letters to her, and in 1850 she readily answered his queries concerning the events of 25 September 1828. She died in 1856.

Bolívar's body was embalmed and people crowded into its resting place in the Custom House to view it. The funeral, on 20 December, drew further crowds to the streets in Santa Marta, where the funeral procession led by Bolívar's horses draped in black made its way to the cathedral. Solemn marches were played and bells tolled, and a Requiem Mass committed the Liberator to eternity. The cathedral itself housed his tomb. The news of his death was slow in travelling and subdued in its reception. An obituary in *The*

Times of London recorded: 'It would probably have been impossible for the most skilful political architect to have constructed a permanent edifice of social order and freedom with such materials as were placed in the hands of Bolivar; but whatever could be done he accomplished, and whatever good exists in the present arrangements of Colombia and Peru may be traced to his superior knowledge and capacity.'[89] Venezuelans were divided in their sympathies and at that date few would have described his qualities as superior. It would be twelve years before his body was returned to Caracas, twelve years of disillusion with post-Bolivarian politics, when Venezuelans began to learn that there were worse choices than Bolívar. He was buried in the Cathedral of Caracas in December 1842, and in the National Pantheon in October 1876.

Chapter 12

THE LEGACY

Man and Myth

The history of Bolívar is not a seamless web from first protest to last battle. His life unfolded in three stages: revolution, independence and state building. In the first, from 1810 to 1818, the young, enlightened Venezuelan was a revolutionary leader, who fought and legislated for his native land and its neighbour New Granada. In the second, from 1819 to 1826, he was the universal liberator who saw beyond national boundaries and took the revolution to its limit. In the third, from 1827 to 1830, he was the statesman who sought institutions, security and reform for Americans, and left a legacy of national liberation, imperfect in his own mind but recognized as a great achievement by the rest of the world.

Across the chronological divisions there was remarkable continuity in his political ideas from the Cartagena Manifesto of 1812 to the Address to the Admirable Congress of 1830. But each phase had its own character, and in each he faced distinct challenges and responded with specific policies, accumulating experience and adapting to the times, before moving on to the next challenge and the next project. The revolutionary who fought his way through the *campaña admirable* only to become mired in conflicts with the caudillos and the confusion of his own strategy, had to learn that he could not defeat the Spaniards on the northern coast of Venezuela but needed to open another front in the interior. The liberator who then won independence for Colombia had to secure it by taking the revolution into the heart of royalist Peru, thereby overstretching his lines of military control and exposing his political position at home. The statesman who struggled to shore up the revolution's defences was finally left with the task of state building in a society deeply divided by region, race and ideology, conscious that his own presence was a further source of division. Was he a man of immutable strategies? Did he defy time and place? Or did he renew his policies as he moved from one phase to the next, deploying further weapons in his armoury and adopting further positions in his project? He was ever the pragmatist, the politician, who was ready to compromise to achieve his aim; he preferred a successful deal to the constraints of dogma, and he advocated 'not the best system of government, but the one that is most likely to work'.[1]

Interpretations of Bolívar have occupied writers of history, fiction and polemics from his day to ours, and models of political behaviour have been sought from the materials of his career. No single theory can encompass his life. Historians run the risk of distortion if they enclose him in a conceptual framework and look for models to recreate his past. Psychobiography would devalue the story of his life by forcing it into a structure determined in advance of its actual course. Better to interpret the life of the Liberator after it had run its time rather than to look for clues before it had happened. As he himself advised, 'To understand revolutions and their participants we must observe them at close range and judge them at great distance.'[2] The history of Bolívar has to follow a narrative line, with breaks for analysis and interpretation, and a final pause for appraisal.

The historian of Bolívar cannot ignore the flaws. In his personal life these were common enough, in his relations with people, with colleagues, with women, and do not call for particular comment or censure. His moods could veer between lively and morose, according to his preoccupations, and if he had a short temper his rages were brief and hardly surprising in a leader who had to take political and military decisions in emergency conditions and against the inertia or resistance of colleagues inferior to himself.[3] In his leisure moments he tended to gossip about absent colleagues and express his wit at their expense in quick, cutting phrases, a tendency not unknown among those involved in a common enterprise. But in general his instincts were generous and so was his care for others, for war widows and dependants, whom he quietly helped with payments from his own income.

His public life is a different matter and his record of political and military decisions was not impeccable. Once the revolution began he gave signs of impatience with rivals and intolerance of other opinions, concomitants of leadership and conditions of success perhaps, but deadly in their effects. His readiness to write off Miranda and betray him to his enemies was unworthy, no way to treat a precursor of the revolution who at that time had done more to put Spanish America on the map of international awareness than had Bolívar. This was a deep hatred, not a passing resentment, and the anger continued even when he knew the fate of Miranda; for years he denounced him as a coward and refused to let anyone forget it. His vendetta against the Precursor's memory answered apparently to some sombre interior need to erase a rival's record. He ignored the possibility that Miranda's motives were not so different from his own – to live to fight another day – and he seemed to treat Miranda's decision to capitulate as an action that robbed him of the opportunity to turn defeat into personal triumph and decisive victory.

Liberal opinion in the nineteenth century and later was quick to condemn the war to the death, without considering the imperatives of fighting a ruthless colonial power. The greatest outrage was not the policy itself but its application to non-combatants. The practice veered out of control when, in 1817, the Capuchin missions of southern Venezuela were inadvertently caught in the crossfire between royalist and republican forces and accused of taking part in the defence of Spanish Guayana. Twenty of the captive priests were executed by machete and lance, and their bodies burned. Bolívar was not personally involved but he was the overall commander and he issued no public proclamation on the outrage. The two republican officers directly responsible for the massacre were never punished, and one rose to senior rank in the Liberator's army. Bolívar was not easily moved to pity. He was a military commander who accepted the casualties of war, whether of his own soldiers at Bomboná and Pantano de Vargas, or among the enemy ranks at Taguanes and Carabobo, or among the helpless victims of atrocities on both sides. He was confident of his moral position. If Spain withdrew from America and Spanish generals showed humanity on the battlefield, all this would end. The war of liberation was a just war. Of that he had not the slightest doubt.

In the course of the revolution Bolívar had to associate with many crass characters, but it was usually their military or political offences that outraged him, not their personal behaviour. So the wild Córdova was his protégé until he came out in rebellion in 1829. 'Fighting like a lion, he fell and expired sternly, proud and unrepentant,' wrote O'Leary, who may have had a guilty conscience over the gruesome death of his late comrade in arms.[4] On people, Bolívar's sense of judgement was not impeccable. How otherwise could he describe José María Pando as one of the best men in Peru, 'a man incapable of flattery, utterly straight, and above all well informed and resolute'? That was in 1826. Four years and an act of disloyalty later he had become 'a scoundrel who would not hold back anything that might reflect upon me'.[5] And how account for his lifelong attachment to the eccentric Simón Rodríguez, whose behaviour in Bolivia was no model for the Bolivarian Enlightenment and whose latent talents the long-suffering Sucre could never discover? Bolívar's judgement of people, however, was normally sound and served him well throughout his life. His selection of Sucre as his leading general and heir presumptive was an inspired decision and said much for the values of Bolívar as well as the qualities of Sucre. His most emotional choice, and one that reveals another side of Bolívar, was his commitment to Manuela Sáenz, friend, adviser, consoler, as well as lover. A free spirit, as independent as he, she was a model for a later age rather than her own; her partnership with Bolívar exemplified a love that was not exploitative and suggests that his views on women did not entirely conform to the culture of the times. Or was she an exception to his more traditional views on women and his concern for reputation? He wanted his niece to marry an honourable and patriotic man, 'for the family is a treasure in which we all have an interest', and he once remarked to his sister Antonia that women should not get involved in politics.[6]

The great objective and ultimate hope of Bolívar, the union of Venezuela, New Granada and Quito in one great Colombia governed by his own constitution, was already illusory in his lifetime, and historians have not failed to criticize his pursuit of a lost cause as a lapse of judgement. Andrés Bello in a positive, but cool, appraisal of Bolívar in 1847 drew attention to the impermanence of Colombia and the defects of the Bolivian Constitution, and concluded that policies derived from his great ideals could not be sustained.[7] But Colombia was born of necessity more than ideals. He saw that the liberation of Venezuela and New Granada could not be accomplished separately, granted Spain's ability to exploit the dividing line and defend each as a single battlefield, and that it needed a greater strategy and greater resources. This implied a united front. A unified Colombia then had to be protected against Spanish counter-revolution from the south, and so Ecuador had to be won and brought into the union. For its own security against royalist Peru, Colombia had to remain united, pool its resources and secure its defences. The original creation, therefore, was based on military strategy, then prolonged as a matter of national identity and international credibility, before succumbing to realities that Bolívar himself recognized.

The great decisions of Bolívar and the commanding heights of his career overshadow individual lapses of judgement and taste. In pointing the finger at Spain he was not alone. Awareness of the colonial condition of Americans, their pent-up grievances and their growing sense of identity, was shared by many of his compatriots and expressed in many parts of the Americas. But Bolívar began with an advantage over his fellows, not simply in his aristocratic status, independent wealth and European experience, but in his understanding of the international conjuncture. The Spanish American revolution was served, though not driven, by the state of Europe in 1808: a weak Spain, an aggressive France and a watchful Britain. Bolívar understood the weakness of Spain as an imperial power, the danger of a takeover by France and the importance of Britain as a friend in need. This was a beginning, the first incentive to action. Subsequently Spain lost its imperial grip and in compensation looked to France and the Holy Alliance. Bolívar appreciated that

Britain, without the need of a great diplomatic gesture, already provided the basic protection Spanish America needed: the British navy, acting in British interests, would prevent any European aggression in the Americas far more effectively than the Monroe Doctrine. Bolívar's sense of judgement showed itself first in seizing the moment, when Spain's decline had reached its nadir, and Spanish America had gained a shield. His dominance was then displayed in his military role, in his grand strategic decisions and tactical responses certainly, but also in his place at the head of his armies and his determination always to be available, leading from the front.

Ideas and Ideals

What made Bolívar's greatness? First, his cause. Not simply his hostility to Spain. The Spanish empire was not an evil empire. As Andrés Bello pointed out, the Spanish colonial regime was not totally tyrannical; like other colonial regimes, it was a mixture of severity, moderation and inefficiency.[8] But colonies do not stand still; they have within them the seeds of their own destruction, demands for office, for equality of opportunity, for freer economies, all signs of a growing self-awareness, an increasing sense of nationality. Bolívar recognized that the time had come to release these demands and express them in absolute independence. Liberation was his objective, and liberation itself was a great cause, to free Spanish America from colonial occupation and its peoples from foreign laws. Liberty and equality, these were his pivotal themes, and he made them the foundation of his revolution. He thus advanced beyond those creoles who would have been satisfied with autonomy within the Spanish monarchy and whose commitment to equality was always dubious. He also led with the mind as well as the will. It was Bolívar, the intellectual, the political theorist, who gave Spanish American independence its intellectual underpinning, in works whose style and eloquence resound to this day.

Liberty, he said, is 'the only object worth the sacrifice of a man's life', not simply freedom from absolutism but freedom from colonial power.[9] From Montesquieu he inherited a hatred of despotism and a belief in moderate constitutional government, in the separation of powers and the rule of law. But liberty in itself is not the key to his political system. He distrusted theoretical concepts of liberty, and his hatred of tyranny did not lead him to the glorification of anarchy. 'Abstract theories create the pernicious idea of unlimited freedom,' he said, and he was convinced that absolute liberty invariably deteriorated into absolute power. His search for freedom therefore was a search for a mean between the extremes of anarchy and tyranny, between the rights of the individual and the needs of society. This would be secured essentially by the administration of justice and the rule of law, so that the just and weak could live without fear, and merit and virtue could receive their due reward.[10] He believed, with Rousseau, that only the law can be sovereign, and law is the result not of divine or despotic authority but of human will and the sovereignty of the people.

Equality too was a right and an objective in Bolívar's project. First, equality of Americans with Spaniards, of Venezuela and Colombia with Spain. This equality was absolute, and was the basis of his argument for independence. Second, equality between Americans. European political theorists wrote for communities of relative social homogeneity and appealed to fairly distinct classes, such as the petty bourgeoisie favoured by Rousseau. Bolívar had no such advantage. He had to begin with more complex human material and to legislate for a society with a special racial formation. Americans, he was never tired of saying, were neither European nor indigenous people but a mixture of Spanish, Africans and Indians. 'All differ visibly in the colour of their skin, a difference which places upon us an obligation of the greatest importance.'[11] This obligation was to correct the disparity imposed by nature and inheritance, by making men equal before the law and the constitution. 'Men are born with equal rights to share the benefits of society,' he observed, but obviously they do not possess equal talents, virtue, intelligence and strength. This physical, moral and intellectual inequality must be corrected by laws, so that the individual may enjoy political and social equality; thus by education and other opportunities an individual may gain the equality denied him by nature. It was Bolívar's opinion that 'the fundamental basis of our political system turns directly and exclusively upon the establishment and practice of equality in Venezuela'. And he explicitly denied that this was inspired by France or North America, where in his view equality had not been a political dogma, a debatable opinion probably influenced by his determination to produce American solutions for American problems. The logic of his own principles led him to conclude that the greater the social inequality, the greater the need for legal equality. Among the practical steps which he envisaged was the extension of free public education to all the people and particular reforms for those sectors who were especially disadvantaged, such as the landless and the slaves.

Liberty and equality, these were the essential objectives. But how could they be realized without sacrificing security, property and stability, those other rights by which society protected the persons and possessions of its citizens? In principle Bolívar was a democrat and he believed that government should be responsible to the people. As he moved into Venezuela to confront the rebellion of Páez in December 1826 he warned the people against warlords and their parties: 'Only the majority is sovereign; he who takes the place of the people is a tyrant and his power is usurpation.'[12] But Bolívar was not such an idealist as to imagine that America was ready for pure democracy, or that the law could instantly annul inequalities of nature and society. Until our people acquire the political virtues of our brothers in North America, he said, I fear that popular systems of government, far from helping us, will be our ruin. He had no confidence in the people en masse as they came out of the colonial system; they had to be re-educated under the tutelage of a strong executive before they could be fit for liberty. Meanwhile: 'Complete liberty and absolute democracy are but reefs upon which all republican hopes have foundered.'[13] He spent his whole political career developing his principles and applying them to American conditions in his own version of the age of revolution. 'His principle was not to expect too much from a people who unhappily might still be considered little better than a nation of slaves, to give them no more power than they were able to direct, and to have wholesome checks on those who held such power.'[14] Until they were educated into political society his solution lay not in a federal system, which he consistently opposed, nor in monarchy, of which he was accused, but in his Bolivian Constitution, though even about this he was more diffident than is often supposed.

Bolívar's revolution did not resemble revolutionary movements in Europe or the Atlantic world. These reflected conditions and claims which were appropriate to themselves but had only limited application to the political, social and economic problems of America. The European Enlightenment and its liberal aftermath, well known to Bolívar, were too self-absorbed to offer political ideas or services to colonial peoples. The economic interests of industrial Europe, being those of a metropolis, involved some opportunities for primary producers but also disadvantages, and if industrialization was a medium of social change in western Europe, it played no such role in early nineteenth-century Spanish America, whose concern was to strengthen the traditional export sector – and with it the landed oligarchy – in order to import manufactures made by others. For these reasons Bolívar, who in many respects had a deep affinity with the age of revolution, could not imitate its intellectual and political leaders, even had he wished to do so. While the Enlightenment confirmed his attachment to reason and inspired his struggle for liberty and equality, he had to employ his own intellectual resources to fashion a theory of colonial emancipation, and then to find the appropriate limits for liberty and equality, and in the process we can see traces of enlightened absolutism as well as democratic revolution. Democratic forms in Europe and North America evoked his respect, but he insisted on writing his own constitutions, designed to conform to Spanish American conditions, not to outside models. These conditions, especially in the post-war period, when social and racial divisions, lack of consensus and absence of political traditions placed liberal constitutions under severe strain and brought the new republics to the edge of anarchy, caused serious problems for Bolívar. Now we see the realistic Bolívar – his democratic ideals tempered by experience of popular protest, race conflict, and elite factionalism – the man who declared Spanish America to be ungovernable.

The Bolivarian model of government, designed around the life presidency, appealed to the military but otherwise made few friends: it excluded too many vested interests from political life and decisions to gain wide acceptance. The civilian elites preferred more liberal constitutions, though even these and their authors were affected by that bias towards authority and centralism that was a feature of the republican as it had been of the colonial state. Most Venezuelan constitutions allowed the president extraordinary powers of intervention in time of crisis or rebellion, and most defined the political nation in the narrowest of terms, establishing property and literacy qualifications for those entitled to stand for election and even to vote. Bolívar had nothing to be ashamed of in any comparison of his constitutional principles with those of his liberal enemies. Historians have suggested that he abandoned the search for liberty, or at least postponed it in favour of order and security. But the evidence shows that his principles in 1828–30 were not basically different from those he had developed from 1812 onwards, that his insistence on liberty and equality was always accompanied by a search for strong government.

Bolívar conceived the American revolution as more than a fight for political independence. He also thought of it as a social movement, which would improve as well as liberate, and would respond to both the radical and liberal demands of the age. For him a free government had to be an active government, moving beyond dispensing privileges and patronage into the more positive work of giving Americans a better life. Strong government was essential for the new states if they were to impose reforms, an incomprehensible synthesis for the liberals of his day, but better understood by later generations of Latin Americans. Many of them came to believe that powerful presidential government and one-party states were suitable, or at least inevitable, constitutional forms for new nations in formation. Bolivarian absolutism, therefore, was not an end in itself. The bias towards strong government, in the interests of reform as well as of order, and as a necessary framework for post-colonial development, was a quality rather than a flaw in Bolívar's policy, and endows him with a modernity beyond the confines of the age of revolution.

The Realist of the Revolution

Bolívar did not promote a social revolution, and never claimed to do so. Land distribution, racial equality, abolition of slavery, pro-Indian decrees, were policies of a reformist – not a revolutionary – character. He was too much of a realist to believe that he could change the social structure of America by legislation or by imposing policies unacceptable to the major interest groups. In the age of democratic revolution, no other regime in the Atlantic world had accomplished a social revolution. The possible exception was Haiti, and for Bolívar, as for many North Americans, Haiti was a warning, not a model, a clear lesson in the consequences of recklessly dismantling strong institutions and unleashing slaves into a fool's paradise.[15] The Spanish American revolution was ambiguous on slavery, prepared to abolish the slave trade but reluctant to release slaves into a free society, where they might not conform to creole rules on law and order and would leave their masters without labour in mines and plantations. This was not Bolívar's position. The Liberator, with a firmer moral instinct than Thomas Jefferson, thought it 'madness that a revolution for liberty should seek to maintain slavery'.[16] He freed his own slaves, first for service in the army of liberation, for it was right that slaves too should be prepared to die for liberty, then unconditionally as an absolute right to freedom. He then sought to write abolition into law but in practice he did not succeed, either in Colombia or Bolivia, for the landed oligarchies in both countries were too strongly rooted in social and economic life to be coerced by mere legislation. Bolívar never had the power to do as he pleased. At the very time he was being denounced as a 'tyrant' by his liberal enemies, the limits on his power were only too obvious, when the oligarchies, from which his enemies also came, rejected his liberal social policies. The chronology of abolition was determined in practice by the number of slaves in a country, by their importance to its economy, and sometimes by arguments over compensation. Freedom for Venezuela's forty thousand slaves waited until 1854, when landowners appreciated that slaves were expensive and uneconomical workers, and that a cheaper labour force could be obtained by turning them into 'free' peons tied to estates by laws against vagrancy or by a coercive agrarian regime. Colombia and Peru also delayed abolition until the 1850s.

Liberal sentiments gave way to rational calculation in matters of race. The opposite was true in his Indian policy. Basically the Indians were losers from independence. In a formal sense, enshrined in Bolivarian legislation, they were emancipated, for they were now free citizens and released from payment of tribute and the obligation of forced labour. But Indians in Peru, Ecuador and Bolivia did not automatically welcome abolition of tribute in exchange for paying the same taxes as other citizens – for they saw tribute as a legal proof of their landholdings, from the surplus of which they paid their dues. And their land was now under threat. The liberals of post-independence regarded the Indians as an obstacle to national development, and believed that the autonomy they had inherited from the colonial regime should be ended by integrating them into the nation. In Colombia and Peru the new legislators sought to destroy corporate entities in order to release Indian lands and mobilize Indian labour. The policy involved the division of communal lands among individual owners, theoretically among the Indians themselves, but in practice among their more powerful neighbours. Bolívar legislated along these lines when he was in Cuzco and ordered that community land be distributed, and each Indian, 'of whatever sex or age', be given a *topo* of land in the best places.[17] But the Andean agrarian structure did not allow for benevolence and legislative enactments were not enough to change it. The Indians, it is true, had their own mechanisms of survival and could not be legislated out of existence. But their community lands were left without protection and eventually became one of the victims of land concentration and the export economy.

The revolution failed to reach out to Indians and slaves, even as it also stopped short of the mixed races. Since the middle of the eighteenth century the hopes of the *pardos* for advance had rested with the metropolis. It was Spanish policy that had first introduced a degree of social mobility against the protest and resistance of the creoles. Now the creoles were in power, it was the same families who had denounced the opening of doors to the *pardos* in the university, the Church, and civil and military office. For the mass of the *pardos* independence was, if anything, a regression. Political mobilization ended with the end of the war, and social mobility was thwarted by plutocratic prejudice and their own poverty. Yet their claims to education, office and political rights could not be ignored, for in numbers alone they were indispensable to the whites in the wars of independence. In the army they qualified for promotion up to officer of middle rank. Finally they obtained legal equality – the new republican constitutions abolished all outward signs of racial discrimination and made everyone equal before the law. But this was the limit of equality, as many agencies of social mobility remained closed to *pardos*. In Venezuela the rules of university entrance were still restrictive: a certificate of *limpieza* (purity of blood) was demanded until 1822; after that, proof of legitimacy, relatively high entrance fees, and de facto discrimination all placed higher education beyond the reach of the majority of people.[18]

The popular sectors in general were the outcasts of the revolution. In rural occupations they were subject to greater pressures, from land concentration, liberal legislation in favour of private property, and the renewed attack on vagrancy. In towns no doubt the retail and service sectors expanded with the expansion of international trade. But local industry suffered, or failed to develop. In Venezuela and Colombia local industry declined, except in regional markets; in the Andean countries it survived only for local consumption. Artisans remained an unemployed or underemployed group; together with the rural poor, they were regarded as outside the political nation. Bolívar was absolutely committed to racial equality; his political thought and constitutional enactments were clear that whites, *mestizos*, blacks, *pardos* and

Indians were equal before the law, and in practice too he appointed and promoted officials and military regardless of their racial origin. But he could not change the structure of society and he was well aware that there were masses of poor blacks and *pardos* on the fringes of social and economic life and resentful of practical discrimination by their wealthier neighbours – not only whites.

The *pardos* wanted more than equality before the law. 'Equality before the law,' he warned, 'is not enough for the people in their present mood. They want absolute equality as a public and a social right. Next they will demand *pardocracia*, that they, the *pardos*, should rule. This is a very natural inclination which will ultimately lead to the extermination of the privileged class.'[19] He was ruthless towards any attempt to exploit racial divisions and acted promptly to suppress black rebellion and incipient race war. The execution of Piar and Padilla weighed on his conscience, but as he looked at the racial composition of Venezuela and Colombia he believed that they were victims of their own extremism and that existing society could not withstand black rebellion. In the pessimism of his final years he feared that only excesses could result from granting any political powers to *pardos*. The threat of *pardocracia* haunted him: he considered it as abhorrent as the *albocracia*, or white rule, which was 'absolute dogma' in the south. On race the idealist had to give way to the realist. He knew that he could not carry the oligarchy with him in any excess of social liberalism, and any attempt to force the issue would risk the advances he had already made. The ruling classes of Venezuela and Colombia, the alliance of landowners, merchants, officials and lawyers, far from facing 'extermination', were more than capable of withstanding social rebellion and preserving power for themselves, as they proved in the course of the nineteenth century and beyond.

While it may be agreed that Bolívar did not promote a social revolution, Germán Carrera Damas goes further and argues that Bolívar's policy was in effect a variation of that of the creole elite. The argument is subtle. The creole elite were driven by an overriding objective: to preserve the internal power structure in Venezuela, namely the predominant power of the white propertied classes, formed in the colony and now threatened by the social convulsions unleashed by the war. To preserve their power amidst these tensions, and to confront the demand of the slaves for freedom and the *pardos* for social equality, the creoles were prepared to make minimum concessions, to abolish the slave trade and to declare legal equality of all citizens. But this controlled and peaceful change was brutally broken by the rising of the slaves in 1812 and 1814, the rebellion of the *pardos* in 1811, 1812 and 1814, the war to the death, and the near destruction of the white dominant class. Carrera Damas argues that Bolívar shared these objectives, but not the policies to achieve them.

Fearing the risk of social war turning into racial war, he became permanently committed to absolute abolition of slavery. Abolition would remove the threat posed by the struggle of the slaves for freedom and enable him to reconstruct and preserve the internal power structure. But there remained another danger, the unsatisfied demands of the *pardos*. He confronted this through the centralist and aristocratic character of his constitutional projects, those of Angostura and the Bolivian Constitution, and in his partiality towards monarchy at the end of his life, all designed to restore the structure of internal power. As for republican forms, they threatened to become vehicles of *pardocracia*; from 1821 he criticized the effectiveness of republican institutions and democratic liberalism, and saw them as obstacles to the restoration of order in Venezuela, that is, 'the re-establishment of the internal structure of power'. The argument concludes by underlining the contrast in Bolívar's career: his failure to produce a project for the organization of Venezuelan society of the same order of creativity as he had demonstrated in his formulation of the theory of independence.[20]

Nevertheless, another interpretation is possible. Bolívar was an exception to the theory of the internal power structure. The reason is that from a position of leadership he had to struggle with events and conditions, and he had to make decisions while subject to intolerable pressure from conflicting demands. He could overcome adverse circumstances, and thus he fought the Spaniards to a standstill and won independence. But he could not be expected to win a completely new order in society and economy, for these were founded on long-term conditions rooted in history, environment and people, and not easily changed by mere legislation, much less in a short period of ten to fifteen years. To describe society as an internal power structure, moreover, cannot ignore the details of social and economic life. Bolívar presided over some racial mobility and in practice admitted *pardos* to new opportunities in the army and the administration. What he refused to countenance was *pardocracia*, rule by *pardos*, overturning in two decades three centuries of Venezuela's history. The question to ask is not why did he say no to *pardocracia*, but would *pardocracia* have given Venezuela better government and greater peace and stability? The lesson from Haiti was not reassuring.

Bolívar was also subject to another condition, recently highlighted as the 'chaos of the revolution'. Bolívar was caught in a constant struggle against chaos, a chaos unleashed by a long and violent war and by the simultaneous upheaval in social relations. The chaos theory argues that Bolívar succeeded as a military leader because he was able to direct his armed forces through this chaos and reach his goals, but that he failed as a post-revolutionary leader because he could no longer survive in a chaotic world.[21] The second part of this argument is less convincing than the first, for again it introduces, or

restates, the notion of failure. Bolívar, credited with superhuman achievements, is also expected to have superhuman qualities. The problem with all
concepts of failure is that no person, party or government ever produces a
perfect model of society, and all solutions depend on the willingness of people
to collaborate in their own salvation.

To criticize Bolívar, as he was criticized in his own time and since, for not
being a liberal democrat rather than a conservative absolutist, is to leave conditions out of the argument. He once protested to those who wanted to make
him a monarch, 'I am not Napoleon, and Colombia is not France.' He could
equally have said to his liberal critics, 'I am not Washington and Colombia is
not the United States.' North Americans had already travelled the road of independence and made progress towards a democratic and egalitarian society
where education, literacy and the suffrage were more advanced than anything
so far achieved in Colombia. But Bolívar had won independence by mobilizing
an army of *pardos*, blacks, and former slaves, all with post-war expectations.[22]
This was not the homogeneous society of the North, but a multiracial people,
each race with its own interest and its own intolerance. He could not satisfy
every interest and he was not so idealist as to destroy the historic Colombia in
a vain search for equality. His political revolution, therefore, was accompanied
by social reform and no more.

Paths of Glory

Did Bolívar have an inner life, hidden from immediate view? Can we capture
his character and motivation? What inspired and enlightened him? Bolívar
spent his whole public life philosophizing; he took few actions and prepared
few policies without theorizing about them. 'My unhappiness,' he said, 'comes
from my philosophy, and I am more the philosopher in success than in
misfortune. If I am unhappy, it is for others, because my fate has lifted me to
such a height that it is difficult for me to be unhappy. Even were I to lose
everything on earth, I would still have the glory of having fulfilled my duty to
my last breath. And this glory will be my boon and my happiness for ever.'[23]
He wrote these words as he approached the summit of his campaign in Peru,
invulnerable to success or failure; supreme self-reliance made him indifferent
to fortune, for he was sustained by confidence in his glory. Yet the historian
has to beware of judging Bolívar's mind and actions from his own words
alone. The myriad words of Bolívar are difficult to avoid and there are few
other guides to his mind, especially to his glory. But was glory a deep enough
faith to sustain greatness?

Glory was a ruling passion, a constant theme of his self-appraisal, and he
sometimes seemed to desire glory as much as, perhaps even more than, power.

When did the obsession begin? It was not something a creole was likely to acquire under Spanish rule, and Bolívar did not emerge from his youth trailing clouds of glory. It was an indication of the ambition of Bolívar, of his post-colonial mentality, his exposure to Europe and his awareness of Napoleon, his reading of history, his anxiety to emulate the heroes of the ancient and modern worlds, and his determination to equal the greatest of contemporary leaders. From the very beginning of his public life he wanted glory, believed that he had earned glory, and demanded that others recognize his glory. He was not embarrassed when, after the victory of Carabobo, Santander called him 'the chosen son of glory'. On the contrary, he agreed. His concern for glory, his awareness of his own greatness, was not simply one aspect of his inner self: it defined his character and inspired his actions. It seemed to be the wellspring of his life.

What did glory mean in the Bolivarian vocabulary? It was not, of course, a new concept. Ancients and moderns alike strove for glory. As every school-child knows, la gloire was the favourite motive of Louis XIV. For centuries glory was regarded as an attribute of God, though humans too could acquire glory through exceptional actions. St Augustine looked long and hard at glory, through the eyes of theology and history. His description of the Roman emperors could almost have been written for Bolívar, take away the word 'empire'. 'They felt it would be shameful for their country to be enslaved, but glorious for her to have dominion and empire; and so they set their hearts on making her free, then on making her sovereign. It was this greed for praise, this passion for glory, that gave rise to those marvellous achievements, which were, no doubt, praiseworthy and glorious in men's estimation.' But the love of glory, he continues, is a flawed passion, inferior to virtue, which bears the witness not of others but of a man's own conscience. So the greed for glory is a vice, overtaken in the Christian world by the love of justice. And his conclusion? 'Glory may not be a female voluptuary, but she is puffed up with empty conceit.'[24]

For Bolívar love of glory was a conviction, if not a vice. Even his great admirer O'Leary saw it as a weakness. In the months before Cúcuta in 1821 Bolívar was furious at the calumnies being spread about him by his enemies at the expense of his reputation. 'No one was more sensitive to such attacks as Bolívar. Neither his own knowledge of their injustice nor the insignificance of their authors were enough to assuage the pain. I often saw him full of anger or rather suffering terrible torment as the result of reading an article written against him in some worthless rag. This may not be the mark of a great soul, but it does reveal a high regard for public opinion.'[25] His republic was inter-national and he had an international audience. Volume 12 of O'Leary's Memorias, 'Correspondencia de hombres notables con el Libertador', is an anthology of admiration from the wider world; it includes the names of Sir Robert Wilson, Lafayette, the Abbé de Pradt, Humboldt, Joseph Lancaster, Daniel O'Connell, Jeremy Bentham and numerous others. He was jealous of his reputation in Europe, and in 1830 he instructed the Colombian envoy in London to guard it at all costs against slander.

Bolívar's sense of glory was not simply an anxiety about what people thought of him but a love of glory in itself, for his own satisfaction. It was his own opinion of himself, rather than that of others, that counted with Bolívar. Glory was a compound of fame, honour and recognition, something won in battle and then after the war something recorded with pride. It was also an honourable achievement. 'Glory consists in being great and useful,' he admonished Sucre after the battle of Junín, when his colleague regarded some tasks as too menial for him.[26] During his days and nights of illness in Pativilca he mused dementedly on his labours for liberty in the south, the ingratitude of its leaders and the temptation to leave it all. 'Until now I have fought for liberty: in future I will fight for my glory, no matter what it costs. My glory now consists in ruling no more and in thinking of nothing but myself; I have always had this intention but it increases progressively by the day. My years, my ill health, and my disillusion with all the dreams of youth prevent me from taking any other way.'[27] He always kept glory in reserve, and glory could survive without power.

But glory could not overcome everything. Later in 1824, when the glory won at Junín was tempered by depressing news from Colombia, he wrote to his friend Fernando Peñalver, 'In this ill-fated revolution, as ill-fated in victory as in defeat, we must always shed tears over our destiny. The Spaniards will soon be finished. But when will it end for us? Like a wounded hind we receive the arrow in our breast, deadly for us, for our own blood is our poison. Happy are those who die before the final outcome of this bloody drama. . . . Console yourself with the thought that however sad our death, it will always be happier than our life.'[28] Bolívar's glory was not mere military glory, limited to the battlefield. And it was not the same as ambition. When relations with Santander and Congress were tense over his wish to return to Bolivia to present his constitution, he declared, 'In this century of philosophy no one acquires or conserves glory except by scrupulous adherence to principles.' Then, referring to the schemes of a crown for Bolívar concocted in Venezuela, he insisted, 'My enemies and foolish friends refuse to believe that I detest ruling as strongly as I love glory, and that glory consists not in ruling but in exercising great virtues. I have sought glory and freedom, and having achieved both I have no further desires.'[29] Almost an echo of St Augustine.

Liberation for Americans, glory for himself. Bolívar led one of the first movements of decolonization in the modern world. But liberation brought

problems, some of them beyond his control, and in the aftermath of liberation there were fewer opportunities for glory. Comparison of Bolívar's revolution with national liberation movements in the twentieth century reveals
some common ground in the years after victory. One-party systems, failed
experiments in social reform, corruption and ethnic clashes can all find paral-
lels in Bolívar's world, and even the economies had similar problems: foreign
debt, failing infrastructure, economic mismanagement, bad government. In
both cases there was a tendency for people to look back on the imperial power
– Spain, or Britain – with nostalgia for a previous paradise, and to reassess the
history of imperial rule. In Spanish America perceptions of the past changed
from rejection to acceptance, and traditional institutions returned to favour.
Monarchy re-emerged as a subject for discussion. Liberals threw up their
hands, or drew their guns, in horror; for them it was a return to tyranny.
Pragmatists were ready to consider it, and Bolívar was not afraid to look at it
and to speak of it to British diplomats. It is clear from O'Leary's correspondence in 1829 that advice from the Bolivarians was mixed and that Bolívar was
hearing arguments in favour of monarchy as well as against.[30] He had to make
his own decision, taking into account public opinion, the history of the revolution and his own reputation. The man who denounced Spain as a tyrant
never seriously considered the adoption of monarchy; in any case constitutional monarchy was not strong enough for him. Basically he was looking for
some form of monocracy. Everything came back to the life-term president,
described in his Bolivian Constitution.

Dynamics of Leadership

Beyond the ideas, the proclamations, the decrees and the constitutions, and
behind the glory, the driving force of Bolívar was the power of his will, the
passion to command. The revolution threw up a whole range of military and
political figures who fought to reach the top, and it soon brought forth an
array of virtue and talent, of heroes and heroines, worthies and mediocrities,
the dull, the wicked and the mad. There were, too, essential and anonymous
collaborators, the unsung heroes of logistics, who mobilized troops, supplied
horses and mules and assembled supplies. But at whatever level of command,
and even among the revolution's elite, no one else emerged with the genius of
Bolívar. He was conscious of his superiority and confident enough to speak of
it. He warned the rebellious Páez not to join the losers: 'General Castillo
opposed me and lost; General Piar opposed me and lost; General Mariño
opposed me and lost; General Riva Agüero opposed me and lost; and General
Torre Tagle opposed me and lost. Providence seems to bring down my
personal enemies, whether they are Americans or Spaniards.'[31] He was the

supreme leader, who advanced beyond others, impelled by his iron determination. His instinct for leadership was displayed in small things as well as great, in tactics as well as strategy, and in the end it was his leadership that prevailed and took the revolution to its conclusion in independence. Revolutions require some to lead and some to follow. People will always follow whoever has the clearest ideas and the strongest sense of purpose. These were the qualities that enabled Bolívar to dominate the elites and direct the hordes.

In Thomas Carlyle's discourse on heroes, hero-worship is presented as a natural tendency in a world of instability and disorder, answering to a deep need in people for a great man to guide and rule them. The ultimate hero embodies virtually the whole typology: prophet, priest, poet, teacher and ruler of men, 'he to whose wills our wills are to be subordinated'. The rule of the hero is superior to any other form of government. 'Find in any country the Ablest Man that exists there; raise *him* to the supreme place, and loyally reverence him; you have a perfect government for that country; no ballot-box, parliamentary eloquence, voting, constitution-building, or other machinery whatsoever can improve it a whit. It is in the perfect state; an ideal country.' Bolívar did not conform in every respect to Carlyle's hero. He was not exactly one of the silent men of history, inhabiting a great 'Empire of Silence', silently thinking, silently working amidst the noisy inanity of the world. Yet in other respects Bolívar was Carlyle's indispensable man, who would 'tell us for the day and the hour what we are to *do*'.[32]

Bolívar's power of leadership was innate, not learned, improved through experience but not acquired from others. The strong sense of destiny and mission was already ingrained in him from the time of his return to Venezuela from Europe, and became more deeply embedded within him as he advanced through the years of revolution. No doubt the way was prepared by others, by precursors and patriots, who created a platform from which Bolívar could launch his project of liberation. But his was the creative spirit that was needed to articulate and direct the revolution. Did Bolívar make the revolution, or did the revolution make Bolívar? The question is superfluous. The events around 1810, it is true, produced a historical opportunity, but the opportunity needed a *jefe supremo* with leadership qualities to supply the ideas and direct the action. Bolívar quickly showed the mental determination and physical skills required by the situation. He was the intellectual leader of the Spanish American revolution, the prime source of its ideas, the theorist of liberation whose arguments clarified and legitimized independence during and after the war.

He was also the man of action, though he himself seems to have been indifferent to the quality that distinguished him above others: his physical endurance and durability. The travels and travails of the great campaigner were not things that he boasted about – on the contrary, he admitted that he had wanted for nothing throughout his life – but sheer will power was an ingredient of his greatness. This sustained him through twenty years of unremitting struggle, driving him tens of thousands of miles along primitive roads and tracks across plains and mountains in one of the longest of colonial wars. His odyssey culminated in the painful journey in 1829 from Bogotá to Pasto and from Quito to Guayaquil, at a time when he was aware of his growing infirmity as well as of hostility along the route, but determined to overcome both for Colombia. This was heroism on a grand scale. The way back was a struggle against the elements, the rain relentless from Guayaquil to Popayán, the roads almost impassable and the riding difficult; from there to Bogotá the political problems of his rule poured in, oppressing the mind and testing the spirit. But he was still the leader, and who was his equal?

Bolívar's leadership was revealed in the compelling powers of his oratory, when his fusion of reason and emotion lifted his arguments to heights not previously experienced by his audiences. We have, of course, no recordings of his speeches to tell us the tone of his voice, the resonance, the inflections, the ironies and the emotions. But we know that in the earliest debates of the patriots his voice rose loud and clear, his ideas cut through the arguments over loyalty, autonomy and independence. His great speeches, which he prepared in full written versions, appealed to the heart as well as the mind, and his address to the congress of Angostura was said to have moved his listeners to tears. Yet he did not harangue or lecture his audiences, often legislators, and he was never condescending, though his allusions and references assumed knowledge of ancient, modern and contemporary history that probably few of his listeners possessed. And he could speak to the troops as well as to politicians. At Cerro de Pasco, before the battle of Junín, he roused the ranks to cheers: 'Soldiers! You are going to free an entire world from slavery, you are invincible!' On campaign he stayed close to his troops, especially to his loyal Venezuelans, and when they left him to return to Venezuela in 1830, he knew his war was over.

The Bolivarian style emerged not only in his oratory but also in his writings. Words flowed from him in a flood, letters on different subjects dictated simultaneously to different secretaries, political documents, proclamations, constitutional speeches, decrees, from the sublime to the trivial in a few sentences. His prose was unique, a singular mixture of styles, clear, allusive, rich in metaphor, and suddenly lyrical. Bolívar was honest and direct, but he was also a propagandist, and his writings, including his correspondence, display a concern to persuade as well as to analyse; for him dissemination was as important as description. Moreover his message was designed for each individual correspondent and could differ from one to the other. So he was quite capable of saying different things to different people at different times, or even at the same time. A dangerous temptation to the historian, a trap for the unwary, his words are also an honest guide, transparent, opening his world frankly and generously. 'I have revealed my opinions publicly and solemnly on all occasions,' he protested. 'If anyone wants to consult them I have no need to repeat them, for they can be found in the documents of my public life.'[33]

'I am the man of difficulties,' Bolívar told Santander, 'you are the man of law.' An exquisite distinction, making it clear that he was the supreme leader, his rival the subordinate administrator. Dealing effectively with difficulties was essential to leadership and that usually meant dealing with people. What today is called people management was second nature to Bolívar. His sensibilities were finely tuned to his colleagues' strengths and weaknesses: he knew what would please and what would offend, and he conducted his relations with his senior officers and officials with a sure sense of the appropriate, using frankness, flattery and rebuke according to the man and the occasion. He did not shirk difficult decisions, and his orders on appointments and promotions were tactful but firm. Quick to command and to mollify, he was also ready to listen. Marching into Venezuela in December 1826 to recall his country to union, he made it clear to Páez who was chief and who was subordinate, but quickly recognized how far the chief could go.

He disliked accepting advice from inferiors such as Páez, but from Sucre, whom he recognized and promoted as a leader in the making with talents comparable to his own, he sought and accepted advice and treated his decisions with respect. And to Sucre, though to few others, he was also ready to delegate responsibility, up to the point of entrusting to him the final campaign of the war and the administration of the last liberated country. Sucre was his alter ego, a protégé whom he treated as an equal, a subordinate from whom he hid nothing. Santander, on the other hand, was the bane of his life, a nemesis he could neither shun nor sack, ironically one of his greatest 'difficulties'. Bolívar had the political sense to know that he had to make Santander next in seniority to himself, a New Granadan to govern New Granadans, an administrator mean enough to assume the bureaucratic responsibilities of the revolution while the Liberator concentrated on liberation. Neither trusted the other, but the relationship remained apparently civilized and friendly and left a correspondence which reveals some of the frankest and most personal thoughts of Bolívar on the people and problems of the revolution. But the façade broke into honest recriminations in 1827–8 and first principles came out loud and clear.

In styling himself the man of difficulties, Bolívar was also expressing his readiness to take responsibility, for failures as well as successes. Failure itself was a challenge, another obstacle to be overcome; his ability to pick himself up from adversity was notorious and helps to account for his soldiers' faith in him and their acceptance of his defeats. In the 'Manifesto of Carúpano', which brought to an end the miserable campaign of 1814, he acknowledged that he was not blameless for the collapse of resistance. At Pasto in 1822 his reluctance to accept less praise than Sucre was simply an admission that a leader could not afford to diminish his glory if he wanted to retain allegiance. There was, however, a limit to his willingness to accept blame for constitutional failure and the difficulty of finding a solution to the political problems of the Union. For this he blamed a series of enemies ranging from Santander and his political cronies in Bogotá, to caudillos in the regions, and in the final analysis to an immature people. Who can say he was wrong?

Leadership is a variable concept and makes different demands in different ages. But one constant is the ability to inspire people, to excite the mind and stir the heart, and to make everything seem possible. Many of Bolívar's projects, creations of his own mind, looked like madness to others. To restart the revolution from New Granada, to invade Venezuela from Haiti, to abandon Caracas for Angostura, and then, most mind-boggling of all, to switch strategy westwards across the Andes, were not ideas immediately understood by his followers or accepted by his colleagues. And more was to come: mobilization for a campaign in the south and then for the invasion of Peru, a foreign country in the eyes of most Colombians, and finally a leading role in Bolivia. Many of these projects appeared risky or even impossible, and they demanded constant sacrifices from the people. Bolívar had to convince critics, motivate doubters, reassure the clergy, and keep warlords in line. The case was not always easy to argue, but thanks to his eloquence, his reputation and his position at the front, in short to his supreme leadership, each call was answered and the revolution could advance again. This was not blind obedience. People followed, if not out of conviction then from faith in Bolívar, inspired by what O'Leary called 'the magic of his prestige'.[34]

The Cult of Bolívar

The days of triumph passed and his leadership was challenged. He had always had 'enemies' but after his return to Bogotá in 1826, bringing with him his Bolivian Constitution, now for universal consumption, he began to lose prestige as well as support. The historic victories had created and nurtured his glory. Boyacá, a great triumph over Spain and over nature, raised him to the summit: now he was the *Padre de la Patria*, the soul of the nation's independence and nationality, the accepted saviour of Colombia as well as of Venezuela. But the time came when his victories were a memory, a time when people began to look ahead and think of a future without Bolívar. Then his glory became even more precious and in greater need of protection. This was the mood of his waning years. The man who seized the moment in 1810 also timed his exit in 1830. The tragedy of his premature death was his final glory, a glory undimmed by longevity and the fate of an unsuccessful administrator.

The story of Bolívar reached its nadir in his compatriots' refusal to have him on Colombian territory, followed by his melancholy journey into exile, and final days on the Caribbean coast. The irony of the following years would not have been lost on Bolívar: author of Colombian unity and victim of its collapse, he depended for his rehabilitation in his native land on his enemy's campaign for his return. He owed few favours to Páez but the instability of post-Bolivarian Venezuela persuaded the caudillo to seek once more the saving hand of the Liberator. After a first gesture in 1833, it was February 1842 before Páez made a serious effort to have the remains of the Liberator repatriated. He urged congress that it would be appropriate and a matter of political duty to restore Bolívar 'so that in future public esteem for the memory of the Liberator may rest on the national vote legitimately expressed, and the demonstrations of thanks and admiration for his great deeds of patriotism and humanity shall be in accord with the wishes of the legislators'.[35] At a time when civil unrest was never far away and the opposition readily reached for weapons rather than arguments, it was to the advantage of Páez and other politicians to bathe themselves in vicarious glory and associate themselves with the record of Bolívar.

In November 1842 the body of Bolívar was exhumed from the Cathedral of Santa Marta, escorted in a small fleet to La Guaira and from there transported to Caracas, where it arrived on 16 December. Amidst exuberant funeral honours the body was followed in procession by leaders of the government, the Church, the military, the administration, the foreign envoys and 'an elegant body of citizens'; it was received in a solemn requiem liturgy and entombed first in the church of San Francisco then in the cathedral of Caracas, an occasion described and interpreted by Fermín Toro, politician, journalist and spokesman for the conservative oligarchy. To extol Bolívar without criticizing the congress that had delayed his return required a careful approach, as he weaved his argument around the unity between Bolívar and the nation. Homage to the Father and Liberator was homage to the fatherland; the voice of the people had broken through and twelve years of error, envy and calumny now ended in a supreme national celebration. Who is great in these days? Who is strong as a rock? He who bequeathed to Venezuelans and to the *masas populares* the liberty won in battle and left them the means to defend it.[36] Páez himself added the final touch. 'The prosperity of Venezuela was the first thought of Bolívar, the first motive of his heroic deeds; we have omitted nothing we could possibly do in honouring his memory. It is not only the triumph of Bolívar that we celebrate: it is also the triumph of Venezuela. We have witnessed the arrival on our shores of the great Bolívar escorted by the warships of powerful nations mixing their flags with ours in honour of the Hero, in honour of Venezuela.'[37]

So the cult of Bolívar was born, and he was reunited with his native Venezuela, a country without a distinguished prehistory or an outstanding colonial experience, and great only in the independence he had won for it. In his lifetime he had gathered around him the Bolivarians, a select group of soldiers and officials who had served him loyally out of respect for his talents and deference to his leadership. Now there were new Bolivarians – historians, journalists, priests, politicians and presidents – who created and guarded a cult around an idealized Bolívar, who served the needs of an abject people. The cultists had a good story. A hero of pure Venezuelan lineage, after a tragic marriage and golden youth in Europe, assumes the leadership of national independence, provides the intellectual base of a continental revolution, and then the military and political talents to create a union of states and win international respect, all the time asserting his manhood as a glorious lover. There were many Bolívars here, with any of whom people could identify. Venezuelan nationalist, American hero, macho male, Bolívar conformed to the roles. But hero-worship was not the same as the cult. This had a greater purpose. Bolívar was a model for the nation. A post-colonial people who, through no fault of their own, had been rendered incapable of improvement or of enjoying the liberty he had won for them, could be saved by his example and his guidance. Listen to his words and Venezuela can escape from the abyss. He is not God: that would be blasphemy. But he is a saint with a cult parallel to religion, teaching political virtues complementary to the religious truths of the Catholic faith.

The original outpouring of popular and spontaneous feeling for Bolívar was succeeded by a new phase of the cult, more regimented and government-inspired, which passed from a cult of the people to a cult for the people, and in which he was presented as a democrat, a revolutionary, a moral guide and a Catholic.[38] The doctrine was preached from on high and taught in the schools. A Catechism of Venezuelan History gave the correct version of Independence. Referring to the London mission of Simón Bolívar, Luis López Méndez and Andrés Bello in 1810, it asks: Who were the commissioners?

And it answers: The principal was Colonel Simón Bolívar, to whose exertions and talents was subsequently due not only the independence of Venezuela but of almost the whole of South America, and whose glory rose to become the first and most brilliant of the world of Columbus.

As the cult developed, presidents pushed forward to become its leading advocates. Antonio Guzmán Blanco, Illustrious American, dictator in the positivist 'order and progress' style, and far from the Bolivarian model of ruler, took the cult to new heights. In 1874 the equestrian statue of the Liberator was erected in the Plaza Bolívar in Caracas. In October 1876 the remains of Bolívar were solemnly transferred from the cathedral to the new National Pantheon. In 1879 the publication of the *Memorias* of O'Leary was decreed, fulfilling the duty 'to exalt the glories of Venezuela's most illustrious hero'. The high point of Guzmán Blanco's Bolivarianism was reached in July 1883 when he presided over the centenary of Bolívar's birth with extraordinary pomp; a plethora of speeches, articles, celebrations and new statues marked the glorification of the Liberator by a ruler who personified many of the Liberator's notorious aversions. The man who tried to establish a national Venezuelan Church free from Rome, something that Bolívar specifically rejected, exemplified the division between the cult of Bolívar and the real history of the Liberator.

In 1876 Guzmán Blanco had bought the historic town house of the Bolívar family, birthplace of the Liberator, which had been badly damaged in the earthquake of 1812. With the help of public subscription this was later acquired from the dictator's heirs and in October 1912 formally accepted for the nation by Juan Vicente Gómez, another caudillo turned president. Reconstructed and embellished, the Casa Natal del Libertador in the centre of Caracas was inaugurated on 5 July 1921, the anniversary of the battle of Carabobo; it became an archive and gallery, housing the Archivo del Libertador and the works of Tito Salas in celebration of the life of the hero, the whole a shrine to the Liberator. Meanwhile, the Sociedad Bolivariana de Venezuela was promoted to the status of a national institution under the patronage of General Eleazar López Contreras and became the official depositary and guardian of the glory of the Liberator.[39] And Vicente Lecuna, the scholarly custodian of the cult, laid down the authorized version in a series of works designed to dispel doubt and resist dissent.[40]

So Bolívar defies history, 'doomed to death though fated not to die'. The apotheosis has gone far beyond the real Liberator, creating an ideal and a myth, a fiction to serve its authors. Bolívar himself did not establish the cult. Guardian of his own glory, he would have been scornful of any attempt by his fellow Americans to glorify him. Yet his life, his achievements, his great battles became embedded in their culture almost as soon as they happened. The memory of them had many layers. It was kept alive first in pure admiration. Then out of respect. And finally as propaganda, serving a number of needs. He symbolized what Venezuela could be and had so far failed to be; he was the national conscience against which Venezuelans could be judged in their efforts to secure good government and a just society. He was a boon to governments. When Venezuelans were bewildered and needed instant guidance, it was easier to rely on Bolívar to tell them what to do than to develop new policies. Fear of anarchy found consolation in Bolívar, who expressed a similar fear every year of his leadership.

Bolívar compensated for a national feeling of inferiority to the world, especially to Europe. He enabled Venezuelans to raise themselves in international esteem. He was the first Latin American of real universal dimension who enabled them to escape from the tendency to self-deprecation. As a white Venezuelan he could speak to Europe and the United States on equal terms. The thoughts of Bolívar on Spanish American unity and his efforts on behalf of the Congress of Panama were hailed as relevant beyond his own time. In the words of a leading Bolivarian historian, 'Without violent internal crises, without racial hatreds, without religious conflicts, without class struggles, with positive and solid political liberty and equality, Spanish America will be able to devote itself to the peaceful and vigorous conquest and domination of its environment and a realization of its own being by applying the revolutionary plan prepared by Bolívar.'[41]

Juan Vicente González (1810–66), politician and journalist, and fervent admirer of Bolívar, came closest to deifying the Liberator and recommending him to the adoration of Venezuelans, miserable creatures dedicated to the absurd destruction of the great work of one who by his eloquence alone set an example to his countrymen. There was no one his superior, no one his equal. Take away Bolívar, he asked, and what have we left? A crucial question in any explanation of the cult. There were no other great heroes. González was followed closely by Guzmán Blanco, who described him as 'an incomparable man', a 'Semigod': 'Bolívar, like Jesus Christ, is not a hero of a fantastic epic. He is the Liberator of the continent, the Creator of the American republics, the Father of free citizens. He was born for this; for this God endowed him with all the talents, with courage, daring, and perseverance found no where else on earth, in the past, in the present, and in the future.'[42] This interpretation was taken a stage further in more recent times when, in 1980, the Cardinal Archbishop of Caracas referred to the 'sin of Venezuela' in demanding Bolívar's exile in 1830 and thus repudiating his character as the chosen of God: 'The infamous proposal of exile against the Father of the Patria, accepted without protest by the Venezuelan nation, was a clear rejection of his character as the divine chosen one. And this is the reason why ever since 1830, when this iniquity was committed, our national history for the whole of the past century can be summarized as one of devastating civil wars and prolonged tyrannies, barely separated by brief and precarious periods of peace.'[43] Not a word about the carnage of liberation.

Venezuelan homage to Bolívar culminated in the memorable year 1983. The bicentenary of the Liberator's birth brought together the whole gamut of Bolivarian interest. Government, politicians, the military, academics, the arts, business and somewhere perhaps the people, joined to pay homage to the Liberator in a series of public acts, performances, congresses, publications and endless receptions, all worthy of the hero and a fitting salute to his memory. Serious scholarship had a role, and research as well as adulation paid homage to the Liberator. Ironically, the celebrations were held in the midst of a national crisis, when, with its financial world collapsing, Venezuela continued to spend in style, opening a new metro, hosting international congresses, staging the bicentenary and holding a decisive election. Was 1983 the last year of the cult? From the Liberator there was only silence, no answers, no rescue, and from his admirers no petitions for guidance. But there was still time for a new twist to the story, a modern perversion of the cult.

In 1998 Venezuelans were astonished to learn that their country had been renamed 'the Bolivarian Republic of Venezuela' by decree of President Hugo Chávez, who called himself a 'revolutionary Bolivarian'. Authoritarian populists, or neo-caudillos, or Bolivarian militarists, whatever their designation, invoke Bolívar no less ardently than did previous rulers, though it is doubtful whether he would have responded to their calls. The traditional cult of Bolívar had been used as a convenient ideology by military dictators, culminating in the regimes of Juan Vicente Gómez and Eleazar López Contreras; these had at least more or less respected the basic thought of the Liberator, even when they misrepresented its meaning. But the new heresy, far from maintaining continuity with the constitutional ideas of Bolívar, as was claimed, invented a new attribute, the populist Bolívar, and in the case of Cuba gave him a new identity, the socialist Bolívar. By exploiting the authoritarian tendency, which certainly existed in the thought and action of Bolívar, regimes in Cuba and Venezuela claim the Liberator as a patron for their policies, distorting his ideas in the process.[44] Thus the Bolívar of liberty and equality is appropriated by a Marxist regime, which does not hold liberty and equality in high esteem but needs a substitute for the failed Soviet model. And in Venezuela a populist regime of the twenty-first century, looking for political legitimacy, is drawn to Bolívar as to a magnet, another victim of the spell. Who is to say that it will be the last?

NOTES

Abbreviations

AGN   Archivo General de la Nación, Caracas
BAGN   *Boletín del Archivo General de la Nación*
BANH   Biblioteca de la Academia Nacional de la Historia, Venezuela
BHN   Biblioteca de Historia Nacional, Colombia
BOLANH *Boletín de la Academia Nacional de la Historia*, Caracas
FJB, AL   Fundación John Boulton, Caracas, Archivo del Libertador
HAHR   *Hispanic American Historical Review*
ILAS   Institute of Latin American Studies, London
JLAS   *Journal of Latin American Studies*
PRO   Public Record Office, the National Archives, London

Chapter 1

1. José Domingo Díaz, *Recuerdos sobre la rebelión de Caracas* (BANH, 38, Caracas, 1961), 98–9.
2. Alexander von Humboldt, *Personal Narrative of Travels to the Equinoctial Regions of the New Continent during the Years 1799–1804*, trans. Helen Maria Williams, 6 vols (London, 1814–29), IV, 12–17. Humboldt was not present during the earthquake but used a manuscript narrative of events in Caracas in 1812 by Luis Delpeche.
3. *Gaceta de Caracas*, 25 April 1812.
4. The 'Detached Recollections' of General D. F. O'Leary, ed. R. A. Humphreys (London, 1969), 36.
5. Robert J. Ferry, *The Colonial Elite of Early Caracas: Formation and Crisis 1567–1767* (Berkeley and Los Angeles, 1989), 208–11.
6. Message to the Constituent Congress of the Republic of Colombia, Bogotá, 20 January 1830, Simón Bolívar, *Obras completas*, ed. Vicente Lecuna and Esther Barret de Nazarís, 3 vols (2nd edn, Havana, 1950), III, 812.
7. Alexander von Humboldt, *Personal Narrative*, trans. Jason Wilson (London, 1995), 163.
8. John V. Lombardi, *People and Places in Colonial Venezuela* (Bloomington, Indiana, 1976).
9. Ildefonso Leal, *La Universidad de Caracas en los años de Bolívar 1783–1830*, 2 vols (Caracas, 1983), I, 27–33.
10. Humboldt, *Personal Narrative*, trans. Helen Maria Williams, III, 472–6.

11. Merle E. Simmons, 'Los escritos de Juan Pablo Viscardo y Guzmán, Precursor de la Independencia Hispanoamericana' (Caracas, 1983), *Esquisse Politique*, 236, and *La Paix et le bonheur*, 332–3.

12. Jamaica Letter, or 'Contestación de un americano meridonial a un caballero de esta isla', Kingston, setiembre 6 de 1815, Sociedad Bolivariana de Venezuela, *Escritos del Libertador*, VIII (Caracas, 1972), 233.

13. Mark A. Burkholder and D.S. Chandler, *From Impotence to Authority: The Spanish Crown and the American Audiencias, 1687–1808* (Columbia, Missouri, 1977), 191–2.

14. Jamaica Letter, *Escritos*, VIII, 233–4.

15. A verdict from within by Manuel Godoy, Príncipe de la Paz, *Memorias*, 2 vols (Biblioteca de Autores Españoles, 88–9, Madrid, 1956), I, 416.

16. Ferry, *The Colonial Elite of Early Caracas*, 254.

17. Juan Vicente de Bolívar, Martín de Tobar, and marqués de Mixares to Miranda, Caracas, 24 February 1782, Francisco de Miranda, *Colombeia*, II (Caracas, 1979), 533–4. In Bogotá and Cuzco popular movements had recently failed when the creoles withdrew their support and left them to be crushed by the royal authorities. The editor of the Miranda documentation, *Colombeia*, II, 31–45, concludes that this 'mysterious' letter is unlikely to be authentic. The Precursor's latest biographer believes it may be a forgery; see Karen Racine, *Francisco de Miranda: A Transatlantic Life in the Age of Revolution* (Wilmington, Delaware, 2003), 27–8.

18. Salvador de Madariaga, *Bolívar* (London, 1968), 23–4; Tomás Polanco Alcántara, *Simón Bolívar: Ensayo de interpretación biográfica a través de sus documentos* (Caracas, 1994), 38.

19. F. Depons, *Viaje a la parte oriental de Tierra Firme en la América Meridional*, 2 vols (Caracas, 1960), II, 14–92; Federico Brito Figueroa, *Historia económica y social de Venezuela*, 2 vols (Caracas, 1966), I, 63–121, 160.

20. Humboldt, *Personal Narrative*, trans. Helen Maria Williams, III, 472–6.

21. Racine, *Francisco de Miranda*, 5–6; María del Pilar Rodríguez Mesa, 'Los blancos pobres', *BOLANH*, 80, 317 (1997), 133–88.

22. P. Michael McKinley, *Pre-revolutionary Caracas: Politics, Economy, and Society 1777–1811* (Cambridge, 1985), 80–2.

23. Laureano Vallenilla Lanz, *Obras completas, I. Cesarismo democrático* (Caracas, 1983), 48–50.

24. Santos R. Cortés, *El Régimen de las 'Gracias al Sacar' en Venezuela durante el período hispánico*, 2 vols (Caracas, 1978), I, 469.

25. 'Informe que el ayuntamiento de Caracas hace al rey de España referente a la real cédula de 10 de febrero de 1795', José Félix Blanco and Ramón Azpurúa, eds, *Documentos para la historia de la vida pública del Libertador*, 14 vols (Caracas, 1875–88), I, 267–75.

26. AGN, Gobernación y Capitanía General, lvi, 1795, f. 13, 149, 244.

27. Federico Brito Figueroa, *La estructura económica de Venezuela colonial* (Caracas, 1978), 123–4.

28. Ildefonso Leal, 'La aristocracia criolla venezolana y el código negrero de 1789', *Revista de Historia*, 2 (Caracas, 1961), 61–81.

29. Mariano Arcaya, city attorney of cabildo of Coro, in Federico Brito Figueroa, *Las insurrecciones de los esclavos negros en la sociedad colonial venezolana* (Caracas, 1961), 61–2.

30. Pedro M. Arcaya, *Insurrección de los negros en la serranía de Coro* (Caracas, 1949), 38; Brito, *Insurrecciones de los esclavos negros*, 41–88.

31. For *Las Ordenanzas*, see Pedro Grases, *La Conspiración de Gual y España y el ideario de la Independencia*, in *Preindependencia y Emancipación* (*Obras*, III, Barcelona, 1981), 51–3, 172–7. Detail on the role of Picornell and the action of Dolores Gil in AGN, Gobernación y Capitanía General, lxiv, f. 71, 127.

32. Quoted by Josefina Rodríguez de Alonso in Miranda, *Colombeia*, II, 37.

33. Humboldt, *Personal Narrative*, trans. Helen Maria Williams, III, 414–15.
34. Kathy Waldron, 'The Sinners and the Bishop in Colonial Venezuela: The *Visita* of Bishop Mariano Martí, 1771–1784', Asunción Lavrin, ed., *Sexuality and Marriage in Colonial Latin America* (Lincoln, Nebraska, 1989), 165–6, 170–2.
35. Mariano Martí, *Documentos relativos a su visita pastoral de la diócesis de Caracas, 1771–1784*, 7 vols (ANH, Caracas, 1969), II, 188, 215, 276, 289, 581.
36. Bolívar to Palacios, Cuzco, 10 July 1825, *Obras completas*, II, 163.
37. Bolívar to María Antonia, Cuzco, 10 July 1825, *Obras completas*, II, 162–3.
38. Bolívar to Santander, Arequipa, 20 May 1825, Francisco de Paula Santander, *Cartas Santander-Bolívar*, 6 vols (Bogotá, 1988–90), IV, 378.
39. Polanco Alcántara, *Simón Bolívar*, 13–17.
40. N.E. Navarro, 'Un episodio divertido de la primera educación de Bolívar', BOLANH, 38, 149 (1955), 3–15; Real Audiencia de Caracas, 'Transcipción del expediente', July 1795, ibid., 21–2.
41. Antonio Cussen, *Bello and Bolívar: Poetry and Politics in the Spanish American Revolution* (Cambridge, 1992), 4.
42. Carlos Palacios to Esteban Palacios, 8 October 1799, Vicente Lecuna, 'Adolescencia y juventud de Bolívar. Documentos', BOLANH, 13, 52 (1930), 562.
43. Simón Bolívar to Pedro Palacios Blanco, Veracruz, 20 March 1799, *Obras completas*, I, 13–14, his earliest extant letter.
44. John Lynch, *Bourbon Spain 1700–1808* (Oxford, 1993), 376, 392–5.
45. *Memorias del General Daniel Florencio O'Leary: Narración*, 3 vols (Caracas, 1952), I, 57.
46. Bolívar to Pedro Palacios Blanco, 30 September 1800, in Germán Carrera Damas, ed., *Simón Bolívar Fundamental*, 2 vols (Caracas, 1993), I, 54.
47. Polanco Alcántara, *Simón Bolívar*, 69–70, 74.
48. Marriage documents in Simón Bolívar, *Escritos del Libertador* (Caracas, 1964–), II, 102–6, and BOLANH, 35, 139 (1952), 253; description in O'Leary, *Narración*, I, 57; Marriage declaration in Carrera Damas, *Simón Bolívar Fundamental*, II, 9.
49. O'Leary, *Narración*, I, 59.
50. L. Peru de Lacroix, *Diario de Bucaramanga* (Ediciones Centauro, Caracas, 1976), 62–6.

Chapter 2

1. O'Leary, '*Detached Recollections*', 29–30; Alfredo Boulton, *Los retratos de Bolívar* (2nd edn, Caracas, 1964), 25–8.
2. Suggestions elaborated in Polanco Alcántara, *Simón Bolívar*, 151–6.
3. Fanny du Villars to Bolívar, Paris, 6 April, 14 May 1826, O'Leary, *Memorias del General O'Leary*, 34 vols (Caracas, 1981) XII, 293–300.
4. Charles Minguet, 'Las relaciones entre Alexander von Humboldt y Simón Bolívar', *Bolívar y Europa en las crónicas, el pensamiento politico y la historiografía*, ed. Alberto Filippi, 2 vols (Caracas, 1986–92), I, 743–54.
5. Humboldt to O'Leary, Berlin, 1853, in Minguet, op cit., 746.
6. Bolívar to Humboldt, 10 November 1821, Carrera Damas, *Simón Bolívar Fundamental*, I, 205.
7. O'Leary, *Narración*, I, 61.
8. Peru de Lacroix, *Diario de Bucaramanga*, 64–6.
9. Bolívar to Rodríguez, Pativilca, 19 January 1824, *Obras completas*, I, 881–2.
10. O'Leary, *Narración*, I, 66–7.
11. O'Leary, *Narración*, I, 67–8.
12. Mario Laserna, *Bolívar: Un euro-americano frente a la ilustración* (Bogotá, 1986), 76–7.
13. *Escritos*, IV, 14–16; the text of this vow, the *Juramento de Roma*, was reconstructed years later from memory by Rodríguez and given to Manuel Uribe in 1850, who published it in *Homenaje de Colombia al Libertador* (Bogotá, 1884).

14. Bolívar to Rodríguez, Pativilca, 19 January 1824, Simón Bolívar, *Cartas del Libertador*, ed. Vicente Lecuna (vols 1–10, Caracas, 1929–30; vol. 11, New York, 1948; vol. 12, ed. Manuel Pérez Vila, Caracas, 1959), IV, 32–4.
15. O'Leary, *Narración*, I, 68.
16. Peru de Lacroix, *Diario de Bucaramanga*, 63.
17. Bolívar to Santander, Arequipa, 20 May 1825, *Cartas Santander–Bolívar*, IV, 378; see also Manuel Pérez Vila, *La formación intelectual del Libertador* (2nd edn, Caracas, 1979), 16–20.
18. Pérez Vila, *La formación intelectual del Libertador*, 189–216, identifies eight lists of books, 299 in all.
19. O'Leary, *Narración*, I, 63–4, II, 34; Bolívar, 'Método que se debe seguir en la educación de mi sobrino Fernando Bolívar', Carrera Damas, *Simón Bolívar Fundamental*, II, 157–8.
20. Angostura Address, 15 February 1819, *Obras completas*, III, 683.
21. R. R. Palmer, *The Age of the Democratic Revolution. A Political History of Europe and America, 1760–1800*, 2 vols (Princeton, 1959–64); E. J. Hobsbawm, *The Age of Revolution. Europe 1789–1848* (London, 1962), 53.
22. John Lynch, 'Simón Bolívar and the Age of Revolution', *Latin America between Colony and Nation* (London, 2001), 134–46, 161–2.
23. Miranda to Gual, 31 December 1799, *Archivo del General Miranda*, 24 vols (Caracas, 1929–50), XV, 404.
24. Grases, *Preindependencia y Emancipación*, 378.
25. Cartagena Manifesto, 15 December 1812, *Escritos*, IV, 123.
26. Leal, *La Universidad de Caracas en los años de Bolívar 1783–1830*, I, 64–5.
27. Luis Castro Leiva, *La Gran Colombia: Una ilusion ilustrada* (Caracas, 1985), 66, 74–6.
28. Pérez Vila, *La formación intelectual del Libertador*, 184–5.
29. 'The Second Treatise of Government', 2: 102–3, 217, in John Locke, *Two Treatises of Government*, ed. Peter Laslett (Cambridge, 1989), 334–5, 419.
30. Baron de Montesquieu, *The Spirit of the Laws*, ed. Anne M. Cohlen and others (Cambridge, 1989), 328–89, 396.
31. Angostura Address, 15 February 1819, *Obras completas*, III, 683; Ildefonso Méndez Salcedo, *Dos estudios sobre Montesquieu y Bolívar* (Caracas, 1995), 65–75.
32. Luis Castro Leiva, *De la patria boba a la teología bolivariana* (Caracas, 1991), 46–8.
33. Jean-Jacques Rousseau, *The Social Contract and the Discourses*, trans. G.D.H. Cole (London, 1993), 190–1.
34. Norman Hampson, 'The Enlightenment in France', in Roy Porter and Mikulas Teich, *The Enlightenment in National Context* (Cambridge, 1981), 49–50.
35. Frank Holl, 'El científico independiente y su crítica al colonialismo', *Debate y Perspectivas, Cuadernos de Historia y Ciencias Sociales*, 1 (Madrid, 2000), 101–23.
36. Humboldt, *Personal Narrative*, trans. Williams, III, 472–6.
37. Humboldt to O'Leary, Berlin, 1853, in Minguet, 'Las relaciones entre Alexander von Humboldt y Simón Bolívar', 746.
38. *The Collected Works of Jeremy Bentham. Colonies, Commerce, and Constitutional Law: Rid Yourselves of Ultramaria and other Writings on Spain and Spanish America*, ed. Philip Schofield (Oxford, 1995), 124–8.
39. 'Common Sense', in Thomas Paine, *Political Writings*, ed. Bruce Kuklick (Cambridge, 1989), 23, 37–8, 101; 'Rights of Man', ibid., 140–1.
40. Manuel García de Sena, *La Independencia de la Costa Firme justificada por Thomas Paine treinta años ha*, ed. Pedro Grases (Caracas, 1949); see also Pedro Grases, *Libros y libertad* (Caracas, 1974), 21–6.
41. Guillaume Thomas François Raynal, *A Philosophical and Political History of the Settlement and Trade of the Europeans in the East and West Indies, By the Abbé Raynal. To which is added the Revolution of America*, 6 vols (Edinburgh, 1782), VI, 265, 300–1, 346.

42. Dominique Dufour De Pradt, *Les trois âges des colonies, ou leur état passé, present et à venir*, 3 vols (Paris, 1801–02), I, v–xi, II, 188–211, III, 299, 316–17, 352–3, 371–2, 508–9.
43. O'Leary, '*Detached Recollections*', 28, and *Narración*, I, 53, 63–4; Peru de Lacroix, *Diario de Bucaramanga*, 114–15.
44. P. Schwartz and C. Rodríguez Braun, 'Las relaciones entre Jeremías Bentham y S. Bolívar', *Bolívar y Europa*, I, 445–60; Jamaica Letter, 6 September 1815, *Escritos*, VIII, 239; Angostura Address, 15 February 1819, *Obras completas*, III, 683; Bolívar to Santander, Tulcán, 31 December 1822, *Cartas Santander–Bolívar*, III, 290–1.
45. Pérez Vila, *La formación intelectual del Libertador*, 81.
46. The theory of overstretch is not a recent invention. It was stated seventy years ago by Richard Pares, *War and Trade in the West Indies 1739–1763* (Oxford, 1936), 1: 'The greatest fault of Spanish imperialism was attempting too much. Its claims vastly exceeded its performance.'
47. Peru de Lacroix, *Diario de Bucaramanga*, 65.

Chapter 3

1. Antonio García-Baquero González, *El comercio colonial en la época del absolutismo ilustrado: Problemas y debates* (Granada, 2003), 324–5; John Fisher, *Commercial Relations between Spain and Spanish America in the Era of Free Trade, 1778–1796* (Liverpool, 1985), 76.
2. E. Arcila Farías, *Economía colonial de Venezuela* (Mexico, 1946), 368–9.
3. García-Baquero González, *El comercio colonial en la época del absolutismo ilustrado*, 333–68.
4. Bolívar to Páez, 4 August 1826, *Obras completas*, II, 445.
5. Recollections of Bello given to Miguel Luis Amunátegui, *Vida de don Andrés Bello* (Santiago, 1882), 37–51.
6. Beaver to Sir Alexander Cochrane, quoted by O'Leary, *Narración*, I, 40.
7. *Conjuración de 1808 en Caracas para la formación de una junta suprema gubernativa (documentos completos)*, Instituto Panamericano de Geografía e Historia, Comisión de Historia, 2 vols (Caracas, 1969), I, 351–77; on the junta movement see Andrés F. Ponte, *La revolución de Caracas y sus próceres* (Caracas, 1960), 46–52.
8. Caracciolo Parra-Pérez, *Historia de la Primera República de Venezuela*, 2 vols (2nd edn, Caracas, 1959), I, 317; Ponte, *La revolución de Caracas*, 29.
9. *Conjuración de 1808*, I, 41–112, 351–77.
10. Ponte, *La revolución de Caracas*, 48–50.
11. Parra-Pérez, *Historia de la Primera República*, I, 333.
12. José Francisco Heredia, *Memorias del regente Heredia* (Caracas, 1986), 64; Parra-Pérez, *Historia de la Primera República*, I, 337–42.
13. Polanco Alcántara, *Simón Bolívar*, 195–7.
14. *Gaceta de Caracas*, 7, 14 April, 5, 20 May 1809.
15. *Textos oficiales de la Primera República de Venezuela*, 2 vols (BANH, 1–2, Caracas, 1959), I, 99–103.
16. Intendant Vicente Basadre, report of 4 July 1810, in *Causas de infidencia*, 2 vols (BANH, 31–2, Caracas, 1960), I, 128.
17. Miranda, circular letter to 'nuestras Américas', 24 March 1810, *Archivo del General Miranda*, XXIII, 367–8.
18. López Méndez to Venezuelan secretary of state, London, 3 October 1810, quoted by María Teresa Berruezo León, *La lucha de Hispanoamérica por su independencia en Inglaterra, 1800–1830* (Madrid, 1989), 91–2.
19. Amunátegui, *Vida de don Andrés Bello*, 93, 95–6.
20. O'Leary, *Narración*, I, 77.

21. On Bolívar in London, see Racine, *Francisco de Miranda*, 200–6, and Polanco Alcántara, *Simón Bolívar*, 226–46.
22. Peru de Lacroix, *Diario de Bucaramanga*, 57–8.
23. Notes on the Caraccas, 5 August 1810, National Archives, PRO, London, FO 72/106.
24. On the Apsley House conversations, see Cristóbal L. Mendoza, *Las primeras misiones diplomáticas de Venezuela*, 2 vols (Caracas, 1962), I, 240–8, 260–9; D. A. G. Waddell, *Gran Bretaña y la Independencia de Venezuela y Colombia* (Caracas, 1983), 63–72.
25. Notes on the Caraccas, 5 August 1810, National Archives, PRO, FO 72/106.
26. 21 July 1810, National Archives, PRO, FO 72/106.
27. Díaz, *Recuerdos sobre la rebelión de Caracas*, 88.
28. Racine, *Francisco de Miranda*, 212–13, 219.
29. Simón Bolívar, *Proclamas y Discursos del Libertador*, ed. Vicente Lecuna (Caracas, 1939), 3.
30. Acta de la Independencia, in *La Constitución Federal de Venezuela de 1811* (BANH, 6, Caracas, 1959), 89–96.
31. Roscio to Bello, 31 August 1811, Amunátegui, *Vida de don Andrés Bello*, 111; Parra-Pérez, *Historia de la Primera República*, II, 80–2.
32. *Constitución Federal*, 151–211; Parra-Pérez, *Historia de la Primera República*, II, 113–20, 131.
33. *Textos oficiales de la Primera República*, II, 95; Parra-Pérez, *Historia de la Primera República*, II, 113–20.
34. *Textos oficiales de la Primera República*, II, 36, 38.
35. Constitution of 1811, II, ii, 26, IX, 203, in *Constitución Federal*, 159–60, 205.
36. Decree of 26 June 1811, *Textos oficiales de la Primera República*, II, 42–3.
37. Narciso Coll y Prat, *Memoriales sobre la independencia de Venezuela* (BANH, 23, Caracas, 1959), 59–60, 63–7.
38. Manifesto to the Nations of the World, 30 September 1813, Carrera Damas, *Simón Bolívar Fundamental*, II, 26.
39. Bolívar to congress of New Granada, Cartagena, 27 November. 1812, O'Leary, *Memorias*, XIII, 57–60.
40. José de Austria, *Bosquejo de la historia militar de Venezuela*, 2 vols (BANH, 29–30, Caracas, 1960), I, 299.
41. Miranda to Sata, secretary of war, 24 July, 13 August 1811, *Selected Writings of Bolívar*, compiled by Vicente Lecuna, ed. Harold A. Bierck Jr., 2 vols (2nd edn, New York, 1951), I, 6–10.
42. Díaz, *Recuerdos sobre la rebelión de Caracas*, 96, 98–9. See Chapter 1.
43. Humboldt, *Personal Narrative*, trans. Williams, IV, 12–17.
44. Austria, *Bosquejo de la historia militar de Venezuela*, I, 298.
45. Vicente Lecuna, *Crónica razonada de las guerras de Bolívar*, 3 vols (New York, 1950), I, xix–xxi.
46. Bolívar to Miranda, 12 July, 14 July 1812, O'Leary, *Memorias*, XXIX, 11–13.
47. Austria, *Bosquejo de la historia militar de Venezuela*, I, 307, 316, 321–2.
48. Racine, *Francisco de Miranda*, 238.
49. Carlos Pi Sunyer, *Patriotas Americanos en Londres* (Caracas, 1978), 89–95; Polanco Alcántara, *Simón Bolívar*, 271–3.
50. O'Leary, *Narración*, I, 113–14, including letter of Wilson to O'Leary, London, 14 July 1832.
51. O'Leary, *Narración*, I, 118; Bolívar, Manifesto to the Nations of the World, Carrera, *Simón Bolívar Fundamental*, II, 29–30.
52. Pedro Gual, personal secretary and confidant of Miranda, was with him in La Guaira at the fateful time; he reports that Miranda was reading an urgent request for assistance from President Torrices of Cartagena and proposing to go there; Gual, Bogotá, 15 February 1843, in Blanco and Azpurúa, eds, *Documentos para la historia de la vida pública del Libertador*, III, 760–1.

53. Cussen, *Bello and Bolívar*, 106–7.
54. Polanco Alcántara, *Simón Bolívar*, 289–95.
55. Bolívar to Iturbe, Curaçao, 10, 19 September 1812, O'Leary, *Memorias*, XXIX, 13–16.

Chapter 4

1. Hermes Tovar Pinzón, 'La lenta ruptura con el pasado colonial (1810–1850)', *Historia económica de Colombia*, ed. José Antonio Ocampo (Bogotá, 1987), 88.
2. Rebecca A. Earle, *Spain and the Independence of Colombia 1810–1825* (Exeter, 2000), 23–4.
3. Simón Bolívar and Vicente Tejera, Cartagena, 27 November 1812, O'Leary, *Memorias*, XIII, 57–60.
4. Bolívar, *Memoria dirigida a los ciudadanos de la Nueva Granada por un caraqueño*, Cartagena, 15 December 1812, *Escritos*, IV, 116–27.
5. Mario Laserna, *Bolívar: Un euro-americano frente a la ilustración*, 90–2.
6. Anthony McFarlane, 'Identity, Enlightenment and Political Dissent in Late Colonial Spanish America', *Transactions of the Royal Historical Society*, sixth series, 8 (1998), 309–35.
7. Speech to the people of Tenerife on the banks of the Magdalena, 24 December 1812, *Escritos*, IV, 127–30; Manuel Pérez Vila, *Simón Bolívar, Doctrina del Libertador* (2nd edn, Caracas, 1979), 17–19.
8. O'Leary, *Narración*, I, 133–9.
9. Bolívar to the army of Cartagena and the Union, 10 March 1813, O'Leary, *Memorias*, XIII, 151–2.
10. O'Leary, *Narración*, I, 154–5.
11. José Francisco Heredia, *Memorias del regente Heredia* (BANH, 186, Caracas, 1986), 67.
12. On this, the *campaña admirable*, see Lecuna, *Crónica razonada*, I, 1–73.
13. Pedro de Urquinaona y Pardo, *Memorias de Urquinaona* (Madrid, 1917), 254; Heredia, *Memorias*, 97, 145; Bolívar to President of the Union, Cúcuta, 6 April 1813, O'Leary, *Memorias*, XIII, 172; Bolívar, Manifesto to the Nations of the World, Valencia, 20 September 1813, Carrera Damas, *Simón Bolívar Fundamental*, II, 25–35; Gabriel E. Muñoz, *Monteverde: cuatro años de historia patria 1812–1816*, 2 vols (BANH, 42–3, Caracas, 1987), I, 429.
14. Bolívar, 'Aprobación con reservas', Cúcuta, 20 March 1813, *Escritos*, IV, 166–73.
15. O'Leary, *Narración*, I, 156.
16. Proclamation, Mérida, 8 June 1813, O'Leary, *Memorias*, XIII, 246–7; see also *Narración*, I, 158.
17. Decree of War to the Death, Trujillo, 15 June 1813, *Escritos*, IV, 305–7.
18. Manifiesto de Carúpano, 7 September 1814, *Escritos*, VI, 390–5.
19. Bolívar to President of the Union, Mérida, 31 May 1813, O'Leary, *Memorias*, XIII, 238.
20. Bolívar to Governor of Trujillo, 22 June 1813, O'Leary, *Memorias*, XIII, 278.
21. Bolívar, Proclamation, Trujillo, 22 June 1813, O'Leary, *Memorias*, XIII, 270.
22. O'Leary, *Narración*, I, 172.
23. *Gaceta de Caracas*, No. 1, 26 August 1813, 4, a more trustworthy account than the sensational story spread by Ducoudray-Holstein which has Bolívar riding in a chariot drawn by the girls.
24. H.L.V. Ducoudray-Holstein, *Memoirs of Simón Bolívar, President, Liberator of the Republic of Colombia*, 2 vols (London, 1830), I, 151, 156–7.
25. Bolívar, Proclamation of General of Army of Liberation, Caracas, 8 August 1813, O'Leary, *Memorias*, XIII, 332–3.
26. Caracciolo Parra-Pérez, *Mariño y la independencia de Venezuela*, 5 vols (Madrid, 1954–7), I, 134–8.

27. Ibid., I, 245.
28. Bolívar to Mariño, Valencia, 16 December 1813, *Cartas del Libertador*, I, 88.
29. Heredia, *Memorias*, 159.
30. Decoudray-Holstein, *Memoirs of Simón Bolívar*, I, 156–7.
31. Bolívar to Richard Wellesley, 14 January 1814, *Escritos*, VI, 63.
32. Speech to assembly in the convent of San Jacinto, Caracas, 2 January 1814, *Escritos*, VI, 8–9.
33. Parra-Pérez, *Mariño y la independencia de Venezuela*, I, 325–6.
34. Bolívar to Coll y Prat, Caracas, 10 August 1813, Carrera Damas, *Simón Bolívar Fundamental*, I, 70–1; Alberto Gutiérrez, *La Iglesia que entendió el Libertador Simón Bolívar* (Bogotá, 1981), 70–4.
35. Bolívar to municipality of Caracas, 18 October 1813, O'Leary, *Memorias*, XIII, 397.
36. Heredia, *Memorias*, 66.
37. Heredia, *Memorias*, 97, 145; Urquinaona, *Memorias*, 86, 114, 254.
38. Bolívar to governor of Curaçao, 2 October, 9 October 1813, *Escritos*, V, 12–14, 113, 204.
39. Richard Vowell, *Campaigns and Cruises in Venezuela and New Grenada and in the Pacific Ocean from 1817 to 1830*, 3 vols (London, 1831), I, 76.
40. Bolívar to president of congress of New Granada, Caracas, 14 August 1813, *Escritos*, V, 29.
41. Bolívar to governor of Valencia, 9 September 1813, O'Leary, *Memorias*, XIII, 357; Bolívar to Santander, Pamplona, 1 November 1819, *Cartas Santander–Bolívar*, I, 186–7.
42. Bolívar to congress of New Granada, 4 September 1813, O'Leary, *Memorias*, XIII, 355.
43. Bolívar to governor of Curaçao, 2 October, 9 October 1813, *Escritos*, V, 204–5.
44. Bolívar to Coll y Prat, 8 February 1814, Carrera Damas, *Simón Bolívar Fundamental*, I, 75–6.
45. O'Leary, *Narración*, I, 201–2.
46. Quoted by Germán Carrera Damas, 'Segunda República venezolana', *Tres temas de historia* (2nd edn, Caracas, 1978), 141–3.
47. 'Reflexiones sobre el estado actual de los Llanos', 6 December 1813, quoted by Germán Carrera Damas, *Boves, aspectos socio-económicos de su acción histórica* (2nd edn, Caracas, 1968), 158.
48. O'Leary, *Narración*, I, 195–7, 225–36; O'Leary, '*Detached Recollections*', 34–6.
49. Carrera Damas, *Boves*, 170–88.
50. 'Memorial presentado al Rey en Madrid por el Pbro. Doctor don José Ambrosio Llamozas, Vicario General del Ejército de Barlovento, en las provincias de Venezuela', *BOLANH*, 18, 71 (1935), 168.
51. Ibid., 169.
52. Heredia, *Memorias*, 41–51, 239.
53. Austria, *Bosquejo de la historia militar de Venezuela*, II, 256.
54. Bolívar to the Editor, *Royal Gazette*, Kingston, Jamaica, 28 September 1815, in Pérez Vila, *Doctrina del Libertador*, 75–9; Heredia, *Memorias*, 172.
55. Austria, *Bosquejo de la historia militar de Venezuela*, II, 222, 226.
56. O'Leary, *Narración*, I, 212–13.
57. O'Leary, *Narración*, I, 230–1.
58. Díaz, *Recuerdos sobre la rebelión de Caracas*, 308–12.
59. Ibid., 311.
60. Polanco Alcántara, *Simón Bolívar*, 356–7.
61. Bolívar, Manifiesto de Carúpano, 7 September 1814, *Escritos*, VI, 390–5.
62. Bolívar to division of Urdaneta, Pamplona, 12 November 1814, *Obras completas*, III, 614.
63. Camilo Torres, in Bolívar, *Escritos*, X, 458.
64. Bolívar to Juan Jurado, 8 December 1814; Pey and Duquesne to citizens of Bogotá, 16 December 1814, O'Leary, *Memorias*, XIII, 558; Peru de Lacroix, *Diario de Bucaramanga*, 185.

65. Bolívar, Address on inauguration of government of United Provinces of New Granada, 23 January 1815, Pérez Vila, *Doctrina del Libertador*, 46–50.
66. Bolívar, Proclamation in La Popa, 8 May 1815, O'Leary, *Memorias*, XV, 14–15.
67. Bolívar, Jamaica Letter, 6 September 1815, *Escritos*, VIII, 222–48.

Chapter 5

1. The total for the whole war of independence would be about 41,000, regarded as small for an imperial army in a large region; see Earle, *Spain and the Independence of Colombia*, 30–1, 70–1.
2. Margaret L. Woodward, 'The Spanish Army and the Loss of America, 1810–1824', *HAHR*, 48 (1968), 586–607.
3. O'Leary, *Narración*, I, 297–8; Stephen K. Stoan, *Pablo Morillo and Venezuela, 1815–1820* (Columbus, Ohio, 1974), 83–4, 163.
4. Bolívar to Richard Wellesley, Kingston, 27 May 1815, O'Leary, *Memorias*, XXIX, 46.
5. Bolívar, *Escritos*, VIII, 222–48; the Jamaica Letter was first published in English in the *Jamaica Quarterly Journal and Literary Gazette* in July 1818 and in a Spanish version in Caracas in 1833.
6. Mark A. Burkholder and D.S. Chandler, *From Impotence to Authority: The Spanish Crown and the American Audiencias, 1687–1808*, 10–11, 74–5, 104–6.
7. O'Leary, '*Detached Recollections*', 38.
8. Bolívar to the Editor, *Royal Gazette*, 28 September 1815, *Selected Writings*, I, 125.
9. To the Editor, *Royal Gazette*, 15 August 1815, O'Leary, *Memorias*, XXIX, 54–60.
10. El Americano, after 28 September 1815, Pérez Vila, *Doctrina del Libertador*, 75–9.
11. R.A. Humphreys, 'British Merchants and South American Independence', *Tradition and Revolt in Latin America* (London, 1969), 117–20.
12. Bolívar to Maxwell Hyslop, 19 May 1815, O'Leary, *Memorias*, XXIX, 45–6.
13. Bolívar to Maxwell Hyslop, 30 October, 8 November 1815, O'Leary, *Memorias*, XXIX, 66–7.
14. Bolívar to Maxwell Hyslop, 3 December 1815, O'Leary, *Memorias*, XXIX, 67–8.
15. *Royal Gazette*, Kingston, 16, 23 December 1815, O'Leary, *Memorias*, XV, 28–33; *Narración*, I, 333.
16. Paul Verna, *Pétion y Bolívar* (Caracas, 1969), 157–61; Lecuna, *Crónica razonada*, I, 418.
17. John Lynch, *Caudillos in Spanish America 1800–1850* (Oxford, 1992), 4–6, 35–6.
18. O'Leary, *Narración*, I, 350.
19. Francisco Rivas Vicuña, *Las guerras de Bolívar*, 7 vols (Bogotá, 1934–8, Santiago, 1940), II, 85–95.
20. Austria, *Bosquejo de la historia militar de Venezuela*, II, 454–6.
21. Ibid., II, 388.
22. Ibid., II, 385.
23. 'Acta de Reconocimiento de Bolívar como Jefe Supremo', 6 May 1816, *Escritos*, IX, 123–6.
24. Bolívar, Ocumare, 6 July 1816, O'Leary, *Memorias*, XV, 84; *Escritos*, IX, 188, 352.
25. Bolívar to Fernández Madrid, Bogotá, 6 March 1830, Carrera Damas, *Simón Bolívar Fundamental*, I, 611–13. Soublette refers discreetly to the 'love' factor, a remark which enraged Lecuna: O'Leary, *Narración*, I, 469; Lecuna, *Crónica razonada*, I, 469, II, 17.
26. O'Leary, *Narración*, I, 371–2.
27. Ibid., I, 385.
28. Bolívar to Piar, 10 January 1817, *Escritos*, X, 46.
29. Bolívar to Pétion, on board the *Indio Libre*, Jacmel, 4 September 1816, *Escritos*, IX, 341–2, 344–5.
30. Bolívar to Páez, Angostura, 15 September 1817, O'Leary, *Memorias*, XV, 295–7.

31. Bolívar to Páez, 4 October, 4 November 1817, ibid., XV, 324–6, 445–7.
32. Díaz, *Recuerdos sobre la rebelión de Caracas*, 328.
33. Buenaventura de Carrocera, *Misión de los Capuchinos en Guayana*, 3 vols (BANH, Caracas, 1979), III, 13–14, 318–23; O'Leary, *Narración*, I, 390–1.
34. Blanco y Azpurúa, *Documentos para la historia de la vida pública del Libertador*, V, 646–7.
35. See the account in Tomás Cipriano de Mosquera, *Memoria sobre la vida del General Simón Bolívar, Libertador de Colombia, Perú y Bolivia* (Bogotá, 1954), 221–2, who adds, 'Many years later I heard the Liberator again condemn the Caroní massacre in our presence with the utmost severity.'
36. Bolívar to Nariño, Barinas, 21 April 1821, Carrera Damas, *Simón Bolívar Fundamental*, I, 187.
37. Manifesto to the Peoples of Venezuela, 5 August 1817, *Escritos*, X, 338; Bolívar to O'Leary, Guayaquil, 13 September 1829, Carrera Damas, *Simón Bolívar Fundamental*, I, 588–94.
38. Parra-Pérez, *Mariño y la independencia de Venezuela*, II, 368.
39. Díaz, *Recuerdos sobre la rebelión de Caracas*, 336.
40. Piar to Bolívar, San Felipe, 31 January 1817, O'Leary, *Memorias*, XV, 150–5.
41. Bolívar to Piar, 19 June 1817, *Escritos*, X, 264.
42. Morillo to Minister of War, 8 May 1817, Antonio Rodríguez Villa, *El teniente general don Pablo Morillo, primer conde de Cartagena, marqués de La Puerta*, 4 vols (Madrid, 1908–10), III, 379–85.
43. Bolívar to Briceño Méndez, 19 June 1817, O'Leary, *Memorias*, XXIX, 113–14.
44. Manifesto to the Peoples of Venezuela, 5 August 1817, *Escritos*, X, 335–40.
45. Bolívar to Cedeño, 24 September 1817, *Escritos*, XI, 91.
46. Bolívar, Manifesto to the peoples of Venezuela, 5 August 1817, ibid., X, 337.
47. Peru de Lacroix, *Diario de Bucaramanga*, 116–17.
48. Bolívar, Manifesto to the peoples of Venezuela, 5 August 1817, *Escritos*, X, 339.
49. Proclamation, 17 October 1817, *Escritos*, XI, 253–4.
50. Peru de Lacroix, *Diario de Bucaramanga*, 58–9.
51. Díaz, *Recuerdos sobre la rebelión de Caracas*, 353.
52. O'Leary, *Narración*, I, 223.
53. Bolívar, Villa del Norte, 23 May 1816, *Obras completas*, III, 634–5; Carúpano, 2 June 1816, *Decretos del Libertador*, ed. Vicente Lecuna, 3 vols (Caracas, 1961), I, 55–6.
54. Austria, *Bosquejo de la historia militar de Venezuela*, II, 448.
55. Decree, 24 September 1817, *Escritos*, XI, 94–5.
56. Regulation, 7 June 1817, Decree, 23 September 1817, O'Leary, *Memorias*, XV, 264–8, 304–7.
57. Bolívar to Bermúdez, 7 November 1817, O'Leary, *Memorias*, XV, 449–50; Rivas Vicuña, *Las guerras de Bolívar*, III, 63–4.
58. Clément Thibaud, *Repúblicas en armas: Los ejércitos bolivarianos en la Guerra de Independencia (Colombia–Venezuela, 1810–1821)*, (Bogotá, 2003), 44, 282–7.
59. Decree, 30 October 1817, *Escritos*, XI, 318–20.
60. Bolívar to Mariño, 17 September 1817, *Escritos*, XI, 27; Bolívar to Mariño, 11 November 1817, O'Leary, *Memorias*, XV, 454–5.
61. Bolívar to Zaraza, 3 October 1817, to Monagas, 30 October 1817, *Escritos*, XI, 157–8, 160.
62. Parra-Pérez, *Mariño y la independencia de Venezuela*, II, 497–8.
63. Proclamation, 17 July 1817, Simón Bolívar, *Proclamas y Discursos del Libertador*, 157–8.
64. José Antonio Páez, *Autobiografía del General José Antonio Páez*, 2 vols (Caracas, 1973), I, 86–7.
65. O'Leary, *Narración*, I, 397.

66. Páez, *Autobiografía*, I, 124.
67. O'Leary, *Narración*, I, 451–2; Lecuna, *Crónica razonada*, II, 122–30.
68. Quoted by R.B. Cunninghame Graham, *José Antonio Páez* (London, 1929), 108–9, 114–15, 134; O'Leary, *Narración*, I, 451.
69. Díaz, *Recuerdos sobre la rebelión de Caracas*, 324.
70. Páez, *Autobiografía*, I, 128.
71. Richard Vowell, *Campaigns and Cruises in Venezuela and New Grenada*, I, 65–8. Spelt Vawell in the British Library catalogue. On the experienced mercenaries as an influential component of a new generation of officers, see Thibaud, *Repúblicas en armas*, 411–25.
72. Bolívar to Morillo, 13 February 1818, O'Leary, *Memorias*, XV, 571.
73. Bolívar to Páez, Calabozo, 24 February, 28 February 1818, O'Leary, *Memorias*, XV, 600, 601.
74. O'Leary, '*Detached Recollections*', 39–40.
75. Páez, *Autobiografía*., I, 153–4; O'Leary, *Narración*, I, 489–91, '*Detached Recollections*', 19–20; Bolívar to Páez, Angostura, 25 June 1818, O'Leary, *Memorias*, XVI, 58.
76. O'Leary, *Narración*, I, 461.
77. Speech to council of state, Angostura, 1 October 1818, O'Leary, *Memorias*, XVI, 103.
78. Polanco Alcántara, *Simón Bolívar*, 412–14.
79. Rodríguez Villa, *Pablo Morillo*, IV, 626–9; Earle, *Spain and the Independence of Colombia*, 70, 86.
80. Bolívar, Declaration of Angostura, 20 November 1818, Carrera Damas, *Simón Bolívar Fundamental*, II, 68–71.

Chapter 6

1. O'Leary, *Narración*, I, 496.
2. *Correo del Orinoco*, 20 February 1819.
3. Angostura Address, 15 February 1819, Simón Bolívar, *Obras completas*, III, 674–97; first published in abridged form in the *Correo del Orinoco*, 20, 27 February, 6, 13 March 1819; an English version was published at the same time in Angostura, and a Spanish version, revised by Bolívar, in Bogotá in April 1820. See Pedro Grases, *El Libertador y la Constitución de Angostura de 1819* (Caracas, 1970).
4. Angostura Address, *Obras completas*, III, 679.
5. Jamaica Letter, *Escritos*, VIII, 241.
6. Contract with H.C. Wilson, 1 July 1817, with G. Hippisley, 15 October 1817, O'Leary, *Memorias*, XV, 270–3, 345–7. In addition to the soldiers some 1,000 sailors also served.
7. Eric Lambert, 'Los legionarios británicos', *Bello y Londres*, Segundo Congreso del Bicentenario, 2 vols (Caracas, 1980–81), I, 355–76; see also the same author's *Voluntarios británicos e irlandeses en la gesta bolivariana*, 3 vols. (Caracas, 1983–93). For a conceptual as well as narrative assessment of the foreign adventurers see Matthew Brown, 'Esclavitud, castas y extranjeros en las guerras de la Independencia de Colombia', *Historia y Sociedad*, 10 (2004), 109–25.
8. D.A.G. Waddell, 'British Neutrality and Spanish-American Independence: The Problem of Foreign Enlistment', *JLAS*, 19, 1 (1987), 1–18.
9. Proclama de Morillo a los Jefes ingleses, Achaguas, 26 March 1819, Rodríguez Villa, *Pablo Morillo*, IV, 108–9, as quoted.
10. A British Officer in the service of Venezuela, Margarita, 1 July 1819, *Correo del Orinoco*, 27 November 1819.
11. John P. Hamilton, *Travels through the Interior Provinces of Colombia*, 2 vols (London, 1827), I, 31.
12. Charles Stuart Cochrane, *Journal of a Residence and Travels in Colombia, during the years 1823 and 1824*, 2 vols (London, 1825), I, 496.

13. Carlos Pi Sunyer, *Patriotas americanos en Londres*, 242.
14. Barreiro to Sámano, 13, 23 March 1819, Alberto Lee López, ed., *Los Ejércitos del Rey*, 2 vols (Bogotá, 1989), II, 7–8, 29–32; Santander to Bolívar, 29 April, 5 May 1819, *Cartas Santander–Bolívar*, I, 83–9.
15. Angostura Address, 15 February 1819, *Obras completas*, III, 695–6.
16. Earle, *Spain and the Independence of Colombia*, 133, and the same author's 'Popular Participation in the Wars of Independence in New Granada', Anthony McFarlane and Eduardo Posada-Carbó, eds, *Independence and Revolution in Spanish America: Perspectives and Problems* (ILAS, London, 1999), 87–101.
17. Bolívar to Páez, Angostura, 19 August 1818, O'Leary, *Memorias*, XVI, 86; to Granadinos, 15 August 1818, ibid., XVI, 84.
18. O'Leary, *Narración*, I, 543.
19. O'Leary, '*Detached Recollections*', 40, who does not give a date for this incident in the *llanos*.
20. Bolívar to Santander, Cañafistola, 20 May 1819, *Cartas Santander–Bolívar*, I, 92; Morillo to Secretary of War, Calabozo, 12 May 1819, Rodríguez Villa, *Pablo Morillo*, II, 401, IV, 25–32.
21. O'Leary, '*Detached Recollections*', 20–1, 54–5; *Narración*, I, 546–51.
22. Bolívar to Páez, Arauca, 4 and 5 June 1819, O'Leary, *Memorias*, XVI, 391–6; Páez to Bolívar, 24 May, 15, 28 June, 21 July 1819, ibid., II, 28–35.
23. O'Leary, *Narración*, I, 555.
24. Bolívar to Vice-President Paya, 30 June 1819, O'Leary, *Memorias*, XVI, 406.
25. Vowell, *Campaigns and Cruises in Venezuela and New Grenada*, I, 163.
26. Bolívar to Zea, Bolívar to Páez, 30 June 1819, to the inhabitants of New Granada, Paya, 30 June 1819, O'Leary, *Memorias*, XVI, 404–7.
27. Francisco de Paula Santander, *Escritos autobiográficos 1820–1840*, ed. Guillermo Hernández de Alba (Bogotá, 1988), 7.
28. O'Leary, *Narración*, I, 572.
29. Lambert, *Voluntarios británicos e irlandeses en la gesta bolivariana*, I, 32.
30. O'Leary, *Narración*, I, 576–9; Soublette, *Boletín del Ejército Libertador*, 8 August 1819, O'Leary, *Memorias*, XVI, 429–30.
31. Earle, *Spain and the Independence of Colombia*, 136–7.
32. *Boletín del Ejército Libertador*, 11 August 1819, O'Leary, *Memorias*, XVI, 431.
33. Rodríguez Villa, *Pablo Morillo*, IV, 70–1.
34. Bolívar to Santander, 8 November 1819, *Cartas Santander–Bolívar*, I, 204.
35. Bolívar, Proclamation, Santa Fe, 26 August 1819, O'Leary, *Memorias*, XVI, 576.
36. O'Leary, *Narración*, II, 8.
37. O'Leary, '*Detached Recollections*', 12.
38. Santander to Bolívar, 17 October 1819, *Cartas Santander–Bolívar*, I, 156.
39. O'Leary, *Narración*, I, 584–8; Santander to Bolívar, 17 October 1819, *Cartas Santander–Bolívar*, I, 154–8.
40. Bolívar to Santander, Pamplona, 26 October 1819, *Cartas Santander–Bolívar*, I, 176–8; Zea to Bolívar, St Thomas, 30 March 1820, O'Leary, *Memorias*, IX, 255.
41. Santander, *Escritos autobiográficos*, 15.
42. O'Leary, *Narración*, I, 552–5.
43. Bolívar to Santander, 30 May, 22 July 1820, *Cartas Santander–Bolívar*, II, 167–9, 244.
44. *Correo del Orinoco*, 11 December 1819.
45. Bolívar to congress, Angostura, 14 December 1819, O'Leary, *Memorias*, XVI, 565, XXVIII, 18.
46. Santander to Bolívar, 15 February 1820, *Cartas Santander–Bolívar*, II, 10–15.
47. O'Leary, *Narración*, II, 32–6.
48. Bolívar to Santander, 1 June 1820, Carrera Damas, *Simón Bolívar Fundamental*, I, 170.

49. Bolívar to Santander, 19 June, 1 August 1820, Santander to Bolívar, 13 August 1820, *Cartas Santander–Bolívar*, II, 188, 259, 270–1.
50. See Chapter 7.
51. O'Leary, '*Detached Recollections*', 12.
52. Morillo to minister of war, 30 September 1819, Rodríguez Villa, *Pablo Morillo*, IV, 70.
53. Bolívar to Gabriel de Torres, Turbaco, 29 August 1820, O'Leary, *Narración*, II, 44; Bolívar to Soublette, Rosario, 19 June 1820, O'Leary, *Memorias*, XXIX, 162.
54. Lecuna, *Crónica razonada*, II, 463–6; O'Leary, *Narración*, II, 58.
55. Bolívar to Morillo, 30 November 1820, O'Leary, *Memorias*, XXIX, 177; Peru de Lacroix, *Diario de Bucaramanga*, 121–2.
56. Relación de la entrevista de Santa Ana, Rodríguez Villa, *Pablo Morillo*, IV, 320–3.
57. O'Leary, *Narración*, I, 4.
58. Bolívar to Santander, 29 November 1820, *Cartas Santander–Bolívar*, III, 71–4.
59. Resumen sucinto de la vida del General Sucre, 1825, *Archivo de Sucre* (Caracas, 1973), I, xli.
60. Sucre to Bolívar, 17 October 1817, ibid,. I, 12.
61. O'Leary, *Narración*, II, 68.
62. Briceño Méndez to Sucre, Bogotá, 21 January 1821, Bolívar, Instrucciones, 21 January 1821, O'Leary, *Memorias*, XVIII, 30–5.
63. O'Leary, *Narración*, II, 68–9.
64. Bolívar to La Torre, 19 February 1821, O'Leary, *Memorias*, XVIII, 77–80.
65. Proclamation, 17 April 1821, Simón Bolívar, *Proclamas y Discursos del Libertador*, 256–7.
66. Bolívar to Santander, Valencia, 25 June 1821, *Cartas Santander–Bolívar*, III, 115–17.
67. Bolívar to Gual, Guanare, 24 May 1821, O'Leary, *Memorias*, XXIX, 207.
68. O'Leary, *Narración*, II, 81–3; see also Briceño Méndez, Caracas, 30 June, 1821, O'Leary, *Memorias*, XVIII, 350–5; Lecuna, *Crónica Reservada*, III, 39–56.
69. *Carabobo 24 June 1821: Some Accounts Written in English*, ed. Eric Lambert (Caracas, 1974), 25.
70. La Torre, Puerto Cabello, 6 July 1821, O'Leary, *Memorias*, XVIII, 368.
71. Lambert, 'Los legionarios británicos', 369.
72. O'Leary, *Narración*, II, 94; elsewhere, O'Leary says that he does not know the exact number but that they were not less than a hundred, '*Detached Recollections*', 51.
73. Bolívar to Santander, 10 July 1821, *Cartas Santander–Bolívar*, III, 119–20.
74. On land policy see Chapter 7.
75. Bolívar to vice-president, Valencia, 16 July 1821, O'Leary, *Memorias*, XVIII, 390–1.

Chapter 7

1. Bolívar to Nariño, 21 April 1821, Carrera Damas, *Simón Bolívar Fundamental*, I, 187.
2. Bolívar to Santander, San Carlos, 13 June 1821, *Cartas Santander–Bolívar*, III, 113–14.
3. O'Leary, *Narración*, II, 99–104.
4. Bolívar to Azuola, 9 March 1821, to Peñalver, 21 April 1821, Carrera Damas, *Simón Bolívar Fundamental*, I, 184–5.
5. Bolívar to Gual, Maracaibo, 16 September 1821, O'Leary, *Memorias*, XXIX, 219–20.
6. Bolívar to president of congress of Colombia, 1 October, Speech to congress, 3 October 1821, O'Leary, *Memorias*, XVIII, 540–3.
7. Cochrane, *Journal of a Residence and Travels in Colombia*, II, 42; John Miller, ed., *Memoirs of General Miller in the Service of the Republic of Peru*, 2 vols (2nd edn, London, 1829), II, 285.
8. Some sources indicate a lower post-war figure. See John V. Lombardi, *People and Places in Colonial Venezuela*, 132; Miguel Izard, *Series estadísticas para la historia de Venezuela*

(Mérida, 1970), 9, and the same author's *El Miedo a la Revolución: La lucha por la libertad en Venezuela (1777–1830)*, 45–7.

9. O'Leary, '*Detached Recollections*', 37–8.
10. Sutherland to Bidwell, Maracaibo, 28 July 1827, National Archives, PRO, FO 18/41.
11. Ker Porter, 15 January 1832, *Sir Robert Ker Porter's Caracas Diary, 1825–1842*, ed. Walter Dupouy, (Caracas, 1966), 597.
12. Andrés Level de Goda, 'Antapodosis', *BOLANH*, 16 (1933), 631.
13. J.A. Polanco Páez to Páez, 8 January 1826, AGN, Intendencia de Venezuela, vol. cclxxxvi.
14. Páez, *Autobiografía*, I, 464.
15. Ker Porter, 21 March, 5 April 1827, 16 December 1830, *Caracas Diary*, 229, 233, 517.
16. Reglamento para Hacendados y criadores del Llano, 25 August 1828, Universidad Central de Venezuela, *Materiales para el estudio de la cuestión agraria en Venezuela (1800–1830)*, vol. I (Caracas, 1964), 511–16.
17. *Decretos del Libertador*, I, 55–6; John V. Lombardi, *The Decline and Abolition of Negro Slavery in Venezuela, 1820–1854* (Westport, 1971), 41–6. On Bolívar's earlier efforts on behalf of the slaves, see Chapter 5.
18. Bolívar to Santander, 10 May, 30 May 1820, *Cartas Santander–Bolívar*, II, 137, 167–8.
19. *Correo del Orinoco*, 5 February 1820.
20. Santander to Bolívar, 2 April 1820, Bolívar to Santander, 18 April 1820, *Cartas Santander–Bolívar*, II, 64, 85–6.
21. Harold H. Bierck, 'The Struggle for Abolition in Gran Colombia', *HAHR*, 33 (1953), 365–86; Lombardi, *Decline and Abolition of Negro Slavery in Venezuela*, 48–50.
22. O'Leary, *Narración*, II, 102–3.
23. *Decretos del Libertador*, II, 345–52; Sutherland to Bidwell, 18 December 1827, National Archives, PRO, FO 18/46.
24. Message to congress of Bolivia, 25 May 1826, *Obras completas*, III, 768–9.
25. Bolívar to Santander, Zumbique, 29 December 1821, *Cartas Santander–Bolívar*, III, 178.
26. Juan Paz del Castillo, Memoria sobre el estado político y militar del Ecuador, Quito, 6 September 1825, O'Leary, *Memorias*, XXIII, 309.
27. Decrees of 20 May 1820 and 12 February 1821, *Decretos del Libertador*, I, 194–7, 227–30.
28. *Actas del Congreso de Cúcuta 1821*, Biblioteca de la Presidencia de la República, 3 vols (Bogotá, 1989), III, 201–3.
29. Timothy E. Anna, *The Fall of the Royal Government in Peru* (Lincoln, Nebraska, 1979), 62–3.
30. Decrees of 8 April, 4 July 1825, *Decretos del Libertador*, I, 295–6, 410–11.
31. Decree of 4 July 1825, *Decretos del Libertador*, I, 407–8.
32. Decree of 15 October 1828, *Decretos del Libertador*, III, 171–8.
33. Bolívar to Santander, 28 June 1825, *Cartas Santander–Bolívar*, V, 1.
34. Decrees, 3 September, 10 October 1817, *Escritos*, XI, 75–7, 219–21; *Materiales para el estudio de la cuestión agraria*, I, 201–2, 204–5; Bolívar to Zaraza, 11 October 1817, *Escritos*, XI, 227.
35. Angostura Address, *Obras completas*, III, 694.
36. Bolívar to Land Commission, 3 December 1817, *Materiales para el estudio de la cuestión agraria*, I, 211; Parra-Pérez, *Mariño y la independencia de Venezuela*, III, 225.
37. Soublette to Minister of Finance, 5 October 1821, *Materiales para el estudio de la cuestión agraria*, I, 311.
38. Briceño Méndez to Gual, 17 July 1821, O'Leary, *Memorias*, XVIII, 393–5. See also Francisco Miguel López, *Contribución al estudio de la ley de haberes militares y sus repercusiones* (Caracas, 1987), 16–36.
39. Bolívar to Santander, 30 May 1820, *Cartas Santander–Bolívar*, II, 168; Bolívar to Gual, 24 May 1821, O'Leary, *Memorias*, XXIX, 207.
40. Briceño Méndez to Gual, 20 July 1821, O'Leary, *Memorias*, XVIII, 399.
41. Decree, 18 January 1821, *Decretos del Libertador*, I, 222–3.
42. Páez to Santander, February–March 1825, *Materiales para el estudio de la cuestión*

agraria, I, 421–2; David Bushnell, *The Santander Regime in Gran Colombia* (Newark, Delaware, 1954), 281; Izard, *La lucha por la libertad en Venezuela*, 158–63.

43. Antonio M. Briceño to Senate, Bogotá, 30 March 1825, in Bushnell, *Santander Regime*, 279.
44. Briceño Méndez to Gual, 17 July 1821, O'Leary, *Memorias*, XVIII, 39.
45. *El Venezolano*, Caracas, 2 September 1822, *Materiales para el estudio de la cuestión agraria*, I, 327.
46. Peru de Lacroix, *Diario de Bucaramanga*, 112–13.
47. On the economic impact of the war, see Hermes Tovar Pinzón, 'La lenta ruptura con el pasado colonial, 87–117; Anthony McFarlane, 'Economía política y política económica en Colombia, 1819–1850', Antonio Annino, ed., *America Latina: Dallo Stato Coloniale allo Stato Nazione*, 2 vols (Milan, 1987), I, 187–208; Earle, *Spain and the Independence of Colombia*, 92–104.
48. Miguel Izard, 'Período de la Independencia y la Gran Colombia, 1810–1830', *Política y Economía en Venezuela 1810–1976* (Fundación John Boulton, Caracas, 1976), 1–31.
49. Tupper to Canning, La Guaira, 21 February 1824, *British Consular Reports on the Trade and Politics of Latin America 1824–1826*, ed. R.A. Humphreys (London, 1940), 275.
50. Hamilton, *Travels through the Interior Provinces of Colombia*, I, 244–5.
51. Ricketts to Canning, 27 December 1826, *British Consular Reports*, 101–206.
52. Ibid., 195.
53. Captain Basil Hall, *Extracts from a Journal written on the coasts of Chili, Peru, and Mexico in the years 1820, 1821, 1822*, 2 vols (3rd edn, Edinburgh, 1824), I, 268.
54. Jamaica Letter, *Escritos*, VIII, 233–4.
55. Decree, Lima, 12 January 1824, *Decretos del Libertador*, I, 283; Watts to Canning, Cartagena, 9 May 1824, *British Consular Reports*, 258.
56. Cochrane, *Journal of a Residence and Travel in Colombia*, II, 44–5.
57. Hamilton, *Travels through the Interior Provinces of Colombia*, I, 74.
58. Hamilton to Planta, 7 March 1825, National Archives, PRO, FO 18/3.
59. Decree, Quito, 25 June 1822, *Decretos del Libertador*, I, 260–1; Wood to Canning, 28 February 1826, *British Consular Reports*, 226–7.
60. Tupper to Canning, La Guaira, 21 Feb. 1824, *British Consular Reports*, 275–7.
61. Decree, Coro, 20 December 1826, *Decretos del Libertador*, II, 68.
62. Decrees, Cuzco, 5 July 1825, *Decretos del Libertador*, I, 413–15.
63. Decree of 23 December 1828, *Decretos del Libertador*, III, 270.
64. Revenga to Director General de Rentas, José Rafael Revenga, *La hacienda pública de Venezuela en 1828–1830* (Caracas, 1953), 218.
65. Anthony McFarlane, *Colombia before Independence: Economy, Society, and Politics under Bourbon Rule* (Cambridge, 1993), 347–52.
66. Frank Griffith Dawson, *The First Latin American Debt Crisis: The City of London and the 1822–25 Loan Bubble* (New Haven, 1990), 34–7, 56–9, 75–6, 249.
67. Tovar, 'La lenta ruptura con el pasado colonial', 116.
68. Hamilton, *Travels through the Interior Provinces of Colombia*, II, 4.
69. Ibid., I, 34, 259–60.
70. Luis Ospina Vásquez, *Industria y protección en Colombia 1810–1930* (Medellín, 1955), 132–5.
71. Revenga, 5 May, 7 August 1829, *Hacienda pública de Venezuela*, 95–6, 203.
72. Bolívar to Santander, 28 June, 10 July 1825, *Cartas Santander–Bolívar*, V, 1–4, 8–9.
73. Bolívar to Sucre, 22 January 1826, *Obras completas*, II, 296–7.
74. Bolívar to Santander, Potosí, 21 October 1825, *Cartas Santander–Bolívar*, V, 86.
75. Bolívar to Páez, Bogotá, 16 August 1828, *Obras completas*, II, 945.
76. Charles Milner Ricketts to Canning, Lima, 27 December 1826, *British Consular Reports*, 145.

Chapter 8

1. Proclamation to the people of Colombia, 21 July 1821, O'Leary, *Memorias*, III, 457.
2. Bolívar to Santander, Tocuyo, 16 August 1821, *Cartas Santander–Bolívar*, III, 132.
3. O'Leary, *Narración*, II, 118.
4. See Chapter 6.
5. For an interesting though not entirely accurate account of royalist resistance in Pasto by the British consul in Guayaquil, see 'History of events in Pasto', Henry Wood to Canning, Popayán, 30 June 1825, National Archives, PRO, FO 18/21.
6. Earle, *Spain and the Independence of Colombia*, 47–54.
7. O'Leary, *Narración*, II, 122–3; Hamilton, *Travels through the Interior Provinces of Colombia*, II, 44–5.
8. Bolívar to Santander, Popayán, 29 January 1822, Santander to Bolívar, 30 January 1822, *Cartas Santander–Bolívar*, III, 194–8, 203–4.
9. Proclamation, 18 February 1822, O'Leary, *Memorias*, XIX, 187.
10. Salom, *Boletín del Ejército Libertador*, 8 April 1822, Bolívar to Col. Lara, Cariaco, 15 April 1822, O'Leary, *Memorias*, XIX, 236–40, 251.
11. Bolívar to bishop of Popayán, 10 June 1822, Carrera Damas, *Simón Bolívar Fundamental*, I, 214.
12. Sucre, *Documentos relativos a la campaña del sur*, Quito, 28 May 1822, O'Leary, *Memorias*, XIX, 290–2.
13. Bolívar to Santander, Pasto, 9 June 1822, *Cartas Santander–Bolívar*, III, 225–8.
14. *Escritos*, XXIII, 233–4. The first known copy of the document is dated 13 October 1822, and the first publication 1833; the original has not been found. See Pedro Grases, *Estudios Bolivarianos* (*Obras*, IV, Barcelona, 1981), 367–86, 666. Polanco Alcántara, *Simón Bolívar*, 649–54, presents the event as a possibility. For a sceptical view of the document's authenticity, see Gerhard Masur, *Simón Bolívar* (Albuquerque, 1948) 463, n. 45.
15. Bolívar to Olmedo, Cali, 2 January 1822, *Obras completas*, I, 612–13.
16. Decree, 13 July 1822, O'Leary, *Memorias*, XIX, 333–4, *Narración*, II, 148–51, '*Detached Recollections*', 31–3.
17. See John Lynch, *San Martín: Argentine Patriot, American Liberator* (ILAS, London, 2001), 2–4.
18. Bolívar to San Martín, Trujillo, 23 August 1821, O'Leary, *Memorias*, XXIX, 214.
19. Bolívar to San Martín, Quito, 17 June 1822, O'Leary, *Memorias*, XIX, 307; Bolívar to San Martín, 22 June 1822, *Cartas del Libertador*, III, 50–2.
20. San Martín to Bolívar, Lima, 13 July 1822, O'Leary, *Memorias*, XIX, 335–6.
21. On the Guayaquil interview, one of the most controversial and least documented events of the War of Independence, see Vicente Lecuna, *La entrevista de Guayaquil*, 2 vols (4th edn, Caracas, 1962–3); and Gerhard Masur, 'The Conference of Guayaquil', *HAHR*, 31 (1951), 189–229, the most convincing interpretation.
22. J.G. Pérez to Gual, Guayaquil, 29 July 1822, *Obras completas*, I, 655–9.
23. San Martín to William Miller, Brussels, April 1827, Lecuna, *La entrevista de Guayaquil*, II, 467.
24. San Martín to Bolívar, 29 August 1822, a letter whose authenticity is disputed. See A.J. Pérez Amuchástegui, *La 'carta de Lafond' y la perceptiva historiográfica* (Córdoba, 1962), 141–50, and *Ideología y acción de San Martín* (Buenos Aires, 1966), 55–7.
25. San Martín to Guido, 18 December 1826, 21 June 1827, Museo Mitre, *Documentos del Archivo de San Martín*, 12 vols (Buenos Aires, 1910–11), VI, 504, 529.
26. Ruben Vargas Ugarte, *Historia general del Perú*, 6 vols (Barcelona, 1966), VI, 240.
27. San Martín to Guido, 18 December 1826, *Documentos del Archivo de San Martín*, VI, 503.
28. Bolívar to San Martín, Guayaquil, 25 July 1822, O'Leary, *Memorias*, XIX, 338.
29. Bolívar to Santander, Guayaquil, 29 July 1822, *Cartas Santander–Bolívar*, III, 243.
30. Bolívar to Santander, Quito, 6 December 1822, *Cartas Santander–Bolívar*, III, 282.

31. Bolívar to Fernando Toro, Cuenca, 23 September 1822, *Obras completas*, I, 683–5.
32. O'Leary, '*Detached Recollections*', 23–6, 37.
33. Earle, *Spain and the Independence of Colombia*, 164–5.
34. Decrees, 13 January 1823, *Decretos del Libertador*, I, 273–5.
35. Bolívar to Santander, Ibarra, 23 December 1822, *Cartas Santander–Bolívar*, III, 288.
36. Bolívar to Santander, Quito, 6 December 1822, *Cartas Santander–Bolívar*, III, 283.
37. Bolívar to Santander, Tulcán, 31 December 1822, *Cartas Santander–Bolívar*, III, 290–1; O'Leary, *Narración*, II, 182–4.
38. He later said to friends that he had no heirs, 'for his wife died very early, and he did not marry again, but that did not mean he was sterile, for he had proof to the contrary'. Peru de Lacroix, *Diario de Bucaramanga*, 96.
39. Bolívar to Bernardina Ibáñez, Cali, 5 January 1822, Carrera Damas, *Simón Bolívar Fundamental*, I, 212–13.
40. Alfonso Rumazo González, *Manuela Sáenz: La libertadora del Libertador* (6th edn, Caracas, 1962); Cornelio Hispano, *Historia secreta de Bolívar, su gloria y sus amores* (Medellín, 1977); Blanca Gaitán de Paris, *La mujer en la vida pública del Libertador* (Bogotá, 1980); Victor Wolfgang von Hagen, *The Four Seasons of Manuela: The Love Story of Manuela Saenz and Simon Bolivar* (London, 1966) are a few examples of the tendency to mix fact and fiction. In preference see Bernardo J. Caicedo, 'El supuesto rapto de Manuelita Sáenz', *BAGN*, 71 (1981), 130–5, Jorge Villalba Freire, *Manuela Sáenz en la leyenda y en la historia* (Caracas, 1988), *Manuela Sáenz, Epistolario* (Quito, 1986), and especially Pamela S. Murray, ' "Loca" or "Libertadora"? Manuela Sáenz in the Eyes of History and Historians, 1900–c.1990', *JLAS*, 33, 2 (2001), 291–310, an expert and original interpretation.
41. Bolívar to Garaycoa family, Quito, 16 November 1822, Babahoyo, 16 June 1823, Carrera Damas, *Simón Bolívar Fundamental*, I ,230, 254–5.
42. Bolívar to Garaycoas ladies, Cuenca, 14 September 1822, Carrera Damas, *Simón Bolívar Fundamental*, I, 223; Cartas de mujeres, *BOLANH*, 16, 62 (1933), 335, 339, 341.
43. Manuela Garaycoa, Guayquil, 15 June 1826, 2 January 1827, 14 August 1828, Cartas de mujeres, *BOLANH*, 16, 62 (1933), 337, 338–9, 340.
44. Bolívar to Garaycoa family, Bogotá, 16 November 1827, Carrera Damas, *Simón Bolívar Fundamental*, I, 498.
45. La Gloriosa to Bolívar, Guayaquil, 13 June 1830, *BOLANH*, 16, 62 (1933), 341.
46. J-B. Boussingault, *Memorias* (Caracas, 1974), 303, 306. On Boussingault see the essay by Germán Carrera Damas, *La Disputa de la Independencia* (Caracas, 1995), 87–116.
47. Manuela Sáenz to Bolívar, Quito, 30 December 1822, Cartas de mujeres, *BOLANH*, 16, 62 (1933), 332.
48. Bolívar to Santander, Huamachuco, 6 May 1824, *Cartas Santander–Bolívar*, IV, 240–1.
49. Manuela Sáenz to Captain Santana, Huamachuco, 28 May 1824 (BANH, 16, 62 (1823), 332).
50. Manuela Sáenz to Thorne, October 1823, Vicente Lecuna, 'Papeles de Manuela Sáenz', *BOLANH*, 28, 112 (1945), 501–2; Bolívar to Manuela Sáenz, La Plata, 26 November 1825, *Cartas del Libertador*, V, 180; see also O'Leary, *Narración*, III, 338–9, note.
51. Bolívar to Manuela Sáenz, Ica, 20 April 1825, *Cartas del Libertador*, IV, 315–16.
52. Bolívar to Manuela Sáenz, 13 October 1825, *Cartas del Libertador*, V, 121–2; Manuela Sáenz to Bolívar, Lima, 27 November 1825, *BOLANH*, 16, 62 (1933), 334.
53. Bolívar to Manuela Sáenz, Lima, 6 April, 1826, *Obras completas*, II, 345; Bolívar to Manuela Sáenz, La Magdalena, July 1826, Carrera Damas, *Simón Bolívar Fundamental*, I, 422–3.
54. Manuela Sáenz to Bolívar, Lima, 27 November 1825, Cartas de mujeres, *BOLANH*, XVI, 334.
55. Bolívar to Manuela Sáenz, Ibarra, 6 October 1826, *Cartas del Libertador*, VI, 80.
56. Bolívar to Manuela Sáenz, Bucaramanga, 3 April 1828, *Cartas del Libertador*, VI, 80.

57. Bolívar to Manuela Sáenz, end of July 1828, *Cartas del Libertador*, VII, 377; Bolívar to Manuela Sáenz, 11 May 1830, *Cartas del Libertador*, IX, 265.
58. Jorge Basadre, *Historia de la República del Perú*, 10 vols (5th edn, Lima, 1961–4), I, 332.
59. Susy Sánchez, 'Clima, hambre y enfermedad en Lima durante la Guerra independentista (1817–1826)', *La Independencia en el Perú: De los Borbones a Bolívar*, ed. Scarlett O'Phelan Godoy (Lima, 2001), 237–63.
60. Bolívar to Santander, 12–14 March 1823, *Cartas Santander–Bolívar*, IV, 31.
61. Bolívar to Riva Agüero, Guayaquil, 13 April 1823, *Obras completas*, I, 731–3.
62. Sucre to Bolívar, El Callao, 19 June 1823, O'Leary, *Memorias*, I, 47.
63. O'Leary, *Narración*, II, 211.
64. Bolívar to Santander, Quito, 3 July 1823, *Cartas Santander–Bolívar*, IV, 87.
65. O'Leary, '*Detached Recollections*', 29.
66. Bolívar to Santander, Lima, 11 September, 20 September 1823, *Cartas Santander–Bolívar*, IV, 127, 135–6.
67. Miller, *Memoirs*, II, 102–4.
68. Bolívar to Santander, Lima, 11 September 1823, *Cartas Santander–Bolívar*, IV, 127–8.
69. Bolívar to Santander, Trujillo, 21 December 1823, *Cartas Santander–Bolívar*, IV, 187; Proclamation, 25 December 1824, *Proclamas y discursos del Libertador*, 298.
70. Bolívar to Santander, Pallasca, 8 December 1823, *Cartas Santander–Bolívar*, IV, 174.
71. Bolívar to Santander, Pativilca, 9 January 1824, *Cartas Santander–Bolívar*, IV, 196–9.
72. Bolívar to Torre Tagle, Pativilca, 7 January 1824, *Obras completas*, I, 861–3.
73. O'Leary, *Narración*, II, 241–4; Anna, *Fall of the Royal Government in Peru*, 222–5.
74. Bolívar to Santander, Pativilca, 23 January 1824, *Cartas Santander–Bolívar*, IV, 202–5.
75. Mosquero to Restrepo, 2 August 1854, Blanco y Azpurúa, *Documentos para la historia de la vida pública del Libertador*, IX, 343–4.
76. O'Leary, *Narración*, II, 240.
77. Bolívar to Santander, Trujillo, 16 March 1824, *Cartas Santander–Bolívar*, IV, 227.
78. Bolívar to Santander, Lima, 13 October 1823, *Cartas Santander–Bolívar*, IV, 150.
79. Scarlett O'Phelan, 'Sucre en el Perú: Entre Riva Agüero y Torre Tagle', *La Independencia del Perú*, 379–406.
80. Bolívar to Sucre, Pativilca, 26 January 1824, O'Leary, *Memorias*, XXIX, 409–17.
81. James Dunkerley, *The Third Man: Francisco Burdett O'Connor and the Emancipation of the Americas* (ILAS, London, 1999), 15–17; Celia Wu, *Generals and Diplomats: Great Britain and Peru 1820–40* (Cambridge, 1991), 9–23.
82. Anna, *Fall of the Royal Government in Peru*, 228–31.
83. Bolívar to Sucre, Huaraz, 9 June 1824, O'Leary, *Memorias*, XXIX, 507.
84. Miller, *Memoirs*, II, 148–9.
85. Proclamation, Pasco, 29 July 1824, O'Leary, *Memorias*, XXII, 413.
86. Santa Cruz, Parte oficial, 7 August 1824, O'Leary, *Memorias*, XXII, 423.
87. Bolívar to Sucre, Huamanga, 4 September 1824, O'Leary, *Memorias*, XXIX, 513–15; Bolívar, Resumen sucinto de la vida del General Sucre, 1825, *Archivo de Sucre*, I, xli.
88. Bolívar to Santander, Lima, 20 December 1824, 6 January 1825, *Cartas Santander–Bolívar*, IV, 275–84.
89. O'Leary, *Narración*, II, 282, '*Detached Recollections*', 17.
90. Miller, *Memoirs*, II, 191–2, 200.
91. Sucre, Parte de la batalla de Ayacucho, 11 December 1824, O'Leary, *Memorias*, XXII, 569–75.
92. Bolívar to Santander, Lima, 9 February 1825, *Cartas Santander–Bolívar*, IV, 297.
93. Proclama, 25 December 1824, Decreto, 27 December 1824, O'Leary, *Memorias*, XXII, 602, 605–6.
94. Bolívar, Resumen sucinto de la vida del General Sucre, *Archivo de Sucre*, xlvii–xlviii.
95. O'Leary, *Narración*, II, 333.
96. J. Gabriel Pérez to bishop of Arequipa, 26 May 1825, O'Leary, *Memorias*, XXIII, 161–3.

97. Decrees, Cuzco, 4 July 1825, Urubamba, 20 July 1825, *Decretos del Libertador*, I, 407–9, 427–8.
98. Kathryn Burns, *Colonial Habits: Convents and the Spiritual Economy of Cuzco* (Durham, North Carolina, 1999), 187–8, 193–4.
99. Bolívar to Peñalver, Cuzco, 11 July 1825, O'Leary, *Memorias*, XXX, 93.
100. Bolívar to Olmedo, Cuzco, 12 July 1825, O'Leary, *Memorias*, IV, 388–91.

Chapter 9

1. José Santos Vargas, *Diario de un comandante de la independencia Americana 1814–1825*, ed. Gunnar Mendoza L. (Mexico, 1982), 242.
2. Sucre, Decree, 9 February 1825, Bolívar to Sucre, 21 February 1825, O'Leary, *Narración*, II, 366–78.
3. Bolívar to Santander, Lima, 18 [23] February 1825, *Cartas Santander–Bolívar*, IV, 307.
4. Charcas, La Plata and, from 1839, Sucre.
5. O'Leary, *Narración*, II, 383; O'Leary, '*Detached Recollections*', 18, 28.
6. O'Leary, *Narración*, II, 384.
7. Miller, *Memoirs*, II, 302–09.
8. Joseph Andrews, *Journey from Buenos Ayres, through the provinces of Córdoba, Tucuman, and Salta, to Potosi*, 2 vols (London, 1827), II, 90–5.
9. Palabras en Potosí, 26 October 1825, *Itinerario documental de Simón Bolívar. Escritos selectos* (Caracas, 1970), 280–1.
10. Antonio Cacua Prada, *Los hijos secretos de Bolívar* (Bogotá, 1992), 251–3.
11. Decrees, Chuquisaca, 16 November, 29 December 1825, *Decretos del Libertador*, I, 436–9.
12. Bolívar to Santander, Plata, 12 December 1825, *Cartas Santander–Bolívar*, V, 122.
13. Bolívar to Briceño Méndez, 27 February 1826, O'Leary, *Memorias*, III, 175–7.
14. Sucre to Bolívar, Chuquisaca, 6 June 1826, O'Leary, *Memorias*, I, 335–40.
15. *Proyecto de Constitución para la República Boliviana, Lima, 1826, con adiciones manuscritas de Antonio José de Sucre* (Caracas, 1978).
16. Ricketts to Canning, Lima, 25 April 1826, National Archives, PRO, FO 61/7.
17. O'Leary, *Narración*, II, 428–9.
18. Message to the Congress of Bolivia, 25 May 1826, *Obras completas*, III, 765–7.
19. Ricketts to Canning, 30 May 1826, National Archives, PRO, FO 61/7.
20. Sir Robert Wilson, London, 31 January 1827, O'Leary, *Memorias*, XII, 150.
21. This was not, of course, a hereditary president. The successor came to power by appointment, not by hereditary right.
22. Sucre to Bolívar, Chuquisaca, 20 May 1826, O'Leary, *Memorias*, I, 327.
23. *Proyecto de Constitución*, 102–3, 128.
24. Ibid., 99–103.
25. Bolívar to Sucre, 12 May 1826, *Cartas del Libertador*, V, 291.
26. Circular letter to people of influence in Colombia, 3 August 1826, O'Leary, *Memorias*, XXIV, 62–3.
27. O'Leary, *Narración*, II, 431.
28. William L. Lofstrom, *La presidencia de Sucre en Bolivia* (BANH, Caracas, 1987), 371–422, especially 415.
29. Sucre to Bolívar, Chuquisaca, 4 August 1826, O'Leary, *Memorias*, I, 368.
30. Ricketts to Canning, 30 May 1826, *British Consular Reports*, 219–20.
31. Miller, *Memoirs*, II, 283, 293–4. According to Pentland, Potosí produced only $900,000 in 1826; the mines of all Bolivia produced in 1826 $2,619,918 in silver and $800,000 in gold; see J.B. Pentland, Report on Bolivia, 2 December 1827, National Archives, PRO, FO 61/12.

32. R. A. Humphreys, *Liberation in South America 1806–1827: The Career of James Paroissien* (London, 1952), 139–44, 155–61; Dawson, *The First Latin American Debt Crisis*, 120, 218.
33. Andrews, *Journey from Buenos Ayres*, II, 113–26; Miller, *Memoirs*, II, 291–4.
34. Ricketts to Canning, 30 May 1826, *British Consular Reports*, 217–18; Lofstrom, *La presidencia de Sucre*, 356–65.
35. According to Pentland the population of Bolivia was 1,100,000, divided as follows: 200,000 whites; 800,000 Indians; 100,000 *mestizos*; 7,000 Negroes, of whom 4,700 were slaves. Pentland to Ricketts, 2 December 1827, National Archives, PRO, FO 61/12.
36. Miller, *Memoirs*, II, 284.
37. Decree, Chuquisaca, 14 December 1825, Lecuna, ed., *Documentos referentes a la creación de Bolivia*, 2 vols (Caracas, 1924), I, 442–3.
38. Miller, *Memoirs*, II, 299.
39. *Proyecto de Constitución*, 114; Lecuna, *Documentos referentes a la creación de Bolivia*, II, 324, 346.
40. Sucre to Bolívar, Chuquisaca, 20 August 1826, O'Leary, *Memorias*, I, 377.
41. Sucre to Bolívar, Chuquisaca, 27 May, 10 July 1826, O'Leary, *Memorias*, I, 332, 347–57; Sucre to O'Leary, Quito, 7 November 1828, ibid., IV, 491; Lofstrom, *La presidencia de Sucre*, 242–68, 301–2.
42. See Inés Quintero, *Antonio José de Sucre: Biografía política* (BANH, Caracas, 1998), 189–210.
43. Sucre to Bolívar, 20 June 1827, O'Leary, *Memorias*, I, 436; Bolívar to Sucre, 8 June 1827, O'Leary, *Memorias*, XXX, 409.
44. Sucre to Bolívar, Chuquisaca, 27 April 1828, O'Leary, *Memorias*, I, 496–7; Lofstrom, *La presidencia de Sucre*, 498–9.
45. Ninavilca, Proclama, Canta, 16 November 1823, O'Leary, *Memorias*, XXI, 48–9.
46. Bolívar to Briceño Méndez, 2 August 1826, O'Leary, *Memorias*, XXX, 244–7.
47. Printed in *British Consular Reports*, 198–206.
48. Ricketts to Canning, 18 February 1826, C. K. Webster, ed., *Britain and the Independence of Latin America 1812–1830: Select Documents from the Foreign Office Archives*, 2 vols (London, 1938), I, 533.
49. Bolívar to Santander, 7, 8 June 1826, Carrera Damas, *Simón Bolívar Fundamental*, I, 421.
50. Peter Blanchard, *Slavery and Abolition in Early Republican Peru* (Wilmington, Delaware, 1992), 9–15, 42–3.
51. Ricketts to Canning, 19 December 1826, National Archives, PRO, FO 61/8.
52. O'Leary, '*Detached Recollections*', 28; Bolívar to Santander, 7 April 1826, *Cartas Santander–Bolívar*, V, 177; Bolívar to Sucre, Magdalena, 12 May 1826, *Obras completas*, II, 361.
53. Willemott to Ricketts, 31 January 1828, National Archives, PRO, FO 61/15.
54. Message to the Constituent Congress of Colombia, 20 January 1830, *Proclamas y Discursos del Libertador*, 398.
55. Hugh Seton-Watson, *Nations and States* (London, 1977), 1–9.
56. Proclama a los Venezolanos, Angostura, 22 October 1818, O'Leary, *Memorias*, XVI, 113–15.
57. Jamaica Letter, *Escritos*, VIII, 240.
58. Bolívar to Mariño, 16 December 1813, *Cartas del Libertador*, I, 88.
59. Simon Collier, 'Nationality, Nationalism, and Supranationalism in the Writings of Simón Bolívar', *HAHR*, 63, 1 (1983), 37–64.
60. Jamaica Letter, *Escritos*, VIII, 244–5.
61. Bolívar to O'Higgins, 8 January 1822, *Obras completas*, I, 619.
62. Bolívar to Santander, Arequipa, 6–7 June 1825, *Cartas Santander–Bolívar*, IV, 388.
63. Bolívar to Santander, Cuzco, 28 June 1825, *Cartas Santander–Bolívar*, V, 3.

64. Lima, 7 December 1824, O'Leary, *Memorias*, XXIV, 251–3.
65. Thoughts on the Congress to be held in Panama, *Obras completas*, III, 756–7; Carrera Damas, *Simón Bolívar Fundamental*, II, 111–12.
66. Dawkins to Canning, London, 15 October 1826, Webster, *Britain and the Independence of Latin America*, I, 424.
67. O'Leary, *Narración*, II, 564.
68. Peru de Lacroix, *Diario de Bucaramanga*, 119.
69. Bolívar to Santander, Magdalena, 8 July 1826, *Cartas Santander–Bolívar*, V, 242.
70. Bolívar to Santander, Magdalena, 7 May 1826, *Cartas Santander–Bolívar*, V, 197–8; Bolívar to Sucre, 12 May 1826, *Obras completas*, II, 360–4; Bolívar to Gutiérrez de la Fuente, 12 May 1826, *Obras completas*, II, 365.
71. Bolívar to Santa Cruz, Popayán, 26 October 1826, O'Leary, *Memorias*, XXX, 271–4.
72. Bolívar to Mariño, 16 December 1813, *Cartas del Libertador*, I, 88.
73. Bolívar to Santander, Pasto, 8 January 1823, *Cartas Santander–Bolívar*, IV, 3.
74. Bolívar to Santander, Angostura, 20 December 1819, O'Leary, *Memorias*, XVII, 11.
75. Bolívar to Santander, Guayaquil, 30 May 1823, *Cartas Santander–Bolívar*, IV, 64. *Trigarantes*, a reference to Iturbide's Army of the Three Guarantees in Mexico: Religion, Unity, Independence.
76. Bolívar to Maxwell Hyslop, 19 May 1815, O'Leary, *Memorias*, XXIX, 42–7.
77. Bolívar to Campbell, Bogotá, 29 October 1827, National Archives, PRO, FO 18/42.
78. Humphreys, *Tradition and Revolt in Latin America*, 148–9.
79. Bolívar to Santander, Babahoyo, 14 June 1823, *Cartas Santander–Bolívar*, IV, 71, Cuzco, 28 June, 10 July 1825, ibid., V, 3–4, 9.
80. Bolívar to Revenga, Cuzco, 10 July 1825, *Obras completas*, 166.
81. *Obras completas*, III, 756–7.
82. Bolívar to Santander, Magdalena, 8 July 1826, *Cartas Santander–Bolívar*, V, 243–4.
83. Santander to Bolívar, 9 June 1826, *Cartas Santander–Bolívar*, V, 222.
84. Bolívar to Santander, Ibarra, 8 October 1826, *Cartas Santander–Bolívar*, VI, 42–6.
85. Campbell to Canning, 5 November, 13 December 1826, National Archives, PRO, FO 18/28.
86. Watts to Canning, Cartagena, 27 May 1825, National Archives, PRO, FO 18/18.
87. The balance of population in the union also favoured New Granada; José Manuel Restrepo, *Historia de la revolución de la república de Colombia*, 10 vols (Paris, 1827) I, xiv, estimated New Granada 1.4 million, Venezuela 900,000, Quito 600,000; Campbell to Planta, 6 November 1824, National Archives, PRO, FO 18/3, estimated 2,650,000 for greater Colombia.
88. Victor M. Uribe-Uran, *Honorable Lives: Lawyers, Family, and Politics in Colombia, 1780–1850* (Pittsburgh, 2000), 75, 89.
89. In 1825 Páez declined to recruit six hundred men from Apure ordered by Escalona. AGN, Papeles de Guerra y Marina, ci, f. 92.
90. Bolívar to Santander, Potosí, 13 October 1825, *Cartas Santander–Bolívar*, V, 72–3.
91. Campbell to Canning, 6 October 1826, National Archives, PRO, FO 18/27.
92. Páez to Bolívar, 1 October 1825, O'Leary, *Memorias*, II, 57–60.
93. Bolívar to Páez, Magdalena, Peru, 6 March 1826, O'Leary, *Memorias*, XXX, 183–5; Bolívar to Páez, 26 May 1826, *Obras completas*, II, 378; Bolívar to Santander, 21 February 1826, *Cartas Santander–Bolívar*, V, 149–50.
94. Antonia to Bolívar, Caracas, 30 October 1825, *BOLANH*, 16, 61 (1933), 275.
95. Sucre to Bolívar, Chuquisaca, 27 April 1826, O'Leary, *Memorias*, I, 314–17.
96. Santander to Bolívar, 21 April 1826, *Cartas Santander–Bolívar*, V, 182–3.
97. Santander, *Escritos autobiográficos*, 49–51.
98. Santander to Bolívar, 6 May 1826, *Cartas Santander–Bolívar*, VI, 316.
99. Sutherland to Canning, Maracaibo, 1 September 1826, Sutherland to HM Chargé d'affaires, Maracaibo, 2 October 1826, National Archives, PRO, FO 18/33.

100. O'Leary, *Narración*, III, 66; '*Detached Recollections*', 22; Manuel Pérez Vila, *Vida de Daniel Florencio O'Leary, primer edecán del Libertador* (Caracas, 1957), 302–4.
101. Campbell to Canning, 6 October 1826, National Archives, PRO, FO 18/28.
102. Bolívar to Santander, Magdalena, 7 and 8 June 1826, *Cartas Santander–Bolívar*, V, 215–17.
103. See above, note 82.
104. Bolívar to Páez, Lima, 4 August 1826, *Cartas del Libertador*, VI, 32–34, 8 August 1826, *Cartas del Libertador*, VI, 49–52, *Obras completas*. II, 455–8.
105. Bolívar to Santander, Ibarra, 8 October 1826, *Cartas Santander–Bolívar*, VI, 45.
106. Ricketts to Canning, Lima, 18 February 1826, Webster, *Britain and the Independence of Latin America*, I, 530.
107. Ker Porter to Canning, Caracas, 9 April 1827, National Archives, PRO, FO 18/47.
108. Bolívar to Páez, 11 December 1826, *Obras completas*, II, 505–6.
109. Bolívar to Páez, 23 December 1826, O'Leary, *Memorias*, XXX, 295–8; *Obras completas*, II, 514–16.
110. Watts to Bidwell, Cartagena, 5 August 1826, National Archives, PRO, FO 18/31.

Chapter 10

1. Bolívar to Santander, Guayaquil, 21 August 1822, *Cartas Santander–Bolívar*, III, 254.
2. Páez, *Autobiografía*, I, 335–7.
3. As reported by Ker Porter to Canning, Caracas, 24 January 1827, National Archives, PRO, FO 18/47.
4. Ker Porter to Canning, Caracas, 7 April 1827, National Archives, PRO, FO 18/47.
5. Peru de Lacroix, *Diario de Bucaramanga*, 71–2.
6. Ker Porter to Canning, Caracas, 9 April 1827, National Archives, PRO, FO 18/47.
7. Campbell to Canning, Bogotá, 3 January 1827, National Archives, PRO, FO 18/40; Santander to Bolívar, 6 July 1826, *Cartas Santander–Bolívar*, V, 239.
8. Bolívar to Santander, Caracas, [16] January 1827, *Cartas Santander–Bolívar*, VI, 161.
9. Bolívar to Soublette, Caracas, 16 March 1827, O'Leary, *Memorias*, XXX, 359–60.
10. Santander to Bolívar, 16 March 1827, *Cartas Santander–Bolívar*, VI, 207–13.
11. Bolívar to Páez, Caracas, 20 March 1827, *Obras completas*, II, 588.
12. Decrees, 22 January 1827, 24 June 1827, *Decretos del Libertador*, II, 88–9, 276–341.
13. Santander, *Escritos autobiográficos*, 69.
14. Drusilla Scott, *Mary English: A Friend of Bolívar* (Lewes, 1991), 150–4, 167–9, 170–1.
15. Bolívar to Santa Cruz, Caracas, 8 June 1827, *Obras completas*, II, 630.
16. O'Leary, *Narración*, II, 601.
17. Bolívar to Páez, Bogotá, 29 January 1828, *Obras completas*, II, 761.
18. Bolívar, Message to the congress of Ocaña, 29 February 1828, *Obras completas*, III, 789–96.
19. Roulin, 'El retrato físico de Bolívar,' Blanco y Azpurúa, *Documentos para la historia de la vida públicá del Libertador*, XIV, 485–7; Boulton, *Los retratos de Bolívar*, 86–98; O'Leary, '*Detached Recollections*', 41.
20. Paul Verna, 'Bello y las minas del Libertador,' *Bello y Londres*, I, 469–86.
21. Peru de Lacroix, *Diario de Bucaramanga*, 116. See Cussen, *Bello and Bolívar*, 140–2, and Iván Jaksić, *Andrés Bello: Scholarship and Nation-Building in Nineteenth-Century Latin America* (Cambridge, 2001), 53–8, 89–91.
22. Proclamation, Caracas, 19 June 1827, O'Leary, *Memorias*, XXV, 394–5.
23. Campbell to Dudley, Bogotá, 29 September 1827, Ker Porter to Dudley, Caracas, 22 October 1827, National Archives, PRO, FO 18/42, 18/47.
24. Bolívar to Wilson, Bogotá, 22 January 1828, O'Leary, *Memorias*, XXXI, 23.
25. Mosquera, *Memoria sobre la vida del General Simón Bolívar*, 557.

26. Campbell to Dudley, Bogotá, 8 October 1828, National Archives, PRO, FO 18/54; Uribe-Uran, *Honorable Lives*, 89.
27. Bolívar to Páez, Bogotá, 16 February 1828, *Obras completas*, II, 783.
28. AGN, Papeles de Guerra y Marina, lxv, f. 169, shows Venezuelan pride in Padilla's naval victory. See also Joaquín Posada Gutiérrez, *Memorias histórico-políticas*, 4 vols (2nd edn, BHN 41–4, Bogotá, 1929), I, 123.
29. See Aline Helg, 'Simón Bolívar and the Spectre of *Pardocracia*: José Padilla in Post-Independence Cartagena', *JLAS*, 35, 3 (2003), 447–71.
30. Bolívar to Santander, Lima, 7 April 1825, *Cartas Santander–Bolívar*, IV, 344. Bolívar was well aware of the Montilla-Padilla dichotomy: 'Ambos parecen muy adictos a mí: el primero no puede nada; el segundo lo puede todo.' Bolívar to Santander, Lima, 7 May 1826, ibid., V, 197–8.
31. O'Leary to Bolívar, Ocaña, 5 April 1828, O'Leary, *Memorias*, XXXII, 191.
32. O'Leary, '*Detached Recollections*', 37; Posada Gutiérrez, *Memorias histórico-políticas*, I, 127; José Manuel Restrepo, *Diario político y militar desde 1819 para adelante*, 4 vols (Bogotá, 1954), I, 379.
33. Manuel Valdés to Juan José Flores, Cartagena, 8 April 1828, *Archivo Santander*, 24 vols (Bogotá, 1913), XVII, 295.
34. Manuela Sáenz to Bolívar, 28 March 1828, *BOLANH*, 16, 335.
35. Bolívar to Manuela Sáenz, Bucaramanga, 3 April 1828, *Obras completas*, II, 811.
36. Peru de Lacroix, *Diario de Bucaramanga*, 144–5, 148–9, 161–2, 172–4.
37. Ibid., 64–6.
38. Ibid., 114–15.
39. Briceño Méndez to Bolívar, Ocaña, 9 April 1828, O'Leary, *Memorias*, VIII, 239; Bolívar to Briceño Méndez, Bucaramanga, 15 April 1828, ibid., XXXI, 68.
40. O'Leary, '*Detached Recollections*', 56–7; Santander, *Escritos autobiográficos*, 78.
41. Bolívar to Páez, 12 April 1828, *Obras completas*, II, 820–2.
42. Bolívar to Arboleda, Bucaramanga, 1 June, to Páez, 2 June 1828, O'Leary, *Memorias*, XXXII, 315–19.
43. Campbell to Dudley, 13 April 1828, National Archives, PRO, FO 18/53.
44. Acta del pronunciamento de Bogotá, 13 June 1828, O'Leary, *Memorias*, XXVI, 306–9.
45. Blanco and Azpurúa, *Documentos para la historia de la vida pública del Libertador*, XII, 705–20.
46. Mosquera, *Memoria sobre la vida del General Simón Bolívar*, 567.
47. Campbell to Dudley, Bogotá, 14 June 1828, National Archives, PRO, FO 18/53.
48. See Chapter 9.
49. Organic Decree, 27 August 1828, *Decretos del Libertador*, III, 137–44; Proclamation, 27 August 1828, O'Leary, *Memorias*, XXVI, 368–9. See David Bushnell, 'The Last Dictatorship: Betrayal or Consummation?', *HAHR*, 63, 1 (1983), 65–105.
50. Message to Congress, 20 January 1830, *Obras completas*, III, 812–17.
51. *Gaceta de Colombia*, 31 August 1828.
52. José M. de Mier, *La Gran Colombia*, 7 vols (Bogotá, 1983), III, 841–2.
53. Jamaica Letter, *Escritos*, VIII, 242–3; Angostura Address, *Obras completas*, III, 685.
54. Restrepo to Bolívar, 5 December 1828, O'Leary, *Memorias*, VII, 271.
55. Bolívar to Córdova, Bogotá, end of July 1828, *Obras completas*, II, 931; Bolívar to Manuela Sáenz, end of July 1828, ibid., 932.
56. 'Relación de un testigo ocular', O'Leary, *Memorias*, XXXII, 363–9.
57. Santander, *Escritos autobiográficos*, 87–8.
58. Restrepo to Montilla, Bogotá, 28 September 1828, O'Leary, *Memorias*, VII, 312–13.
59. Mosquera, *Memoria sobre la vida del General Simón Bolívar*, 575.
60. Bolívar to Fernández Madrid, 14 October 1828, *Itinerario documental*, 325–6; Bolívar to O'Leary, 22 October 1828, O'Leary, *Memorias*, app. XXXII, 465; Manuela Sáenz to

O'Leary, Paita, 10 August 1850, O'Leary, *Memorias*, XXXII, 370–5; *Gaceta de Colombia*, Suplemento, 28 September 1828.

61. Urdaneta to Montilla, 21 October 1828, O'Leary, *Memorias*, VI, 177–8.
62. Sentence, 7 November 1828, O'Leary, *Memorias*, XXVI, 450–2; on Carujo see O'Leary to Bolívar, 9 September 1829, FJB, AL, C-643.
63. Bolívar to Briceño Méndez, Bogotá, 16 November 1828, O'Leary, *Memorias*, XXXI, 239–40.
64. Santander, *Escritos autobiográficos*, 88.
65. Sucre to Bolívar, Quito, 7 October 1829, O'Leary, *Memorias*, I, 557.
66. Páez to Bolívar, 7 August 1828, O'Leary, *Memorias*, II, 150.
67. Soublette to Bolívar, 28 August 1828, 12 January 1829, 21 January 1829, O'Leary, *Memorias*, VIII, 65, 76, 77–9.
68. Bolívar to O'Leary, 13 September 1829, *Cartas del Libertador*, IX, 125.
69. Bolívar to Páez, Bogotá, 30 June 1828, *Obras completas*, II, 905.
70. Cartagena Manifesto, 15 December 1812, *Escritos*, IV, 122.
71. John Lynch, 'Revolution as a Sin: the Church and Spanish American Independence', *Latin America between Colony and Nation*, 124.
72. Message to the Congress of Bolivia, 25 May 1826, *Obras completas*, III, 529.
73. Miriam Williford, *Jeremy Bentham on South America: An Account of His Letters and Proposals to the New World* (Baton Rouge, 1980), 115, 121, 125. See Chapter 2.
74. Bolívar to Bentham, 27 September 1822, Bentham to Bolívar, 6 January, 4 June 1823, *The Correspondence of Jeremy Bentham, Volume 11*, ed. Catherine Fuller (Oxford, 2000), 154–5, 185–9, 238–56.
75. Bentham to Bolívar, 24 January 1820 (not sent), Pedro Schwartz, ed., *The Iberian Correspondence of Jeremy Bentham*, 2 vols (London, 1979), I, 122–7. See also 'Las relaciones entre Jeremías Bentham y S. Bolívar', *Bolívar y Europa*, I, 445–60.
76. Bentham to Bolívar, London, 13 August 1825, *The Correspondence of Jeremy Bentham, Volume 12*, Letter 0088; O'Leary, *Memorias*, XII, 265–79.
77. Bolívar to Bentham, Caracas, 15 January 1827, O'Leary, *Memorias*, XXX, 318–19.
78. Santander, Decree 8 November 1825, Mier, *La Gran Colombia*, II, 442–3.
79. Bolívar to Archbishop Méndez, Bogotá, October 1828, *Obras completas*, II, 472.
80. Mier, *La Gran Colombia*, III, 883–4; Decrees 12 March 1828, 29 October 1828, *Decretos del Libertador*, III, 53–4, 182–4.
81. Hamilton, *Travels through the Interior Provinces of Colombia*, I, 140.
82. *Diario del General Francisco de Paula Santander en Europa y los EE.UU. 1829–1832*, ed. Rafael Martínez Briceño (Bogotá, 1963), 172–5; Bentham to Santander, 9 July 1830, Santander to Bentham, 10 July 1830, 29 July 1830, *Correspondence of Jeremy Bentham, Volume 13*, letters 0252, 0253, 0263. See also *Obra Educativa: La Querella Benthamista, 1748–1832* (Bogotá, 1993), 88–94.
83. *Gaceta de Colombia*, 24 July 1828, 27 July 1828.
84. *Decretos del Libertador*, III, 143.
85. Message to Congress, 20 January 1830, *Obras completas*, III, 816.
86. O'Leary, '*Detached Recollections*', 31.
87. Tomás C. Mosquera to Bolívar, Popayán, 22 July 1828, O'Leary, *Memorias*, IX, 129.
88. See Lynch, 'Revolution as a Sin', *Latin America between Colony and Nation*, 124, 109–33.
89. Quoted by Gutiérrez, *La Iglesia que entendió el Libertador*, 259.
90. Pedro de Leturia, *Relaciones entre la Santa Sede e Hispanoamérica 1493–1835*, 3 vols (Rome, Caracas, 1959–60), II, 110–13, 215, 265–71, III, 432.
91. Bolívar to Council of State, Angostura, 10 November 1817, Pérez Vila, *Doctrina del Libertador*, 95.
92. Bolívar to bishop of Popayán, Pasto, 10 June 1822, Bolívar to Santander, 10 June 1822, Carrera Damas, *Simón Bolívar Fundamental*, I, 213–16, *Cartas Santander–Bolívar*, III, 228–9.

93. Toast of the Liberator to the bishops at the banquet in Bogotá, 28 October 1827, O'Leary, *Memorias*, XXV, 588.
94. Bolívar to Pius VIII, Bogotá, 14 September 1829, *Bolívar y Europa*, I, 657; Gutiérrez, *La Iglesia que entendió el Libertador*, 254–7.
95. Bolívar to Gutiérrez, Bogotá, October 1828, *Obras completas*, III, 15.
96. Bolívar to Briceño Méndez, Bucaramanga, 15 April 1828, O'Leary, *Memorias*, XXXI, 69.
97. Carrera Damas, Prologue, Castro Leiva, *La Gran Colombia*, 14.

Chapter 11

1. Bolívar to Vergara, Guayaquil, 31 August 1829, O'Leary, *Memorias*, XXXI, 495.
2. Posada Gutiérrez, *Memorias histórico-políticas*, I, 194.
3. Obando to La Mar, Pasto, 14 December 1828, Guáitara, 29 December 1828, O'Leary, *Memorias*, IV, 431, 432.
4. Bolívar to Santander, Potosí, 21 October 1825, *Cartas Santander–Bolívar*, V, 86.
5. Decree, Bogotá, 24 December 1828, *Decretos del Libertador*, III, 300.
6. Posada Gutiérrez, *Memorias histórico-políticas*, I, 201–3.
7. Bolívar to Urdaneta, Pasto, 9 March 1829, O'Leary, *Memorias*, XXXI, 330.
8. Obando to Bolívar, Pasto, 17, 28 March 28 April, 13, 28 May 1829, O'Leary, *Memorias*, IV, 414–18.
9. Proclama, Bogotá, 3 July, Manifesto, 15 July, 1828, O'Leary, *Memorias*, XXVI, 334–5, 340–6.
10. O'Leary to Bolívar, Guayaquil, 28 November 1828, O'Leary, *Memorias*, XXXII, 475.
11. Sucre to Bolívar, Quito, 7 October 1828, O'Leary, *Memorias*, IV, 490.
12. O'Leary, '*Detached Recollections*', 17–19, 37.
13. O'Leary to Bolívar, Guayaquil, 20 October 1828, O'Leary, *Memorias*, XXXII, 456.
14. O'Leary to Bolívar, Rosario, 6 March 1830, FJB, AL, C-653.
15. Bolívar to Sucre, Bogotá, 28 October 1828, O'Leary, *Memorias*, XXXI, 230–3.
16. Bolívar to Flores, Bogotá, 8 October 1828, O'Leary, *Memorias*, XXXI, 223–4.
17. Sucre, Report on battle of Tarqui, 2 March 1829, O'Leary, *Memorias*, XXXII, 499–508.
18. O'Leary, '*Detached Recollections*', 17.
19. Sucre to Bolívar, Cuenca, 3 March, Quito, 11 March 1829, O'Leary, *Memorias*, I, 521–3.
20. See Quintero, *Antonio José de Sucre*, 234–5.
21. Una Mirada sobre la América Española, April–June, 1829, Pérez Vila, *Doctrina del Libertador*, 286–7.
22. Una Mirada sobre la América Española, ibid., 282.
23. Sucre to Bolívar, Quito, 14 August 1829, O'Leary, *Memorias*, I, 547–9.
24. Bolívar to O'Leary, Guayaquil, 21 August 1829, O'Leary, *Memorias*, XXXI, 484–5.
25. Bolívar to Mosquera, 3 September 1829, O'Leary, *Memorias*, XXXI, 501–2.
26. Bolívar to O'Leary, 4 September 1829, O'Leary, *Memorias*, XXXI, 506–8.
27. Bolívar to O'Leary, Guayaquil, 13 September 1829, Carrera Damas, *Simón Bolívar Fundamental*, I, 588–94.
28. Bolívar to O'Leary, Babahoyo, 28 September 1829, O'Leary, *Memorias*, XXXI, 526; O'Leary to Bolívar, Medellín, 31 October 1829, FJB, AL, C-648.
29. O'Leary to Bolívar, 9 May, 18 August 1829, FJB, AL, C-633, C-641. Nicolasa Ibáñez was the sister of Bernardina Ibáñez, Bolívar's old flame.
30. O'Leary to Bolívar, 9 September, 6 November, 14 November 1829, FJB, AL, C-643, C-650, C-651; 'Detached Recollections', 13–15; Posada Gutiérrez, *Memorias histórico-políticas*, I, 263, 282.
31. Restrepo to Bolívar, Bogotá, 8 April 1829, O'Leary, *Memorias*, VII, 280; Bolívar to Restrepo, Quito, 6 May 1829, O'Leary, *Memorias*, XXXI, 365.
32. Restrepo to Bolívar, 8 June 1829, O'Leary, *Memorias*, VII, 285.

33. Restrepo to Bolívar, 15 July 1829, O'Leary, *Memorias,* VII, 286.
34. Bolívar to Campbell, Guayaquil, 5 August 1829, *Obras completas,* III, 278–9.
35. See pp. 261–2.
36. Mosquera, *Memoria sobre la vida del General Simón Bolívar,* 581–2, 598.
37. O'Leary to Bolívar, 14 June 1829, FJB, AL, C-635; '*Detached Recollections*', 13.
38. Córdova, Manifesto, Medellín, 16 September 1829; to Council of Ministers, 21 September 1829, O'Leary, *Narración,* III, 462–7.
39. Bolívar to Sucre, Babahoyo, 28 September 1829, Carrera Damas, *Simón Bolívar Fundamental,* I, 597–8.
40. O'Leary to Bolívar, Marinilla, 17 October 1829, FJB, AL, C-645, a letter described by Lecuna as 'apocryphal', containing sentiments unworthy of 'a perfect gentleman like O'Leary', *Narración,* III, 505–10.
41. O'Leary to Bolívar, Medellín, 23 October 1829, FJB, AL, C-647.
42. Posada Gutiérrez, *Memorias histórico-políticas,* I, 307–8, who describes Hand as 'un hombre de la ínfima plebe de Irlanda'; Mosquera, *Memoria sobre la vida del General Simón Bolívar,* 635; see also *Diccionario de Historia de Venezuela,* 3 vols (Caracas, 1988) E–O, 448–9.
43. Bolívar to Vergara, Popayán, 22 Nov. 1829, to Urdaneta, 22, 28 November 1829, *Obras completas,* III, 365, 367, 370; Posada Gutiérrez, *Memorias histórico-políticas,* I, 310–11.
44. O'Leary, '*Detached Recollections*', 16–17. On the letter to Campbell and the monarchy idea, see the discussion in Urbaneja, *El Alcalde de San Mateo,* 103–9, who concludes that Bolívar was 'consistently antimonarchical'.
45. José Gil Fortoul, *Historia constitucional de Venezuela,* 3 vols (2nd edn, Caracas, 1930), I, 650–63.
46. Bolívar to Páez, 25 March 1829, *Obras completas,* III, 157–8.
47. Sucre to Bolívar, 17 September 1829, O'Leary, *Memorias,* I, 552.
48. Lievesley to Aberdeen, La Guaira, 27 November 1829, National Archives, PRO, FO 18/72; Ker Porter to Aberdeen, Esher, 10 February 1830, FO 18/78.
49. Francisco A. Labastida to Páez, 23 February 1830, AGN, Secretaría del Interior y Justicia, v, f 421, *BAGN,* 10, 37 (1929), 49–50.
50. Acta del Cantón de Valencia, 23 November 1829, Gil Fortoul, *Historia constitucional de Venezuela,* I, 653.
51. Páez to Bolívar, Valencia, 1 December 1829, O'Leary, *Memorias,* II, 224; Bolívar to Castillo Rada, Cartago, 4 January 1830, Carrera Damas, *Simón Bolívar Fundamental,* I, 608.
52. Bermúdez, Proclamation, Cumaná, 16 January 1830, Parra-Pérez, *Mariño y la independencia de Venezuela,* V, 46; Mariño to Quintero, 2 September 1829, ibid., IV, 478.
53. Ker Porter to Aberdeen, Caracas, 12 June 1830, National Archives, PRO, FO 18/78; Parra-Pérez, *Mariño y la independencia de Venezuela,* V, 180.
54. Bolívar to Vergara, 25 September 1830, *Obras completas,* III, 465; Carrera Damas, *Simón Bolívar Fundamental,* I, 627.
55. Wood to Canning, Guayaquil, 28 February 1826, *British Consular Reports,* 228–9.
56. Uribe-Uran, *Honorable Lives,* 90–1.
57. Message to the Constituent Congress, Bogotá, 20 January 1830, *Obras completas,* III, 812–17.
58. Bolívar to Fernández Madrid, Bogotá, 13 February, 6 March 1830, Carrera Damas, *Simón Bolívar Fundamental,* I, 609–10, 611–13.
59. He went on to specify Ocumare, which still rankled. See Chapter 5.
60. Posada Gutiérrez, *Memorias histórico-políticas,* I, 369–70.
61. Bolívar to Congress, Bogotá, 27 April 1830, *Obras completas,* III, 821–2.
62. O'Leary to Bolívar, Rosario, 6–8 March 1830, FJB, AL, C-653.
63. AGN, Hacienda Pública, xviii, f. 333, 341.
64. The Colombian authorities had given Sucre eight copies of the project of a constitution 'to seek the collaboration of the eastern departments', a vain hope. AGN, Hacienda

Pública, xvi, f. 317. Ker Porter to Aberdeen, Caracas, 20 August 1830, National Archives, PRO, FO 18/78.

65. The mines were not sold until 1832, when a contract was signed in Caracas between the heirs of Bolívar and an English company for a sum of £38,000. See Paul Verna, *Las minas del Libertador* (Caracas, 1977).
66. Posada Gutiérrez, *Memorias histórico-políticas*, II, 71–2.
67. O'Leary, '*Detached Recollections*', 17.
68. Posada Gutiérrez, *Memorias histórico-políticas*, II, 78–9.
69. Sucre to Bolívar, Bogotá, 8 May 1830, O'Leary, *Memorias*, I, 571; Bolívar to Sucre, Turbaco, 26 May 1830, *Itinerario documental*, 349.
70. Bolívar to Manuela Sáenz, 11 May 1830, *Cartas del Libertador*, IX, 265.
71. Posada Gutiérrez, *Memorias histórico-políticas*, II, 91–4. The College was a hotbed of liberalism.
72. Posada Gutiérrez, *Memorias histórico-políticas*, II, 222; Mosquera, *Memoria sobre la vida del General Simón Bolívar*, 671.
73. Estéban Febres Cordero to Obando, Guayaquil, 16 June 1830, O'Leary, *Memorias*, IV, 436; Mosquera, *Memorias sobre la vida del General Simón Bolívar*, 668–72; Antonio José de Irisarri, *Historia crítica del asesinato cometido en la persona del Gran Mariscal de Ayacucho* (Caracas, 1846), 45–50, 121–38.
74. Bolívar to Mariana Carcelén de Sucre, Cartagena, 2 July 1830, *Itinerario documental*, 349–50. Sucre's widow lost face in Ecuador when, just over a year later, she married in what some thought unseemly haste General Isidoro Barriga, a New Granadan bon vivant.
75. Bolívar to Flores, Barranquilla, 9 November 1830, *Obras completas*, III, 502.
76. Bolívar to Urdaneta, Cartagena, 18 September 1830, *Obras completas*, III, 457–9; Bolívar to Briceño Méndez, 20 September 1830, *Obras completas*, III, 461–2.
77. Bolívar to Santa Cruz, 14 September 1830, *Obras completas*, III, 452.
78. Bolívar to Vergara, Cartagena, 25 September 1830, *Obras completas*, III, 463–6.
79. Bolívar to Mariano Montilla, 27 October, 8 November 1830, *Obras completas*, III, 483–4, 498–500.
80. Bolívar to Urdaneta, Soledad, 16 October 1830, *Obras completas*, III, 473–6; Wilson to O'Leary, 13 October, 25 October 1830, O'Leary, *Memorias*, XII, 125, 131.
81. Bolívar to Flores, Barranquilla, 9 November 1830, *Obras completas*, III, 501–2; Pérez Vila, *Doctrina del Libertador*, 321–6.
82. Bolívar to O'Leary, Barranquilla, 25 November 1830, *Itinerario documental*, 355.
83. Alejandro Próspero Reverend, Bulletins, in Blanco and Azpurúa, *Documentos para la historia de la vida pública del Libertador*, XIV, 464–74.
84. Bolívar to Urdaneta, Santa Marta, San Pedro, 6, 7, 8 December 1830, *Obras completas*, III, 520–3, 524–5.
85. Testamento del Libertador, Hacienda de San Pedro Alejandrino, 10 December 1830, *Obras completas*, III, 529–31; Gutiérrez, *La Iglesia que entendió el Libertador*, 262–7.
86. The Last Proclamation of the Liberator, Hacienda de San Pedro, Santa Marta, 10 December 1830, *Obras completas*, III, 823–4.
87. Reverend, in Blanco and Azpurúa, *Documentos para le historia de la vida pública del Libertador*, XIV, 468–72.
88. O'Leary, '*Detached Recollections*', 48.
89. *The Times*, London, 19 February 1831, p. 5.

Chapter 12

1. Jamaica Letter, *Escritos*, VIII, 241.
2. Bolívar to Pedro Gual, Mompós, 9 February 1815, O'Leary, *Memorias*, XIV, 67–9.

3. Ricketts to Canning, Lima, 18 February 1826, Webster, *Britain and the Independence of Latin America*, I, 527.
4. O'Leary, '*Detached Recollections*', 26.
5. Bolívar to Sucre, Magdalena, 12 May 1826, Bolívar to Santa Cruz, Popayán, 26 October 1826, *Obras completas*, II, 361, 487–8; Bolívar to Fernández Madrid, Bogotá, 6 March 1830, Carrera Damas, *Simón Bolívar Fundamental*, I, 612.
6. Bolívar to María Antonia Bolívar, April 1825, 10 July 1826, Carrera Damas, *Simón Bolívar Fundamental*, I, 316. 424.
7. Cussen, *Bello and Bolívar*, 152–3.
8. Jaksić, *Andrés Bello*, 135–6.
9. Speech of Bolívar in Bogotá, 23 January 1815, *Escritos*, VII, 264.
10. Speech of Bolívar in Bogotá, 24 June 1828, *Obras completas*, III, 804.
11. Angostura Address, 15 February 1819, *Obras completas*, III, 682.
12. Bolívar, Proclamation to Venezuelans, Maracaibo, 16 December 1826, O'Leary, *Memorias*, XXIV, 573–4.
13. Angostura Address, 15 February 1819, *Obras completas*, III, 690.
14. Ricketts to Canning, 18 February 1826, Webster, *Britain and the Independence of Latin America*, I, 530.
15. Lester D. Langley, *The Americas in the Age of Revolution 1750–1850* (New Haven, 1996), 242.
16. Bolívar to Santander, Cúcuta, 10 May 1820, *Cartas Santander–Bolívar*, II, 137.
17. Decree, Cuzco, 4 July 1825, *Decretos del Libertador*, I, 410–11.
18. Ildefonso Leal, *Historia de la Universidad de Caracas (1721–1827)* (Caracas, 1963), 332–8.
19. Bolívar to Santander, Lima, 7 April 1825, *Cartas Santander–Bolívar*, IV, 344.
20. Germán Carrera Damas, *Venezuela: Proyecto Nacional y Poder Social* (Barcelona, 1986), 111–43; *La Disputa de la Independencia*, 25–8; and 'Casos de continuidad y ruptura: Génesis teórica y práctica del proyecto americano de Simón Bolívar', *Historia General de América Latina*, Volumen V (UNESCO, Paris, 2003), 288–90.
21. Langley, *The Americas in the Age of Revolution*, 286.
22. Ibid., 47–8, 195–6.
23. Bolívar to marqués del Toro, Chancay, 10 November 1824, *Obras Completas*, II, 37–8.
24. St Augustine, *Concerning the City of God against the Pagan*, trans. Henry Bettenson (Penguin Books, London, 1984), 197–9, 202–4, 215.
25. O'Leary, *Narración*, II, 95.
26. Bolívar to Sucre, Huamanga, 4 September 1824, O'Leary, *Memorias*, XXIX, 513–15.
27. Bolívar to Santander, Pativilca, 23 January 1824, *Cartas Santander–Bolívar*, IV, 202–5.
28. Bolívar to Peñalver, Chancay, 10 November 1824, O'Leary, *Memorias*, XXX, 10–11.
29. Bolívar to Santander, Magdalena, 7 April 1826, *Cartas Santander–Bolívar*, V, 177.
30. O'Leary to Bolívar, 20 March, 9 May, 8 June, 9 September, 6, 14 November 1829, FJB, AL, C-632, C-633, C-634, C-643, C-650, C-651.
31. Bolívar to Páez, Cúcuta, 11 December 1826, *Obras completas*, II, 505–6.
32. Thomas Carlyle, *On Heroes, Hero-Worship and the Heroic in History* (1841) (Lincoln, Nebraska, 1966), 196–7, 203–4, 224.
33. Bolívar to Estanislao Vergara, Guayaquil, 31 August 1829, O'Leary, *Memorias*, XXXI, 495.
34. O'Leary, *Narración*, II, 601.
35. Páez, *Autobiografía*, II, 350–1.
36. Germán Carrera Damas, *El Culto a Bolívar* (Caracas, 1969), 55–8.
37. Speech of Páez at Government House, at the conclusion of the public ceremonies, 23 December 1842, *Autobiografía*, II, 356.
38. Carrera Damas, *El Culto a Bolívar*, 226–7, 229–30, 232.
39. Ibid., 245–7.

40. See especially Vicente Lecuna, *Catálogo de errores y calumnias en la historia de Bolívar* 3 vols (New York, 1956–58).
41. J.L. Salcedo-Bastardo, *Visión y Revisión de Bolívar*, 2 vols (Caracas, 1977) II, 162.
42. Carrera Damas, *El Culto a Bolívar*, 194–6, 206.
43. Quoted by Germán Carrera Damas, 'Simón Bolívar, el Culto Heroico y la Nación', *Venezuela: Proyecto nacional y poder social*, 178–9.
44. Germán Carrera Damas, *El Bolivarianismo-Militarismo: Una Ideología de Reemplazo* (Caracas, 2005), 191–210.

BIBLIOGRAPHY

Sources

The sources for the life and times of Simón Bolívar in all their variety and abundance are best described by Manuel Pérez Vila, 'Contribución a la bibliografía de los escritos del Libertador, manuscritos y ediciones', Sociedad Bolivariana de Venezuela, *Escritos del Libertador*, vol. I, *Introducción general* (Caracas, 1964), 61–290. Archival and printed sources are expertly surveyed by Pedro Grases, *El Archivo de Bolívar (manuscritos y ediciones)* (Caracas, 1978). Among the published primary sources, which are the basis of the present work, two classic nineteenth-century collections are still indispensable: José Félix Blanco and Ramón Azpurúa, *Documentos para la historia de la vida pública del Libertador de Colombia, Perú y Bolivia*, 14 vols (Caracas, 1875–8), and Daniel Florencio O'Leary, *Memorias del General O'Leary*, 32 vols (Caracas, 1879–88, republished in 34 vols, 1981, by the Ministerio de la Defensa, the last two volumes being an index by Manuel Pérez Vila). *The 'Detached Recollections' of General D.F. O'Leary*, ed. R.A. Humphreys (London, 1969) adds valuable insights to the larger collection. Vicente Lecuna compiled a number of worthy successors to the preceding works, including *Cartas del Libertador*, 10 vols (Caracas, 1929–30, vol. 11, New York, 1948; vol. 12, ed. Manuel Pérez Vila, Caracas, 1959), *Decretos del Libertador*, 3 vols (Caracas, 1961) and especially *Obras completas*, ed. Vicente Lecuna and Esther Barret de Nazarís, 2nd edn, 3 vols (Havana, 1950). In a final search for perfection the Sociedad Bolivariana de Venezuela has undertaken a definitive and critical edition of all known Bolivarian documents, *Escritos del Libertador* (Caracas, 1964–, still in progress and reaching to the mid 1820s.) Bolívar's correspondence with Santander has been excellently edited in *Cartas Santander–Bolívar*, Biblioteca de la Presidencia de la República, 6 vols (Bogotá, 1988–90).

There are two further compilations representing the selections of historians whose distinguished scholarship and expert knowledge give them a particular value: Manuel Pérez Vila, *Doctrina del Libertador*, (2nd edn, Caracas, 1979), and Germán Carrera Damas, *Simón Bolívar Fundamental*, 2 vols (Caracas, 1993).

Finally, a number of English translations have served Bolivarian studies, notably Simón Bolívar, *Selected Writings*, comp. Vicente Lecuna, ed. Harold A. Bierck Jr., trans. Lewis Bertrand, 2 vols (New York, 1951), and *El Libertador: Writings of Simón Bolívar*, trans. Frederick H. Fornoff, ed. David Bushnell (Oxford, 2003).

Guides to Sources

Aljure Chalela, Simón, *Bibliografía bolivariana* (Bogotá, 1983).
Fundación John Boulton, *Colección bolivariana* (Caracas, 1983).
— *Sección venezolana del archivo de la Gran Colombia. Indice sucinto* (Caracas, 1960).
Grases, Pedro, *El Archivo de Bolívar (manuscritos y ediciones)* (Caracas, 1978).
— *Los papeles de Bolívar y Sucre* (Caracas, 1985).

Pérez Vila, Manuel, 'Contribución a la bibliografía de los escritos del Libertador, manuscritos y ediciones', Sociedad Bolivariana de Venezuela, *Escritos del Libertador*, vol. I, *Introducción general* (Caracas, 1964), 61–290.
— *Simón Bolívar, 1783–1830: Bibliografía básica* (Bogotá, 1983).

Archives

Fundación John Boulton, Caracas
    Archivo del Libertador
    Signatura: C-632–C-655

Archivo General de la Nación, Caracas
    Gobernación y Capitanía General
    Papeles de Guerra y Marina
    Hacienda Pública
    Secretaría del Interior y Justicia

National Archives, Public Record Office, London
    FO 72, Spain
    FO 18, Colombia
    FO 61, Peru

Published Documents and Contemporary Works

Andrews, Joseph, *Journey from Buenos Ayres, through the provinces of Córdoba, Tucuman, and Salta, to Potosi*, 2 vols (London, 1827).
Austria, José de, *Bosquejo de la historia militar de Venezuela*, 2 vols (BANH, 29–30, Caracas, 1960).
Blanco, José Félix, and Azpurúa, Ramón, eds, *Documentos para la historia de la vida pública del Libertador de Colombia, Perú y Bolivia*, 14 vols (Caracas, 1875–8).
Bolívar, Simón, *Cartas del Libertador*, ed. Vicente Lecuna (vols 1–10, Caracas, 1929–30, vol. 11, New York, 1948; vol. 12, ed. Manuel Pérez Vila, Caracas, 1959).
— *Decretos del Libertador*, ed. Vicente Lecuna, 3 vols (Caracas, 1961).
— *Doctrina del Libertador*, ed. Manuel Pérez Vila (2nd edn, Caracas, 1979).
— *Escritos del Libertador*, Sociedad Bolivariana de Venezuela (Caracas, 1964–).
— *El Libertador: Writings of Simón Bolívar*, trans. Frederick H. Fornoff, ed. David Bushnell (Oxford, 2003).
— *El Libertador y la Constitución de Angostura de 1819*, ed. Pedro Grases (Caracas, 1970).
— *Itinerario documental de Simón Bolívar. Escritos selectos* (Caracas 1970).
— *Obras completas*, ed. Vicente Lecuna and Esther Barret de Nazarís, 3 vols (2nd edn, Havana, 1950).
— *Proclamas y Discursos del Libertador*, ed. Vicente Lecuna (Caracas, 1939).
— *Proyecto de Constitución para la República Boliviana, con adiciones manuscritas de Antonio José de Sucre. Edición facsimilar, Lima, 1826* (Caracas, 1978).
— *Selected Writings*, compiled by Vicente Lecuna, ed. Harold A. Bierck Jr., trans. by Lewis Bertrand, 2 vols (New York, 1951).
— *Simón Bolívar Fundamental*, ed. Germán Carrera Damas, 2 vols (Caracas, 1993).
Boussingault, J-B, *Memorias* (Caracas, 1974).
'Cartas de Mujeres', *BOLANH*, 16, 62 (Caracas, 1933), 332–99.
Cochrane, Charles Stuart, *Journal of a Residence and Travels in Colombia, during the years 1823 and 1824*, 2 vols (London, 1825).
Conjuración de 1808 en Caracas para la formación de una junta suprema gubernativa (documentos completos), Instituto Panamericano de Geografía e Historia, Comisión de Historia, 2 vols (Caracas, 1969).

336 BIBLIOGRAPHY

Correo del Orinoco, Angostura, 1818–21, reproducción facsimilar (Paris, 1939).
De Pradt, Dominique Dufour, Les trois âges des colonies, ou leur état passé, présent et à venir, 3 vols (Paris, 1801–2).
Díaz, José Domingo, Recuerdos sobre la rebelión de Caracas (BANH, 38, Caracas, 1961).
Ducoudray-Holstein, H. La Fayette Villaume, Memoirs of Simón Bolívar president, liberator of the Republic of Colombia, 2 vols (London, 1830).
Epistolario de la Primera República, 2 vols (BANH, Caracas, 1960).
Espinosa Apolo, Manuel, ed., Simón Bolívar y Manuela Sáenz: Correspondencia íntima (Quito, 1996).
Fuller, Catherine, ed., The Correspondence of Jeremy Bentham, vols 11–12 (Oxford, 2000–5).
Gaceta de Colombia, Rosario de Cúcuta and Bogotá, 1821–4, 1821–9, 1831 (Bogotá, 1973).
Gazeta de Caracas, facsimile, 1808–12, 2 vols (BANH, 21–22, Caracas, 1960).
Grases, Pedro, ed., Pensamiento político de la emancipación venezolana (Caracas, 1988).
Hall, Francis, Colombia: Its Present State (London, 1824).
Hamilton, John P., Travels through the Interior Provinces of Colombia, 2 vols (London, 1827).
Heredia, José Francisco, Memorias del regente Heredia (BANH, 186, Caracas, 1986).
Humboldt, Alexander von, Cartas americanas, ed. Charles Minguet (Caracas, 1980).
— Personal Narrative of Travels to the Equinoctial Regions of the New Continent during the Years 1799–1804, trans. Helen Maria Williams, 6 vols (London, 1814–29).
— Personal Narrative of a Journey to the Equinoctial Regions of the New Continent, trans. Jason Wilson (London, 1995).
Humphreys, R.A., ed., British Consular Reports on the Trade and Politics of Latin America 1824–1826 (London, 1940).
Lecuna, Vicente, ed., Documentos referentes a la creación de Bolivia, 2 vols (Caracas, 1924).
— 'Papeles de Manuela Sáenz', BOLANH, Caracas, 28, 112 (1945), 494–525.
— ed., Relaciones diplomáticas de Bolívar con Chile y Buenos Aires, 2 vols (Caracas, 1954).
Lee López, Alberto, ed., Los Ejércitos del Rey, 2 vols (Bogotá, 1989).
Mendoza, Cristóbal, ed., Las primeras misiones diplomáticas de Venezuela: documentos, 2 vols (Caracas, 1962).
Mier, José M. de, ed., La Gran Colombia, 7 vols (Bogotá, 1983).
Miller, John, Memoirs of General Miller in the Service of the Republic of Peru, 2 vols (2nd edn, London, 1829).
Miranda, Francisco de, Archivo del General Miranda, 24 vols (Caracas, 1929–50).
— Colombeia (Caracas, 1978–).
Muñoz, Gabriel E., Monteverde: cuatro años de historia patria 1812–1816 2 vols (BANH 42–3, Caracas, 1987).
Obra Educativa: La Querella Benthamista, 1748–1832. Biblioteca de la Presidencia de la República, Documentos, No. 72 (Bogotá, 1993).
O'Connor, Francisco Burdett, Independencia Americana: recuerdos de Francisco Burdett O'Connor (Madrid, 1915).
O'Leary, Daniel Florencio, The 'Detached Recollections' of General D.F. O'Leary, ed. R.A. Humphreys (London, 1969).
— Memorias del General O'Leary, 34 vols (Caracas, 1981).
— Memorias del General Daniel Florencio O'Leary: Narración, 3 vols (Caracas, 1952).
— Memorias del General Daniel Florencio O'Leary: Narración, Abridged Version, trans. and ed. Robert F. McNerney, Jr. (Austin, Texas, 1970).
Páez, José Antonio, Autobiografía del General José Antonio Páez, 2 vols (BANH, Caracas, 1973).
Peru de Lacroix, Louis, Diario de Bucaramanga, ed. Mons. Nicolás E. Navarro, prolog. J.L. Salcedo-Bastardo (Caracas, 1982).
— Diario de Bucaramanga. Vida pública y privada del Libertador. Versión sin mutilaciones (Ediciones Centauro, Caracas, 1976).
Porter, Robert Ker, Sir Robert Ker Porter's Caracas Diary, 1825–1842, ed. Walter Dupouy (Caracas, 1966).
Posada Gutiérrez, Joaquín, Memorias histórico-políticas, 4 vols (2nd edn, BHN 41–4, Bogotá, 1929).

Presidencia de la República, *Las fuerzas armadas de Venezuela en el siglo xix: Textos para su estudio*, 12 vols (Caracas, 1963–71).
— *Pensamiento político venezolano del siglo xix: Textos para su estudio*, 15 vols (Caracas, 1960–2).
Raynal, Guillaume Thomas François, *A Philosophical and Political History of the Settlements and Trade of the Europeans in the East and West Indies, By the Abbé Raynal, To which is added the Revolution of America*, 6 vols (Edinburgh, 1782).
Restrepo, José Manuel, *Diario político y militar, 1819–1858*, 5 vols (Bogotá, 1954).
— *Historia de la revolución de la república de Colombia*, 10 vols (Paris, 1827).
Revenga, José R., *La hacienda pública de Venezuela en 1828–1830*, ed. Pedro Grases and Manuel Pérez Vila (Caracas, 1953).
Roscio, Juan Germán, *Obras*, 3 vols (Caracas, 1953).
Santander, Francisco de Paula, *Archivo Santander*, 24 vols (Bogotá, 1913–32).
— *Cartas y mensajes*, ed. Roberto Cortázar, 10 vols (Bogotá, 1953–6).
— *Cartas Santander–Bolívar*, Biblioteca de la Presidencia de la República, 6 vols (Bogotá, 1988–90).
— *Correspondencia dirigida al general Francisco de Paula Santander*, ed. Roberto Cortázar, 14 vols (Bogotá, 1964–70).
— *Escritos autobiográficos 1820–1840*, ed. Guillermo Hernández de Alba (Bogotá, 1988).
Simmons, Merle E., *Los escritos de Juan Pablo Viscardo y Guzmán: Precursor de la Independencia Hispanoamericana* (Caracas, 1983).
Stevenson, William Bennet, *A Historical and Descriptive Narrative of Twenty Years' Residence in South America*, 3 vols (London, 1825).
Sucre, Antonio José de, *Archivo de Sucre*, Fundación Vicente Lecuna, Banco de Venezuela, 15 vols (Caracas, 1973–8).
Textos oficiales de la Primera República de Venezuela, 2 vols (BANH 1–2, Caracas, 1959).
Universidad Central de Venezuela, *Materiales para el estudio de la cuestión agraria en Venezuela (1800–1830)*, I, (Caracas, 1964).
Urquinaona y Pardo, Pedro de, *Memorias de Urquinaona* (Madrid, 1917).
Vowell, Richard, *Campaigns and Cruises in Venezuela and New Grenada and in the Pacific Ocean from 1817 to 1830*, 3 vols (London, 1831).
Webster, C.K., ed., *Britain and the Independence of Latin America 1812–1830*, 2 vols (London, 1938).
Yanes, Francisco Javier, *Relación documentada de los principales sucesos ocurridos en Venezuela desde que se declaró estado independiente hasta el año 1821* (Caracas, 1943).

Secondary Works

Amunátegui Reyes, Miguel Luis, *Vida de Don Andrés Bello* (Santiago, 1882).
Andrien, Kenneth J., and Johnson, Lyman L., eds, *The Political Economy of Spanish America in the Age of Revolution, 1750–1850* (Albuquerque, 1994).
Anna, Timothy E., *The Fall of the Royal Government in Peru* (Lincoln, Nebraska, 1979).
Belaunde, Víctor Andrés, *Bolívar and the Political Thought of the Spanish American Revolution* (Baltimore, 1938).
Berruezo León, María Teresa, *La lucha de Hispanoamérica por su independencia en Inglaterra, 1800–1830* (Madrid, 1989).
Bierck, Harold A., Jr., 'The Struggle for Abolition in Gran Colombia', *HAHR*, 33, 3 (1953), 365–86.
Bonilla, Heraclio, 'Bolívar y las guerrillas indígenas en el Perú', *Cultura*, Revista del Banco Central del Ecuador, 6, 16 (1983), 81–95.
Boulton, Afredo, *Iconografía del Libertador* (Caracas, 1992).
— *Los retratos de Bolívar*, (2nd edn, Caracas, 1964).
Brito Figueroa, Federico, *Historia económica y social de Venezuela*, 2 vols (Caracas, 1966).
Brown, Matthew, 'Esclavitud, castas y extranjeros en las guerras de la Independencia de Colombia', *Historia y Sociedad*, 10 (2004), 109–25.

Bushnell, David, 'Independence Compared: the Americas North and South', MacFarlane and Posada-Carbó, *Independence and Revolution in Spanish America*, 69–83.
— 'The Last Dictatorship: Betrayal or Consummation?' *HAHR*, 63, 1 (1983), 65–105.
— ed., *The Liberator, Simón Bolívar: Man and Image* (New York, 1970).
— *The Santander Regime in Gran Colombia* (Newark, Delaware, 1954).
— *Simón Bolívar: Liberation and Disappointment* (London, 2004).
Cacua Prada, Antonio, *Los hijos secretos de Bolívar* (Bogotá, 1992).
Caicedo, Bernardo J., 'El supuesto rapto de Manuelita Sáenz', *BAGN*, 71 (1981), 130–5.
Carrera Damas, Germán, *Boves: Aspectos socio-económicos de su acción histórica* (Caracas, 1968).
— *El Bolivarianismo–Militarismo: Una Ideología de Reemplazo* (Caracas, 2005).
— 'Casos de continuidad y ruptura: Génesis teórica y práctica del proyecto americano de Simón Bolívar', *Historia General de América Latina*, Volumen V (UNESCO, Paris, 2003), 287–315.
— *El culto a Bolívar* (Caracas, 1969).
— *La disputa de la independencia y otros peripecias del método crítico en historia de ayer y de hoy* (Caracas, 1995).
— *Historia de la historiografía venezolana (Textos para su estudio)* (2nd edn, vol. I, Caracas, 1985, vol. III, Caracas, 1997).
— ed., *Historia General de América Latina. Volumen V, La crisis estructural de las sociedades implantadas* (UNESCO, Paris, 2003).
— *Tres temas de historia* (Caracas, 1961).
— *Venezuela: Proyecto Nacional y poder social* (Barcelona, 1986).
Castro Leiva, Luis, *De la patria boba a la teología bolivariana* (Caracas, 1991).
— *La Gran Colombia: Una ilusión ilustrada* (Caracas, 1985).
Collier, Simon, 'Nationality, Nationalism and Supranationalism in the Writings of Simón Bolívar', *HAHR*, 63, 1 (1983), 37–64.
Cortés, Santos R., *El régimen de las 'gracias al sacar' en Venezuela durante el período hispánico*, 2 vols (Caracas, 1978).
Cussen, Antonio, *Bello and Bolívar: Poetry and Politics in the Spanish American Revolution* (Cambridge, 1992).
Dawson, Frank Griffith, *The First Latin American Debt Crisis: The City of London and the 1822–25 Loan Bubble* (New Haven and London, 1990).
De Grummond, Jane Lucas, *Renato Beluche: Smuggler, Privateer and Patriot 1780–1860* (Baton Rouge, 1983).
Diccionario de Historia de Venezuela, Fundación Polar, 3 vols (Caracas, 1988).
Earle, Rebecca A., 'Popular Participation in the Wars of Independence in New Granada', McFarlane and Posada-Carbó, eds, *Independence and Revolution in Spanish America: Perspectives and Problems* (ILAS, London, 1999) 87–101.
— *Spain and the Independence of Colombia 1810–1825* (Exeter, 2000).
Filippi, Alberto, ed., *Bolívar y Europa en las crónicas, el pensamiento político y la historiografía*, 2 vols (Caracas, 1986–92).
Gaitán de Paris, Blanca, ed., *La mujer en la vida del Libertador* (Bogotá, 1980).
García Márquez, Gabriel, *The General in his Labyrinth* (London, 1992).
González, Eloy G., *Historias Bolivarianas* (Caracas, 1976).
Grases, Pedro, *Estudios Bolivarianos Obras*, IV (Caracas, Barcelona, 1981).
— *Preindependencia y Emancipación: Protagonistas y testimonios Obras*, III (Caracas, Barcelona, 1981).
Groot, José Manuel, *Historia eclesiástica y civil de Nueva Granada*, 5 vols (Bogotá, 1953).
Guerra, François-Xavier, *Modernidad e Independencia. Ensayos sobre las revoluciones hispánicas* (Madrid, 1992).
Gutiérrez, Alberto, *La Iglesia que entendió el Libertador Simón Bolívar* (Bogotá, 1981).
Halperin Donghi, Tulio, *Reforma y disolución de los imperios ibéricos 1750–1850* (Madrid, 1985).
Harvey, Robert, *Liberators: Latin America's Struggle for Independence 1810–1830* (London, 2000).
Helg, Aline, 'Simón Bolívar and the Spectre of *Pardocracia*: José Padilla in Post-Independence Cartagena', *JLAS*, 35, 3 (2003), 447–71.
Hildebrandt, Martha, *La lengua de Bolívar* (Caracas, 1961).
Hispano, Cornelio, *Historia secreta de Bolívar, su gloria y sus amores* (Medellín, 1977).

Irisarri, Antonio José de, *Historia crítica del asesinato cometido en la persona del Gran Mariscal de Ayacucho* (Caracas, 1846).

Izard, Miguel, *El miedo a la Revolución: La lucha por la libertad en Venezuela (1777–1830)* (Madrid, 1979).

Jaksić, Iván, *Andrés Bello: Scholarship and Nation-Building in Nineteenth-Century Latin America* (Cambridge, 2001).

Kinsbruner, Jay, *Independence in Spanish America: Civil Wars, Revolutions, and Underdevelopment* (Albuquerque, 1994).

Lambert, Eric, 'Los legionarios británicos', Fundación La Casa de Bello, *Bello y Londres*, 2 vols (Caracas, 1980–1), I, 355–76.

— *Voluntarios británicos e irlandeses en la gesta bolivariana*, 3 vols (Caracas, 1983–93).

Langley, Lester D., *The Americas in the Age of Revolution, 1750–1850* (New Haven, 1996).

Larrazábal, Felipe, *La vida y correspondencia general del Libertador Simón Bolívar*, 2 vols (New York, 1865).

Laserna, Mario, *Bolívar: Un euro-americano frente a la Ilustración* (Bogotá, 1986).

Leal, Ildefonso, *La Universidad de Caracas en los años de Bolívar 1783–1830*, 2 vols (Caracas, 1983).

Lecuna, Vicente, *Breviario de ideas bolivarianas* (Caracas, 1970).

— *Catálogo de errores y calumnias en la historia de Bolívar*, 3 vols (New York, 1956–8).

— *Crónica razonada de las guerras de Bolívar*, 3 vols (New York, 1950).

— *La entrevista de Guayaquil: restablecimiento de la verdad histórica*, 2 vols (4th edn, Caracas, 1962–3).

Leturia, Pedro de, *Relaciones entre la Santa Sede e Hispanoamérica, 1493–1835*, 3 vols (Rome, Caracas, 1959–60).

Lloréns Casani, Milagro, *Sebastian del Toro, ascendiente de los heroes de la independencia de Venezuela* (2 vols, Jaén, 1998).

Lofstrom, William L., *La presidencia de Sucre en Bolivia* (BANH, Caracas, 1987).

Lombardi, John V., *The Decline and Abolition of Negro Slavery in Venezuela 1820–1854* (Westport, 1971).

— People and Places in Colonial Venezuela (Bloomington, 1977).

López, Francisco Miguel, *Contribución al estudio de la ley de haberes militares y sus repercusiones* (Caracas, 1987).

Löschner, Renata, *Bellermann y el paisaje venezolano 1842–1845* (Caracas, 1977).

Lynch, John, 'Bolívar and the Caudillos', *HAHR*, 63,1 (1983), 3–35.

— *Caudillos in Spanish America 1800–1850* (Oxford, 1992).

— 'Los factores estructurales de la crisis: la crisis del orden colonial', *Historia General de América Latina*, Volumen V (UNESCO, Paris, 2003), 31–54.

— *Simón Bolívar and the Age of Revolution* (ILAS Working Papers, London, 1983).

— 'Spanish American Independence in Recent Historiography', McFarlane and Posada-Carbó, *Independence and Revolution in Spanish America*, 87–101.

— *The Spanish American Revolutions 1808–1826*, (2nd edn, New York, 1986).

McFarlane, Anthony, *Colombia before Independence: Economy, Society, and Politics under Bourbon Rule* (Cambridge, 1993).

— 'Identity, Enlightenment and Political Dissent in Late Colonial Spanish America', *Transactions of the Royal Historical Society*, Sixth series, 8 (1998), 309–35.

— and Eduardo Posada-Carbó, eds., *Independence and Revolution in Spanish America: Perspectives and Problems* (ILAS, London, 1999).

McKinley, P. Michael, *Pre-Revolutionary Caracas: Politics, Economy, and Society 1777–1811* (Cambridge, 1985).

Madariaga, Salvador de, *Bolívar* (London, 1968).

Masur, Gerhard, *Simón Bolívar* (Albuquerque, 1948).

— 'The Conference of Guayaquil', *HAHR*, 31, 2 (1951), 189–229.

Mijares, Augusto, *El Libertador* (Caracas, 1987).

Mosquera, Tomás Cipriano de, *Memoria sobre la vida de General Simón Bolívar, Libertador de Colombia, Perú y Bolivia*, (Bogotá, 1954).

Murray, Pamela S., '"Loca" or "Libertadora"? Manuela Sáenz in the Eyes of History and Historians, 1900–c.1990', *JLAS*, 33, 2 (2001), 291–310.

Navarro, Nicolás E., *La cristiana muerte del Libertador* (Caracas, 1955).

O'Phelan Godoy, Scarlett, ed., *La Independencia en el Perú: De los Borbones a Bolívar* (Lima, 2001).

Parra-Pérez, Caracciolo, *Historia de la Primera República de Venezuela*, (2nd edn, BANH, 19–20, 2 vols, Caracas, 1959).

— *Mariño y la independencia de Venezuela*, 5 vols (Madrid, 1954–7).

Pérez Amuchástegui, A.J., *La 'Carta de Lafond' y la perceptiva historiográfica* (Córdoba, 1962).

Pérez Vila, Manuel, *La formación intelectual del Libertador*, (2nd edn, Caracas, 1979).

— *Vida de Daniel Florencio O'Leary, primer edecán del Libertador* (Caracas, 1957).

Polanco Alcántara, Tomás, *Simón Bolívar: Ensayo de una interpretación biográfica a través de sus documentos* (Caracas, 1994).

Ponte, Andrés F., *La revolución de Caracas y sus próceres* (Caracas, 1960).

Puente Candamo, José A. de la, *San Martín y el Perú* (Lima, 1948).

Quintero, Inés, *Antonio José de Sucre: Biografía política* (BANH, 73, Caracas, 1998).

Racine, Karen, *Francisco de Miranda: A Transatlantic Life in the Age of Revolution* (Wilmington, Delaware, 2003).

Ramos, Demetrio, *España y la Independencia de América* (Madrid, 1996).

Rivas Vicuña, Francisco, *Las guerras de Bolívar*, 7 vols (Bogotá, 1834–8, Santiago, 1940).

Rodríguez Villa, Antonio, *El teniente general don Pablo Morillo, primer conde de Cartagena, marqués de La Puerta (1778–1837)*, 4 vols (Madrid, 1908–10).

Rumazo González, Alfonso, *Manuela Sáenz: La libertadora del Libertador* (6th edn, Caracas, 1972).

Salcedo-Bastardo, J.L., *Bolívar: A Continent and its Destiny* (Richmond, 1978).

— *Visión y revisión de Bolívar*, 2 vols (Caracas, 1977).

— and others, *Bolívar en Francia* (Caracas, 1984).

Scott, Drusilla, *Mary English: A Friend of Bolívar* (Lewes, 1991).

Slatta, Richard W. and De Grummond, Jane Lucas, *Simón Bolívar's Quest for Glory* (Texas A&M University Press, College Station, 2003).

Stoan, Stephen K., *Pablo Morillo and Venezuela, 1815–1820* (Columbus, Ohio, 1974).

Thibaud, Clément, *Repúblicas en armas: Los ejércitos bolivarianas en la Guerra de Independencia (Colombia–Venezuela, 1810–1821)* (Bogotá, 2003).

Urbaneja, Diego Bautista, *El Alcalde de San Mateo. Posibilidad y sentido de la presencia de lo hispánico en el pensamiento y la acción del Libertador* (Caracas, 1990).

Uribe-Urán, Victor M., *Honorable Lives: Lawyers, Family, and Politics in Colombia, 1780–1850* (Pittsburgh, 2000).

— ed., *State and Society in Spanish America during the Age of Revolution* (Wilmington, Delaware, 2001).

Uslar Pietri, Juan, *Historia de la rebelión popular de 1814: contribución al estudio de la historia de Venezuela* (2nd edn, Caracas, 1962).

Vargas Ugarte, Rubén, *Historia del Perú. Emancipación, 1809–1825* (Buenos Aires, 1958).

Verna, Paul, *Las minas del Libertador* (Caracas, 1977).

— *Pétion y Bolívar* (Caracas, 1969).

Vittorino, Antonio, *Relaciones colombo-británicas de 1823 a 1825, según los documentos del Foreign Office* (Barranquilla, 1990).

Von Hagen, Victor Wolfgang, *The Four Seasons of Manuela: The Love Story of Manuela Saenz and Simon Bolivar* (London, 1966).

Waddell, D.A.G., 'British Neutrality and Spanish-American Independence: The Problem of Foreign Enlistment', *JLAS*, 19, 1 (1987), 1–18.

— *Gran Bretaña y la Independencia de Venezuela y Colombia* (Caracas, 1983).

Williford, Miriam, *Jeremy Bentham on Spanish America* (Baton Rouge, 1980).

Wu, Celia, *Generals and Diplomats: Great Britain and Peru 1820–40* (Cambridge, 1991).

Zeuske, Michael, '¿Padre de la Independencia? Humboldt y la transformación a la modernidad en la América española', *Debate y Perspectivas. Cuadernos de Historia y Ciencias Sociales*, 1 (Madrid, 2000), 67–99.

GLOSSARY

albocracia: white rule

alcabala: sales tax

antioqueño: of Antioquia, inhabitant of Antioquia

audiencia: high court of justice with administrative functions

bandidos: bandits

bejuco: liana

blancos de orilla: poor whites

boga: boatman, in present context on the river Magdalena

caballero: gentleman

cabildo: town council

cachucha: popular Andalusian dance

cacique: Indian chieftain

canarios: people from the Canary Islands, such immigrants in Venezuela

caudillo: leader, whose rule is based on personal power rather than on constitutional form

cédula: royal decree issued by council

cédula de gracias al sacar: a royal decree granting an exemption

censos: mortgage-type loans

cholos: *mestizos* (Peruvian)

cobarde: coward

consulado: merchant guild and commercial tribunal

convencionistas: delegates at the Ocaña Convention

conventos menores: small monasteries with fewer than eight members

coyote: person of mixed *mestizo* and *mulatto* descent

criollo: creole, Spanish American

cundinamarquis: inhabitant of Cundinamarca

curiales: lawyers

doctrinas populistas: theories of popular sovereignty

encomienda: grant of Indian labour

estanco: state monopoly

familias afectas al sistema: republican supporters

fanegada: unit of area

flechera: long, narrow canoe

fuero: right, privilege or immunity, conferred by membership of a profession or community

gente de color: coloured people

gentes de pueblo: common people

godos: reactionaries

granadino: native of New Granada

guayaquileños: inhabitants of Guayaquil

guerra a muerte: war to the death

hacienda: large landed estate, plantation

hacendado: owner of *hacienda*

hato: ranch (Venezuelan)

huasos: Chilean horsemen

independentista: pro-Independence, supporter of Independence

isleños: people or immigrants from the Canary islands

jefe: chief, chieftain

jefe político: political governor

jefe supremo: supreme chief
junta: committee, board
juntista: of a *junta* or committee

limeño: of Lima, inhabitant of Lima
limpieza: purity of blood
llanos: plains
llaneros: plainsmen

mantuanos: white elite of Caracas, from the mantilla worn to church
mayordomo: steward, overseer
mestizo: of mixed white and Indian descent
mita: forced labour recruitment of Indians in rotation, especially for work in mines
mulato: of mixed white and black descent (*mulatto* in English)

novio: fiancé

olañetistas: followers of Olañeta

páramo: high plateau, bleak moorland
pardo: mulatto, of mixed white and black descent, free coloureds
pardocracia: pardo rule
pastusos: of Pasto, inhabitants of Pasto
patria: native land, mother country, fatherland
patria boba: 'foolish fatherland', Venezuela's brief first republic

patrón: patron, master or boss
peninsular: Spaniard born in Spain
poder moral: moral power
pongueaje: forced domestic service owed to landlord in Andes
porteños: of Buenos Aires, inhabitants of Buenos Aires
pueblo: people, village

quiteño: of Quito, inhabitant of Quito

repartimiento: forced sale of goods to Indians; allotting of Indians as labourers
resguardos: reservations, Indian community lands
ruana: poncho or cape

sabanas: savannah
santanderistas: supporters of Santander
soroche: altitude sickness

topo: Indian measurement of distance, 1.5 leagues
tribunal de secuestros: confiscations tribunal
tunales: land growing nopal cacti

visita: tour of inspection

zambo: of mixed black and Indian descent

INDEX